M & E HANDBOOKS

M & E Handbooks are recommended reading for examination syllabuses all over the world. Because each Handbook covers its subject clearly and concisely books in the series form a vital part of many college, university, school and home study courses.

Handbooks contain detailed information stripped of unnecessary padding, making each title a comprehensive self-tuition course. They are amplified with numerous self-testing questions in the form of Progress Tests at the end of each chapter, each text-referenced for easy checking. Every Handbook closes with an appendix which advises on examination technique. For all these reasons, Handbooks are ideal for pre-examination revision.

The handy pocket-book size and competitive price make Handbooks the perfect choice for anyone who wants to grasp the essentials of a subject quickly and easily.

D0727002

THE M & E HANDBOOK SERIES

European History 1789–1914

C. A. Leeds,

MA, B.Sc (Econ)

Lecturer, University of Nancy II

SECOND EDITION

MACDONALD AND EVANS

Macdonald & Evans Ltd.
Estover, Plymouth PL6 7PZ

First published 1971
Reprinted 1973
Reprinted 1974
Reprinted 1975
Reprinted 1977
Second edition 1979
Reprinted 1980
Reprinted 1982
Reprinted 1983

© Macdonald & Evans Ltd. 1979

7121 0575 1

Printed in Great Britain by
Richard Clay (The Chaucer Press) Ltd.,
Bungay, Suffolk

Preface to the Second Edition

There is renewed interest today in attempting to solve the question "What is history?" Voltaire is said to have commented that "it is a parcel of tricks which we play upon our ancestors". Briefly, it is the story of the past which researchers try to piece together in as accurate a fashion as possible. As a subject it has close links with the humanities, sociology and geography, which has been highlighted by the number of integrated programmes developed in education in recent years.

This HANDBOOK is intended for the student who wishes to study in some detail the political events of nineteenth-century European history. While "O" Level candidates should derive some benefit from the book, it is primarily intended for persons studying for "A" Level, university degree examinations, and other examinations of a similar nature. The particular arrangement should be especially helpful to students who have limited time for undertaking extensive reading and note-taking of their own.

Decisions in domestic and foreign policy are usually affected by political, economic and strategic factors and motives. In this book some attention is given to diplomatic history, which is basically a study of the interaction of the foreign policies of the powers and which requires an understanding of the factors involved in the formulation of any state's foreign policy. Though military and constitutional factors are considered, shortage of space makes it impossible to discuss in any detail economic, social and cultural aspects, though these are undoubtedly important. While the impact of political ideas prior to 1848 is considered, students who wish to study in more detail the influence on events of nineteenth-century political ideas should read the author's *Political Studies*, which is also published in the HANDBOOK series. Students should make use of a historical atlas and note the influence of certain geographical factors (location, climate, distribution of resources, type of terrain, etc.) on historical events.

This book covers the period from 1789 to 1914, both of these dates being considered by the author appropriate starting and finishing points for analysing the ideas and institutions of the nineteenth century. Broadly speaking, the 1790s were marked by the collapse of the rule of the enlightened despots, and the 1910s were characterised by the disappearance of many of the ideas and accepted standards of the nineteenth century and marked the advent of new political and technical forces.

Questions reprinted by kind permission of various examining bodies have been grouped together in Appendix III under various topics. Acknowledgments in this connection are due to the following: the Associated Examining Board; the Joint Matriculation Board; the Senate and the Schools Department of the University of London; the Oxford and Cambridge Joint Board; the Senate of the University of Cambridge; the University of Cambridge Local Examinations Syndicate; the Oxford Delegacy of Local Examinations; and the University of Southampton.

March 1979   C.A.L.

Contents

List of Maps

CHAPTER I

The French Revolution

CAUSES AND SIGNIFICANCE
OF THE REVOLUTION

1. Introduction. The French Revolution profoundly affected the fortunes of Europe. The following were the major European powers on the eve of revolution in 1789.

(*a*) *France.* Her past policies and ideas had exerted considerable influence on other European countries. However, her colonial ambitions had received a setback in 1763 when Britain became the leading European power in Canada and India.

(*b*) *Austria.* This was the strongest power in Central Europe, ruled by a famous dynasty, the Hapsburgs, who possessed a large European empire. As a leading Catholic power, and as a German state, Austria exercised considerable influence in German affairs.

(*c*) *Prussia.* This state became a major military power as a result of the efforts of Frederick the Great (1740–86). In 1740 he had taken Silesia from Austria. From that time Prussian influence in north Germany had increased.

(*d*) *Russia.* On the eastern fringe of Europe, Russia became the strongest power as a result of the activities of Peter the Great (1682–1725). He destroyed the power of his strongest rival in north-eastern Europe, Sweden. During the eighteenth century Russia began to expand at the expense of Poland and Turkey.

(*e*) *Britain.* Through her Continental alliances and sea power Britain made her influence felt in European affairs. In contrast to France, who had important European as well as colonial interests, Britain's interests were primarily centred outside Europe.

NOTE: Spain had ceased to be an important power though she still retained extensive colonial possessions. Holland and Portugal were important trading and colonial powers.

2. Why the French Revolution is the starting-point. The year 1789 has been taken as the main date to start nineteenth-century European history, for two reasons. These are as follows.

(*a*) *It was the dawn of a new age.* In the past it had been the accepted principle that rulers could govern their subjects as they chose. The king had claimed to rule by divine right and demanded obedience from his subjects to his wishes. The year 1789 marked the fall of the *ancien régime* in Europe, and the first serious challenge to the monarchical and aristocratic traditions which had descended from the Middle Ages. The new age brought great industrial change, and greater political and social freedom.

(*b*) *New political ideas were popularised.* These resulted in considerable change in the economic, political and social conditions not only in France but also in the rest of Europe.

3. Why the Revolution started in France. The English Parliament had already won substantial powers from the king as a result of struggles in the seventeenth century. The theory of the divine right of kings had been discredited and the government was a constitutional monarchy. Though it was elected by only a small section of the population, the English Parliament was regarded as a model by people of other countries who aspired to control their governments.

In Europe the kings ruled as powerful autocrats. The Revolution occurred in France for the following reasons.

(*a*) *Existence of a numerous and educated middle class.* Apart from Britain, France was the only country to have a rich and influential group of bankers, merchants, lawyers and doctors. Commerce had helped create this new class. The middle class supplied much of the funds for government but disliked its exclusion from politics.

(*b*) *Incompetent government.* The system of government was not so much tyrannical as inefficient and unsuited to the needs of a large commercial and agricultural state. Most people were excluded from participation in government. No accurate financial accounts were kept and constant resort was made to borrowing. As a result of wars and past extravagances of her kings, the government became bankrupt in 1789.

(*c*) *Discontent among the lower class.* Peasants were almost wholly free and in many regions possessed land. They took part in the Revolution not because they were hopelessly downtrodden but because they were sufficiently well off to wish to better themselves. They disliked:

   (*i*) the disproportionately heavy burden of taxation, especially the *taille* (land tax) from which the nobles and clergy were exempt;

(*ii*) the existence of feudal dues.

(*d*) *Influence of the American Revolution.* The French had been interested in the struggle of the thirteen American colonies between 1776 and 1783 to be independent of Britain. As a result of travel abroad, many Frenchmen who played a prominent part in the early stages of the French Revolution, especially the Marquis de Lafayette, exchanged ideas with leaders of the American Revolution.

(*e*) *Intellectual influences.* The middle classes were influenced by certain writers who had criticised many of the established conventions and organisations of Church and State during the eighteenth century. Three notable thinkers were:

(*i*) Montesquieu, who ridiculed the principle of divine right;

(*ii*) Rousseau, who spread ideas of equality and of the rights man possessed to life, liberty and property;

(*iii*) Voltaire, who praised England for her limited monarchy and civil liberties while denouncing the despotism of the French government.

(*f*) *Revolt of the Nobles.* The attempts of Calonne in 1787 and Lomenie de Brienne in 1788 to abolish privileged exemptions from taxation led to a revolt of the nobles. Their resistance to the new reforms of the monarchy set in motion events leading to the Revolution.

4. Political ideas of the French Revolution. During the period 1789–1871, the history of France was partly also the history of every other European country. For example, the outbreak of revolution in France in 1830 and 1848 led to similar outbreaks in other countries.

Ideas popularised during the Revolution were as follows.

(*a*) *Democratic principles.* The rallying cry of the French revolutionaries was *"Liberté, égalité, fraternité"*. *The Declaration of the Rights of Man* was approved by the French Assembly on 17th August 1789. It stated that men are born free and equal, and that law is the expression of the sovereign will of the people. Important ideas thrown up by the Revolution were as follows.

(*i*) Sovereignty of the people. The Revolution asserted the principle that people should rule themselves.

(*ii*) Liberty. This implied freedom from tyrannical government, unjust arrest and imprisonment. The right was claimed to certain freedoms, for example, of speech, press and religion. The French were determined to state the basic liberties of the people and the role of government in a written constitution. This led to demands for constitutions in other countries after 1815.

(*iii*) Equality. This meant individual rights to equal opportunity in all aspects of life. Though the Jacobins and Napoleon restricted individual liberties, the removal of the inequalities of feudalism, guild regulations and social distinctions resulted ultimately in greater liberty.

Eventually feudal restrictions were removed in Prussia (after 1806), Austria (1848) and Russia (1861).

(*b*) *Spirit of nationalism.* In the past patriotism existed on a local basis. People were loyal to their immediate feudal lord. In France, for example, people considered themselves as Gascon, Norman, Provençal, etc., rather than French. When in the Middle Ages kings subdued feudal lords and consolidated their own power, people then gave their loyalty to these kings.

During 1789–95 the removal of class privileges in France, the abolition of provinces and the existence of threats at home and abroad all contributed to the growth of French nationalism. The French Revolution contributed two elements necessary for the national ideal: the first was implicit in the stated objects of the Revolution; the second occurred as a result of the activities of the French abroad. These two elements were as follows.

(*i*) The belief that a country's welfare was the concern of all the people, not just of the king and his advisers. In addition, it became accepted that an individual's supreme loyalty should be given to his country, and that this should override any family, local or international loyalties.

(*ii*) The belief in the right to self-government for nations. The French desire to impose their ideas abroad led, after 1806, to the demand in Europe for liberation not only from oppressive rule but also from foreign rule (*see* II, **20** and IV, **2**).

5. Influence of the Revolution outside Europe. The French Revolution stirred people's imagination as a success story of the struggles against oppression. Its ideas were carried far afield, and influenced events particularly in the following continents.

(*a*) *Latin America* (after 1808). This continent was under the colonial rule of the Spanish and Portuguese (*see* IV, **14**).

(*b*) *Asia.* China suffered from the imperialism of European powers, and India from British colonialism. In time, discontented subjects felt justified in promoting revolution to overthrow what they considered to be unjust rule.

It was interesting that the first successful revolt against European colonisation took place on 22nd August 1791. It was led by the negro leader Toussaint l'Ouverture on the island of Hispaniola, which was shared between France and Spain. The economy was based on sugar plantations and African slave labour working in chain gangs. In January 1804 the island became independent as the Republic of Haiti.

6. Stages of the Revolution. The French Revolution can be divided into distinct periods. These are distinguished by changes both in the form of government in France and in France's relations with other powers.

(*a*) *Monarchical rule and Allied intervention* (1789–92). (*See* **7–16**.)

    (*i*) The Constituent Assembly (May 1789–September 1791). The system of government was a limited monarchy and was dominated by upper-middle-class rule.

    (*ii*) The Legislative Assembly (October 1791–September 1792). The influence of the lower classes became greater. France was soon at war with six foreign powers and eventually the King was deposed and a republic declared.

(*b*) *Jacobin rule and collapse of the First Allied Coalition* (1792–5). (*See* **17–24**.) During this period, France was theoretically controlled by the National Convention, but in practice was ruled tyrannically by a small clique of the Jacobin Party.

(*c*) *The rise of Napoleon and defeat of the Second Allied Coalition* (1795–1801). (*See* **25–32**.) This period was noted for the rise to power of Napoleon Bonaparte and his remarkable victories over the Allies. The forms of government in France in this period were as follows.

    (*i*) The Directory of five (1795–9).

    (*ii*) The Consulate (1799–1802). This was rule by three persons, of whom Napoleon was the most important (*see* **28**).

MONARCHICAL RULE AND ALLIED INTERVENTION

7. Meeting of the Estates-General. Pressure from the aristocracy led to the King summoning the Estates-General on the 5th May 1789, the first time since 1614. The nobility hoped that the adoption of the traditional method of voting by order and not by head would enable them to prevent radical reform and to achieve victory over both the Crown and the "Third Estate".

The Third Estate represented most of the people. Under the leadership of the Abbé Sieyès, it demanded an end to voting by estates, for under this system the other two houses, representing the Church and the nobility, were in a position to outvote measures of the Third Estate by two to one.

The King rejected this demand. The Third Estate then declared itself to be the National Assembly, together with such members of the other estates who wished to join. On 20th June, in the Tennis Court Oath, they vowed they would not dissolve until they had drawn up a constitution for France. Principal orator was the comte de Mirabeau, a man of noble birth who had consented to represent the commoners. On 23rd June the King ordered the representatives of the clergy and nobility to join the commoners in the National Assembly.

8. Outbreak of the Revolution. Riots broke out in Paris when it was rumoured that the King planned to use troops to dissolve the Assembly. On 14th July a Parisian mob stormed the Bastille, a notorious prison which symbolised the oppression of the *ancien régime*.

In Paris the tricolour (blue, white and red) was adopted as the flag of the Revolution and of the people's army, the newly formed National Guard. Nobles began to leave the country as peasant uprisings broke out everywhere. Those who left in this way were known as the *émigrés*.

9. Reforms of the National Assembly. During the period 1789–91 a number of important measures were taken by the National Assembly. These were as follows.

(*a*) *Abolition of feudalism and the special privileges of the nobility.* In addition, hereditary titles and coats-of-arms were no longer recognised.

(*b*) *Approval of a Civil Constitution of the Clergy.* The King was forced, very much against his will, to give his consent to this. It made the clergy elected public officials, and thus under state control.

(*c*) *Dissolution of most ecclesiastical orders.* Those concerned with education or care of the sick were exempted.

(*d*) *Appropriation of church lands as public property.* This measure was taken to alleviate financial distress. It provided the government with funds since:

(*i*) the lands were security to back *assignats*, a new paper currency (these soon became worthless, owing to the fall in the value of land following a market slump);

(*ii*) the lands were sold to the peasants at low prices.

(*e*) *Decentralisation of local government.* France was divided into eighty-three departments, each of which had the power to elect its own officials.

(*f*) *Creation of an elective judiciary.* This replaced the system by which judges had bought their positions.

(*g*) *Provision of a new constitution for France* (1791). This gave France a limited monarchy in which:

(*i*) the chief executive, the king, had only a temporary veto over legislation;

(*ii*) the unicameral (one-chamber) legislature had all power to make laws;

(*iii*) the right to vote was restricted to tax-paying citizens.

10. The attempted flight of the King. In June 1791, before the constitution was finally completed, the King tried to escape with his family to the north-east frontier. Reasons for the King's attempted escape were as follows.

(*a*) *His dislike of the Civil Constitution of the Clergy.* This had split the French Catholic Church into two sections, the Dissidents, who refused to take the oath, and the Constitutionalists, who did take it. The Pope threatened to excommunicate all those who adhered to the Civil Constitution. At Easter the King had been prevented by a suspicious crowd from going to St. Cloud to avoid receiving Communion from a "constitutional" priest.

(*b*) *His desire to make constitutional changes.* Mirabeau, before his death in April 1791, had urged the King to act decisively to make changes in government before it was too late. The King felt his only chance was to escape to the protection of loyal troops. With their support, he could then make constitutional changes, increasing the powers of the nobility and the Church.

(*c*) *The difficulty of his position at home.* The King's weak political position made it difficult for him to reject the ideals of the Revolution. Until he broke with the revolutionaries, however, the French *émigrés* in the Rhineland did not have complete justification for any attempted military support for the King. The

King wanted to break the deadlock by taking action which would eventually unite all groups to his cause.

11. Weakened position of the monarch. The King was caught at Varennes and brought back to Paris. He was suspended from office until the constitution had been finished. Many "royalist" officers then deserted from the army, and increased unrest occurred in Paris. In one incident, known as the Massacre of the Champ de Mars (17th July), the National Guard was forced to fire to disperse the crowd.

The people's confidence in the monarch was now severely shaken. A small group in the Assembly demanded the deposition of the King and the forming of a republic. Until this time such a step had never been contemplated.

On 14th September 1791 the King agreed to the new constitution. The National Assembly dissolved itself, after voting that none of its members would be eligible for re-election.

12. The new Legislative Assembly. This met in October. As the members were elected by tax-paying citizens, they represented primarily the middle classes. Right-wing parties (constitutionalists, royalists, etc.) became steadily weaker.

The left-wing parties were in the majority. They felt that the Revolution had not gone far enough. The chief parties of the Left were the following.

(*a*) *The Girondists*, led by able members from Bordeaux, such as Brissot. They accepted the monarchy temporarily, but regarded a republic under middle-class rule as the ideal.

(*b*) *The Jacobins*, led by Robespierre, Danton and Marat. They wanted a republic where the lower class would have the strongest voice.

The King at first chose a ministry from the Right. He refused to assent to a law condemning to death all emigrant nobles who did not return before January 1792, or to a severe law against dissident clergy. This was regarded as a sign of sympathy with the enemies of the Revolution, and he was finally forced to appoint a ministry from the Girondists.

13. Reaction of other powers to the French Revolution. It was difficult for the great powers, Britain, Russia, Austria and Prussia, to come to any agreed understanding about the attitude to adopt to France. At the time, no formal machinery for joint consultation existed. The position of the powers during the first months of the Revolution may be summarised as follows.

(*a*) *They were not unduly alarmed by French events.* France had been the traditional rival of other powers. For the French king to be involved in domestic upheaval was not unwelcome news. Diplomatic relations between states were primarily concerned with questions of dynastic security and the acquisition of territories. As the French Assembly at first renounced war as an aim of the government, there seemed little to fear from France. In fact, among much of the educated and enlightened opinion of Europe, there was a great deal of sympathy. Charles James Fox described the fall of the Bastille as the greatest event in the history of the world.

(*b*) *They were preoccupied with other affairs.*

(*i*) Poland (*see* **23**(*c*)).

(*ii*) Turkey: Prussia was perturbed by Austria's involvement in the Turkish war in support of Russia (*see* XIV, **10**).

(*iii*) Sweden: this country fought Russia in 1788–90 to regain parts of Finland lost in earlier wars (in 1713 and 1743). Russia, aided by Denmark, defeated Sweden, who had to cede the rest of Finland.

14. Austro-Prussian collaboration. Eventually the Austrian emperor, Leopold II, became concerned lest ideas of the French Revolution spread to his territories. He already had domestic unrest, particularly in the Austrian Netherlands (Belgium) and Hungary. Also it was not easy to ignore the likely repercussions of the French abandonment of the "divine right" principle, and the indignities which had been suffered by a fellow sovereign.

In August 1791 the Austrian and Prussian rulers met and settled their differences over the Balkans (*see* **13**(*b*)(*ii*)). They then issued the Declaration of Pillnitz, in which they stated their intention of intervening to help the French king if other countries, particularly Britain, joined them.

15. The start of European war. At first there was little prospect of war as Britain refused to be involved. However, the French interpreted the Declaration of Pillnitz as a bold threat of intervention. Relations between France and Austria deteriorated, so that when France declared war in April 1792 it was welcomed by both sides. Some of the factors contributing to the war are listed below.

(a) *Austria.* Emperor Leopold of Austria wanted to avoid war. In February 1792 he concluded a defensive alliance with Prussia, hoping to deter France. He died on 1st March. His son, Francis II, was keen on war. He demanded the restoration to the German princes in Alsace of their feudal rights lost as a result of the French decree of August 1789 (*see* 9(a)).

(b) *French émigrés.* They had been trying to provoke Austrian intervention and in 1791 had formed an *émigré* army in the German Rhineland. Their leader was the comte d'Artois, younger brother of the King. They were particularly offended by the abolition of all titles to nobility by the National Assembly in 1790. Austria took no action to disperse them from German territory when requested by France.

(c) *France.* The Girondist government in France wanted war. The King's supporters also advocated this, hoping it would render Louis popular if a victorious campaign was fought. There were also domestic considerations. France was in the midst of famine and disorder. Unemployment was rife as industry had collapsed. Marat observed that war was necessary to "rid France of 300,000 armed brigands".

16. Fall of the Girondists. During the summer and autumn of 1792 the Girondists and the Legislative Assembly became increasingly unable to control French affairs, particularly events in Paris. The various factors contributing to their downfall were as follows.

(a) *French reverses.* France failed to gain any foreign support. An advance into the Austrian Netherlands was a complete failure. The troops were ill-disciplined and the officers unenthusiastic. There was a shortage of experienced leaders.

In a manifesto issued on 25th July 1792, the Austrian Duke of Brunswick threatened the destruction of Paris if further violence were offered to the royal family. In August an Allied force, under Brunswick, invaded France. The Allies won victories at Longwy and Verdun.

(b) *Domestic unrest.* Defeats abroad increased the revolutionary excitement in Paris. The Parisians were maddened with hunger. They hated the King's Austrian wife, Marie-Antoinette, whose behaviour seemed to epitomise the *ancien régime.* Louis XVI refused to make concessions.

(c) *Lack of organisation and power to keep order.* The Girondists did not prevent:

(*i*) the penetration of the palace of the Tuileries by a mob on 20th June and the humiliation of the royal family;

(*ii*) the storming of the Tuileries on 10th August by a mob which forced the King to take refuge in the National Assembly;

(*iii*) the execution of some thousand prisoners (known as the September Massacres) when the Parisians feared an Allied advance on Paris.

(*d*) *Rise of the Jacobins.* During 1792 the influence of the Jacobins, supported by the working class, increased. The Assembly approved the election of a National Convention by universal suffrage. This met on 20th September. Though the Girondists, supported by the provinces, were numerically the stronger, the extreme Jacobins, who believed in strong rule, gained the ascendancy. This was due to:

(*i*) their capable leaders, Robespierre, Danton and Marat;

(*ii*) the support of the Paris Commune (town council) and an effective network of clubs throughout France;

(*iii*) their influence with the Paris artillerymen;

(*iv*) the use of the press and demonstrations to spread their ideas.

(*e*) *Ineffective policies.* The Girondists did not appear to have any policies appropriate to the critical times. Their belief in middle-class rule was not as appealing to the masses as the Jacobin doctrine of "the sovereignty of the people".

RULE OF THE NATIONAL CONVENTION AND THE JACOBINS

17. Abolition of monarchy. In August 1792 the King was suspended from office and his ministers dismissed. The new Convention, composed mostly of republicans, decided by unanimous vote to establish a republic on 21st September 1792. The Girondists tried to prevent strong measures being taken against the King, but they lost influence to the Jacobins. In December the latter had the King tried on the charge of plotting against the nation: he was found guilty. By a majority of one, the death penalty was imposed and Louis was guillotined on 21st January 1793.

This action hardened opinion abroad against France, particularly in Britain.

18. French initiative abroad. On 20th September 1792 the French under Dumouriez defeated the Prussians at Valmy, after which the withdrawal of the Prussians from France was arranged. This gave heart to the French armies. In October Savoy and Nice were annexed. In November the Austrian Netherlands were captured after the victory of Jemappes.

The new government took a number of political measures likely to undermine the *status quo* abroad, and these increased the prospects of European war.

(*a*) *The Edict of Fraternity.* In November 1792 France offered help abroad to peoples wishing to gain freedom by overthrowing their kings. The French Revolution thus became of European concern.

(*b*) *Instructions to French generals.* The military commanders were told that the occupation of any territory was to be accompanied by:

(*i*) the ending of feudalism and the confiscation of clerical and aristocratic property;

(*ii*) the proclamation of the sovereignty of the people.

(*c*) *The statement of the doctrine of "natural frontiers".* In January 1793 France claimed an extension of her territory by right with boundaries extending to the Rhine, the Pyrenees and the Alps. This ambition brought her into conflict with Holland, Spain and Austria.

(*d*) *Violation of treaty provisions concerning the Netherlands.* Specifically these provisions referred to Dutch neutrality, the closure of the Scheldt to warships and Antwerp to international trade. The French sent warships down the Scheldt and started to develop Antwerp. This was a direct threat to the British position.

19. Critical position of France. In early 1793 France declared war on numerous European powers. The French position soon became desperate as the result of the following factors.

(*a*) *Reverses abroad.* France had to fight a coalition of six powers, Austria, Prussia, Sardinia, Holland, Britain and Spain. In March 1793 the Austrians defeated Dumouriez at Neerwinden and captured Brussels. Dumouriez and Louis-Philippe, Duke of Chartres, went over to the Austrians.

(*b*) *Domestic unrest.* Many revolutionaries feared that "royalist" intrigues might overthrow the Revolution. For example, "royalist" risings took place in La Vendée and in Toulon. The latter proclaimed the Dauphin (a prisoner in Paris) King Louis XVII and sought the aid of the British fleet.

(*c*) *Economic crisis.* Confidence in the economy was shaken by numerous political upheavals. The *assignats* fell to 22 per cent of their original value. The rapid rise in prices encouraged hoarders and speculators.

20. The Reign of Terror. The people were prepared to support strong measures to deal with the perilous position of the French. As a result, the National Convention delegated powers to a Committee of Public Safety (April 1793). This body, in conjunction with commissioners of the Convention and various special committees, soon exercised considerable authority over the people.

During the period 1793–5 Robespierre and the Jacobin leaders gained almost absolute power. Under their rule, Paris dominated French affairs. The influence of the Girondists was extinguished and many were executed. The period is known as the "Reign of Terror", as its tyranny was worse even than that of the *ancien régime*.

(*a*) All opposition to the government was ruthlessly suppressed. By the Law of Suspects (September 1793), persons could be imprisoned without trial.

(*b*) Revolutionary tribunals were empowered to award the death penalty with scant regard for legal justice. Their powers were increased by the Law of Prairial (June 1793), which permitted juries to convict without hearing evidence.

(*c*) Some 13,000 people were beheaded by the guillotine.

21. Reforms of the National Convention. Despite its preoccupation with preserving the gains of the Revolution, the Convention was able to pass some useful measures. These resulted in the following:

(*a*) the start of a national system of education;

(*b*) the simplification of commercial and financial transactions, thus benefiting trade;

(*c*) the introduction of a metric system of weights and measures;

(*d*) the abolition of negro slavery in the colonies;

(*e*) the repeal of the law of primogeniture: this had stated that property could not be divided among heirs, but had to be left to the eldest son.

22. Military successes. The French forces made a remarkable recovery under the National Convention.

(*a*) *Position in France secured.* Uprisings in France were suppressed. Toulon was recaptured from the British at the end of 1793. A royalist *émigré* landing at Quiberon Bay, aided by Britain in 1793, was routed by Hoche.

(*b*) *Defeat of the Allies.* During 1794 the Allies were driven back across the Rhine. Holland, Prussia and Spain withdrew from the war. The following points may be noted.

(*i*) The Austrians had to evacuate the Austrian Netherlands after their defeat at Fleurus in June 1794.

(*ii*) By the Treaty of Basle (April 1795), the Prussians promised France a free hand on the left bank of the Rhine. In return, France promised that she would respect the neutrality of northern Germany, which Prussia wanted to control.

In May 1795 some of the German states in the south-west made peace with France. They feared possible Austrian designs on Bavaria and hoped to receive some benefits from France.

23. Factors contributing to the French success.

(*a*) *Efficient French organisation and leadership.* Under the able leadership of Carnot, armies were quickly trained. Brissot fired the imagination of the French by saying they were fighting against the privileged cliques of Europe. The *Marseillaise* became the national anthem, inspiring the French to make personal sacrifices for their country.

All the resources of the nation were harnessed by the government in defence of the Revolution. All unmarried men aged 18–25 were conscripted into the army while married men worked in factories and women also contributed to the cause.

(*b*) *Superiority of the French armies.* The troops were imbued with a sense of nationalism and freedom. In contrast, their opponents were either the unwilling conscripts of absolute monarchs or mercenaries. The enthusiastic French armies were led by talented young generals who knew that failures were severely penalised. Allied leadership was mediocre.

(*i*) Disagreements between the Prussian king and the Austrian Duke of Brunswick on strategy slowed up the original Allied advance into France.

(*ii*) The Duke of York was an incompetent leader of the British expedition to Flanders in 1795.

(*c*) *Preoccupation of the Allies with Eastern Europe.* Mutual jealousies and rivalry prevented Austria and Prussia following any co-ordinated policy towards France. Prussia was primarily interested in Northern and Eastern Europe. She entered the war against France only to keep pace with Austria.

Polish independence vanished in the three partitions of 1772, 1792 and 1795. Russia took the initiative in occupying Poland, and Prussia and Austria intervened to prevent Russia gaining too much power. During the French war, the preoccupation with eastern Europe had harmful effects for the Allies.

(*i*) Prussia sent most of her troops to Poland and British troops sent by Pitt were also used there. (Thus Pitt stopped sending subsidies to Prussia in October 1794.)

(*ii*) Austria had to evacuate Flanders in March 1794 owing to the Russian intervention in Poland. This contributed to the failure of the British expedition to Flanders, which was left in an exposed position.

24. End of the Jacobin regime. Robespierre gradually became increasingly unpopular. In addition to executing suspected opponents of the Revolution, he started to eliminate persons likely to usurp his powers: Hébert and Danton were guillotined. In June 1794 he introduced the "Cult of the Supreme Being" and the "Republic of Virtue". The French tired of the struggles for power within the party and the excesses of the Revolution. After the downfall of Robespierre (July 1794) his successors were forced to adopt more moderate policies.

In 1795 the moderates (Thermidoreans) dominated the Convention and proceeded to break the power of the Jacobins. The following events then took place.

(*a*) *New constitution approved.* The Convention accepted a new constitution vesting executive power in a Directory of five. There were to be two houses of the legislature. Two-thirds of the members were to be taken from the rolls of the Convention. This last proviso led to opposition in the provinces and Paris, instigated by royalists.

(*b*) *Paris uprising.* On the suggestion of Barras, the Convention placed Bonaparte in charge of its troops. He crushed the Paris rising with the skilful use of artillery and thus saved the Convention and the Directory.

NOTE: Napoleon Bonaparte had been born in Corsica in 1769, a year after it had been annexed by the French. He had attended a military academy and served in an artillery regiment. As he had entertained revolutionary ideas, including a scheme for the independence of Corsica, he had lost his position in the army under the *ancien régime*. In 1792 he had been given a command in Paris and distinguished himself at the French recovery of Toulon in 1793.

(*c*) *Dissolution of the Convention*. The Convention then dissolved itself. This left complete power in the hands of the Directory.

THE DIRECTORY AND THE RISE OF NAPOLEON

25. Strategy of Britain. The basic plan of the British Prime Minister, William Pitt, was as follows.

(*a*) *To encourage small expeditions to Europe to harass the enemy*. The expeditions to Toulon (1793), Quiberon Bay and Flanders (1795) all failed (*see* **22**).

(*b*) *To support European allies with subsidies*.

(*c*) *To capture enemy possessions*. This helped reimburse Britain for the drain on her financial resources to Europe and increased her power abroad.

(*i*) Martinique, St. Lucia and Tobago were captured from the French (1794).

(*ii*) Ceylon and the Cape of Good Hope were captured from the Dutch (1795).

(*iii*) Trinidad was taken from Spain (1797).

(*d*) *To preserve mastery of the sea*. On 1st June 1794 Lord Howe defeated the French off Ushant.

26. The war in 1796-7. William Pitt, owing to the exhaustion of Austria and financial difficulties at home, wanted to negotiate peace terms with France (1796). The Directory, however, was determined to continue the war to defeat Britain and to attack Austria. This led to the following developments.

(*a*) *French defeat in Germany by the Austrians*. Two French forces under Jourdan and Moreau invaded southern Germany. They were eventually driven back by the Archduke Charles of Austria.

(*b*) *French victory over the Austrians in Italy*. Napoleon was given command of an Italian expedition. He drove a wedge between the Austrian and Sardinian armies and defeated them both separately.

The Austrians were defeated at Rivoli in January 1797. Napoleon forced the Pope to make the Peace of Tolentino in February. The Pope agreed to cede Avignon to France and

Bologna, Ferrara and Romagna to a new state in northern Italy created by Napoleon, the Cisalpine Republic. Sardinia was forced to make peace in April, ceding Savoy and Nice to France.

On 17th October 1797, by the Treaty of Campo-Formio, the Austrians agreed to certain terms:

(*i*) to recognise the French conquest of the Austrian Netherlands and her newly won Rhine frontier;

(*ii*) to cede Lombardy to the Cisalpine Republic: though this was nominally independent, it was effectively under French control;

(*iii*) to accept in return the independent republic of Venice as a bribe.

(*c*) *Isolation of Britain.* In 1797 Britain alone remained of the original six-power coalition against France. There was unrest in Ireland. The government, weakened by the previous drain of subsidies to Prussia and Austria, was forced to suspend payments in gold and institute a paper currency. Mutinies occurred at Spithead and the Nore owing to bad naval conditions.

Spain had declared war on Britain in 1796. Napoleon forced the Batavian Republic in Holland into war against Britain.

(*d*) *French invasion attempt of Ireland and Britain foiled.* In 1797 Napoleon planned to defeat the island power of Britain. However, the French fleet was prevented from combining with her allies for an invasion of Britain owing to the following events:

(*i*) defeat of the Spanish fleet by Jervis off Cape St. Vincent (February);

(*ii*) defeat of the Dutch fleet by Duncan at Camperdown (October).

NOTE: Napoleon tried to defeat Britain by launching a campaign in Egypt. For details, *see* XIV, **11–12**.

27. Formation of the Second Coalition. The Tsar Paul I was offended when Malta was taken by Napoleon (*see* XIV, **12**). The Tsar and Pitt were largely responsible for the forming of a second coalition. Besides Russia and Britain it included Austria, Portugal, Naples and Turkey.

The coalition was successful while Napoleon was absent in Egypt. The Archduke Charles defeated the French near Lake Constance (March 1799). The Russian general, Suvorov, supported by the Austrians, defeated the French at the battles of the Trebbia (June) and Novi (August) and drove them out of Italy.

28. The Directory overthrown. The Directory had proved in-capable of continuing the war in Europe while Napoleon was in Egypt. It was not generally popular, its members being largely undistinguished apart from Carnot. On his return from Egypt in 1799, Napoleon carried out a *coup d'état* with the aid of Barras and Sieyès. The Directory was overthrown and a Consulate of three established, in which Napoleon was Chief Consul with special powers.

29. Napoleon's rise to power. In 1799 Sieyès is reported to have said: "Gentlemen, you have got a master – a man who knows everything, wants everything and can do everything." The following factors contributed to Napoleon's rise to power.

(*a*) *Weakness of the Directory*. Its leadership had been poor and it seemed unable to cope with the increased unrest in 1799.

(*b*) *Popular support for stable rule*. France had suffered years of upheaval. The people wanted a leader capable of consolidating the gains while providing orderly government. Napoleon proved that he possessed qualities of leadership and could win the respect of others.

(*c*) *Napoleon's strength of character*. Napoleon had ability, un-limited energy and ambition, was a gifted speaker and could absorb details quickly and make rapid decisions.

Believing he was a "man of destiny", he was unscrupulous with those who opposed him. He said: "There is only one secret for ruling; that is to be strong, because in force there is neither error nor illusion."

(*d*) *Napoleon's military ability*. Napoleon had the ability to gain the loyalty of his troops and to win battles. He was a clever strategist and developed a successful technique for out-manoeuvring his enemies so that only a small portion of their forces faced his army at any one time. Relying on speed of move-ment, his forces would attack the enemy at their weakest point, the connecting link. This tactic had been employed effectively in the Italian campaign. The Duke of Wellington remarked that "his presence in the field was worth a difference of 40,000 men". Bernadotte, one of Napoleon's marshals who became King of Sweden, commented to military allies that "when you face the marshals, attack; when you face Napoleon, retreat".

30. Collapse of the Second Coalition. The following were the reasons for the collapse of the Second Coalition.

(*a*) *Withdrawal of Russia.* In 1799 Masséna had defeated a combined Russo-Austrian army at Zürich, and Suvorov had evacuated Switzerland. The Tsar Paul, encouraged by Napoleon and having quarrelled with Austria, decided in 1800 to retire from the war. He was also annoyed since Britain had now seized Malta from France.

(*b*) *Allied reverses.* The Duke of York was forced to evacuate Holland in 1799. In 1800 Napoleon beat the Austrians at Marengo and recovered northern Italy. Moreau defeated the Austrians in Germany at Hohenlinden.

By the Treaty of Lunéville in 1801, Austria had to recognise the French republics in Italy, Switzerland and Holland and the cession of all territory on the left bank of the Rhine to France.

31. The Armed Neutrality against Britain. In 1799 a defensive alliance was concluded between Russia and Sweden. In 1800 they were joined by Prussia and Denmark in a convention, the Armed Neutrality of the North. This was opposed to the extensive "right of search" that Britain claimed over ships of neutral powers. The Danish fleet was defeated by Nelson at Copenhagen (1801).

32. The Peace of Amiens. By the beginning of 1802 the Anglo-French war had reached stalemate. Neither power could effectively attack the other. Britain had checked Napoleon's designs in Ireland and Egypt, but was in financial difficulties. The French were disappointed at the loss of their colonies, the collapse of the Armed Neutrality and their failures against Britain. By the Peace of Amiens (March 1802) the following terms were agreed.

(*a*) Britain should return Malta to the Knights of St. John and all her colonial conquests, except Ceylon and Trinidad, to the countries from which she had taken them. She also recognised the French Republic.

(*b*) France was to restore Egypt to Turkey and to evacuate Rome and southern Italy.

PROGRESS TEST 1

1. What were the major European powers in 1789? Which two had most recently become major powers? **(1)**

2. What were the main causes of the French Revolution? **(3)**

3. Why was the French Revolution a significant influence in

Europe and elsewhere?	(4–5)

4. What was the immediate cause of the French Revolution? (7–8)

5. Describe the major achievements of the National Assembly. (9)

6. Why did King Louis XVI try to escape? What results followed from his capture?	(10–11)

7. Why were the European powers not unduly alarmed at first by the outbreak of revolution in France?	(13)

8. Why did France declare war on Austria in 1792?	(15)

9. Account for the fall from power of the Girondists.	(16)

10. Why did France soon have to fight a European coalition? (17–18)

11. Account for the Reign of Terror.	(19–20)

12. Why did the First Coalition collapse?	(22–23)

13. Describe the fall of the Jacobin regime.	(24)

14. How did Pitt intend to defeat France?	(25)

15. Account for the rise to power of Napoleon.	(28–29)

16. What influences led Britain to conclude an armistice with France?	(30–32)

CHAPTER II

Europe and Napoleon Bonaparte, 1801–14

1. Introduction. The period 1801–14 can be subdivided as follows.

(*a*) *Period of peace in Europe and domestic reforms in France* (1801–3). Napoleon's most constructive work at home was achieved during the period of peace. He stayed in France and devoted himself to the initiation of various reforms. Some were not implemented until later, but they owed much to his original encouragement (*see* **31–35**).

(*b*) *Napoleon at the height of his power* (1804–7). France was unable to achieve control of the sea and could neither develop a colonial empire nor defeat Britain as Napoleon earnestly desired. On land, however, Napoleon inflicted heavy defeats on the Third Coalition and achieved mastery in Europe.

(*c*) *Downfall of Napoleon* (1807–14). The origins of Napoleon's downfall might be taken as earlier or later than 1807. However, it was in this year that he suffered his first serious reverses. He had problems in enforcing the Continental System and in maintaining his authority in Spain and Portugal (*see* **10** and **13–15**).

NAPOLEON AT THE HEIGHT OF HIS POWER

2. The Napoleonic Era. Between 1799, when Napoleon became First Consul, and 1814, he exerted such a great influence on European affairs that this period has been known as the Napoleonic Era.

For convenience, the Age of Napoleon starts in this book in 1801. This was the beginning of many of Napoleon's notable domestic achievements (*see* **31–35**) and the interlude of peace in Europe. However, it might be argued that it did not truly start until 1804. In this year Napoleon's power became hereditary. On 18th May he was made "Emperor of the French". With the formation of the Empire, France became a monarchy again in a new guise. The Republic was overthrown.

3. Causes for the renewal of war. Peace between Britain and France lasted until May 1803. Both sides regarded the peace as a temporary lull, a breathing space. They were intensely suspicious of each other and failed to co-operate. Friction was caused by the following factors.

(*a*) Napoleon's plan to extend French influence overseas. Britain was not prepared to see the growth of a strong colonial power. In 1801 Napoleon forced Spain to cede Louisiana to France. In 1803, fearing its capture by Britain, he sold it to the United States. Britain disliked Napoleon for various reasons:

(*i*) his support of rebellious Mahratta princes in India;

(*ii*) his attempt to establish French influence in Australia (1800–3);

(*iii*) his attempted capture of San Domingo in the Caribbean (1802).

(*b*) British determination to retain Malta until Napoleon had abandoned schemes for invading Egypt again.

(*c*) Napoleon's determination to keep southern Italy until Britain had left Malta.

(*d*) The shelter given to the French *émigrés* in Britain and the personal attacks on Napoleon in the British press.

(*e*) British dislike of the growth of French power.

(*i*) In Holland French troops were permitted into Dutch fortresses.

(*ii*) In Italy French troops annexed Piedmont and seized Parma. Napoleon was elected President of the Cisalpine Republic.

(*iii*) In Switzerland Napoleon gained extensive powers over that country's army.

4. The Third Coalition.

(*a*) *Formation of Allied coalition.* In April 1805 Russia and Britain combined forces to drive the French from Switzerland and Holland. Austria, annoyed at the annexation of Genoa by the French, joined the coalition in August. Sweden also joined.

(*b*) *Frustration of Napoleon's invasion plans.* Napoleon collected a vast army at Boulogne in 1804 for the invasion of Britain. However, the French and Spanish fleets under Villeneuve were defeated by Nelson at Trafalgar on 21st October 1805. Napoleon thus had to abandon his invasion plan in the west. Instead, his troops were sent to defeat the European coalition in the east.

(c) *Austro-Russian defeat.* On 20th October 1805 the Austrian army was defeated at Ulm. The Russian general, Kutusov, then counselled delay until Prussia could be brought effectively into the war, but the headstrong young Tsar, Alexander I, wished to secure a quick success. However, the combined Austro-Russian forces were utterly routed at Austerlitz on 2nd December. This disaster is said to have contributed to the death of the over-worked Pitt, who declared at the time: "Roll up the map of Europe; it will not be needed these ten years." The Russian forces retreated.

Napoleon decided on harsh peace terms with Austria, who wanted a truce. This was perhaps unwise, for, as Talleyrand suggested, France might have gained an Austrian alliance against either Britain or Russia. The Treaty of Pressburg was signed on 26th December 1805.

(i) Austria agreed to cede Venice to Italy and the Tyrol to Bavaria.

(ii) The Bavarian and Württemberg rulers were elevated to the title of king and their states were freed from obligations to the Austrian Empire. They agreed to provide Napoleon with forces for any future war.

(iii) Austria had to accept a war indemnity of 40 million francs which was intended to make her military recovery impossible.

(d) *Prussian defeat.* Prussia had been neutral during the 1805 hostilities, since Napoleon had promised her Hanover. By the Treaty of Schönbrunn (15th December) this was carried out, and in return Prussia agreed to cede Ansbach to Bavaria.

Pitt died on 23rd January 1806. His successor, Fox, opened peace negotiations with France. Napoleon offered to return Hanover to Britain. Prussia was furious and demanded that French troops evacuate Hanover. The Prussians were heavily defeated at Jena on 14th October 1806 and Napoleon occupied Berlin.

(e) *Russian defeat.* The Russian forces were defeated by the French at Friedland on 14th June 1807. The Tsar decided to come to terms with Napoleon. He was annoyed at the lack of support from Britain, who had diverted her energies to unsuccessful expeditions to the Dardanelles, Buenos Aires and Alexandria. The seizing of Russian merchant vessels under the Orders in Council made matters worse (*see* **10**(*b*)).

5. The Peace of Tilsit. In July 1807 Napoleon, Alexander I of Russia and Frederick William III of Prussia met privately on a raft in the river Niemen. By 9th July the peace provisions had been settled.

(*a*) Prussian territory was depleted by about one-third.

(*i*) Jerome Bonaparte was recognised as king of a new kingdom, Westphalia, in the west.

(*ii*) The King of Saxony was to be the nominal ruler of Prussia's Polish lands, which now formed a buffer state – the Grand Duchy of Warsaw.

(*b*) *The Continental System was enforced.* Prussia agreed not to trade with Britain. The Tsar agreed to enforce the system if his offer of mediation between France and Britain was rejected.

(*c*) Napoleon promised to mediate in the Russo-Turkish War (*see* XIV, **14**).

(*d*) *Prussia and Russia agreed to recognise the following:*

(*i*) Joseph Bonaparte as King of Naples;

(*ii*) Louis Bonaparte as King of Holland;

(*iii*) a Confederation of the Rhine.

6. War between Britain and Russia. In 1807 Britain rejected the proffered mediation of Alexander I. The British government heard that Napoleon planned to seize the Danish navy. The Danes were ordered to hand over their fleet to the British until the end of the war. When they refused, Copenhagen was bombarded and the Danish fleet and naval stores seized in September. As a result, Russia declared war on Britain.

7. War between Austria and France. In 1809 Austria felt ready to challenge France again. The moment was considered opportune by the Chancellor, Stadion, since Napoleon was involved in Spain, the Austrian army had been reorganised and he (Stadion) hoped the German princes would render aid. Also Austria resented the control of her trade from Italian and Dalmatian ports (*see* **10**).

Archduke Charles invaded Bavaria, but was defeated by Napoleon at Wagram (6th July). Neither Prussia nor the German princes gave help. The latter seemed either too servile to Napoleon or too jealous of Hapsburg power to lend support. A diversionary British expedition to the Netherlands in July ended in disaster. It was badly organised and the last of the fever-stricken troops were evacuated from Walcheren in December, two months after peace had been signed between France and Austria.

(a) *Treaty of Schönbrunn.* In October 1809 the Emperor agreed to humiliating peace terms. Austria lost $3\frac{1}{2}$ million people and was deprived of access to the sea. She had to agree to the following provisions.

(i) Cession of the "Illyrian Provinces" (including Croatia, Dalmatia and Slovenia) and Trieste to France.

(ii) Cession of her Polish territories. West Galicia, including Cracow, went to the Duchy of Warsaw. Russia received East Galicia.

(iii) Reduction of her army to 15,000 men and the payment of another large indemnity.

(b) *Results of the war.* France gained territorially. Other results were as follows.

(i) Formation of Austro-French alliance. Metternich became Chancellor in 1809. He supported the marriage of Marie-Louise (daughter of the Emperor) to Napoleon, a French alliance and the adoption of the Continental System by Austria as the only protection for the country during its period of recuperation. In turn Napoleon hoped the alliance would give him security against another Austrian attack.

(ii) Collapse of revolt in the Tyrol. Hofer had been leading a movement protesting against the transference of the Tyrol to Bavaria after Pressburg. Abandoned by Austria, his movement now collapsed. Napoleon joined the area to the North Italian Kingdom in 1810.

(iii) Increased friction between France and Russia (*see* **16**).

THE DOWNFALL OF NAPOLEON

8. Napoleon's achievements abroad. If Napoleon had died in 1807 after Tilsit, his career would have seemed the most miraculous in military history. He had acquired wealth and power for himself and his family.

Territorially, he was at the peak of his power in 1810 after defeating Austria once more (*see* map on p. 26). He regarded his marriage to Marie-Louise as one of his greatest triumphs, for to marry into the Hapsburg family was regarded as the ultimate mark of respectability in Europe.

His achievements may be summarised as follows.

(a) *French territory had been substantially increased.* Annexations included all land on the west bank of the Rhine, Savoy and Nice.

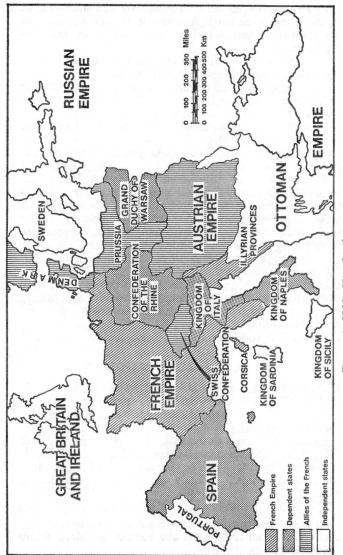

Europe in 1810: Napoleon's empire

(b) *Poland* was largely contained in the Grand Duchy of Warsaw under Napoleon's ally the King of Saxony.

(c) *Austria, Prussia and Russia* had acknowledged the territorial arrangements established by Napoleon.

(d) *Italy*. French authority in Italy was paramount.

    (i) Napoleon himself was crowned King of Italy in 1805.

    (ii) Napoleon's brother Joseph was made King of Naples in 1806.

(e) *Germany*. French influence was also paramount in Germany. The King of Saxony was allied to France, while Jerome Bonaparte was made king of a new state, Westphalia, in 1807. On 16th July sixteen German states, including Bavaria, Württemberg and Baden, were formed into the Confederation of the Rhine, of which Napoleon was president.

(f) *Holland* (the Batavian Republic) was under the rule of Louis Bonaparte from 1806.

(g) *Switzerland* was subservient to French interests.

(h) *In Sweden*, Marshal Bernadotte (related to Napoleon by marriage) was firstly crown prince and then king.

9. Causes of the downfall of Napoleon. The chief factors contributing to Napoleon's defeat were as follows.

(a) *British naval supremacy* (*see* **11**). The conflict between Britain and France has been called the struggle between "the shark and the tiger", as Britain controlled the sea and France the land. Owing to his failure to defeat Britain, Napoleon resorted to the Continental System (*see* (b)).

(b) *The Continental System* (*see* **10**). Napoleon hoped to bring Britain ("the nation of shopkeepers", as he called her) to heel through the use of non-military methods.

Britain was not affected as disastrously as Napoleon anticipated. Napoleon underestimated the following two factors.

    (i) The financial resources and naval strength of Britain. Britain soon developed a system of smuggling and illicit trade through Sicily, Gibraltar, the Channel Isles, Heligoland, etc.

    (ii) The determination of many countries, notably Holland and Sicily, not to enforce the system. Its enforcement would have caused great hardship to these countries, as their prosperity depended on trade with Britain.

Napoleon's attempt to enforce the system led to two disastrous campaigns (*see* (c)–(d)).

(c) *The Peninsular War* (*see* 13).

(d) *The Moscow campaign* (*see* 17).

(e) *Napoleon's policies after* 1805 (*see* 12).

(f) *The rise of nationalism.* This was partly caused by all the factors mentioned in (b)–(e): *see* 20.

(g) *The exhaustion of France.* During 1813–14 France and her allies were not able to supply troops in adequate numbers to replace the loss of the seasoned veteran armies of earlier years. Napoleon's marshals no longer had noble ideals with which to inspire their forces. They continually lost battles when he was not present.

10. Economic warfare. Since neither France nor Britain was able to take effective military action against the other, economic measures were implemented. In June 1803 Napoleon occupied Hanover and closed the Elbe and Weser and all French ports to British goods and to colonial goods transported in British ships. In reply, Britain declared a blockade of the mouths of the Elbe and Weser. This was extended in 1804 to all French ports on the English Channel and the North Sea. In May 1806 Britain attempted to commence a blockade of the entire European coastline from Brest to the Elbe. More serious measures followed.

(a) *Continental System.* After Trafalgar (1805) and the destruction of French naval power, Napoleon gave up the attempt to conquer Britain through an invasion. He concentrated on economic measures to damage her trade and bankrupt her instead. Napoleon had aimed to exclude Britain's exports from markets abroad while she was still able to obtain necessary imports, for she would then have to pay out in gold, which would soon weaken her financially. In 1806 the Continental System was introduced.

(i) Berlin Decrees: on 21st November France, Italy, Spain, Switzerland, Holland and the Rhine Confederation were forbidden to trade with Britain.

(ii) Milan Decrees: on 23rd November any neutral ship which called at a British port was declared subject to seizure and colonial goods were declared liable to be treated as British.

The Continental System was extended to include Denmark, Russia and Prussia in 1807 and Austria in 1808. Napoleon soon was in the position where he had to control the whole of Europe to make the system work against Britain.

(b) *Orders in Council.* Britain retaliated to the Berlin Decrees with similar measures against Napoleon. The object was to starve the Continent of alternative sources of supply and cause rising prices and hardship which would result in growing discontent against Napoleon.

(*i*) First Order: all neutral ships were forbidden to trade with French ports or with countries observing the Berlin Decrees.

(*ii*) Second Order: this declared all countries which excluded British goods to be in a state of blockade.

11. British naval supremacy. Britain's ability to retain "mastery of the seas" contributed to the defeat of Napoleon's plans and thus to his downfall. Examples of the effects of British sea power on Napoleon were as follows.

(*a*) The defeat of his invasion fleets destined for Britain in 1797 and 1805.

(*b*) A decisive contribution to the failure of his plans to conquer Egypt and his designs on India in 1799 (*see* XIV, 11–12).

(*c*) Resisting his ambition to make France a large colonial power.

(*d*) Making the Orders in Council effective, thus resulting in hardship in Europe and encouraging nations to resist Napoleon's Continental System.

(*e*) Supporting the Peninsular campaign with supplies and reinforcements (*see* 15).

12. Napoleon's policies. Napoleon's ideas became increasingly negative. He relied mainly on the sword to maintain his rule and felt a single defeat would end his career. He said: "At home and abroad, I reign only by the fear I inspire."

At home he ruled with the support of a powerful police, which crushed all opposition, and of civil servants who owed their positions to him. After Austerlitz (1805), no foreign ventures had much popular support at home. Thiers (a historian and politician of a later period) believed that Napoleon's further campaigns against Prussia and Russia deviated from France's true interests: he ceased to be the symbol of the French Revolution and aspired to being a European and then a world figure. One observer commented that his aims were not a policy but a "state of mind". They changed as new opportunities appeared. The failure of his policies towards Britain and the implementation of the Continental System have been noted.

After 1807 and 1810 respectively, he was without his two chief aides, Talleyrand (Foreign Minister) and Fouché (Minister of Police). They had felt his policies would end in defeat and were dismissed after intriguing against him.

Napoleon, a great military leader, without Talleyrand's help was an inflexible and poor diplomatist. This was shown in two ways.

(a) His imposition of harsh terms on his enemies when he was successful. His treatment of Austria in 1805 and 1809 was not conducive to securing the permanent friendship of that country. It also helped to alienate sympathy for Napoleon in other states.

(b) His failure to accept good terms when they were offered to him by Metternich in 1813 and 1814 (see 25).

13. Causes of the Peninsular War. Both the Spanish and the Portuguese were determined to resist Napoleon, and he was equally determined to conquer the Peninsula. The main factors which brought Britain and France actively into war in the Peninsula were as follows.

(a) The Continental System. Portugal, an old commercial ally of Britain, refused to accept the Berlin Decrees. Britain decided to reverse her past military strategy and embark on an active land campaign to aid the Portuguese.

(b) Spanish resistance to the new King of Spain. Spain had been actively allied to France since the Treaty of Madrid in 1801. In 1807 France and Spain secretly agreed to divide Portugal. When Ferdinand forced his father Charles IV of Spain to abdicate in 1808, Napoleon failed to give Ferdinand the expected support and decided to offer his own brother, Joseph, King of Naples since 1806, the Spanish crown.

Joseph was expelled from Madrid in July 1808, having been king for one month. The French were defeated at Baylen by the Spanish on 19th July. Napoleon was thus involved in a prolonged war when he had originally thought that only 12,000 troops would be adequate to impose his brother on the reluctant Spanish. The Spanish king, Ferdinand VII, was kept virtually a prisoner of the French.

14. French evacuation of Portugal. A British expeditionary force went to Portugal and Sir Arthur Wellesley defeated Marshal Junot at Vimeiro in August 1808. The French were allowed to evacuate Portugal with their spoils by the Convention of Cintra, arranged by Wellesley's chief, Hew Dalrymple.

Sir John Moore advanced into Spain, but received no help from the Spanish. Napoleon entered Spain and reinstalled Joseph on the throne. Soult was left to pursue Moore, who conducted a brilliant retreat and won a rearguard action at Corunna in January 1809, though he was killed in the action.

In Britain there were clamourings for the abandonment of the Peninsular campaign. Canning and Castlereagh supported the sending of Wellesley with 40,000 men to Portugal. The French had some 300,000 men in the Peninsula. Wellesley employed defensive tactics successfully. In July 1809 he defeated the French at Talavera (after which he was created Duke of Wellington). He built strong lines of communication, the Torres-Vedras Lines. Supported by reinforcements, he drove the French out of Portugal in 1811.

15. French retreat from Spain. The French were soon weakened through the loss of experienced troops to the Russian campaign. In June 1813 Wellington defeated Joseph at Vittoria. Soult was defeated by Wellington at the battle of the Pyrenees in July and forced to retreat to France. Wellington then defeated Soult again, after invading France, at Toulouse on 14th April 1814. This was after Napoleon's abdication.

The British initially had problems owing to their small numbers and the unreliability of the Spanish as allies. They triumphed eventually owing to the following factors.

(*a*) *The difficulties of the French.* The French were hampered in fighting by their long lines of communication, the hostile guerrilla warfare of the Spanish, the lack of supplies and the persistent quarrels between commanders. Troops also had to be withdrawn in 1812 for the Moscow campaign (*see* **17–19**).

(*b*) *The able leadership of the Duke of Wellington*, and the quality of his disciplined troops.

(*c*) *The command of the sea* for reinforcements and supplies.

(*d*) *The use of Portugal as a base* with the strong threefold defensive lines of Torres-Vedras, near Lisbon.

16. Causes of war between France and Russia. Napoleon was determined to make the Tsar yield to his wishes. There were differences between the two leaders over various issues.

(*a*) *Poland.* The Tsar strongly resented the grant of the Duchy of Warsaw to the King of Saxony. He also disliked its enlargement in 1809, after the Austrian war, for he feared it might be used as a French springboard for an attack on Russia.

(b) *Marriage issue.* This caused ill-feeling between Napoleon and Alexander. Alexander was reluctant to have Napoleon as a brother-in-law, and thus, when it was rumoured that Napoleon was interested in the Grand Duchess Catherine, she was hastily married to the Duke of Oldenburg. In 1809 Napoleon applied to the Tsar for the hand of his younger sister Anna. Alexander prevaricated and then declined this. He was then annoyed by Napoleon's subsequent marriage to Marie-Louise of Austria.

(c) *Germany.* Here there were two points of contention.

(i) Prussia: Alexander wanted Prussia to be a buffer state against France. After Jena (1806), the Tsar disapproved of the French action of limiting the Prussian army and maintaining a French garrison there.

(ii) Oldenburg: In 1810 Napoleon seized this state, though its duke had married the Tsar's sister. This was an insult to the Tsar and a breach of Tilsit.

(d) *The Near East.* After the decline of Austria in 1809, France soon appeared as a close rival to Russia in establishing influence in the Ottoman Empire (*see* XIV, 13(c)).

(e) *The Continental System.* This damaged the trade of Russian grain for British manufactured goods. The Russian nobles complained and the Tsar relaxed the enforcement in 1810.

17. Invasion of Russia. Napoleon's "Grand Army" of 600,000 men, including strong contingents from Austria and Prussia, crossed the River Niemen between 23rd and 25th June 1812.

(a) *Withdrawal of the Russians.* The Russians avoided battle and withdrew, using the strategy of "distance as their ally". Napoleon failed to obtain a quick victory. There was soon desertion from his army and a shortage of provisions. The latter was due to lengthening lines of communication in infertile areas devastated by the local inhabitants ("scorched earth" policy).

(b) *Borodino.* Eventually the aged Kutusov was placed in command of the Russian army. He was told to stop the delaying tactics and defend Moscow. On 7th September the battle of Borodino was fought with heavy casualties on both sides. The French claimed victory as they remained in control of the ground and the way to Moscow was open. On 14th September the French entered Moscow.

18. Moscow deserted. Moscow was an empty city. There was no government with whom Napoleon could negotiate terms. The Tsar, encouraged by his advisers, remained at St. Petersburg. He insisted that there would be "no peace while a single foreign soldier remained in Russia".

On 16th September three-quarters of the wooden houses of Moscow were burnt in a great fire. No fire engines were available. Each side blamed the other. Napoleon blamed Russian incendiaries, while the Russians blamed the careless behaviour of the French troops. The fire meant that the city would no longer be a suitable place to serve as winter quarters for the French army.

19. Retreat of Napoleon. On 18th October Napoleon decided to withdraw. On the journey back, his troops suffered from lack of food, the intense cold and the constant attacks of the Russian troops which were intended to hurry them on.

Kutusov was sensible enough to keep his main forces at a discreet distance and to avoid a direct confrontation. Marshal Ney, in charge of the French rearguard, earned the title of "bravest of the brave" for his heroic feats against Russian attacks. The Russians caused further hindrance when Napoleon's army crossed the Beresina. Some 12,000 troops were drowned in the river. About 20,000 eventually staggered back out of Russia in December 1812.

20. Napoleon and the rise of nationalism. In his *Memoirs* written on St. Helena, Napoleon posed as the champion of the French Revolution and of nationalism. He certainly helped to end many abuses of the *ancien régime* in countries under French control. He brought efficient government, made legal and educational reforms and abolished feudalism.

Far from implementing the principle of nationalism, however, Napoleon invoked the spirit of nationalism against himself, particularly in Spain and Germany. This was caused by the following aspects of his policies.

(*a*) *Inflicting heavy defeats on European states and then dominating them.* Though Napoleon liberated foreign territories from repressive rulers and antiquated customs, he imposed on them a system just as harsh. For example:

(*i*) he forced states to supply him with money and men: by 1812 Italy was sending two-thirds of her revenue to France;

(*ii*) he deposed his brother Louis for failing to enforce the

Continental System in Holland, and arrested the Pope when he expressed disapproval of the blockade.

Such harshness led people in the conquered states, particularly Prussia, to try to strengthen their governments to throw off French rule.

NOTE: After 1806 the position was the reverse of former years. The French armies were full of unwilling conscripts from various countries. In contrast, the forces of the Allies were composed to an increased extent of soldiers imbued with a new sense of nationalism, as at the battle of Leipzig (1813).

(*b*) *Imposing alien rulers on other states.* He forced countries to accept his brothers or French generals as rulers. Spain was the first state to rebel against this in 1808.

(*c*) *Imposing a uniform pattern on Europe.* Napoleon forced other states to remodel their institutions on French lines or according to some universal criteria. In his desire to make Europe one single, united entity under French influence, he thus opposed the principles of freedom and nationalism. This caused the conquered states to respond by identifying their independence with the preservation of their ancient customs, traditions and historic way of life, language and law, etc. They also wanted to be economically free of such restrictions as the Continental System.

(*d*) *Annexations and territorial changes.* Napoleon aided unification and national feeling in Italy by the creation of the North Italian Kingdom and in Germany by reducing the number of sovereign states. He also encouraged the Poles to fight for their freedom by giving them the illusion of independence in the Grand Duchy of Warsaw.

(*e*) *Using multinational armies.* As a result of ceaseless campaigns across the length and breadth of Europe, Napoleon's soldiers became intensely aware of national differences.

21. The birth of German nationalism. At this stage a summary of the position in Germany will be useful. Napoleon's actions, instead of keeping Germany continually divided, a traditional policy of the French, resulted in something he did not intend. This was a movement for greater national unity.

(*a*) *Germany before Napoleon.*

(*i*) Numerous sovereign states: before 1789 Germany was a collection of over 300 sovereign kingdoms, duchies and free cities. Each had its own government, law, army and tariff. This "divinely ordained confusion" had been caused by religious strife, the mistakes of German rulers and the policies of the French. Only in the distant past had Germany known unity.

Disunity was accentuated in the eighteenth century by the frequent wars between Germany's most powerful states, Austria and Prussia.

(*ii*) Cosmopolitan myth: until the end of the eighteenth century, leading intellectuals took pride in being free of feelings of a purely German nature. They considered themselves spokesmen of humanity though writing in the German language. The myth persisted that Germany was the heir to the Roman Empire, and thus a cosmopolitan entity rather than a nation state.

(*iii*) Pro-French sentiment: before 1789 many Germans, of whom Frederick the Great was a notable example, enjoyed studying French culture and ideas. Immanuel Kant, who died in 1804, was a disciple of Rousseau.

At first the French Revolution was welcomed by many enlightened Germans, including Fichte. They hoped it would allow progressive ideas to percolate into the parochial states of the German princes.

(*b*) *Germany after 1806.* In 1806 Napoleon dissolved the institution of the Holy Roman Empire, and in the same year he inflicted a humiliating defeat upon Prussia at Jena. As a result of his policies (*see* 5) he helped to kindle the flame of nationalism in Germany more firmly than in any other European country. A reaction set in against French ideas and influence. This was particularly so in Prussia.

(*i*) Influence of German intellectuals: poets, historians, philosophers and writers took a renewed interest in Germany's historic past and in finding the foundations for a united state. German Romantics had already been influenced by the ideas of Johann Herder (1744–1803), who had developed the theory of the *Volk* or tribe, united by ties of a common loyalty as the living spiritual force of the State. These ideas were expanded by the successors of Kant at the University of Berlin.

For example, Fichte (1762–1814) argued that the Germans were the creative, original race in Europe, the *Urvolk*. They were the only great nation to have retained its original language intact from foreign influence. Georg Hegel (1770–1831) advocated the creation of a strong, autocratic *Volkstaat*.

NOTE: For further details on Romanticism, *see* IV, 7.

(*ii*) Germany's rapid recovery: There was a patriotic outcry to rebuild the nation. A group of leaders, including Stein, Scharnhorst and Humboldt, persuaded the Prussian King, between 1807 and 1813, to abolish serfdom, to make reforms in education, the army and administration, and to relax economic restrictions.

22. Russian advance into Poland. The Tsar was anxious to lead a triumphant crusade against Napoleon, though his generals were more cautious. The Tsar issued a proclamation in February 1813 which pledged him to bring "peace and independence to nations prepared to face sacrifices to achieve this end". He was stirred by the new nationalistic spirit which was affecting the peoples of Europe.

Russian forces gradually occupied all the Polish territories in Napoleon's Duchy of Warsaw, except the portion which had formerly belonged to Austria. It was clearly not advisable for them to advance further without Prussian support.

23. Prussian alliance with Russia. At first the Prussian people seemed more anxious than their king, Frederick William, to rise against Napoleon. The Prussian diplomat Hardenberg started negotiations with Metternich to acquire Saxony and to oppose the Russian occupation of Poland. General York marched the Prussian army over to the Russian camp. This was an unprecedented step as it was done without prior authorisation from the King and while Prussia was still allied to France. Prussia then dropped negotiations with Austria in favour of an alliance with Russia in the Treaty of Kalisch of February 1813. Russia promised to give Prussia as much territory as she had possessed before 1806, and to provide her with compensation for the loss of her Polish territories.

24. An armistice arranged. Napoleon managed to gather together yet another army, composed of the untrained youth of France, levies from various parts of Europe and Danish troops. Napoleon defeated Prussian and Russian forces in May, but could not follow up his victories owing to lack of cavalry.

Metternich, the Austrian Chancellor since 1809, had avoided participation in the conflict so far. He also wanted to give Austria time to recover her military strength. He disliked Russia's intrusion into Europe and her championing of Germany. He was horrified when Stein, who had entered the service of the Tsar, drew up a proclamation calling upon every German to help in liberating the Fatherland. He proposed an armistice that would prepare the way for a general peace conference. Napoleon agreed to an armistice from 4th June until 20th July.

25. Austrian mediation rejected. Russia and Prussia were persuaded to offer their minimum conditions for a preliminary peace. In the Treaty of Reichenbach of 24th June 1813 these were stated as follows:

(*a*) the Grand Duchy of Warsaw was to be dissolved;
(*b*) Prussia was to be enlarged and Illyria ceded to Austria;
(*c*) Hamburg and Lübeck were to be restored as free cities.

Metternich modified these conditions and then presented them to Napoleon at Dresden on 28th June. They represented the basis on which Austria would be prepared to mediate between the warring powers. This meant the end of the expanded French Empire. France would have the Rhine and the Alps, the "national frontiers", with much of Italy and Spain. However, Napoleon refused to make territorial concessions.

26. The Fourth Coalition. Gradually a new coalition was formed against France. The countries involved were the following.

(*a*) *Russia.*
(*b*) *Prussia.*
(*c*) *Sweden.* Russia had previously taken Sweden's Finnish provinces. In 1812 the Tsar, to retain Sweden's goodwill, promised to give her Norway, which belonged to Denmark. Thus Bernadotte, the Crown Prince of Sweden, was persuaded to join the coalition.
(*d*) *Austria.* News came through of Wellington's victory at Vittoria in Spain on 21st June 1813. This put new heart into Austria. Two days after an extended armistice ended on 10th August. Austria joined the war against France.
(*e*) *Bavaria.* In October she ceased supporting France and joined the coalition.
(*f*) *Britain.* She agreed to contribute subsidies to finance the new coalition.

27. Defeat of Napoleon. Napoleon managed to defeat the Austrians at Dresden on 27th August. However, his subordinates were beaten in subsidiary engagements and he was forced back to Leipzig. There, on 16th–18th October, occurred the decisive "Battle of the Nations" in which over half a million men were involved. During the conflict one Saxon corps deserted Napoleon, and, though this itself had little effect on the outcome, the French were routed. The members of the Confederation of the Rhine then deserted Napoleon and joined the Allied coalition.

Metternich, suspicious of Russian designs on Poland, tried to obtain moderate peace terms for Napoleon. In the Frankfurt Proposals in November, France was to be restored to her "natural frontiers". An independent Holland was to be created and the Spanish Bourbons restored. Napoleon procrastinated and accepted the terms only when it was too late. Soon Allied armies invaded France from Spain (under Wellington), Switzerland and the Rhine.

28. Abdication of Napoleon. It was agreed by the Allies on 29th January 1814, in the Langres Protocol, that the only alternative to Napoleon was the restoration of the Bourbons. However, the Tsar wanted his protégé, Bernadotte, now King of Sweden, to be the new French king.

On 31st March the Allies entered Paris. The Tsar became sympathetic towards the defeated Napoleon and said he would sponsor a regency for his son, the King of Rome. The wily French diplomat Talleyrand persuaded a meeting of the available senators that the Bourbons should return to France. He organised a provisional government which deposed Napoleon on 2nd April.

Talleyrand persuaded the Tsar that only a Bourbon restoration would tranquillise France, and prevent intrigue and the possibilities of a Jacobin republic. He argued that France would be weak if a ruler was imposed on her. The restoration of the Bourbons in accordance with "legitimacy" would make the government strong. As Bonapartist troops began to surrender in increased numbers, the Tsar agreed that Bonapartism was a lost cause. On 6th April Napoleon agreed to unconditional abdication.

29. The Treaty of Fontainebleau. The terms imposed on Napoleon on 12th April were moderate, owing to the generosity, at the time, of the Tsar.

(a) Napoleon was to be granted, in full sovereignty, the Isle of Elba, where he was to be exiled.

(b) An annual revenue of 2 million francs from France was granted to Napoleon.

(c) The Empress Marie-Louise was to retain the duchies of Parma, Piacenza and Guastalla in perpetuity.

(*d*) Numerous members of Napoleon's family were to retain their titles.

30. Return of the Bourbon dynasty. An armistice was signed between France and the Allies on 23rd April 1814. Then the comte de Provence, brother of the guillotined Louis XVI, made his official entry to Paris on 3rd May. The fiction was maintained that he had been recalled by his country to the throne to rule as Louis XVIII.

DOMESTIC ACHIEVEMENTS OF NAPOLEON

31. Code Napoléon. In 1789 France had no common law, only a mixture of local laws and customs. There was much confusion and injustice since the laws were not uniform and favoured the nobility. Napoleon's paramount influence in government was shown in the codification of laws which took place. It embraced the old and new "from Clovis to the Committee of Public Safety", he boasted in 1809.

There were five legal codes. The *Civil Code* (*Code Napoléon*) of 1804 was soon widely adopted by different states in Europe, South America and Louisiana. It was based on Roman law and concerned topics such as civil rights, marriage, divorce and inheritance, and incorporated a statement of the principles governing such matters. It strengthened the authority of parents over the persons and property of their children. A compact document, it was printed in 1810, was translated into Portuguese and Spanish and was perhaps Napoleon's greatest domestic achievement.

The other codes were *Civil Procedure* (1806), the *Commercial Code* (1807), *Criminal Procedure* (1808) and the *Penal Code* (1810). They confirmed certain principles of the Revolution such as the following:

(*a*) equality before the law and the prohibition of special privileges: this meant that all French citizens were now eligible for positions in government;

(*b*) abolition of serfdom and feudalism;

(*c*) guarantee of religious toleration and trial by jury.

32. The Concordat. The attack on the Catholic Church in France had been perhaps the greatest error of the revolutionaries.

Napoleon restored the link with Rome by the Concordat of July 1801. The provisions were as follows.

(a) Catholicism was restored as the official religion, though others were not forbidden. The Pope was recognised as head of the Church.

(b) The State was to pay the salaries of the French clergy. Bishops were to be nominated by the State though appointed by the Pope.

(c) The French Republic received Papal recognition. The Church agreed to give up claims to lands taken during the Revolution.

The Concordat gained popular support for Napoleon because the majority of the French people were Catholic. It also assured the French peasants of the lands taken from the Church and sold to them during the Revolution.

33. Creation of the Legion of Honour. Napoleon had risen to high office largely on the strength of his own abilities. He was determined that the chief positions in the State should be open to men of talent, irrespective of birth. He would not allow the *émigrés* to consider themselves the true nobility of France, and in 1802 he virtually created a new class, distinguished by intellectual gifts in various walks of life, in the Legion of Honour. This was a non-hereditary decoration for military and civil services rendered to the State. It was attacked by some who thought it contrary to the ideals of equality. Napoleon defended it as an incentive and an instrument of government. However, it could be argued that he created a hierarchy of rank which perpetuated the class system in a new form.

34. Other reforms. These were in the following spheres.

(a) *Public education.* He made a step towards state control and the elimination of clerical influence in education. However, the system was never brought fully into force.

(i) Four grades were established: these were primary, secondary and semi-military *lycées*, and technical schools. By 1813 secondary education in France had become the best in Europe, but primary education remained much as it had been before 1789.

(ii) There were changes in curriculum, science and mathematics becoming important subjects in secondary education.

Educational standards were improved, but the close supervision exercised by the State made much of the teaching mechanical.

(*b*) *Finance and commerce*. The following reforms should be noted.

(*i*) The Bank of France was established in 1800. It acted for the government and helped provide a sound currency and financial stability.

(*ii*) The system of tax collection was improved and rigid economies made in government. Commercial exchanges and chambers of commerce were established. Advisory boards were created to help in industrial activities.

(*iii*) Public works: Napoleon embarked on an extensive programme of road, bridge and canal building. Cities were beautified, particularly Paris, where the Louvre was completed and a vast system of arterial roads was planned.

(*c*) *Local government*. This was highly centralised. France was divided into *départements* (under prefects), *arrondissements* (under sub-prefects) and *communes* (under mayors). All the local officials, plus the judges and police chiefs, were appointed by and answerable to the national government. This strengthened the control of the government in securing swift execution of the laws.

35. Assessment of Napoleon's domestic policies. Between 1800 and 1803, when Napoleon was First Consul, the most constructive work at home was done. The notable feature of his statesmanship was not its originality; it was the immense energy and strength of will and attention to detail that he contributed in his encouragement of various measures.

Though Napoleon's policies provided France with a stable and efficient government, he lacked vision or ideals. His work was strictly materialistic, concentrated on the principles of order, discipline and the use of force. He once said: "I am the Revolution". Certainly he tried to realise many of the Revolution's ideas, encouraging religious toleration and equal opportunity for all to progress on the grounds of ability. However, in many ways, his ideas differed from those of the Revolution.

(*a*) He disliked democracy and saw political liberties as merely a disruptive force in the State, likely to imperil its unity and cohesion.

(*i*) The Revolution encouraged liberty of expression; Napoleon believed in a strict censorship of speech, correspondence and the press.

(*ii*) The Revolution believed in no unjust arrests; Napoleon believed in a secret police. In 1810 he created state prisons and allowed arrest without trial.

(*b*) In the Code Napoléon he reversed one of the measures of the Revolution. He repealed the law which stated that an inheritance should be divided equally among the children.

(*c*) In the Legion of Honour he created a hierarchy of rank. This was likely to perpetuate the class system in a different form.

(*d*) In his government reforms he encouraged centralisation. This followed the ideas of the Jacobins who had favoured the dictatorship of Paris over the rest of France. It differed from the policy of the Girondins who had supported decentralisation.

PROGRESS TEST 2

1. When was Napoleon at the height of his power? **(1, 4–5, 7)**

2. Why was war renewed between Britain and France? **(3)**

3. Describe the formation and collapse of the Third Coalition. **(4)**

4. List the provisions of the Peace of Tilsit. **(5)**

5. Why was Austria defeated in 1809? **(7)**

6. What major factors contributed to Napoleon's fall? **(9)**

7. What was the Continental System? **(10)**

8. Describe the war against Napoleon in Spain and Portugal. **(13–15)**

9. Why did Napoleon invade Russia? **(16)**

10. How did Napoleon invoke the "principle of nationality" against himself? **(20)**

11. Account for the rise of Prussia after Jena. **(21(*b*))**

12. Why in 1813 was Austria reluctant to join a European coalition against France? **(24)**

13. Describe the attempts of Metternich to mediate between France and the European powers. **(25, 27)**

14. Why was it decided to restore the Bourbon dynasty? **(28)**

15. What was the *Code Napoléon*? **(31)**

16. Describe the achievements of Napoleon in education and ocal government. **(34)**

CHAPTER III

The Congress of Vienna

HOW A SETTLEMENT WAS REACHED

1. Preliminaries. Before the powers met formally at a general peace conference various provisions for post-war Europe were agreed.

(*a*) *The Treaty of Chaumont* (9th March 1814). While their armies were fighting the disintegrating forces of Napoleon, the Allied diplomats met. Austria, Prussia, Russia and Britain agreed to join for twenty years after the coming of peace to defend any settlement. This resulted from the efforts of Castlereagh, the British Foreign Minister, who wanted to forestall any breakup of the coalition. The powers also agreed to implement the following:

(*i*) an enlarged and independent Holland;

(*ii*) a confederated Germany;

(*iii*) an independent Switzerland;

(*iv*) a Bourbon Spain;

(*v*) the restoration of the Italian states.

(*b*) *First Treaty of Paris* (30th May 1814). After Napoleon's overthrow and the restoration of the Bourbon king, the Allies made a settlement with France before settling outstanding differences between themselves.

The terms of the treaty signed with France were moderate. The Allies hoped it would strengthen the position of the new king.

(*i*) The eastern frontier was reduced to the boundary of 1st January 1792. This included Avignon, parts of Savoy and parts of Germany and Belgium.

(*ii*) France had to surrender Tobago, St. Lucia and Mauritius to Britain and to restore half of San Domingo to Spain.

(*iii*) France was not required to pay an indemnity or reparations.

At this time the Allies invited delegations from nearly every European state to attend a European congress at Vienna to make final territorial settlements.

43

(c) *Further consultations.* For six months prior to the meeting of the congress at Vienna, Britain, Prussia, Austria and Russia discussed the terms of the final peace. They were determined to keep the major issues under their immediate control at the forthcoming congress. As a result a large measure of agreement was reached on colonial questions and western Europe.

2. A congress of notables. The Congress of Vienna comprised eight months of negotiations between the five major powers from October 1814 to May 1815. It proved to be one of the most important diplomatic gatherings in European history. There had never been such an assembly of celebrities. All the powers were represented except Turkey. Emperors, kings, princes and leading diplomats were present.

However, the only occasions on which the majority of delegates assembled were ceremonial or social: Emperor Francis provided lavish entertainments.

3. Aims of the Allied powers. The aims and positions of the Allied diplomats are summarised below.

(a) *Britain.* Castlereagh, the Foreign Minister, was primarily concerned with France and safeguarding British trade and maritime rights. He wanted a moderate peace, which would receive the consent of the French people and preserve the "integrity" of France. His conception of the new Europe was influenced by the following factors.

(i) Pitt's draft of 1804: Pitt had planned that Prussia should expand in north and west Germany, and Austria in Italy, as compensation for the expansion of Russian power westwards. Belgium should be combined with Holland to safeguard the Low Countries against French expansion.

(ii) The desire to create a strong barrier round France.

(b) *Austria.* Metternich emerged as the most commanding personality of the conference. He wanted to preserve the *status quo*. Like Castlereagh, he was totally out of sympathy with national and liberal ideas which were becoming increasingly popular in Europe.

(c) *Russia.* The Tsar, Alexander, handled the major negotiations on the Russian side. He came to the conference supported by numerous gifted advisers of diverse backgrounds and interests to suit his varying moods, such as Stein, Capo d'Istria and Nesselrode. He saw himself as father of peoples struggling for liberation and as guardian of a wider European federation. He failed to see the contradiction implicit in the dual roles of liberator and divine arbiter.

In 1815 the Tsar was generally a liberal and enlightened force in European affairs. For example, he had favoured generous terms to the French and insisted that Louis XVIII grant a constitution.

(d) *Prussia.* Hardenberg and Humboldt were the Prussian representatives. Their position was difficult. Though Prussia had most to lose from a Russian expansion into Europe, she was in no position to protest. Her recovery had been largely due to Russian help, and the Tsar's assistance was needed for any territorial compensation that she might derive for her losses in Poland.

Some advisers favoured plans for Prussian hegemony in northern Germany and favoured the annexation of Saxony. King Frederick William, however, was inclined to a policy of cautious conservatism, so as not to antagonise Austria.

4. The Polish-Saxon problem. No progress was made until the future of Poland and Saxony had been decided. The Tsar had previously committed himself to doubling Prussia's size and population (*see* II, **23**). He was determined to retain the whole of Poland, and Prussia would thus need compensation elsewhere. She was prepared to accept the loss of her Polish territories if she received Saxony, which had remained loyal to Napoleon until after the battle of Leipzig in 1813.

These plans were opposed by Britain and Austria. Deadlock resulted. Castlereagh knew that considerable tact was necessary with the Tsar, who wavered between the world of liberalism and narrowly defined Russian interests. When Castlereagh told Tsar Alexander that it was not the resurrection of a free Poland that Britain opposed but a puppet one under Russian control, he was curtly informed that Russia had an army of 600,000 men (*see* XII, **1-2, 26**).

5. Influence of Talleyrand. The French delegate Talleyrand waited until dissensions between the Allies provided an opportunity for the use of his diplomatic skills. He wanted to end the isolation of France, and restore her to the status of a great power. He achieved this in the following way.

(a) *By gaining the support of the minor powers.* He criticised the claims of the Big Four (Russia, Prussia, Austria and Britain) to control the Congress. He induced them to include the other four signatories of the Treaty of Paris (France, Spain, Portugal and Sweden) in a general council and its various sub-committees.

(b) *By introducing the principle of legitimacy.* Talleyrand, having gained France's admission on equal terms to the preliminary talks, introduced the concept of legitimacy. Since this principle had been applied to his own country with the Bourbon restoration, he suggested it should be the solution of the problems of the Congress.

He hoped to save Saxony and organised a collective protest by the lesser German states. To the Tsar's remark that the King of Saxony, at the time imprisoned, had forfeited his throne by treachery, he replied that this was merely a question of dates.

(c) *By encouraging the formation of a French–British–Austrian coalition.* Castlereagh had failed in all attempts to break the joint understanding between Prussia and Russia. His confidence increased, however, on receipt of the news that the war between Britain and the United States which had begun in 1812 had ended, and he accepted Talleyrand's idea of an alliance. By a secret agreement on 3rd January 1815 the three countries of France, Britain and Austria agreed to support one another in the event of any Russian or Prussian attack on any of them resulting from the peace proposals.

(d) *By gaining admittance to the councils of the Big Four.* The price of French support for the alliance was their inclusion in future detailed negotiations.

6. The Polish-Saxon settlement. The Allies realised they were hopelessly divided among themselves. As a result demands were moderated and the spirit of compromise prevailed.

On 28th January Metternich proposed that Austria and Prussia should agree to certain modifications of their pre-war frontiers in Russia's favour. Part of Saxony was to be given to Prussia in compensation, the remainder returning to its legitimate sovereign. In February a settlement was reached. Most of the other issues were then speedily agreed, particularly since the Allies had reached a broad consensus of opinion prior to the conference.

7. Territorial provisions of the Vienna settlement. The following were the major regions involved.

(a) *Russia.* Her possessions were enlarged by Finland, which had been conquered from Sweden in 1808, and Bessarabia, which had been taken from Turkey. Further, Russia received the major portion of Poland, which the Tsar promised would be made into a separate kingdom.

(*b*) *Prussia*. This state gained two-fifths of Saxony and retained Posen in Poland. As compensation for not getting all of Saxony the Duchy of Westphalia and Swedish Pomerania were also added. To strengthen the barrier against France the conglomeration of minute states in the Rhineland were consolidated into one block under Prussia.

(*c*) *Austria*. As compensation for the loss of Belgium and the loss of her former role in Germany, Austria received Lombardy and Venetia in Italy. It was intended to give her a strong position there to promote stability and so that she could act as a check to French expansion. She also received Salzburg and the Tyrol from Bavaria.

(*d*) *Germany*. No attempt was made to revive the Holy Roman Empire, which Napoleon had destroyed in 1806, and Austria readily agreed to this. The number of German states was reduced from over 300 to thirty-nine. German states which had ceased to exist as far back as 1803 were not restored. The focal point of the new German Confederation was to be a Diet (Parliament), to which the states were to send delegates. It was stipulated that members should establish assemblies of estates.

(*e*) *Holland*. Belgium was united with Holland. This was done to strengthen Holland's border against France and to compensate Holland for the loss of her colonial possessions to Britain. The independent state of Luxembourg was united under the Netherlands Crown and given a Prussian garrison.

(*f*) *Britain*. Non-European gains in the form of colonies from France or her allies, particularly Holland, satisfied Britain. In particular she received Heligoland in the North Sea, Malta and the Ionian Isles in the Mediterranean, Cape Colony in South Africa, and Ceylon.

(*g*) *Sweden*. This state gained Norway. This was done to compensate her for the loss of Finland to Russia, to punish Denmark, who had remained loyal to Napoleon, and as a reward for entering the Fourth Coalition in 1813.

(*h*) *Italy*. Piedmont was given Nice and Genoa to strengthen the north-west border of Italy against France. Italian states which had disappeared by 1798 were not restored, and the Genoan and Venetian republics were not revived. The Tsar made the remark that "republics are no longer fashionable".

OBSERVATIONS ON THE PEACE SETTLEMENT

8. Principles underlying the settlement. The leading diplomats were, to a greater or lesser extent, influenced by the following considerations.

(*a*) *The need to create a barrier round France.* The Allies were determined to strengthen the territories on the borders of France to deter the French from future aggression.

The provisions concerning the Rhine, the Netherlands and Italy have been noted (*see* 7). The Swiss Confederation was strengthened by the addition of three cantons, making twenty-two in all. Her neutrality was guaranteed by a declaration of the major powers.

(*b*) *National self-interest and compensation.* The states that had contributed most to Napoleon's overthrow, the signatories of the Treaty of Chaumont, were determined to make the most gains. When their aims and interests conflicted, the loser was generally compensated by receiving land at the expense of a weaker power.

(*c*) *The preservation of the balance of power.* Metternich and Castlereagh felt the preservation of peace depended on a common front by the victors. Both wanted a "just equilibrium" to exist among European states in terms of territory, population and resources. They were less concerned with obtaining power for their own states than with preventing other states becoming too strong. This would only encourage future unilateral aggression.

The problem was that Russia, the strongest power, made extravagant claims. Since Russia had made gains in Europe, Austria and Prussia had to receive compensation. Both Metternich and Castlereagh agreed that France was not to be unduly weakened.

(*d*) *Legitimacy.* Talleyrand had persuaded the Allies to apply this principle to the restoration of the Bourbons. Later the Allies decided to apply this guiding rule to the territorial provisions. Metternich gave it his own interpretation. Legitimacy meant that a nation had no existence without its ruler, an autocrat with a "right" to the throne which he or his forefathers had occupied.

(*i*) Since the "divine right" theory had been discredited, some approval was given to this doctrine as a theoretical justification for the restoration of old rulers. The Bourbon king returned to Spain, while the rulers of Central Europe, Tuscany, Modena and Sardinia and the Pope also returned to their thrones.

(*ii*) The principle was not applied automatically or consistently. Many defunct German and Italian states were not revived and nor was the Holy Roman Empire. Murat was allowed to remain King of Naples. (However, when he supported Napoleon's revolt in 1815, he was captured and shot, and the legitimate Bourbon king restored.)

(*iii*) The principle was ignored if the considerations of providing safeguards against the French or rewarding the victors intervened. For instance Saxony and Denmark suffered considerable territorial loss.

(*e*) *The acceptance of the fait accompli*. The diplomats made no attempt to return to the position of 1789, the *status quo ante*. Former arrangements between some or all of the Allies, for example the Treaties of Reichenbach, Kalisch and Chaumont, influenced their final decisions. Many changes brought about as a result of Napoleon's influence in Europe were recognised, particularly in Germany. The Allies wanted stability and repose, to accept the inevitable and to restore previous conditions only if it was felt that greater security would be gained.

9. Weaknesses of the settlement. The diplomats were too preoccupied with the distribution of territories which France had been forced to relinquish. No consideration was given to the following factors.

(*a*) *The impact of the ideas of the French Revolution*. The diplomats ignored the following important concepts.

(*i*) The principle of nationalism. Despite their desire for independence, Belgium, Poland and Finland were handed over to governments foreign to them. The language factor was ignored; for example Norwegian was closely allied to Danish, not to Swedish, but Norway was given to Sweden. Little was done to encourage the hopes of some Germans and Italians for greater unity.

(*ii*) Democratic and liberal ideas. No attempt was made to consider the people when determining who their leaders were to be. In many cases unpopular absolute monarchies were restored to power. No effort was made to provide for liberal government. As a result the Spanish king soon abolished the constitutional gains made in 1812 (*see* IV, 9(*a*)).

(*b*) *The need for change in the future*. In time every one of the main decisions was reversed.

(*i*) Belgium gained independence in 1831 (*see* IV, **25**).

(*ii*) Germany and Italy were unified during 1870–1 (*see* IX and XIII).

(*iii*) Norway was separated from Sweden by the Treaty of Carlsbad of 1905.

(*iv*) Poland became a nation in 1919.

(*c*) *The Eastern Question.* It was not sufficiently appreciated that the decline of Turkey was a major problem in Europe (*see* XIV).

10. Justification of the settlement. In the context of its time the peace treaty signed at Vienna was a reasonable and moderate compromise. It contained less flaws than two similarly important settlements: the Treaties of Utrecht (1713) and Versailles (1919). The following were some good points about the settlement.

(*a*) There was no great demand for national unity in 1815. The only exception was in Germany. However, the conflicting interests of Austria, Prussia and the smaller states would have made this impossible to achieve short of war.

(*i*) In Italy a consciousness of nationality hardly existed, as the failure of Murat's last appeal to it showed.

(*ii*) Not all Belgians desired independence. The unification of Holland and Belgium might have proved a success.

(*b*) Peace was preserved for forty years. No major outbreak of hostilities occurred until the Crimean War. Europe was able to recuperate from the wars which had devastated her for twenty-five years.

(*c*) A tradition of international co-operation in periodic conferences was created (*see* 13(*b*)). Though the Conference System lapsed after 1825 the "Concert of Europe" did exert a beneficial influence on European affairs at certain crucial points until 1870. A blueprint had been found which was to be more fully developed after 1919.

(*d*) The settlement was enlightened and progressive in some respects, for example the following:

(*i*) the policy adopted towards German reconstruction (*see* 7(*d*));

(*ii*) the guarantee by the major powers of the neutrality and independence of Switzerland;

(*iii*) the condemnation of the slave trade;

(*iv*) the advocation of the freedom of navigation on international rivers and waterways.

THE HUNDRED DAYS AND THEIR SEQUEL

11. Return of Napoleon. On 1st March 1815 Napoleon, having escaped from Elba, landed at Cannes, with less than a thousand armed men.

(*a*) *Reasons for his escape.*

(*i*) He was bored and dissatisfied with inactivity and the absence of power.

(*ii*) He wanted to exploit the disunity which he knew had existed among the Allies (*see* 4).

(*iii*) He knew that discontent existed in France and that some of his supporters hoped he would return.

(*b*) *The French welcome his return.* The Allies and the French government were surprised that Napoleon was so readily supported by the majority of the people and the troops. This caused the flight of Louis XVIII to Ghent.

Napoleon misled the first troops sent to capture him into believing he had been summoned to Paris by the Allies. The subsequent lack of opposition to his return can be attributed to the following factors.

(*i*) The unpopularity of Louis XVIII (*see* V, 2).

(*ii*) The dynamism of Napoleon. The French could not resist the magic of Bonapartism and the attendant glories it had brought. Many rallied to his support, including Marshal Ney, who had once vowed that he would bring him back in a cage. At one point Napoleon advanced alone towards a battalion sent to capture him, inviting them to kill him if they wished. They ignored the orders to fire and followed him.

(*iii*) Napoleon's promises. He gained popular support when he promised peace and the creation of a parliament.

12. Final defeat of Napoleon. Napoleon hoped to divide the Allies, and thus he made a peace offer to Britain and Austria. However, the Allied leaders in Vienna immediately renewed the Treaty of Chaumont, determined to expel Napoleon.

Only British and Prussian forces were available, since Austrian troops were involved with Murat, who had risen to support Napoleon in Naples, and Russian troops had been withdrawn to Poland.

Napoleon decided to advance into Belgium and to defeat his enemies separately before they could effect a union. He drove the Prussian forces back at Ligny on 16th June, but on the same day Marshal Ney was defeated by the Prince of Orange at Quatre Bras. On 18th June Wellington with an army of British, Dutch, Belgians and Germans held Napoleon's forces all day at Waterloo near Brussels. In the evening Prussian forces under Blücher arrived in the French rear, and this contributed to the Allied victory.

The Emperor fled, failed to escape to America and then surrendered to the British. This time Napoleon was exiled to the British possession of St. Helena in the South Atlantic, where he died in 1821.

13. The Quadruple Alliance. Napoleon's return illustrated the strength of support which the name of Napoleon commanded in France. The Allies were now prepared to accept some form of wider guarantee for the safety of the European settlement.

In October the Tsar proposed that the Big Four should mutually guarantee each other's possessions. Castlereagh opposed this and also the Tsar's demand for a guarantee of the Bourbon dynasty. Instead he persuaded the Allies on 20th November 1815 to accept a treaty perpetuating the Quadruple Alliance as originally established at Chaumont. The main points were as follows.

(*a*) Austria, Prussia, Russia and Britain agreed to maintain by armed force for twenty years the exclusion of the Bonaparte dynasty from France and to uphold the arrangements reached at Vienna and at Paris (*see* **14**).

(*b*) The sixth article pledged the Allies to hold reunions at fixed periods to discuss their "great common interests". They would take any action judged necessary to maintain peace in Europe. In this way the Conference System was born.

14. The Second Treaty of Paris. Increased penalties were imposed on the French. It was some time, however, before agreement could be reached between the Allies over the details. Prussian generals demanded Alsace and Lorraine as well as other French territory and heavy indemnities. On the other hand Castlereagh was determined to preserve the honour and dignity of the French, and not to create a lasting sense of grievance. With the support of the Tsar, he managed to win Austria's acceptance of moderate compromise proposals. Prussia had to give way. The following provisions were agreed on 20th November 1815.

(*a*) France would be reduced to her boundaries of 1790. She lost a few areas on her Belgian and Swiss frontiers and most of Savoy.

(b) France had to agree to pay an indemnity of 700 million francs, to accept an army of occupation for five years and to return works of art seized by French armies.

15. The Holy Alliance proposal. On 25th May 1815, during the general period of turmoil and insecurity following Napoleon's return to France, the Tsar had produced the draft of an extraordinary document.

(a) *Its signatories.* It was to be a personal pact between sovereigns and princes. The three main signatories, the "Holy Allies", were to be Prussia, Austria and Russia. Other states were to be invited to adhere to the pious principles which it espoused.

(b) *Its purpose.* It was an attempt to apply the principles of morality and Christianity to international diplomacy. One clause announced that the monarchs would remain united "by the bonds of a true and indissoluble fraternity". They would regard themselves as "fathers of families towards subjects and armies". Governments and peoples must now behave as "members of one and the same Christian nation".

(c) *Its origins.* The Tsar was experiencing a mood of mysticism and deep religious fervour at the time. The following considerations prompted him in presenting this document.

(i) Past projects: before his death in 1610 Henry IV of France had formed a Grand Design, the idea of which was that delegates from different countries should settle disputes and avoid war. There was also the Abbé de St. Pierre's *Projet de paix perpetuelle* (1713) and Chateaubriand's *Génie du Christianisme* (1802).

(ii) Proposal of 1804: Alexander had suggested to Pitt a pact by which all states should renounce war as an instrument of policy. Pitt expressed interest in having some such arrangement after the war, no doubt intending it to be directed against France.

(iii) Desire to regain the initiative: the Tsar feared that he was losing the political ascendancy in European affairs. Napoleon's escape from Elba had given the initiative to Britain. Wellington had opposed the suggestion that the Tsar should be appointed Allied commander-in-chief.

16. Reaction of the powers to the Holy Alliance. No rulers or diplomats except the Tsar took the document seriously. Castlereagh called it "a piece of sublime mysticism and nonsense", while Metternich scorned the whole idea as a "high-sounding nothing".

However, Metternich saw a means by which the Holy Alliance could be used to turn the Tsar from his liberal sympathies towards support of the Austrian policy of conservatism. He made amendments to the text before the King of Prussia and Emperor of Austria signed the document. They had no objection to signing an agreement which was too general to involve them in any precise commitment.

All other rulers adhered to the Holy Alliance except the Pope, the Sultan of Turkey and George III, who was insane. The Prince Regent pleaded the peculiarities of the British constitution as an excuse for not being involved.

17. Significance of the Holy Alliance. The Tsar was motivated by good intentions when he introduced the document. However, it was as meaningless as the Kellogg Pact of 1928 by which states agreed to outlaw war as an instrument of policy.

The Holy Alliance created alarm and distrust in Europe. It appeared to be against the national and liberal spirit of the age, being confined exclusively to monarchs. It was confused in the public mind with the Quadruple Alliance and also the reactionary policy of the three eastern powers.

The Holy Alliance became an anti-liberal alliance when Metternich, playing adroitly upon the Tsar's wavering personality during the period 1815–20, turned it into an organ of reaction to suppress revolts. It was thus to be a contributory cause of the failure of the Quadruple Alliance and the Conference System as envisaged by Castlereagh (*see* IV, **12**).

PROGRESS TEST 3

1. What were the details of the First Treaty of Paris and of the Treaty of Chaumont? (**1**)

2. Compare and contrast the aims of the various Allied powers at the Congress of Vienna. (**3–4**)

3. Why did the Allies have difficulty initially in reaching agreement? (**4**)

4. What was meant by the principle of legitimacy? (**5**(*b*), **8**(*d*))

5. What territorial gains were made by Russia, Prussia and Austria? (**7**)

6. What factors influenced the diplomats at the Congress of Vienna? **(8)**

7. Discuss the strong and weak points of the Vienna settlement. **(9–10)**

8. Why did Napoleon escape from Elba? **(11)**

9. Which countries contributed to Napoleon's final defeat in 1815? **(12)**

10. On what major issue did Castlereagh and the Tsar fail to agree? **(13)**

11. What was the purpose and significance of the Holy Alliance? Describe Metternich's attitude towards it. **(15–17)**

CHAPTER IV

The Age of Revolution, 1815–48

IDEAS UNDERLYING THE
REVOLUTIONARY MOVEMENTS

1. Introduction. During the period 1815–48 considerable developments took place in the industrial, technical and scientific fields: it was a period of change and growth. In politics many felt it was the "age of progress". They had faith in human nature, and optimistically hoped that man could better his condition and that the ideal of universal brotherhood could be realised. They were hostile to accepted conventions, religion and belief in the supernatural. In particular many of the provisions of the Vienna settlement were disliked (*see* III, 9).

Various ideas motivated rebels in the uprisings which occurred during the period 1815–48 and also influenced political events afterwards. A summary of the main forces is given in 2–7 below.

2. Nationalism. A national group or nation is composed of people who believe that they have common ethnic and historical origins and share certain social and cultural bonds, relating to customs and traditions and possibly also religion and language. Nationalism is a feeling of loyalty and patriotism that a national group or nation has towards its country. When such a group is a minority in an existing multi-nation state, nationalism takes the form of a demand for national self-determination or independence.

After 1815 the people in certain areas of Europe gradually transferred their loyalty from the legitimate ruler to the national ideal and country. This had considerable effects in Europe, as both an integrative and a disintegrative force.

(*a*) *Integrative force.* In Germany and Italy nationalism encouraged separate units to merge together to form one united state.

(*b*) *Disintegrative force.* In other areas nationalism meant the desire for independence from large multi-nation empires or from any existing government considered foreign. Examples of such larger units were:

(*i*) the United Kingdom of the Netherlands (*see* **25**);

(*ii*) the Austrian Empire (*see* XI);

(*iii*) the Ottoman Empire (*see* XIV).

3. Democracy. This meant rule directly by the people or rule by representatives chosen by the people through a majority vote based on universal free suffrage. Owing to the excesses of Jacobin rule during the French Revolution, this idea was associated in the minds of the upper classes with "mob or plebeian rule" or "tyrannical rule by the majority". Thus it was distrusted as an undesirable influence by governments after 1815.

Democracy was closely allied to liberalism and was a powerful force moving the middle classes to gain constitutional rights from the King and nobility in the 1830 July revolution in France. However, the middle classes were not keen to extend the franchise to the lower classes or to ameliorate bad social conditions.

This resulted in a division of opinion among the revolutionaries during the 1848 revolutions in France and Germany.

(*a*) *The middle classes stressed liberty.* They wanted political rights for themselves, "constitutional" control over government, and laws for the preservation of property and existing economic rights.

(*b*) *The working classes stressed equality.* They wanted an extension of the franchise so that they could play an effective role in government, and demanded the implementation of socialist ideas and economic rights.

4. Liberalism. There are many connotations of the words "liberal" and "liberalism". The word "liberal" was first used in Spain in the early 1800s. In essence it denoted a plea for the liberty of the individual and his rights to self-expression. It manifested itself in demands for constitutional rights, first seriously demanded in Europe at the start of the French Revolution. In 1812 the Spanish Parliament (Cortes) established a new constitution, modelled on the French constitution of 1791. It was of an advanced democratic type, providing for a one-chamber parliament, universal suffrage, popular sovereignty, etc.

After 1815 the middle classes, in France particularly, stressed "moderation" in politics. They looked to a *via media* between the absolutism of a king and the despotism of the mob. They felt that in terms of status, income and education they were uniquely qualified to govern. They wanted a "limited democracy", which meant a narrow franchise and "constitutional rights" protecting them against:

(a) arbitrary rule by the king with the aid of his nobility;

(b) tyrannical rule by the masses resulting in the loss of their property rights, etc.

During the 1848 revolutions in France and Germany the middle classes feared the growing influence of the working classes, and the impact of their socialist ideas.

5. Nationalism and liberalism. In Europe both liberal and national ideas were taboo during the period 1815–48. This led many nationalists, particularly in Germany, to believe that a unified state would have a liberal government, where the elected representatives of the people could control legislation and taxation, and where individual liberties were guaranteed. However, it was unfortunate that in Central and Eastern Europe the power of the middle classes was weak. Liberalism was never clearly understood and tended to become confused in Germany with demands for unification or in Hungary and Poland with demands for national emancipation.

In Italy liberal and national movements tended to complement each other. In Germany, however, nationalism was captured for the conservative and autocratic cause after 1848 (*see* IX, 22(*c*)). In the Austrian Empire liberal and national movements were violently opposed in 1848. While the Austrians and Hungarians clamoured for "democratic" or "liberal" rights for themselves, they were not so keen to extend them to national minorities.

6. Socialism. Modern socialist ideas originated in the French Revolution and developed as a direct result of the evils of the competitive *laissez-faire* economic system during the Industrial Revolution. The *laissez-faire* doctrine was prevalent during the nineteenth century. It was argued that the role of government was the negative one of preserving law and order, and that it should not intervene in economic and social matters. Socialists argued that government should take over the management of economic affairs, through the public ownership of economic resources, thus ensuring a fair distribution of the wealth of the State. In 1848 it was the working classes in France and Germany who were primarily influenced by these ideas.

During the latter half of the nineteenth century, socialism developed as a political force in France, Germany and eventually Italy. An extreme form of socialism, "scientific" or "revolutionary" socialism, better known as Communism, also played some part in the French civil wars in 1848 and 1871. It later profoundly influenced events in Russia. Communism owed its modern form to Karl Marx (1818–83), who in collaboration with another German, Engels, wrote *The Manifesto of the Communist Party* (1848).

7. Romanticism. This term was first used in the arts, especially music and literature, and represented a revolt based on faith, sentiment and emotion against the power of reason. It was a symbol of man's desire to be free from religious, political and social restrictions, and of his desire for self-expression. Many poets, musicians, artists and scholars supported the ideals of the French Revolution and later national struggles. An early English Romantic poet was Percy Bysshe Shelley (1792–1822) while Romantic composers included Beethoven, Mahler, Dvořák and Verdi.

Dissatisfaction with European conditions in the late eighteenth century led some intellectuals to idealise the past and to try and remodel the world. This resulted in a cultural renaissance. Scholars brought to light half-forgotten myths, tales and legends of their nation's heroic past. They helped kindle an ardent longing in people to emulate the deeds of their ancestors.

Indirectly Romanticism contributed to the growth of liberalism and nationalism and hence played an important role in the revolutions between 1820 and 1848. It was particularly important in the case of the following groups.

(*a*) *The Greeks.* A literary renaissance preceded their revolt against the Turks in 1821 (*see* XIV, **19**(*a*)). It commanded wide sympathy in Europe. The Greeks were regarded as the descendants of the parents of European civilisation. Considerable publicity surrounded the death of the English poet Lord Byron at Missolonghi (1824) in the cause of Greek freedom.

(*b*) *The Italians.* The "Young Italy" movement of Mazzini appealed to the idealism and heroicism of the hot-headed and flamboyant youth. They were stirred by the fact that in the past Italy had twice given to humanity a sense of unity, based first on the Roman Empire and then on the Catholic Church headed by the Pope.

(c) *The Slavs*. With the exception of the Russians, the Slavs (Poles, Czechs, Croats, Serbs) had all been subjugated by stronger neighbours. Johann Herder (1744–1803), who hated his native Prussia and lived in Riga, gave a tremendous stimulus to the nationalism of the Slav peoples. Their folk-culture was in danger of being swamped by the more powerful and richer civilisations of others. Herder stressed the uniqueness of each people, tribe and language.

Linguistic and literary studies encouraged the Czechs and Croats to seek political rights within the Austrian Empire (*see* XI, **11**(*b*)). For details of the growth of Pan-Slavism, *see* XVI, **1**.

COLLAPSE OF THE QUADRUPLE ALLIANCE AND THE CONGRESS SYSTEM, 1815–25

8. Conference of Aix-la-Chapelle. After 1815 France was prompt in repaying the indemnity and resented the army of occupation. The Allies agreed to a conference to consider French problems. At the Conference of Aix-la-Chapelle in 1818, the powers discussed the following points.

(*a*) *French issues*. The final adjustment of French debts was settled with the aid of a loan from London bankers. It was agreed that the troops would be withdrawn and France admitted once more to the councils of the major powers.

(*b*) *The question of intervention*. The Tsar used the opportunity to raise the question of the future of the alliance. He suggested that all governments should now agree to maintain the territorial settlements concluded at Vienna and to guarantee all legitimate sovereigns everywhere against revolutionary upheaval. Alexander wanted particularly to send an Allied force to help the Spanish king subdue his colonists in revolt (*see* **14**).

The Tsar withdrew his project for the time being owing to opposition from Britain and Austria.

(*i*) Castlereagh insisted that the Spanish colonial revolt was a matter for Spain alone and not the concern of the Allied powers. He felt the Tsar was attempting to substitute as a basis for future Allied action the vague but sweeping principles of the Holy Alliance for the clearly defined obligations of the Quadruple Alliance.

(*ii*) Metternich was fearful lest the Tsar gained too much influence over events in Europe.

9. Spanish revolt of 1820.

(a) *Causes.* Aided by the British, the Spanish had waged successful guerrilla warfare against Napoleon (*see* II, **13–15**). In 1812 a constitution was drawn up. After 1814, however, the government of the restored King Ferdinand stamped out liberal ideas. It was incompetent and failed to improve the conditions of the poor or preserve the integrity of the Empire.

In 1820 trouble started among the troops at Cadiz due for embarkation for South America. The unrest spread and soon the King was forced to restore the 1812 constitution and to promise to govern according to its provisions.

(b) *Attitude of the powers.* The Tsar threatened to march 150,000 troops across Europe to quell the Spanish rising, but wanted collective action by the powers. Metternich, apprehensive of Russia, sounded Castlereagh. The latter, influenced by Canning and a powerful Latin American trade lobby in Parliament, felt that the spread of constitutional government would be in Britain's interests. He declined to be involved.

(c) *British state memorandum.* The British position was stated in the memorandum of 5th May 1820.

(i) Britain was committed only to preventing the return of Napoleon or his dynasty to France and to maintaining the territorial arrangements of Vienna by armed force for twenty years.

(ii) Britain owed her present dynasty and constitution to internal revolution. Therefore she could not deny to other countries the same right of changing their form of government.

10. Conferences of Troppau and Laibach. In July and August 1820 revolts broke out in Naples and Portugal respectively. The Tsar was also alarmed by the student disturbances in Germany and the unrest in Spain and her colonies. He demanded another meeting of the major powers, hoping that a collective force could be organised to crush revolution.

Castlereagh only sent an observer to the Troppau Conference (October 1820). Alexander confirmed Metternich's mistrust of his variable nature when he suggested a liberal constitution for Naples. The Tsar changed his mind following news of mutiny among his personal Semenovsky Russian guards. The following important developments took place.

(a) Russia, Austria and Prussia agreed in a protocol (19th November) that, if developments in any state threatened any other state, then the powers would use peaceful means or arms if necessary to restore the *status quo*.

(*b*) Castlereagh issued a strong protest on 19th January 1821. He pointed out that Austria had a special right to intervene in Italy, but denied any general right of intervention by members of the Quadruple Alliance.

(*c*) Metternich moved the conference to Laibach partly to hear the appeal of King Ferdinand of Naples, who had been forced to grant a constitution. Ferdinand then denounced the rebels and appealed for aid. As Austria had special interests in Italy, she was authorised by the powers to intervene, and her troops put down the rebellion (*see* XIII, 3(*a*)).

(*d*) No decision was taken regarding the Spanish and Portuguese revolts.

11. Conference of Verona. Following the Greek revolt (*see* XIV, 19) another meeting was held at Verona in October 1822.

(*a*) *No decision was reached over Greece.* Alexander was initially sympathetic to the Greek struggle against the old Russian enemy, Turkey. However, Metternich pointed out the inconsistency of approving revolution here and opposing it elsewhere and dissuaded him from taking any action.

(*b*) *No decision was reached over the Spanish colonies.* Austria and Prussia were largely uninterested in Spanish colonial struggles. Britain, France and Russia had different economic and political interests in the Americas (*see* 15).

(*c*) *Britain advocated non-intervention in Spain.* Metternich successfully avoided the Tsar's demands for a European army to crush the Spanish rebels. The British delegate, Wellington, was instructed by Canning, then British Foreign Minister, to reject any military intervention in Spain. Canning was worried lest France secured influence over Spain's American colonies.

(*d*) *France was authorised to intervene in Spain.* Despite British objections, the French were authorised to intervene in Spain. In 1823 a French army of 100,000 men crossed the Pyrenees and restored Ferdinand to absolute power. As a result, all Acts passed by the Cortes since 1820 were annulled. An organisation called the "Society of the Exterminating Angel" began a mad hunt against liberal sympathisers.

12. Collapse of the Conference System. The system did not break down entirely. The great powers held meetings throughout the nineteenth century, though less frequently after 1856. However, they were held on an *ad hoc* basis as circumstances warranted. The principle of regular conferences to discuss common problems, envisaged in the sixth article of the Quadruple Alliance, died for the following reasons.

(*a*) *Removal of the unifying influence among the powers.* Postwar co-operation among the Allied powers worked best while there seemed a threat from France. At first there were no important differences of opinion among them. However, when France was readmitted to the ranks of the major powers in 1818, serious disagreement developed as fresh problems arose.

(*b*) *Liberal and national movements.* In 1815 it had not been foreseen that thorny issues would arise to complicate relations between the powers. However disturbances soon occurred in Spain, Portugal, Italy and Greece (1820–1), while the revolt continued in the Spanish colonies in South America (*see* **16** and **20**).

(*c*) *Division of opinion.* Russia, Austria, Prussia, France and Britain could not agree on how best to deal with revolutionary movements as conflicting interests were involved in both the Ottoman Empire and the Americas (*see* **15** and XIV, **4**).

There were also acute differences on matters of principle, reflecting the distinction between autocratic and constitutional governments.

(*i*) The Holy Alliance powers approved Metternich's doctrine of the "right of general intervention" at Troppau. This meant the powers had the right to put down revolution in any state, against the will of the people or even a sovereign, in the interests of the established monarchical order.

(*ii*) Britain believed in the "principle of non-intervention" as outlined by Castlereagh in 1820 (*see* **9**(*c*)). It was in her interests to pursue this line since most of the revolutionary movements aimed at achieving liberal, constitutional governments, breaking away from autocracy as represented by the Holy Alliance powers.

(*d*) *Exclusion of the minor powers.* The small states had not been consulted on any of the major issues at Vienna. Consequently they did not feel inclined to give the territorial settlement much support.

(*e*) *Isolationist policy of Britain.* After 1815, as the French danger receded, British policy became increasingly isolationist.

Both Castlereagh and Canning, Foreign Ministers during this period, disliked long-term commitments abroad. However, co-operation with European powers did work for a time: Castlereagh, the aristocrat who favoured reaction at home, was in outlook similar to Metternich. On Castlereagh's death, Canning became Foreign Minister in 1821. He was not one of the original framers of the Quadruple Alliance and did not have the same faith in it. Also he was more liberal and tolerant than Castlereagh. Examples of British isolationist policies were the following.

(*i*) Non-attendance at meetings: Canning refused to allow Britain to be represented at two conferences on Spanish affairs (1823–4) and the Eastern Question (1824). As a result, the Congress powers achieved nothing.

(*ii*) Independent action: unlike Castlereagh, Canning was prepared to act without consulting his allies. Examples were his recognition of the Greeks as belligerents (1823) and the independence of South American colonies (1824–5).

EUROPE AND THE COLONIAL REVOLTS IN LATIN AMERICA

13. The Spanish American Empire. Except for Brazil, most of Central and South America had been under Spanish rule for over 300 years. The governing class came from Spain and took for themselves a large share of the wealth of the areas they administered. The next group in the hierarchy was the colonial-born "settler" whites, the creoles. They were often educated and very ambitious, and they resented the power of the leaders, which was often shared with the Church. They regarded the governing class as "foreigners", and disliked the petty economic restrictions and the heavy taxes imposed by Church and State.

As the creoles regarded America as their native land, they were more friendly to the natives than to the rulers. Many marriages took place between creoles and Indians, resulting in a mixed race called *mestizos*.

14. Revolt of the Spanish colonies. In the past, rebellions in the colonies had been suppressed by the army. For example, in 1780, an Indian revolt had been suppressed in Ecuador. This revolt had been caused initially by the use of Indian forced labour in the silver mines.

The following were the major causes of the revolt of the Spanish colonies after 1800.

(a) *Spread of revolutionary ideas.* Though the Church tried to suppress new ideas, inevitably the principles inspiring the American and French Revolutions spread to South America. Rigid barriers existed between the privileged classes (the governing class, the wealthy landowners and the clergy) and the rest of society, comprising the creoles, *mestizos,* Indians and slaves.

The creoles disliked the system of mercantilism which brought wealth to the few and poverty to the many. They were supported by the peasants and slaves who desired freedom.

(b) *French occupation of Spain.* When Napoleon occupied Spain in 1808, many of the Spanish colonies refused to recognise Bonapartist rule. They continued to recognise Ferdinand VII as king. However, this soon set in motion the first serious independence movement in Venezuela (1810).

15. European interests in the Americas. In 1823 rumours circulated that the European powers, led by France and Russia, might attempt through the Holy Alliance or Congress System to restore monarchies in the New World. Britain strongly resisted any such plans. The interests of the powers in the Americas were as follows.

(a) *Russia.* Russia had occupied Alaska in North America since the eighteenth century and even had forts in northern California. In September 1821 the Tsar reaffirmed in an imperial decree claims to the western coastland of North America and to fishing, trading and navigation rights in the North Pacific. This affected the rights of trade, discovery and occupation both of British and of American subjects, and Britain protested. As Russia was then involved in the Eastern Question (*see* XIV, **20**), there was little the Tsar could do to enforce his decree except with the help of the French.

NOTE: Russian settlements in California were abandoned in 1844 and Alaska sold to the United States in 1867.

(b) *France.* This country had plans to benefit from the troubles of the Spanish in America.

(*i*) Economic interests: France saw South America as a potential market for silks and wines.

(*ii*) Political interests: the rebel leaders in South America were divided between monarchists and republicans. In 1822 France suggested that Bourbon princes could be placed on the thrones of Mexico, Colombia, Peru and Chile, and she favoured the use of military force to carry this out. The Spanish government refused to negotiate on such terms and deadlock ensued.

(c) *Britain*. While Britain had been at war with Spain, she had broken the Spanish trading monopoly in South America (1806). Then Britain became allied to Spain (1808), and Spain gave "tacit sanction" to British trade with her colonies.

After 1815 Britain was anxious to increase this trade, especially as trade with the West Indies had declined following the introduction of beet sugar in Europe. Britain feared French designs, however, and in 1822 sent consuls to the Spanish American colonies. A pact with the United States was made to guarantee the colonies against military intervention by European powers.

In October 1823 a French minister committed himself to support Canning by issuing a statement that France had no designs of armed intervention in South America and that the colonies should be independent of Spain. A document known as the Polignac Memorandum was then circulated by Canning to other powers. It was a pledge which France could not easily violate.

16. Dissolution of the Spanish Empire. In 1800 Spain had lost Louisiana, her territory in North America, which she had been forced to cede to Napoleon, who in turn sold it to the United States in 1803. Between 1810 and 1825 large areas in the Americas became free of Spanish rule. Only in the islands of Cuba and Puerto Rico was Spanish colonial rule to survive. The independence movements in the Empire took the following course:

(a) *In South America*.

(i) Northern movement: Simon Bolivar, son of a wealthy creole family, led a revolt in 1810. He deposed the Bonapartist ruler in Caracas, capital of Venezuela. The call to independence was sent to other cities, but full support was not received. The British, allied then to Spain, declined to help. Bolivar fought the supporters of Ferdinand VII, the latter reinforced by the Spanish under Murillo in 1815.

After many reverses, Bolivar won in Venezuela and Colombia (1818) and continued fighting in Ecuador and Upper Peru. When independence was achieved in 1825, one state was called "Bolivia" in his honour.

(ii) Southern movement: In 1810 rebellion occurred in Argentina and spread to Paraguay and Uruguay (1811). In 1816

Argentina declared her independence. The leaders of the movement were José de San Martin and Bernardo O'Higgins. In 1817 Chile was invaded and became independent in 1818. Lord Cochrane, a former British naval officer, contributed to the victory by forming a Chilean navy to defeat the Spanish.

A base was now established to attack Peru. In 1822 San Martin joined Bolivar at Guayaquil and acknowledged him as leader of the independence movement. The Spanish finally surrendered at Ayacucho in December.

(b) *In Central America.* Mexico rebelled in 1810 and in 1821 declared her independence. The former Spanish provinces in the other areas proclaimed themselves the United Provinces of Central America in 1823, independent of both Mexico and Spain.

NOTE: Simon Bolivar had hoped to create a federal United States of South America, similar to the United States of North America. Spanish was a common language except in Brazil. Roman Catholicism was a common religious faith and there was a common culture brought from Spain and Portugal, two closely related countries.

However, rivalries and jealousies existed and after 1825 Central and South America broke up into separate independent sovereign republics.

17. The Monroe Doctrine. The United States was perturbed by the interest shown by European powers in the Americas. After the colonial revolts, she preferred to have weak independent republics in Latin America to the re-creation of European "spheres of influence". This policy was known as the Monroe Doctrine.

(a) *Causes.* Originally Canning and President Monroe favoured a joint Anglo-American declaration directed against the designs of France and Russia in the Americas. However, the American Secretary of State, Adams, favoured a unilateral declaration which would also be directed against Britain, for the following reasons.

(i) Adams felt it would be safe for the United States to act alone. Though the United States was not prepared for war at this stage, he did not believe the "Holy Alliance" was either. Britain, he considered, would in any case fight France if the latter attacked South America.

(*ii*) Adams was suspicious of Britain's ultimate intentions. The United States believed in republicanism and in the independence of nations. Adams felt that Canning was more concerned about preventing French aggrandisement than with setting South America free.

(*b*) *Provisions.* President Monroe in his annual message to Congress on 2nd December 1823 stated the following points.

(*i*) The American continent would not in future be considered an area for colonisation by European powers. If Europe did interfere this would be regarded as "the manifestation of an unfriendly disposition towards the United States".

(*ii*) The United States disclaimed any intention of being involved in European affairs in the future.

(*c*) *Results.* The Monroe Doctrine had no validity in international law and would not have been effective until the 1880s had Britain not given it her moral support backed by her naval supremacy (*see* 18(*a*)). Later the United States became sufficiently strong to enforce the Doctrine herself. The Monroe Doctrine had the following significant results.

(*i*) The independence of South American states was accelerated. European powers abstained from intervention in American affairs. Britain officially recognised numerous Latin American independent republics.

(*ii*) The internal expansion of the United States throughout the northern continent was able to proceed smoothly. Expansionist powers in Europe looked to Africa and Asia as fields for exploration and colonisation.

18. British recognition of independent South American states. The following were the reasons for Canning's decision, on 31st December 1824, to extend general recognition to the rebel colonies in South America.

(*a*) *A desire to co-operate with the United States.* The United States had recognised the South American states much earlier. Canning disliked the particular form the Monroe Doctrine had taken, since it might involve Britain and the United States in later disputes in unoccupied zones of the American north-west. However, he wanted Britain to remain friendly with the United States.

(*b*) *A fear of French designs in the New World.* France had ignored British protests and her troops continued to occupy Spanish soil. Despite the Polignac Memorandum (*see* 15(*c*)),

France still contemplated a possible establishment of French power in South America. In 1824 French troops were sent out secretly to the West Indies, and naval squadrons to Brazil and Peru.

(c) *A desire to preserve favourable trade conditions.* By giving early recognition to the republics, Britain hoped to maintain the favourable position she had established in South American trade. Spain had still refused to recognise the independence of those areas where her forces had clearly been defeated. Her continued resistance was partly attributable to the encouragement of the Holy Alliance powers. In February 1824 Spain had allowed all Europe to trade in South America.

(d) *The fact that the prospects of constitutional monarchies being established were now slight.* While any chance existed of constitutional monarchies being established, Canning had been prepared to delay recognition to encourage that tendency, for it was considered that monarchies would be less susceptible to influence from the United States than would republics. During 1823–4, however, Canning became more favourably inclined towards republicanism as the prospect of French intervention continued to exist.

19. Unrest in Portugal and Brazil.

(a) *In Portugal.* When Napoleon seized Portugal in 1807, the British fleet helped the Regent (afterwards King John VI) to escape to Brazil.

In August 1820 garrisons in Oporto and Lisbon revolted as a protest against the control and influence of Britain and arrested their British officers. A Cortes drew up a constitution based on the 1812 pattern, which abolished feudalism and the Inquisition and guaranteed a free press and equal rights. The royal family were urged to return home.

In 1821 John VI returned to Portugal, leaving Brazil in the charge of his eldest son, Dom Pedro.

(b) *In Brazil.* The separation of Brazil from Portugal was hastened by the determination of Portugal to reduce Brazil again to the status of a dependency. King John tried to impose taxes on Brazil. His son refused to return to Portugal and was proclaimed Emperor Pedro I in Brazil. Brazil declared its independence from Portugal in December 1822.

20. European non-intervention. The revolts in Spain and her colonies had been led by military adventurers and ambitious

generals. Russia and France had been anxious to intervene to preserve the principle of monarchy and to further their own interests. However, the Holy Alliance powers showed a lack of concern over the unrest in Portugal and Brazil, for the following reasons.

(*a*) The position in Portugal and Brazil was different from that in Spain. The forces of both reaction and revolution were headed by members of the royal family. Thus no European power wanted to interfere.

(*b*) Britain might have been expected to intervene because of her special relationship with Portugal. As a result of past treaties, Britain was still committed to protecting Portugal from attack by another power. However, Castlereagh commented that British obligation did not extend to interference in internal revolutions.

21. Turmoil in Portugal. King John's wife and his second son, Dom Miguel, disliked liberal government. Dom Miguel forced the King to cancel the constitution and started a civil war supported by reactionaries.

On 15th July 1823 King John requested British aid to maintain order and suppress the reactionaries. Canning refused on the grounds that British forces were necessary only for external defence, not for internal measures. An unsuccessful attempt was made to assert French influence. The new French ambassador, in October 1823, offered the King an alliance, a guarantee of the House of Braganza and armed aid to recover Brazil if he would break his promise to grant a constitution again.

In February 1824 King John issued a decree for the reassembly of the Cortes. Dom Miguel, encouraged by events in Spain, seized absolute power after a *coup d'état*. King John escaped in a British frigate which was in the River Tagus. He appealed for aid and was restored to his throne by the British. He died in 1826. The throne was left to Dom Pedro, who drew up a charter providing for parliamentary government but refused to leave Brazil. Eventually he handed the Portuguese throne to his daughter Maria.

In 1828 Dom Miguel became king after another *coup d'état* and proceeded to eliminate all vestiges of liberalism. Dom Pedro, who in 1831 was forced to abdicate the throne in Brazil, led an expedition to force him to vacate the Portuguese throne. Pedro was allowed to enlist troops in Britain, and a British fleet under

Admiral Napier defeated Miguel. In 1833 Donna Maria was restored as queen.

22. Causes of success of Latin American revolts. It was understandable that the rebels would be successful until 1815 while Spain and Portugal were occupied in the Napoleonic Wars. The rebels continued to be successful afterwards owing to the following factors.

(*a*) The moral support of the United States, in the form of the Monroe Doctrine.

(*b*) The support of Britain backed by the power of the British navy. This prevented concerted action by the French and the Holy Alliance powers, particularly Russia.

(*c*) Spanish and Portuguese domestic revolts in 1820–1.

THE AREAS OF REVOLT IN EUROPE, 1815–48

23. Revolts of 1820–1. The main forces influencing revolutionary movements between 1815 and 1848 have been noted (*see* 2–7). The early revolts, in 1820 and 1821, were primarily national risings led by military groups, and were in the following areas.

(*a*) *Italy*. Naples and Piedmont were the states involved (*see* XIII, 3).

(*b*) *Spain and Portugal* (*see* **9** and **19**).

(*c*) *The Ottoman Empire* (*see* XIV, **16–18**).

24. Revolts of 1830. In July 1830 the outbreak of a revolt in the Paris streets against Charles X resulted in a series of risings throughout Europe. A chain reaction occurred similar to the events of 1820–1. However, in contrast to the earlier revolts, the movements in 1830 were primarily of a liberal nature, against authoritarian rule. The following were the major areas involved.

(*a*) *The west*. Successful revolts occurred in France, Belgium and Switzerland. After 1828 some Swiss cantons had granted concessions such as universal suffrage, freedom of the press and equality before the law. The movement was strengthened by the Paris revolution. The revolts in Belgium and Switzerland were successful partly owing to the moral support of France and Britain. The principle of Swiss neutrality agreed in 1815 also deterred the Austrians from intervention.

(*b*) *The south and east*. Revolts in Italy and Poland were unsuccessful because of the following factors.

(*i*) The problem of national unification: the lack of national unity meant that the forces of change were too parochial in outlook and too scattered to offer a serious threat to the governments.

(*ii*) The Holy Alliance: the influence of Austria in Italy and of Russia in Poland was so strong that Britain and France could not give much encouragement to the rebels.

(*c*) *Central Europe*. The reactionary influence of Austria and Prussia was sufficient to deter any serious outbreaks of revolution. There were, however, minor repercussions (*see* for example VIII, 7).

25. The Belgian revolt. In 1815 the union of Belgium (formerly the Austrian Netherlands) and Holland had seemed practical from the economic standpoint. It appeared that the maritime trade and colonial possessions of the Dutch would form a good complement to the industrial interests of the south.

However, after 1815 the Belgians were increasingly dissatisfied with the policies of the joint government. This finally culminated in a large-scale revolt in 1830.

(*a*) *Causes*.

(*i*) Social: there were important differences of customs, language (French and Dutch), temperament and religion. The Dutch were Protestant Calvinists in faith, the Belgians Roman Catholics.

(*ii*) Economic: the Dutch agricultural and trading community favoured free trade; the Belgians predominated in manufacturing occupations and preferred protectionist policies. The Belgians disliked the tariff system which gave inadequate protection to their industry.

(*iii*) Political: the Dutch tended to monopolise the offices of government, and their language occupied a privileged position. In the lower house of Parliament, Belgian and Dutch representation was equal, though the Belgian population was nearly twice as large as the Dutch. Belgian liberals disliked the harsh press law.

(*b*) *Course of events*. In August 1830 the Belgians rebelled and in October proclaimed their independence from the Dutch. The Belgians declared the House of Orange deposed, but wanted a continuation of a constitutional hereditary monarchy. In December Palmerston, the British Foreign Minister, backed by Louis-Philippe, induced Austria, Prussia and Russia to abandon the principle of legitimacy and to recognise Belgian independence.

The Belgians at first elected as king the Duke of Nemours, second son of Louis-Philippe. Threats from Palmerston induced the French to reject this and in June 1831 the Belgians finally chose as their ruler Prince Leopold of Saxe-Coburg. The Dutch rejected the terms of separation of the two countries and war took place between Anglo-French forces and the Dutch until 1833. An armistice was then agreed.

(c) *Reasons for the success of the Belgians.*

(i) Russia was preoccupied with the Polish revolt.

(ii) Britain supported the claims of Belgium. Palmerston was determined to resist the spread of French influence.

(iii) Louis-Philippe of France, involved in domestic problems, was prepared to support British policy so as to obtain an ally abroad.

(d) *Final settlement.* Eventually, in 1839, King William of Holland agreed to the terms of settlement, which adopted the frontiers of 1790 except for Luxembourg and Limburg.

(i) Belgium received the western part of Luxembourg: formerly she had claimed the whole. The rest remained a grand duchy with the Dutch king as grand duke.

(ii) Belgium received half of Limburg.

(iii) Belgium was recognised as an "independent and perpetually neutral state" under the collective guarantee of the powers.

26. Unrest between 1830 and 1848. Considerable unrest existed in the Austrian Empire in the years before 1848, while throughout Europe there were many who looked forward to a period of change. There were important events in the following areas.

(a) *Posen and Cracow.*

(i) Prussia managed to prevent a planned rising taking place in Posen in February 1846.

(ii) This sparked off a republican rising in the free city of Cracow, which was suppressed by Austrian and Russian troops. Austria, fearing that revolt might spread to Galicia, annexed Cracow in November 1846.

(b) *Switzerland.* In 1845 the Sonderbund had been formed of the seven Catholic cantons, under Austrian patronage. These cantons favoured a decentralised confederal but autocratic government for Switzerland. The liberals who favoured a strong federal authority succeeded in getting the Diet in 1847 to declare the Catholic organisation contrary to the constitution. After a short civil war the more democratic Swiss cantons overthrew the Sonderbund.

(*c*) *Greece*. An insurrection in 1843 forced Otto I to grant a constitution.

(*d*) *Serbia*. In 1830 the Sultan introduced certain measures which increased Serb independence. Milosh Obrenovich (*see* XIV, 15) was recognised as hereditary prince.

In 1835 the opposition of the nobility to Milosh's autocratic and oppressive rule led to the granting of a constitution and the creation of a popular assembly.

In 1838 the Sultan, supported by Russia, forced the abrogation of the constitution. Autocratic rule returned.

27. The 1848 revolutions. A number of leaders became prominent in the 1840s. Both Frederick William IV of Prussia (after 1840) and Pope Pius IX (after 1846) were influenced by the spirit of Romanticism to carry out useful reforms. They wanted to be accepted as leaders of liberal opinion, but, as they were basically conservative at heart, they only succeeded in raising false hopes among their subjects.

In early 1848 significant sections of Europe's populations had reasons for dissatisfaction. Conditions in various countries were so similar that it was likely that a revolt in one centre would touch off disturbances elsewhere.

(*a*) *Causes of the 1848 revolutions*. Movements were both liberal and national. Economic factors also played an important part in the origins. This led to the influence for the first time in the post-1815 revolutionary movements of the working class, who were motivated by socialist ideas (*see* 6). The following were the most important causes.

(*i*) The Industrial Revolution: rapid industrialisation and the introduction of the factory system led to mass movements of population to the towns. People suffered from appalling living and working conditions. As they were assembled together in large numbers, this led to the discussion of their grievances and the formation of associations.

(*ii*) Agricultural distress: poor corn harvests during 1845–6 coincided with a blight which attacked potato crops from Silesia to Ireland. Prices increased owing to food shortages. Hunger drove people to violent demonstrations in France, the Rhineland and north Italy. Typhus occurred, followed by a wide outbreak of cholera.

(*iii*) Political agitation: the middle classes desired to acquire civil and political rights denied to them or to extend rights already possessed. In Germany and Italy these desires were accompanied by a growing demand for national unity and independence. Many people of talent felt that in the small autocratic provincial states they were denied opportunities for advancement. Only in a democratic, united country, free from foreign influence, would they be able to use their talents and advance to positions of responsibility.

(*b*) *Important centres.* These were as follows:

(*i*) France (*see* V, **19–20**);
(*ii*) Germany (*see* VIII, **11**);
(*iii*) The Austrian Empire (*see* XI, **14–16**);
(*iv*) Italy (*see* XIII, **7**).

(*c*) *Results.* Apart from the revolt in France, the risings failed. In France it led to a republic, but also the restoration of middle-class rule. Conservative and reactionary rule was restored in Italy, Germany and the Austrian Empire. Beneficial results were the abolition of serfdom in the Austrian Empire and the creation of a liberal constitutional monarchy in Piedmont.

PROGRESS TEST 4

1. Compare and contrast liberal and national ideas. (**2, 4–5**)

2. Define "democracy". Which groups demanded an extension of democratic rights after 1815? (**3**)

3. What was the influence of Romanticism on revolutionary movements? (**7**)

4. What were the issues which first caused discord among the Allies after 1815? (**8–9**)

5. Contrast the British state memorandum of 1820 with the Troppau Protocol. (**9(*c*), 10**)

6. Why was it difficult for the Allies to reach agreement at the Verona Conference? (**11**)

7. Account for the collapse of the Quadruple Alliance. (**10–12**)

8. Why did the Spanish colonies in Latin America revolt? (**14**)

9. Discuss the interests of European powers in the Americas. (**15**)

10. What was the importance of the Monroe Doctrine? (**17**)

11. Why did Britain decide to recognise the independence of the Spanish colonies in Latin America? (**18**)

12. Why did the Tsar not advocate European intervention in the revolt in Brazil and Portugal? **(20)**

13. In what ways did the revolts during 1820–1 differ from the revolts in 1830? **(23–24)**

14. Why did Belgium want independence from Holland in 1830? **(25)**

15. Give the causes of the 1848 revolutions in Europe. **(27(*a*), 1–7)**

CHAPTER V

France, 1815–52

THE REIGNS OF LOUIS XVIII AND CHARLES X

1. The Charter of 1814. King Louis XVIII accepted the advice of the Allied powers that France should be ruled in a constitutional manner, and so he granted a Charter which provided for certain liberties. This was a considerable advance on anything known at the time in Eastern Europe, and it recognised the principal changes made by the Revolution. However, it had its weaknesses. Important points to note are as follows.

(*a*) *The Charter restricted popular participation in government.*

(*i*) Voting was limited to male citizens over the age of thirty who paid taxes of about 300 francs or more a year. This meant that only about one in every hundred Frenchmen could vote.

(*ii*) Most people could not be parliamentary candidates. Deputies had to be at least forty years old and substantial property holders.

(*b*) *The King retained sole executive power.* The Charter declared that the King's ministers were "responsible", but it did not state whether this was to the King or the legislature. The following powers were vested in the King alone.

(*i*) The power to make treaties, declare war and make appointments. He was commander of the military forces.

(*ii*) The power to initiate legislation, and to prorogue or dissolve Parliament. He also retained an absolute veto on laws.

(*iii*) The power to issue emergency ordinances "necessary for the . . . safety of the State".

(*c*) *The Charter had some liberal features*, for example the following.

(*i*) There was to be a Parliament consisting of a Chamber of (hereditary) Peers (nominated by the King) and a Chamber of Deputies (elected by the departments in France). It was to be given control over taxation.

(*ii*) Twelve articles were devoted to the "public rights of the French". All Frenchmen were equal before the law, had individual and religious liberty, were eligible for all civil and military positions, and were to have a free press. The security of tenure of judges was guaranteed.

2. Policies of the new king, 1814–15. The period of French history after 1814 was known as the Restoration. In fact little was restored except the Bourbon dynasty. The new king, Louis XVIII, resisted the advice of those counsellors who wanted him to turn back the clock. He knew that too many people had benefited directly from the political, economic and social changes to permit efforts to restore the *ancien régime* as it existed before 1789.

However, some of the King's actions seemed contrary to the ideals of the Revolution. The King caused offence and incurred some unpopularity in the following ways.

(a) *By the nature of the Charter.*

(i) The King professed to grant the Charter "voluntarily" and inserted a long preamble. This recalled the past glories and services of the French monarchs.

(ii) The Charter was dated from "the nineteenth year of my reign". Thus Louis ignored the era of the Napoleonic Empire.

(iii) Louis spoke of himself as king by the grace of God, thus denying the sovereignty of the people. Though the King did not mention the "divine right of kings", the Charter stated that the first duty of the monarch was, in the interests of the people, to preserve the rights of the Crown.

(b) *By certain of his policies.*

(i) Louis took no action against the extravagant claims of the Roman Catholic clergy and the nobles, both of whom hoped to recover lands which had been confiscated and sold to the peasants. This was despite the fact that the Condordat of 1801 and the Charter of 1814 had ratified the changes.

(ii) Louis insisted on levying all the former taxes.

(iii) The white flag of the Bourbons was restored and the tricolour banished.

(iv) Many of Napoleon's troops were retired or put on half-pay. Many former civil servants received a cut in salary or pension.

3. Main political groups. The four main political groups between 1814 and 1830 were as follows.

(a) *The Ultra-royalists (Ultras).* They wanted to restore the absolute powers of the King and the conditions in France as they had existed before 1789. They bitterly opposed the Charter.

(b) *The Doctrinaires.* They accepted the Charter as a reasonable balance between government power and individual freedom.

(c) *The liberals.* They wanted the Charter amended to extend civil liberties and increase the powers of the Chamber of Deputies. They agreed with the Doctrinaires on other points, as both groups opposed any real widening of the franchise and believed that France should be run by the wealthy, educated middle class.

(d) *The radicals.* They wanted to destroy the existing system and to restore the Empire or establish a republic. They were a confused group of varying views, and were not really important until after 1830.

4. Rapid succession of governments. The new French structure of government rested on an uneasy compromise between opposing political ideas. On the one hand were the liberal-democratic ideas surviving from the Revolution and on the other the absolutist-legitimist ideas of the monarchy. It was not surprising, therefore, that government policies oscillated between reaction and moderation.

The King tried to follow a moderate course and to rally the French to the support of the monarchy. However, he was unable to curb completely the demands of the Ultras for reactionary measures. The period 1815–20 can be divided into the following three phases.

(a) *The White Terror of the Ultras.* In the 1816 elections the Talleyrand government was replaced by the royalists. The latter took revenge on former Bonapartist supporters. Some 7,000 were shot, including Marshal Ney, and others lost their government posts.

(b) *Moderate government.* In September 1816 the King dissolved the Chamber of Deputies. As a result of fresh elections the new Chamber contained until 1820 a majority of Doctrinaires and liberals. The post of Chief Minister was held in turn by the following.

(i) The duc de Richelieu (1816–18): his government was fairly liberal but some reactionary measures were passed. These involved, for example, the dissolving of the National Guard and the narrowing of the franchise.

(ii) The duc de Decazes (1818–20): important liberal measures were the Army Law (1818), which provided for army reorganisation, promotion by merit and voluntary enlistment, and the Press Law (1819).

(c) *Return of reaction.* On 13th February 1820 the son of the heir to the throne, the duc de Berri, was murdered by the fanatic Louvel. The Ultras, already infuriated by the measures of Decazes, used this incident to persuade the King to crush liberalism. Censorship of the press was restored and electoral laws were revised. This reduced the power of the liberals, and the Chamber of Deputies became controlled by the Ultras and their Doctrinaire allies.

5. The repressive ministry of Villèle. In 1821 Villèle became Chief Minister. He was supported by the Church and the Ultras. His administration can be divided into the following two phases.

(a) *Period 1821–4.* The King, by this time stricken with a terrible disease, had little energy to resist the demands of the Ultras and allowed their leader, his brother and heir the comte d'Artois, greater initiative in government. Villèle was able to pass a number of repressive measures. It was he who persuaded the hesitant Louis to authorise the expedition into Spain in 1823 (*see* IV, 11(*d*)).

(b) *Period 1824–7.* Louis XVIII died in 1824 and was succeeded by his brother, Charles X. The new king had a pleasant personality, but was intolerant in his beliefs and had limited intelligence in political affairs. He allowed Villèle to advance the programme of the Ultras more rapidly. Examples of Villèle's acts were as follows.

(*i*) Grant of a billion francs as an indemnity to the nobles: this was to compensate them for the lands which had been confiscated and sold by the State during the Revolution.

(*ii*) Sacrilege Law (1826): this unpopular measure was not enforced. It prescribed that burglaries committed in ecclesiastical buildings and the profanation of holy vessels were, under certain conditions, to be punishable by death.

(*iii*) Press Law (1826): this measure was withdrawn, along with a new inheritance law, following vehement opposition from the Chamber of Peers, a liberal stronghold.

(*iv*) Censorship books and journals (1827).

6. The collapse of French government. In 1827 Villèle was forced to resign owing to his general unpopularity. New elections were held and the liberals secured the ascendancy in Parliament. The

King, however, refused to select ministers from their ranks. Instead he relied on the advice of unpopular ministers, including the following, who represented no sizeable body of opinion.

(a) *Martignac.* He made certain concessions to please the liberals. Press censorship was abolished and the Jesuits were deprived of the power to give public instruction. His policy was too progressive for the Ultras and not progressive enough for the liberals, and in 1829 he was defeated.

(b) *Polignac.* After the fall of Martignac, the prince de Polignac, an extreme Ultra, was appointed Chief Minister with a ministry filled almost completely with extreme royalists. He was totally out of touch with French opinion and was full of impractical ideas. For instance, he aimed "to reorganise society, to restore to the clergy its former preponderance in the State, to create a powerful aristocracy and to surround it with privileges".

The results of Polignac's policies were as follows.

(i) In March 1830 the Chamber of Deputies reproached the King for having appointed an "unrepresentative" ministry.

(ii) The King dissolved the Chamber. He hoped that new elections would result in a Chamber more amenable to his wishes. The elections resulted, however, in an even greater majority against Polignac.

7. Ordinances of St. Cloud. Charles decided to issue emergency decrees, provided for in Article 14 of the Charter. On 25th July the following measures were announced.

(a) The liberty of the press was to be suspended.

(b) The Chamber of Deputies was to be dissolved, recent elections being declared null and void.

(c) The electoral system was to be altered, reducing the number of voters from 100,000 to 25,000.

(d) New elections would be held under these changed conditions.

8. Causes of the Paris revolution. On 26th July protests in Paris against the King's measures soon led to a widespread revolt. The chief reasons for the revolution were as follows.

(a) *Failure of the King to respect the spirit of the 1814 Charter.* This was evident when the Ordinances were issued. Two leading forces in the protest whose livelihood was threatened by the new law were:

(*i*) the journalists: they were led by Adolphe Thiers, editor of an anti-government journal *Le National*, founded in January 1830;

(*ii*) the printers.

(*b*) *Government policies which had favoured the Church and nobility.* The middle classes were supported in their opposition to these measures by workers and students.

9. How Louis-Philippe became king. When the revolution started it was not apparent at first what form of government would be established or who would be the ruler.

The reasons for the success of the revolution and the rise of Louis-Philippe were as follows.

(*a*) *Failure of the army to put down the revolution.* There was a shortage of available troops, and they lacked enthusiasm for fighting civilian rebels. In addition they lacked training in street fighting, and knowledge of the layout of the city streets. The rebels erected barricades in the narrow, crooked streets, which made it difficult for artillery to be used effectively and for reinforcements to come to the soldiers. The troops were further demoralised by the fact that possible lines of retreat could easily be cut off.

(*b*) *Abdication of King Charles.* On 29th July the King offered to make concessions, to dismiss Polignac and to restore the Charter. He acted too late and his offer was rejected. Then, on the 31st, he abdicated in favour of his nine-year-old grandson, the son of the murdered duc de Berri.

(*c*) *Desire of the middle-class leaders of the revolution to retain the monarchy.* The majority of the people who did the actual fighting wanted a republic. On 28th July the Hôtel de Ville had been captured and the tricolour hoisted. However, the journalists, deputies, businessmen and professional classes did not want a republic. They feared it would lead to disorder, encourage socialism and result in intervention by the Holy Alliance powers.

Led by Thiers and Talleyrand, the middle classes persuaded Lafayette, leader of the republicans, to support their alternative plan. This was to invite Louis-Philippe, Duke of Orleans, to come to Paris as lieutenant-governor (29th July). When King Charles abdicated, the Chamber of Deputies offered the throne to Louis-Philippe. This was accepted on 3rd August.

To the middle classes, Louis-Philippe represented a satisfactory alternative ruler for the following reasons:

(*i*) He was of royal blood, the head of a younger branch (the Orleanist branch) of the Bourbon line.

(*ii*) He held liberal views in politics. He was the son of "Philippe Egalité", who had welcomed the Revolution of 1789, and he had fought at Jemappes in support of the ideals of the French Revolution.

THE JULY MONARCHY, 1830–48

0. The new political system. The majority of French people soon felt that the July revolution had produced little of political significance. All that had occurred was a change from one ruler to another, and from rule by the aristocracy to rule by the upper middle class.

The tricolour flag replaced the white flag of the Bourbons. On the other hand, a system of heavy fines was introduced which undermined the guarantee of the freedom of the press. Other changes were as follows.

(*a*) *Minor alterations were made to the restored Charter*.

(*i*) The membership of the Chamber of Peers ceased to be hereditary and became nominated.

(*ii*) The preamble on the role of the monarchy was deleted. However, no alternative theory was substituted to give a logical basis for the continuation of monarchical rule.

(*iii*) The paragraph that made Roman Catholicism the official French religion was also removed.

(*b*) *A new electoral law was introduced* (March 1831). The voting age was lowered to twenty-five, and property qualifications were reduced to include the professional classes. The franchise was doubled to about 200,000. However, this was out of a population of about 32 million. The majority of the middle class and all the lower class were still without a vote. (It must be noted that this situation was not unusual in Europe at the time.)

(*c*) *The National Guard was restored*. This contingent nominally included all Frenchmen between the ages of twenty and sixty who paid direct tax. It now became necessary for members to pay for their own uniforms and equipment. This excluded the poor from participation, and it became a middle-class army. It elected its own officers below the rank of lieutenant-colonel.

11. Reasons for growth of unrest. Numerous domestic disturbances occurred during the reign of Louis-Philippe, signifying the growing opposition to the government and its policies. The following aspects of the government's rule were disliked by the people.

(a) *Its unrepresentative character*. Ministers continued to exercise authority without being in any way responsible to the Chamber. The government and Parliament were primarily composed of upper-middle-class businessmen, professional men and intellectuals. Instead of the nobility dominating political posts, it was now the wealthy propertied class. This meant that the following groups were not represented.

(i) The lower middle class and workers: formidable property qualifications for office-holding and voting excluded these groups.

(ii) The Ultra-royalists: this group either ignored the new regime or were excluded from office.

(b) *Its corrupt nature*. From 1840 to 1848, Guizot, leader of the conservative elements in Parliament, was the Chief Minister. He maintained office and gained majority support by giving awards of government posts or business contracts. Thiers led the liberal or progressive element among the deputies.

(c) *Its lack of concern for the conditions of the people*. During the period 1830–48, the economy expanded, industry progressed and the middle classes prospered. However, suffering the evils of the Industrial Revolution, the workers remained as poor as ever.

The government made little effort to remedy slum conditions in towns or poor working conditions in factories. Its main task was considered to be the protection of property from civil disorder, the keeping of legislation to the minimum and the adoption of a *laissez-faire* attitude of non-intervention. In 1831 the Chief Minister, Casimir-Périer, said the government's policy was to represent the *juste milieu*, between clericalism and absolutism on the one hand and republicanism and democracy on the other. The uninspiring government of Guizot after 1840 was nicknamed the "millstone" ministry as it resisted change.

The following legislative measures were passed.

(i) Education Law (1833): the Church was given extensive control over primary education.

(ii) Factory Act (1841): this prohibited the employment of children under eight years of age in certain factories, and it restricted hours of work for those between the ages of eight and sixteen. However, little was done to enforce these limits.

(*d*) *Its unenterprising foreign policies* (*see also* **13**). Spectacular successes abroad might have compensated in part for the inadequate domestic policies. However, France was content to adopt a cautious policy abroad, and seemed subservient to the wishes of the other powers, particularly Britain.

(*i*) Thiers resigned in 1836 over Spain and again in 1840 over Syria when the King refused to allow him to pursue bolder policies.

(*ii*) One notable success in 1846 over the Spanish Marriages lost France her only real ally abroad, Britain. The duplicity of Louis-Philippe in this matter was not admired in some quarters.

(*iii*) In 1847 France failed in her efforts to achieve a conservative Austro-French alliance.

12. Unpopularity of the Orleanist monarch. In almost every year after 1830 there were attempts to assassinate the King. Reasons for the general dissatisfaction with Louis-Philippe were as follows.

(*a*) *His personal character.* The King was clever, kindly, well intentioned and courageous. Though he was rich, he had experienced years of poverty. His weakness was that he did not have the temperament calculated to inspire his people. He was rather colourless and had simple and unaffected habits. For example, he enjoyed walking around the streets armed merely with an umbrella. His "way of life" did not win him the respect of the royalists or the support of the masses hankering after the splendours of bygone days.

(*b*) *His cautious conservative policies.* He seemed to epitomise the class which had taken power. His excessively timid outlook alienated many who looked for a more challenging leader.

(*c*) *His weak basis of authority.* The dynasty rested chiefly on the support of the middle class. It did not have a moral or intellectual claim to the ascendancy of power as compared to:

(*i*) the historically legitimate claims of the Bourbons;

(*ii*) the military renown of a Bonaparte; or

(*iii*) the democratic appeal of an elected president of a republic.

(*d*) *His constant intervention in politics.* Louis-Philippe tried to select ministers whom he felt would be subservient to him. He persistently interposed his ideas on the government, particularly in foreign affairs (*see* **13**).

13. Foreign affairs. Louis-Philippe aimed to preserve peace, and to avoid ambitious policies abroad which would alarm the other major powers. For example, on his accession, he refused to support revolutionary movements in Italy, Poland and Belgium.

The foreign interests of France are covered in other sections. Here they can be summarised as follows.

(*a*) *The Belgian problem* (*see* IV, **25**).

(*b*) *Mehemet Ali and Egypt* (*see* XIV, **29**).

(*c*) *Italy*. Troops were maintained in the Papal States from 1832 to 1838 to match those of the Austrians (*see* XIII, 3(*c*)).

(*d*) *Algeria* (*see* XVIII, **24–25**).

(*e*) *The Spanish Marriages and the Quadruple Alliance* (*see* **14–15**).

(*f*) *Tahiti*. This was annexed by France. When Britain protested, the French withdrew.

(*g*) *The Anglo-French entente cordiale*. During the 1840s increased co-operation took place between Britain and France. Exchange visits consolidated an *entente cordiale* in 1845. This was something novel in the relations of the two countries and provided moral support for the throne of Louis-Philippe. Examples of co-operation were in Belgium (*see* IV, **25**) and in Uruguay between 1843 and 1848. In the latter area Franco-British naval forces supported liberal elements against the dictatorial regime. However, relations soon deteriorated (*see* **15**).

14. The Quadruple Alliance. In Spain and Portugal disputes arose over the royal successions. The background to the events in Portugal has been mentioned elsewhere (*see* IV, **21**).

(*a*) *Origins of the Spanish crisis*. Ferdinand VII, influenced by Queen Christina, revoked the Salic Law and left his throne to his daughter Isabella. This excluded his brother, Don Carlos, the next male heir.

Ferdinand died in September 1833. To help her daughter, Queen Christina adopted the liberal cause.

(*b*) *Quadruple Alliance formed*. The British Foreign Minister, Palmerston, was anxious to erect a liberal bloc in Western Europe. He wanted to counteract the reactionary bloc of the Holy Alliance powers in Eastern Europe.

His offer of an alliance to the Queens of Spain and Portugal to expel their pretenders was accepted. It became known as the Quadruple Alliance when France joined on 22nd April 1834. Eventually the pretenders were expelled.

15. The Spanish Marriages. At the time when the Quadruple Alliance was formed, relations between Britain and France were not good. Each country suspected the motives of the other in the Iberian Peninsula. Relations improved in the 1840s when Aberdeen became British Foreign Minister.

Competition eventually arose between France and Britain to supply a husband for the Spanish queen. In 1843 Louis-Philippe promised Queen Victoria that the Spanish queen's sister would not marry a French prince until Isabella had married and had had children. The recently formed *entente cordiale* was soon broken by the intrigues of the French and British ambassadors in Spain and the policies of Palmerston. The events were as follows.

(*a*) Palmerston, having returned to the Foreign Office in 1846, revived the claim of a German prince, Prince Leopold of Coburg.

(*b*) Louis-Philippe and Guizot then worked out a secret marriage plan. On 10th October two marriages were arranged.

(*i*) Francis, Duke of Cadiz, who was incapable of having children, married the Queen.

(*ii*) The Queen's sister married Louis-Philippe's son, the duc de Montpensier.

(*c*) Britain broke off friendly relations with France. Palmerston was furious about the implementation of the marriage plan, since Louis-Philippe had broken his word to Queen Victoria and had tried to secure the Spanish throne for his descendants.

16. Alternatives to Louis-Philippe. The French government made few positive reforms at home and did not embark on bold ventures abroad. Gradually the working classes felt they had gained nothing from the 1830 revolution. "France is bored," said Alphonse de Lamartine.

Paris had the largest concentration of industrial wage-earners of any European city. It was the gathering-place of the dispossessed, the disenchanted and the exiled. Together with the propertyless proletariat they provided a fertile ground for the ideas of radical reformers and intellectuals.

After 1830 radical movements increased in strength in France. Two of the major seemingly attractive alternatives to the existing regime were as follows.

(*a*) *Socialism.* The indifference of the government to the plight of the workers prompted many thinkers to give more attention to their predicament. In time their ideas received increased popularity among progressive members of the middle class and the lower class. Important contributors were the following.

(*i*) Louis Blanc (1811–82) was the most influential thinker. He advocated that the existing system of competition in business should be replaced by a national economy. In his work *L'Organisation du travail* (1839) he popularised the idea that everyone had the right to work. He explained that the State could take over industry and run National Workshops for the unemployed.

(*ii*) Henri de Saint-Simon advocated a system in which all should be given work according to their talents and rewarded correspondingly. The anarchist P. J. Proudhon believed that "property is theft"; Auguste Blanqui founded secret conspiratorial societies; and Charles Fourier advocated co-operative farming.

(*iii*) Humanitarian novelists such as Victor Hugo and George Sand wrote of the plight of the common man.

(*b*) *Bonapartism.* Though Napoleon had made many constructive reforms he had led France to disaster under his military dictatorship. While in exile on St. Helena, he wrote that he would have given France peace, prosperity and liberal institutions had Europe allowed him. These aspects were later magnified by Bonapartist supporters.

The Bonapartist movement increased in popularity owing to the following factors.

(*i*) Louis Napoleon was the nephew of Napoleon, and, after the death of the Emperor's son, the Bonaparte pretender. In 1836 and 1840 he landed in France, attempting to rally support. He was imprisoned at Ham in 1840. In a series of pamphlets such as *The Extinction of Poverty* he expressed his concern for the poor. He advocated peace, free institutions, schemes of work and the abolition of unemployment.

(*ii*) Historical writings such as the work by Thiers, *History of the Consulate and Empire* (1845), gave a powerful impetus to the Napoleonic legend.

(*iii*) To control the Bonapartist movement the government embarked on a number of projects. The Arc de Triomphe was completed to celebrate the victories of the Empire, and a Museum of Conquests was opened at Versailles. In 1840 the Emperor's body was brought back to Paris. These actions, however, served only to remind the French of past exploits which they compared unfavourably with the drab conditions of the present.

17. Economic crisis. Harvests during the years 1845–6 were poor and agricultural distress was widespread. In addition there was an international financial crisis in 1846. This forced manufacturers to curtail production, and consequently unemployment increased. Previous heavy investments in railways meant that there were no available reserve funds to support the stock market. Prices were high and in 1847 about a third of the Paris working population was starving or being supported by charity.

The government failed to see how serious the situation was. It had no machinery to meet the crisis and was averse to devising any. At the time the government was also discredited by a number of scandals, even though it was not directly involved. One such scandal concerned the duc de Choiseul-Praslin, who, to please his mistress, murdered his wife, and then committed suicide in prison.

18. Reform Banquets. Thiers, leader of the "loyal" opposition in Parliament, decided that the only way to make the government aware of domestic problems was to make it more democratic. The law forbade open political gatherings, and therefore meetings led by the opposition outside the legislature took the form of Reform Banquets. Reformers addressed large assemblies of the lower middle and working classes throughout France in 1847. They demanded parliamentary reform and, notably, universal suffrage.

Gradually some of the reformers began to agitate for more radical changes. The sequence of events leading to the outbreak of revolution was as follows.

(a) A great Reform Banquet and procession were planned for 22nd February 1848.

(i) The government, nervous of incidents occurring, banned the procession.

(ii) The opposition deputies met at the house of Thiers on the 21st and decided finally to call off the procession.

(iii) By the 22nd many of the banqueters did not know whether the banquet was on or off. The Paris masses decided to turn up in the hope that something interesting might happen.

(b) On 23rd February Louis-Philippe dismissed Guizot and recalled Thiers to office.

(c) The same evening a crowd went to the Ministry of Foreign Affairs to demonstrate against Guizot, who was not there.

(i) Someone fired a shot, and the regular troops were

ordered to fire a single volley into the crowd. Fifty-two people were killed.

(*ii*) The demonstrators paraded the dead through the streets. Soon Paris was in open revolt, and barricades were erected.

19. Abdication of the King. On 23rd February the National Guard was called out to restore order. In the past it had been an important basis of power for Louis-Philippe and had put down disturbances throughout his reign. However, it refused to fire on the people, and demonstrated with it instead. The National Guard had grievances of its own. In 1847 a petition demanding the vote for its members had been refused.

The King was not keen to use the regular troops to reinforce his authority. Thiers ordered them to leave Paris so that they would keep their discipline. On 24th February the King abdicated in favour of his ten-year-old grandson.

THE SECOND REPUBLIC, 1848–52

20. Formation of the provisional government. Once again a comparatively bloodless and rapid revolution had taken place in Paris. However, this time months of confusion, civil war and chaos were to follow before stable government finally returned in 1852.

The middle classes, headed by the poet and historian Lamartine, had provided the intellectual spearhead to the rising. The bulk of the fighting had been done by the working classes, led by Louis Blanc, who wanted to establish a socialist programme.

On 25th February Lamartine established a provisional government in the Hôtel de Ville and personally took over responsibility for foreign affairs. The workers established a rival government elsewhere. This was later abandoned when Louis Blanc and two socialist colleagues were admitted to the government of Lamartine.

21. Government measures. The carefree atmosphere in Paris made it difficult for the government to pursue a straightforward policy. It did not want to antagonise the people, but it was necessary to guard against further domestic unrest and to cope with the continued problem of economic distress. The government did not want to provoke intervention by a hostile combination of the other powers.

The government took a number of policy decisions.

(a) *It proclaimed a republic.*

(b) *It strengthened national security.*

(i) It improved conditions of service in the armed forces, which were increased in strength. African troops were recalled to France.

(ii) Service in the National Guard was made compulsory for all Frenchmen. This was to reduce the possibility of fresh mob violence. A new mobile guard was also set up in Paris.

(c) *It established certain liberties of the subject.* These included universal suffrage, freedom of the press and assembly, and the abolition of the death penalty.

(d) *It created National Workshops.* Though inspired by Louis Blanc's ideas, the workshops were little more than open-air public-works projects and not the nationalised industries originally envisaged. They were supervised by Alexandre Marie, who had little interest in them, and not by Blanc. The business classes lost confidence in the economy, trade slackened and unemployment increased. Soon more people demanded work than could be employed by the State. When a dole payment of one franc a day was made, the number of applicants increased. Public revenue was soon insufficient to meet expenses, and increased taxation became necessary. The government refused to give the workers constructive tasks for fear of their competing with ordinary business enterprises.

(e) *It did not intervene abroad.* Soon revolts broke out in other European states. Many Europeans and Frenchmen thought France would, as in 1792, aid revolution abroad. Lamartine acted indecisively, which meant that no one knew what to expect from France. In a "Manifesto to Europe" he made the following ambiguous declarations:

(i) that France no longer felt bound by the 1815 treaties but would still respect them;

(ii) that France would "protect" legitimate national movements abroad but would not resort to arms.

22. National elections won by moderate republicans. On 23rd April 1848 elections by direct male suffrage were held in France for a Constituent Assembly. This was the first such experiment in democracy in Europe. The electorate suddenly leapt from 250,000 to 9 million. The result was a clear victory for the moderate forces. It indicated that, whatever the attitudes of the Parisians, France was a conservative country.

The various political groups were as follows.

(a) *Moderate republicans*. This group won about 500 of the total of 900 seats.

(b) *Monarchists*. Their seats were divided between some 200 Orleanists, 100 legitimists and a few Bonapartists.

(c) *Radical republicans*. This group included socialists and other forces, and won about 100 seats.

23. Reasons for civil war in Paris. The new Assembly had the task of drawing up a new constitution for the Second Republic and to govern France in the meantime. Fresh violence occurred. This time the conflict was not, as in 1789 and 1830, between the nobility or monarchy (who felt the king had the right to govern as he wished) and the forces of liberalism (who believed the king's power should be controlled by an elected Assembly and public opinion). It was a pure struggle for power between the middle and lower classes.

The sequence of events was as follows.

(a) *The extreme Left (radical republicans) were excluded* from the new governing body appointed by the Assembly. The middle classes wished to preserve and not to share the power they had gained as a result of the 1830 and 1848 revolutions.

(b) *The demands of the radicals were ignored.* The "other", un-official, government of France was based on the clubs, the radical coteries of workers headed by Blanc, Raspail and Blanqui. They continued to agitate for far-reaching economic and social reforms. Blanc pleaded in vain for a "Ministry of Progress" while on 15th May the demonstrations in favour of Poland staged by Raspail and the clubs were ignored. That day a group of workers invaded the Assembly and declared it dissolved. The National Guard dispersed the mob and arrested the leaders.

(c) *The National Workshops were abolished.* The workers opposed this. On 22nd June the government gave them the alternative of joining the army or clearing land in the provinces. Force, it was said, would be used if necessary to secure com-pliance.

24. Suppression of the revolt. The barricades appeared again in the streets. For four days (23rd–26th June) there was bitter fighting in Paris, and some 1,500 people were killed. General

Louis Cavaignac, the Minister of War, a strong-willed soldier who had served in Algeria, was given full powers to restore order. He used artillery to blast the insurgents out of fortified positions.

The resistance of the workers was eventually broken. However, a legacy of class hatred remained that was to be a permanent feature of French life. Paris remained in a "state of siege" until 19th October. Cavaignac carried on control, having been voted chief of the executive power by the Assembly. He had the opportunity to establish a permanent dictatorship but he had no ambitions for personal power.

Most of the reforms of the provisional government were revoked. Censorship of the press was reimposed and political clubs were forbidden.

25. The new constitution. The Assembly decided to scrap the "right to work" clause, which had been in the first draft of the constitution. Eventually it was agreed to have an Assembly with supreme legislative power and a president with supreme executive power. Both were to be elected separately and directly by the whole nation. The success of any future government would depend on smooth co-operation between the two branches. The deputies were warned that the nation might elect a president who was unable to work with the Assembly. This was in fact to happen.

The constitution was adopted by the Assembly in November.

26. The triumph of Bonapartism and conservatism. In June Louis Napoleon had been elected to the Assembly by four departments even though he had been in London at the time. The provisional government tried to prevent his entry into politics but the Assembly agreed to admit him.

Gradually Louis Napoleon became the effective force in France as a result of the following factors.

(*a*) *His victory in the presidential elections.* On 10th December elections were held for president. Napoleon secured $5\frac{1}{2}$ million votes. The chief moderate republican candidate, Cavaignac, secured about $1\frac{1}{2}$ million. The other candidates were Ledru-Rollin (350,000), Raspail (37,000), Lamartine (18,000) and Chargarnier (5,000).

(*b*) *His alliance with conservative forces.* Napoleon appointed a ministry dominated by Orleanists, despite the fact that the majority of the National Assembly were republicans. In January 1849 the Assembly, pressured by troops quartered in Paris, voted for its own dissolution.

In April Napoleon sent troops to suppress the Roman Republic and to restore the Pope. When General Oudinot was defeated initially by the Italians (30th April), "the honour of the country and of the army" was used to good account as a slogan by the conservatives. Right-wing and monarchical groups were united on a common programme of "saving society" from the radical and socialist elements of 1848.

(c) *Victory for the Right in new elections.* The results of the May elections were as follows.

(i) The legitimist Bourbon, Orleanist and Bonapartist groups won about 500 seats.

(ii) The socialists, led by Ledru-Rollin, won about 180.

(iii) The moderate republicans won only seventy.

27. Stages in Napoleon's rise to absolute power. According to the constitution the legislature had to be elected every three years, the president every four years. The existing president was not eligible for re-election. In 1852 elections for both the presidency and the legislature would be due.

Napoleon wanted to stay in office, since he felt France needed his services. A more practical consideration was the fact that he was in debt and wanted a continuation of income. He had enemies in the Assembly keen to remove him from office, and yet he managed in a comparatively short space of time to emerge as absolute ruler of France. The various stages in Napoleon's rise to this position were as follows.

(a) *He failed to have his period of office extended* (July 1851). The motion to amend the clause so that his term of office could be increased failed to get the necessary three-quarters majority.

(b) *He organised a successful coup d'état* (2nd December 1851). Plans for this had been made in great secrecy late in November. On the morning of the 2nd, the people of Paris saw the army occupying the Palais Bourbon, the seat of the Assembly, and arresting the remaining deputies. The previous night the following action had been taken.

(i) Some seventy-eight police officers had each separately arrested one of the leaders of the opposition (deputies, journalists, etc.), ignorant of the fact they were part of a large-scale plan.

(ii) Troops had been posted in strategic positions in Paris under Saint-Arnaud. Morny had organised a proclamation which the printers were compelled to issue. This announced the dissolution of the Assembly and the restoration of universal suffrage, and called upon the people to ratify the President's actions and to give him authority to draft a new constitution.

(c) *Opposition* in Paris and the provinces (3rd–4th December 1851) was crushed by the army.

(d) *A plebiscite* showed that 92 per cent of the poll ratified Napoleon's action (21st December 1851). In January 1852 he drew up a constitution which amounted to the introduction of a benevolent dictatorship.

(e) *A triumphant tour of the provinces was made* (September 1852). During 1852 the Bonapartists organised elaborate campaigns to prepare the people for a return to Empire. During this tour, under the influence of paid demonstrators, there were frequent cries of "*Vive l'Empire!*"

(f) *A plebiscite "ratified" a return to Empire* (2nd November 1852). About 8 million people approved this policy, 250,000 opposed it, while 2 million did not vote.

28. Reasons for Napoleon's success. After the experiences of 1848–9 people wearied of parliamentary struggles and the disorders caused by radicalism. The demand for a "strong man" to govern France grew and there seemed to be few suitable alternatives to Napoleon.

Specific points which can be noted about the rise of Bonapartism are as follows.

(a) *The Bonapartists' efficient organisation.* From October 1849 Napoleon had gradually replaced Orleanists holding key posts in government by his own followers. For example, Maupas became Prefect of Police, and General Saint-Arnaud came from Algeria to command the Paris troops. Morny (Napoleon's illegitimate half-brother) exerted influence in the Ministry of the Interior, which controlled internal communications. A journalist friend edited an anti-socialist paper, *Le Spectre rouge*. Since June 1848 Napoleon's followers had been busy among the poor circulating cheap journals containing his ideas. An illustration of the organisation was the comparative smoothness with which the *coup d'état* in 1851 was carried out.

(b) *General support from all classes of society.* Napoleon managed to persuade different groups that he supported their interests, even though some of them would inevitably conflict. In 1848 his election manifesto promised protection of property, religious toleration, free enterprise, a free press, social reform and industrial progress. Just about every interest was fused under the Napoleonic image.

He gained some support from the following sections.

(*i*) The workers, both industrial and agricultural (*see* **16**(*b*)).

(*ii*) The business and commercial classes who looked to Napoleon as the champion of "law and order" against left-wing socialist upheavals. He had supported measures attacking radicalism. In mid 1850 a new electoral law had required three years' residence for voting, which affected the radicals. Other Acts had forbidden clubs and public meetings and imposed a press censorship.

(*iii*) The monarchists: in 1850–1 repressive actions had been taken against prominent supporters of republicanism in government employment and outside. Examples were lawsuits and fines, house-searching, and dismissal from office.

(*iv*) The Ultramontane Catholics: Napoleon had supported the Falloux Law (1850), which gave the clergy a large measure of control in education.

(*c*) *The legend and magic surrounding Napoleon's name.* His personal impact, promises and showy presence, as well as his being a controversial and mysterious character, helped in the unsettled times to appeal to a large section of the people who wanted stability at home and successes abroad. He became well known through his writings, such as *Les Idées Napoléoniennes* (1839), the publicity surrounding his personal attempts at a *coup d'état* (at Strasbourg in 1836 and Boulogne in 1840), and his successful tours in France (1851–2).

PROGRESS TEST 5

1. What were the provisions of the 1814 Charter? **(1)**

2. Why did some of Louis XVIII's initial actions cause unrest among supporters of the Revolution? **(2)**

3. Describe the main political groups between 1814 and 1830. **(3)**

4. Illustrate why it was difficult to form a stable government after 1815. **(4–5)**

5. Give some account of the policies of French ministries between 1821 and 1830. **(5–6)**

6. Account for the 1830 revolution. **(7–8)**

7. Give the reasons why Louis-Philippe became king in 1830. **(9)**

8. What political changes were made as a result of the 1830 revolution? **(10)**

9. Why was the reign of the July monarch one of unrest? **(11–12)**

10. Discuss critically the foreign policies of Louis-Philippe. **(13–15)**

11. Give specific reasons for the growth of Bonapartism. **(16(b))**

12. Why was socialist sentiment particularly strong in Paris? **(16(a), 17)**

13. What was the purpose of the Reform Banquets? **(18)**

14. Were the National Workshops created in 1848 successful? **(21(d))**

15. Explain the causes of the French civil war in 1848. **(23)**

16. Illustrate in what way France believed in moderation in politics. **(22, 26)**

17. Why was Louis Napoleon the main figure in politics from 1848 to 1851? **(27–28)**

CHAPTER VI

Napoleon III and the Second Empire

INTRODUCTION

1. Aims of Napoleon. When the Second Empire was established, Louis Napoleon assumed the title of Napoleon III. His broad objectives were as follows.

(*a*) *The creation of a modern industrial economy.* This would help to raise the material standard of living of the rural and urban masses.

(*b*) *The restoration of French political influence abroad.* Napoleon believed that the main reason why the July Monarchy of Louis-Philippe had failed had been its unambitious foreign policy. He wanted to carry out the policies which he considered his uncle would have followed, and to use the domestic industrial base to secure his foreign policy aims. These aims were:

(*i*) to revise the 1815 peace treaties (*see* **12**);

(*ii*) to support the cause of nationality and liberty in Europe (*see* **12**);

(*iii*) to revive French military prestige;

(*iv*) to extend the French colonial empire.

(*c*) *The maintenance of absolute rule at home.* Napoleon hoped the French would consider national prosperity at home and *la gloire* abroad to be adequate substitutes for the loss of individual liberties.

2. The political system. The constitution of January 1852 had granted Napoleon absolute power for a ten-year period. He commanded the armed forces and the police and he controlled the Civil Service. He alone could initiate legislation, declare war and conclude treaties, and he could rule by decree. He was declared "responsible before the French people", a noticeably vague phrase.

(*a*) *Individual political liberty hardly existed.* Political associations were forbidden to federate, and political meetings could be held only in the presence of government officials. The press decree of 1852 was very harsh. However, rule was not generally oppressive since such a policy would have had few wholehearted supporters.

Napoleon argued that a nation must learn to obey before it can be free. He did "not mind being baptised with the water of universal suffrage" but "refused to live with his feet in it". He promised to curtail his powers gradually, saying liberty would crown the edifice of his work. In fact, failures abroad forced him unwillingly to make concessions earlier than he had anticipated (*see* 9).

(*b*) *The system of government was autocratic.* Ministers in charge of the executive departments had no collective responsibility to the legislature. They were appointed on the basis of personal loyalty and ability and could be dismissed only by the Emperor.

The various institutions were as follows.

(*i*) The *Conseil d'Etat*, composed of senior Civil Servants, was appointed by the Emperor. Its main task was the drafting of legislation.

(*ii*) The Senate: members were leading persons from all sections of the community who were appointed for life by the Emperor.

(*iii*) The Corps Législatif: the deputies were elected by universal male suffrage for six-year terms. This body had the right to accept or reject legislation, but could not introduce or amend it. Debates were not open to the public and no records were kept.

DOMESTIC POLICIES

3. **Material prosperity.** The period 1852–70 was one of the most prosperous in French history. This was due both to world economic conditions and to Napoleon's policies. The Paris Exhibitions (1855 and 1867) showed the world the extent of the industrial progress France had made.

The following examples of Napoleon's policies may be noted.

(*a*) *Private enterprise.* This was encouraged and as a result new businesses multiplied. Napoleon used public bond investments to raise funds for worthwhile business expansion.

Abroad many rail, mining, banking and other industrial projects were established with French capital. A notable example was the digging of the Suez Canal by a company under Ferdinand de Lesseps.

(*b*) *New financial institutions.* The *Crédit Foncier* (mortgage bank) and *Crédit Mobilier* (industrial credit institution) were founded by private enterprise with government support in 1852. They helped finance rail, shipping, mining and metallurgical enterprises.

(*c*) *Communications.* A vast programme of railway, canal and road building was undertaken. Two examples of improvements in communications were the following.

(*i*) The creation of a steamship company with a government subsidy (1855). This eventually became the French steamship line.

(*ii*) The expansion of the telegraph network from 2,000 to over 70,000 kilometres. This enabled prices of stocks to be quoted on the Paris and London exchanges the same day.

(*d*) *Public works.* These projects included the reclaiming of waste land, the drainage of swamps and the preservation of forests. They served the double purpose of improving the land and providing employment.

(*e*) *Agriculture.* Napoleon encouraged scientific farming and selective breeding. Agricultural societies were organised, as also were fairs and model farms.

(*f*) *Social policy.* Help was given to the poor. Workers' dwellings were improved, donations made to charitable institutions, and friendly societies formed.

4. Improvements in Paris. The reconstruction of Paris was one aspect of Napoleon's policy of restoring France to a position of prestige in Europe and covering the Empire with glory. In collaboration with Baron Haussmann, Prefect of the Seine department, he made Paris the most modern capital in Europe. This was done in the following two ways.

(*a*) *By the construction of wide boulevards.* The building of wide avenues on geometric designs relieved congestion and provided work for the unemployed. The erection of barricades, which had been inaccessible to cavalry attacks in the past, was made difficult owing to the width of the avenues.

(*b*) *By various social changes.*

(*i*) Vast slum-clearance projects were carried out, and more than double the number of houses demolished were erected. This improved health conditions and curbed the outbreak of cholera.

(*ii*) Gas lighting was introduced, spacious rail stations built, and the Parc Monceau and Bois de Boulogne developed.

5. Freer trade. Napoleon had been in Britain when the Corn Laws were repealed, and he became a convinced advocate of free trade. This fitted his vision of a Europe of free nationalities living in interdependence. He wanted to widen markets, promote growth and efficiency and reduce the number of incompetent firms. As a result he aroused the hostility of many businesses, especially the smaller ones, which relied on protection.

Between 1853 and 1855 duties on imports of iron, steel, coal and certain other raw materials were reduced. In 1857 the Corps Législatif opposed any further reduction in trade restrictions, but in 1860 Napoleon took advantage of a clause in the constitution which allowed him to sign commercial treaties without reference to the legislature. Foreign trade expanded owing to the following measures.

(*a*) *The Cobden–Chevalier Treaty* (1860). The provisions of this agreement with Britain were as follows.

(*i*) Import duties on British coal, manufactured goods, iron and steel, hardware goods and textiles were to be lowered by 25 per cent over five years.

(*ii*) In exchange French wines, brandy, silks and fancy goods were to enter Britain at reduced tariffs.

(*b*) *Other similar trade agreements.* France made a series of reciprocal trade treaties with other European countries. These were with Belgium (1861), the Zollverein (1862), Italy (1863), Switzerland (1864), Spain and the Netherlands (1865), and Austria and Portugal (1866).

6. The Empire at its peak. By 1859–60 the Second Empire had realised some of the cherished dreams of Napoleon. The Bonapartist government had won considerable support at home and respect abroad.

Napoleon had been successful in the following fields.

(*a*) *Domestic affairs.* Economic and commercial progress had been made and this gained Napoleon the support of the business community and workers. The liberals liked his free-trade measures.

(*b*) *Foreign affairs.* Liberals and nationalists were generally pleased with French successes abroad (*see* **11**).

(*c*) *Personal affairs.*

(*i*) In 1853 Napoleon had married Countess Eugénie de Montijo, daughter of a Spanish grandee. She was vivacious and charming, but also a strict Catholic with little sense over political matters.

(*ii*) In March 1856 the birth of a son, the Prince Imperial, assured the succession to the throne.

7. Growing opposition in France. Napoleon was concerned about the growth of opposition to the government. The problem was that his varied policies could not please all sections of the community. For example, he was never able to reconcile the divergent interests of the French liberals and clericals in his Mexican and Italian policies. His ambiguous and contradictory actions made him unpopular. In addition, his foreign ventures and grandiose public-works projects entailed heavy expenses. He was rapidly losing the support of influential groups of the people and incurring the hostility of others, including the following.

(*a*) *Roman Catholics.*

(*i*) The Ultramontanes disliked Napoleon's aiding of Piedmont in the task of Italian unification. France did nothing to prevent Piedmont entering the Papal States in 1860 and annexing the Papal territory of Romagna. As a result, the clerical press, notably *L'Univers*, was increasingly hostile towards Napoleon.

(*ii*) The liberal wing, under Montalembert, urged the importance of a liberal political system as the only type under which Catholicism could flourish.

(*b*) *Businessmen.* Many of the small traders and artisans disliked Napoleon's free-trade measures.

(*c*) *Republicans.* Opposition from this quarter was reborn in the legislature. Five opponents of Napoleon, including Emile Ollivier, were returned after the elections of 1857–8.

(*d*) *Liberals.*

(*i*) This group disliked Napoleon's personal dictatorship at home.

(*ii*) They resented the abandoning of the Austrian War in 1859.

(*e*) *Legitimists.* Napoleon did nothing to prevent the expulsion of the Neapolitan Bourbon ruler Francis from southern Italy in 1860.

8. The liberal Empire. Napoleon was advised in 1859–60 that the moment was opportune to make the political concessions which he had promised in 1852. The Empire was strong, but it was necessary to conciliate opponents and restore the confidence of the business world. Napoleon also considered it would be to his advantage to allow the legislature to share responsibility for government.

The following concessions were made.

(*a*) *An amnesty* was granted to all political exiles (1859). However, this did not extend to Ledru-Rollin, an extreme republican banished after a Paris rising in 1850.

(*b*) *Parliament* was granted greater legislative and financial freedom (1860–1). Some latitude was given to the press in recording parliamentary debates. Napoleon renounced the right to borrow money while the legislature was not in session, and it was agreed that in future the budget should be voted by section instead of *en bloc*.

(*c*) *Workers were allowed the right to strike* (1864).

9. Further liberal measures. By 1867 the Empire was no longer in its prime but along the path of decline. Further political changes were made.

(*a*) *Causes.* Mounting pressure forced Napoleon to make further political concessions as a result of disastrous foreign policies. Napoleon's original liberal measures, instead of quelling the opposition, had only increased its strength. In 1863 the membership of the opposition in the Chamber increased to thirty-five: no single government supporter was returned from Paris. In 1866 more than forty members of the government majority broke away to form a "Third Party" and agitated for political reform.

Certain liberals, such as Emile Ollivier and Adolphe Thiers, expressed a willingness to support Napoleon if he abandoned autocratic rule. Napoleon gave in, being anxious to remain ruler and to secure the dynasty.

(*b*) *Nature of the changes.*

(*i*) In 1867 increased powers were given to the legislature, including the right of interpellation.

(*ii*) In 1868 an Act encouraged the growth of trade-unionism, while other legislation relaxed the press censorship and permitted a limited right of public meeting.

(*c*) *Results.*

(*i*) There was a growth of the opposition press, both Orleanist and republican. A few extremist papers appeared, including *La Lanterne* and *Le Rappel*.

(*ii*) There was a growth of radicalism and trade-unionism, and an epidemic of strikes.

(*iii*) The government was defeated in the elections of May 1869. Its vote was reduced to only 42 per cent of the total.

10. Introduction of parliamentary democracy. The Third Party, with the co-operation of forty deputies of the Left, now had a majority in the Chamber. They demanded the creation of a responsible ministry. This was granted in September 1869. The Legislative Assembly was allowed to propose laws, to criticise and vote the budget and to choose its own officials. In December, Emile Ollivier, leader of the Third Party, was invited to form a cabinet representative of the majority of the legislature.

In January 1870 a republican journalist, Victor Noir, was shot by a cousin of the Emperor. At his funeral some 100,000 people demonstrated against the Empire. As a result, further political concessions followed. In April the Senate was converted into an upper house, sharing legislative power with the Assembly. As this necessitated a constitutional change, the Bonapartists sought a plebiscite to strengthen the position of the Emperor.

In the May plebiscite, right-wing republicans supported the government. The result showed that $7\frac{1}{2}$ million Frenchmen approved the liberal measures since 1860, $1\frac{1}{2}$ million opposed them, while 2 million had abstained from voting. The negative votes reflected the powerful left-wing republican support in the large cities, notably Paris, Lyons and Marseilles. The Left never forgave Napoleon for the bloodshed incurred in the 1851 *coup d'état*.

The Empire appeared to have gained new strength as a result of the process of liberalisation. However, it was soon to be overthrown following failures in foreign affairs.

FOREIGN POLICIES

11. Successful foreign ventures. Until 1861 Napoleon's foreign policy was successful and French influence and prestige were restored in Europe. France gradually extended her colonial empire, managed to further the cause of nationalism and liberty, secured an extension of French boundaries in the south-east and took part in a victorious war. Areas of interest were as follows.

(*a*) *In Europe.*

(*i*) The Crimea (1854–6): by inflating the dispute over the Holy Places through posing as the protector of Roman Catholics to please the clericals, Napoleon helped provoke war. The Crimean War provided an opportunity for demonstrating French military prowess and for working closely with Britain.

Russia was defeated. In 1856, at the Congress of Paris, France was the diplomatic centre of Europe and was recognised as the leading European military power.

(*ii*) Italy: Napoleon gained from Piedmont the territories of Savoy (Swiss in origin) and Nice (French-speaking) as the price of French support during 1859–60.

(*iii*) Danubian principalities: owing mainly to Napoleon, Moldavia and Wallachia secured regional autonomy in 1856 (*see* XV, **19**(*d*)). In 1857 the Sultan refused the demand of the unionists that these territories should be united as Romania. However, both principalities chose the same person as their king, Colonel Cuza. Napoleon, supported by Russia, dissuaded Turkey and other powers from taking any preventive action. In 1862 the principalities secured ultimate unification and independence as Romania, again with the moral backing of France.

(*b*) *Outside Europe*.

(*i*) Indo-China: Saigon was captured and sovereign rule was gradually extended over the region (*see* XX, **30**).

(*ii*) China: in 1858–60 a successful joint expedition took place with the British (*see* XX, **16**).

(*iii*) Syria and Lebanon: in 1860 a French expedition intervened after a massacre of Christians had occurred. It withdrew shortly afterwards so as not to alienate Britain.

(*iv*) West Africa: the coast of Guinea and Dahomey was occupied under the governorship of Faidherbe.

12. Foreign policies after 1861. After 1861 Napoleon was subjected to increased opposition at home. He felt compelled to pursue certain policies which he hoped would revive his popularity. Unfortunately all his plans went wrong. France gradually lost the ascendant position she had occupied in European affairs since 1856. Napoleon was out-manoeuvred diplomatically by Bismarck and also handicapped after 1866 by bad health. As a result of Napoleon's actions, France failed to gain any diplomatic support among other European states and became completely isolated. The following were the important aspects of Napoleon's policies abroad in this period.

(a) *Revision of the north-east border.* It had been a maxim of French policy that the hegemony, prosperity and unity of France depended on Germany not being politically united and on French control of the Rhineland. This policy received a severe setback in 1815, when Prussia extended into the Rhineland.

Napoleon was not keen to see the emergence of a strong, united Germany under Prussia. However, he devised no plan to forestall this and instead tried to secure compensation for any extension of Prussian power. His first attempts to negotiate something with the Prussian king between 1857 and 1860 had been ignored. Later, in discussions with Bismarck at Biarritz in 1865 (*see* **16**(*a*)), and afterwards, Napoleon persisted in trying to secure territory in the Rhineland, Luxembourg or Belgium, but in vain. He only incurred humiliation and aroused deep suspicion in Germany and Britain as to his intentions (*see* **16**(*d*), **17** and **22**(*a*)).

(b) *Poland.* Napoleon wanted to help the national cause and protested against the Tsar's action in suppressing the revolt in 1863 (*see* XII, **30**), but, as French interests were not directly involved, he took no positive action, fearing that war might occur. However, his policy was enough to bring about the collapse of the Franco-Russian *entente* of 1856, and Bismarck managed to win the friendship of the Tsar (*see* XII, **30–31**).

(c) *Italy.* To placate the Catholics and his empress, Napoleon kept troops in Rome until 1870. This alienated the French liberals and Italian nationalists. Various aspects of his Italian policies annoyed the following powers.

(*i*) Britain: after 1856 Anglo-French relations cooled considerably. Britain suspected French designs in Italy, particularly in the south, and disliked Napoleon's extortion of Nice and Savoy from Piedmont in 1860.

(*ii*) Austria: Napoleon annoyed Francis Joseph by allying with Piedmont in 1859 and then by not taking action to implement the Villafranca agreement.

(*iii*) Italy: by garrisoning Rome with French troops until 1870, Napoleon sacrificed all chances of an Italian alliance after 1866 (*see* **18**).

(d) *Austro-Prussian War* (1866). France failed to mediate between the two powers as Napoleon had hoped, or to gain anything. French prestige suffered a crippling blow as a result (*see* **16**(*d*)).

(e) *Colonial ventures.* Successful expansion took place in West

Africa and Vietnam. However, this did not compensate for failures in Europe. In addition Napoleon was distracted from European events by events in the following areas.

(*i*) Mexico: Napoleon went against the express wishes of the Emperor Francis Joseph in embarking on this venture of starting an expedition to revive French fortunes in the New World. France suffered a humiliating reverse (*see* **13–15**).

(*ii*) Algeria: there was serious unrest in 1865 and Napoleon had to go on a special visit to placate the area.

13. Mexico and European creditors. Since independence in 1823, Mexico had not known stable rule. A rebel leader, Benito Juarez, came to power in 1857 after a successful revolt. He represented the progressive, anti-clerical and anti-aristocratic elements in Mexico. Miramon, representing the clerical and conservative cause, led the opposition. Both parties borrowed money from Europe to fight their civil war.

In 1861 Juarez triumphed over his opponents. Then he refused to pay interest on loans to British, French and Spanish creditors. Because of this a debt-collecting joint expedition by Britain, France and Spain landed troops at Vera Cruz in December. However, Britain and Spain soon withdrew from the dispute as they did not want to enter Mexican territory, they thought Juarez would be amenable to negotiations, and they suspected France of ulterior motives for participating in the expedition. On this last point they guessed correctly.

14. Reasons for the Mexican venture. Napoleon was persuaded by clerical advisers to embark on a crusade, part Catholic, part financial. There was also a slight personal involvement. A Swiss banker in Paris named Jekker had lent money to Miramon and had promised the duc de Morny, the Emperor's half-brother, 30 per cent of the profits.

France decided to take unilateral action in Mexico for the following three reasons.

(*a*) *Economic.* It was expected that the financiers and the Bourse (stock exchange) would welcome the opportunity of establishing trade and markets in a new area that was believed to be wealthy. It was intended that the economic development of Mexico would be assisted by French companies.

(*b*) *Political.* Napoleon planned to revive past French plans of establishing influence in the New World which had been current in the period 1823–5. It was thought the venture would satisfy the public desire for *la gloire*. The moment was considered opportune since the United States was involved in the domestic issue of the Civil War. The throne of Mexico was to be offered to the scientist, traveller and liberal, the Archduke Maximilian, brother of Francis Joseph. This was expected to gain Austria's friendship.

(*c*) *Religious.* It was considered that Mexico, owing to past Spanish influence, was pro-monarchical and supported the Roman Catholic Church. The venture was expected to please clerical opinion and the Vatican.

15. The disastrous Mexican campaign. An army of 23,000 men under General Forey eventually captured Mexico City in 1863, and Maximilian was established as king in 1864. Napoleon had proceeded with the project against the advice of Britain and Francis Joseph.

The French made the following grave miscalculations.

(*a*) The Mexicans were not so keen to be "liberated" as royalist exiles had suggested. As a result the cost in manpower and money of pacifying Mexico and supporting Maximilian on the throne was greater than originally planned.

(*b*) A harsh climate and the outbreak of diseases hampered the troops.

(*c*) It had not been expected that the North would win the American Civil War and that the United States would intervene so quickly. In 1865 the United States accused France of contravening the Monroe Doctrine.

In 1866 Napoleon, tired of this expensive, fruitless venture, ordered the troops, now under Bazaine, to withdraw, as it was expected that they would be needed to strengthen the French position in the approaching Austro-Prussian War. Maximilian refused to leave with the last French troops in February 1867. His supporters quarrelled among themselves, and he was captured by the opposition and shot in June by a firing squad.

16. France and the Austro-Prussian War. In 1865 a war between Austria and Prussia seemed imminent. Napoleon expected the war to be lengthy and wanted France to mediate at the end in favour of the weaker party, whereby, he hoped, she would make some territorial gains.

The following can be noted about the French involvement in the affairs of the German powers.

(a) *Biarritz meeting*. Napoleon reckoned that Prussia was weaker than Austria and decided to open talks with Bismarck. At a meeting at Biarritz in April 1865 he offered French neutrality in the event of a war between Austria and Prussia. If Prussia won, the suggested reward for France would be some territory west of the Rhine and the return of Venetia to Italy. Bismarck was interested but nothing was settled, though it appeared that France would be neutral in a conflict between the German states.

(b) *Austro-French agreement*. In April 1866 Napoleon gave his promise of neutrality to Austria. In return Austria agreed to the amazing condition of handing over Venetia to France for transfer to Italy whether she won or lost the war. In the event of her victory, Austria would be free to make changes in Germany, but would consult France first if these changes disturbed the European balance of power.

(c) *Failure to intervene in time*. The Austro-Prussian War was rapidly concluded, which upset all Napoleon's plans. A settlement was reached before Napoleon could persuade his government to intervene decisively. After the battle of Sadowa he planned to mass an army on the Rhine, but was persuaded to try peaceful mediation instead.

(d) *Failure to gain any benefit from the war*. Before final Austro-Prussian peace terms were settled, Napoleon suggested to Bismarck that there should be some compensation for France. Napoleon was tactless enough to commit himself on paper, not to modest boundary modifications, as Bismarck was led to expect in 1865, but to demands for extensive German territory. This included a frontier up to the Rhine, and perhaps Mainz, Luxembourg and the Bavarian Palatinate. As Bismarck had not committed himself to give Napoleon anything, he rejected these demands.

France was left with the sole satisfaction of being responsible for handing over Venetia to Italy. This had been agreed whatever the outcome of the war (*see* (b)).

17. The Luxembourg crisis. In 1867 Napoleon suggested to the Dutch king, who was the hereditary Grand Duke of French-speaking Luxembourg, that he should sell this duchy to France.

Luxembourg had been a member of the German Confederation until 1866. As it had no army of its own, it was garrisoned by Prussian troops. The King of Holland, who was in debt, was keen on the transaction if the consent of the Prussian king was first secured. Bismarck promised not to oppose the deal, provided it was so engineered that German national feelings were not aroused. (There is some evidence, however, that this was bluff on Bismarck's part, and intended as a trap for Napoleon.)

However, a crisis soon developed which embittered Franco-German relations and nearly led to war. The French mismanaged the affair, and news of the project leaked out. This had the following results.

(a) *Negotiations broke down.* There was a national outcry in Germany, and the King of Holland refused to go through with the arrangements.

(b) *A conference in London was held.* France, wanting to secure some honour from the defeat, suggested the withdrawal of Prussian troops. The situation was ripe for war. Russia suggested a conference, and this met in London in May 1867. The results, which were as follows, displeased both the French and Germans.

(i) Luxembourg was declared a neutral state and its independence was guaranteed by the powers.

(ii) Prussia lost her rights of garrison.

18. Triple Alliance negotiations. Napoleon was determined after the Luxembourg humiliation to prepare for a possible war with Prussia. Negotiations were started for an alliance with Austria, and Napoleon met Francis Joseph at Salzburg in September 1867. Francis Joseph, naturally displeased by the outcome of the Mexican venture, knew that the Hungarians were not keen on a French alliance unless it was to provide security in South-east Europe against Russia. Austria also wanted to protect her flank against a possible attack by Italy. Thus Italy was drawn into the negotiations and a draft treaty was actually prepared in 1869.

Negotiations broke down for the following two reasons.

(a) The reluctance of Austria to commit herself to a dispute between France and Prussia on purely German issues.

(b) The reluctance of Italy to sign any treaty with France until French troops had left Rome. Napoleon would not undertake to evacuate Rome as he did not want to alienate clerical opinion or the Empress Eugénie. The Austrians would not sign any treaty until the Italians had signed first.

19. Dispute over the Spanish succession. In 1868 a Spanish revolt under Serrano and Prim deposed Queen Isabella, who fled into exile in 1869. The provisional government looked round for a successor. A possible candidate was Prince Leopold of Hohen-zollern-Sigmaringen, a Catholic and distant relative of the Prussian king. Napoleon made it clear that the choice of Leopold would be an affront to France. The Prussian king also opposed the candidature. In any case Prince Leopold himself was not keen to embark on such an insecure career as that of a Spanish monarch, and withdrew his candidature.

The following events led up to the immediate cause of war between France and Germany.

(a) *Revival of Leopold's candidature.* Bismarck decided to revive the candidature of Leopold in 1869 and conducted secret negotiations with Prim. According to Lothar Bucher, Bismarck's most intimate collaborator, this step was "a trap for Napoleon", to provoke him or France into indiscreet action.

In 1870 the Spanish government officially offered the throne to Prince Leopold. He accepted the invitation on 3rd July. Bismarck planned to present France with a *fait accompli*.

(b) *Gramont's war speech.* The secret leaked out and France was furious. She feared encirclement if Hohenzollern rule were established on both the Rhine and the Pyrenees. On 6th July the French Foreign Minister, Gramont, stated that, unless Leopold withdrew, France would treat the matter as a cause for war.

(c) *Withdrawal of Leopold's candidature.* Prince Leopold had been advised by the Prussian king not to accept the Spanish throne. This had been after Benedetti, the French ambassador, had spoken to King William. On 12th July Prince Leopold withdrew his candidature for the second time. The news was greeted with general exultation in France.

(d) *French insistence on further guarantees.* An opportunity seemed to have occurred for the French government to gain prestige by exacting revenge on Prussia for past humiliations. If successful it would revive the declining fortunes of the dynasty, as the Empress Eugénie was keen to secure the Spanish throne for the Prince Imperial. On 13th July the French cabinet decided to seek guarantees from King William that the candidature of Leopold would not be renewed. Napoleon, at the time almost incapacitated through illness, accepted the decision.

(e) *Ems meeting.* The Prussian king met the French ambassador, Benedetti, on 13th July and courteously declined to give any guarantee on Leopold's candidature. He would not accept something which seemed to impugn his good faith. Later King

William sent an aide to Benedetti, after receiving official news of Leopold's withdrawal, stating that he regarded the matter as now closed.

20. The Ems telegram. Bismarck wanted war, and regarded the King's mild behaviour as a humiliating surrender to the French. The King sent a telegram to Bismarck, which told of what had taken place with Benedetti at Ems. Bismarck was permitted to give an account of the events to the press. He decided to edit the telegram so that an abridged version would give a different interpretation. He made it appear that the King's refusal to see Benedetti again was due, not to his having heard news of Leopold's withdrawal, but to the nature of Benedetti's original demands. It was made to appear that the King had been curt and not courteous to Benedetti.

There was a general national outcry in both Germany and France when the press broke the news. On 19th July the French cabinet decided to declare war on Germany. The decision was a popular one in France, with the exception of Paris. The importance of the Ems telegram in influencing the French action has been exaggerated. The French cabinet had already decided on 13th July that there must be war if the Prussian king's attitude was anything less than one of capitulation.

21. Role of France and Germany in causing war. The actual circumstances which caused war were complex. In 1870 Europe thought France had been the chief culprit. Later it was realised that Bismarck had also played a leading role. Historians have disagreed on two points. The first concerns how the blame should be apportioned between Prussia and France. The second concerns the degree to which Bismarck had any long-term plan for German unification and intended to fight France as part of the process.

(*a*) *Role of Germany.* In his *Reflections* Bismarck wrote later: "That a war with France would succeed that with Austria lay in the logic of history." On the other hand in 1870 his timetable for future German unification was far from clear. The South German states, Bavaria, Baden and Württemberg, which were Catholic and liberal in sympathy, were friendly to France. They might weaken rather than strengthen the predominance of a Protestant Prussia in Germany which Bismarck desired.

However, Bismarck saw the following advantages in a successful war with France.

(*i*) It would ease the problem of obtaining unity if the South German states took part in the war.

(*ii*) Francis Joseph of Austria would then abandon hope of recovering Austrian ascendancy in Germany.

(*iii*) France would not be able to make territorial demands as compensation for the inclusion of South Germany in a united German state.

(*b*) *Role of France.* In early 1870 French policy was peaceful. The Premier, Ollivier, had frankly and publicly acknowledged the right to unification of the German states. However, French statesmen knew that it had been a constant theme of their policy since 1648 to keep Germany disunited if France were to be secure. The following played important roles.

(*i*) Napoleon felt that, in order to save his declining dynasty, he had to demand from Bismarck, in 1866 and 1867, compensation for the growth in power of Prussia. France appeared to be a barrier in the way of German unity. In 1867 Napoleon said that Germany was divided into two parts, each weaker than France, and that he intended to perpetuate this state of affairs.

(*ii*) The war party, led by Gramont and the Empress Eugénie, utilised every opportunity to produce war.

(*iii*) The French army leaders were confident of their military prowess and of defeating Prussia in any war. In 1869 the cabinet was assured by the War Minister, Leboeuf, that should war take place the French army was ready "to the last gaiter button".

22. France isolated in Europe. In 1870 France found herself without allies in Europe.

(*a*) *Britain.* In 1870, when it appeared that British opinion might support France against Prussia, Bismarck gave a document to the correspondent of *The Times.* This contained a French suggestion, made in August 1866, that Prussia support France if the latter occupied Belgium.

(*b*) *Russia.* The Tsar offered Bismarck Russia's neutrality in the event of a Franco-Prussian war if Prussia would support him in his plan to revise the Black Sea clauses of the Treaty of Paris. Bismarck agreed to this.

(*c*) *South Germany.* In 1866 Bismarck communicated to the French press Napoleon's suggestion for compensation in the

Rhine area and Bavaria. This angered the South Germans. They were thus less inclined to seek the aid of a liberal Catholic France against an autocratic Protestant Prussia.

(*d*) *Austria and Italy*. Russia exerted pressure on Austria to stay neutral in 1870. The failure of the Triple Alliance negotiations in 1869 meant that France could not rely on these countries being her allies in 1870.

23. Collapse of the Second Empire. French forces invaded the Saar, hoping to gain the co-operation of the South German states and perhaps of Austria and Italy. After achieving a minor success at Saarbrücken they were soon subject to fierce counter-attacks by three German armies. The sequence of events was as follows.

(*a*) *Two French defeats on 6th August*.

(*i*) MacMahon was defeated by the Prussian crown prince at Worth and forced to evacuate Alsace.

(*ii*) Bazaine and the Lorraine army were defeated at Spicheren.

(*b*) *Metz*. Napoleon relinquished over-all command of the retreating forces to Bazaine, who was soon encircled by the Germans and besieged at Metz on 18th August.

(*c*) *Sedan*. Napoleon joined forces with MacMahon. The latter wanted to retreat to Paris to fight the next battle with the support of the Paris guns. The Empress Eugénie opposed this, since it meant abandoning the popular Bazaine. While marching to relieve Metz, the French were encircled by the Prussians.

Napoleon realised that resistance to the Prussian guns was hopeless. On 2nd September he and MacMahon surrendered with some 84,000 men.

(*d*) *Republic proclaimed*.

(*i*) On 4th September, when news of the defeat at Sedan arrived, the Paris mobs rioted.

(*ii*) The Assembly deposed Napoleon and proclaimed a republic.

(*iii*) The new government of national defence decided to continue the war under the guidance of the deputies of the Seine department. The rest of France was not consulted.

24. The surrender of the French. The sequence of events leading to the total defeat of France was as follows.

(*a*) *Unsuccessful talks* (18th September). Jules Favre, the new

Minister of the Interior, talked with Bismarck, who wanted French territory ceded to Prussia. Favre resisted this.

(*b*) *Siege of Paris* (20th September). When Paris was besieged by the Germans, Gambetta, a republican leader, escaped in a balloon. His object was to rally the provinces and organise the army of the Loire.

(*c*) *Fall of Metz* (27th October). The civilians and army were keen to continue the defence of Metz as there were still adequate provisions. However, Bazaine, who disliked the change of government in Paris, decided to surrender with some 180,000 troops.

NOTE: After the war Bazaine was found guilty of not doing all that honour required and was sentenced to death. However, the sentence was commuted to imprisonment for twenty years. He escaped, and died in Spain in 1888.

(*d*) *Defeat of the provinces.* German forces released from besieging Metz were able to hinder attempts to rally forces in the provinces to relieve Paris.

(*i*) Chanzy was beaten at Le Mans, Faidherbe was beaten near Saint Quentin (19th January), and Bourbaki failed to relieve Belfort in the south.

(*ii*) Paris was forced to surrender on 28th January 1871.

25. German military superiority. The reasons for Germany's victory are to be found in the superiority of the German army to the French in the following areas.

(*a*) *Leadership.* German leadership was bold and united in purpose. In contrast French leadership was poor, and suffered from lack of co-ordination and from divided counsels. French officers were brave, but also careless and jealous for promotion. The Emperor Napoleon was a sick man and mishandled the opening campaigns. The following points may be noted.

(*i*) Small French armies often fought well but were unsupported. For example, reinforcements were not used at Spicheren.

(*ii*) Political considerations often outweighed military factors. MacMahon was persuaded by the Empress against his better judgment to try to relieve Metz.

(*b*) *Manpower.* In 1870 the small professional French army of 200,000 was outnumbered by over 500,000 Prussians.

(*c*) *Arms.* The French *chassepot* outranged the Prussian needle-gun. However, it was the longer range of the German breach-loading rifled artillery over the French bronze muzzle-loading rifled cannon which was the decisive factor. A single volley was sufficient to shatter the charge of General Gallifet's Chasseurs d'Afrique at Sedan. (Prior to the war the Corps Législatif had refused to vote 13 million francs to buy these guns from the firm of Krupp.)

(*d*) *Organisation.*

(*i*) Germany's arrangements were scientifically prepared ahead of time by Moltke. Good use was made of railways for rapid mobilisation and deployment of German troops.

(*ii*) Confident of victory, the French High Command gave poor guidance to the troops. They had no mobilisation plans, and the troops seemed better supplied with maps of Germany than with maps of France. Transport arrangements were chaotic. In one instance a party of hospital attendants bound for the eastern frontier arrived in Algeria.

(*e*) *Training.* Short-service trained German troops proved superior to the professional French army in discipline and military skill.

FINAL ASSESSMENT OF NAPOLEON III

26. His problems and policies. The aims of Napoleon were ambitious and clear, but also partly contradictory, which give an indication as to why his methods for achieving them were remarkably complex and incurred so much hostility. Perhaps his greatest achievement was in promoting internal prosperity. The following are the reasons why he failed to achieve his other aims, particularly as regards his foreign ambitions.

(*a*) *Public opinion.* Napoleon's greatest strength lay in the fact that he could claim to represent the choice of the French people. He did not want to alienate that support. However, he needed the goodwill of the influential sections of the upper and middle classes, who had accepted him only as a temporary expedient against left-wing rule.

Napoleon tried to satisfy in part all sections of the community. The conflicting aims of various sections of the public and the varying moods of the French fitted in part Napoleon's complex character. Both the French and Napoleon were keen to foster the spirit of nationalism and liberty abroad, so long as France benefited and peace could be secured.

In the end, Napoleon never fully satisfied anybody, since few objectives were ever fully realised.

(b) *Napoleon's character.* Thiers once remarked that the French made two mistakes. The first was when they took Napoleon for a fool; the second was when they took him for a genius. In fact, he was neither.

He was not gifted with either great intellectual capacity or diplomatic skill. Few of his foreign objectives were achieved, since he had a "grasshopper" mind, never giving full attention to one activity before being diverted to the next, and, though he had imagination and ideas, he lacked the resolution to complete any project.

(c) *Napoleon's method of intrigue.* Napoleon was conscious of the suspicions aroused by his name. He knew that if he openly renewed the classical Rhine policy of his predecessors, or adopted policies reminiscent of the Napoleonic Era, the anti-French coalition before which his uncle had succumbed might be brought back. Therefore his method to achieve an extension of French territory was the back-door method of intrigue. His "conspiratorial" tactics in his German and Italian policies only tended to make European diplomats even more cautious and suspicious of him. When it was clear that the Villafranca agreement could not be implemented, Francis Joseph wryly remarked: "The Emperor is, and remains, a scoundrel."

(d) *Napoleon's contradictory policies.*

(i) His shrewd common-sense approach to domestic affairs such as business and trade contrasted with his unrealistic ideas abroad.

(ii) He advocated peace, saying: "*L'Empire, c'est la Paix.*" This aim conflicted with aggressive ventures in the Crimea and Mexico and his schemes for remodelling Europe. The latter could hardly be achieved short of war.

(iii) He performed an undeniable service to the cause of freedom and unity in Romania and Italy. This policy contrasted with his autocratic policies at home, his Mexican venture and his demands for compensation in the Rhineland, Belgium and Luxembourg. In addition he never wanted a strong Italian state to emerge on the French south-east border and kept troops stationed in Rome until 1870.

27. One of Napoleon's visionary schemes. One episode illustrated the impracticality of Napoleon's ideas, his conspiratorial nature and his desire to help the nationalist cause and France at the same time. After preliminary diplomatic feelers, Napoleon on 24th February 1866 suggested to Austria the following plan for the radical alteration of Europe.

(a) *France* was to gain the left bank of the Rhine.

(b) *Austria* was to give Venetia to Italy. She was to be compensated by having Bosnia, Serbia, Silesia and South Germany.

(c) *Russia* was to give up Poland in return for a share of Asiatic Turkey.

(d) *Prussia* was to be compensated for the loss of the left bank of the Rhine and Posen by a boundary rectification in the north.

(e) *Poland* was to be resurrected as a state directed against Russia and Prussia.

The plan was not taken seriously by Austria, and therefore did not progress any further.

PROGRESS TEST 6

1. What were the broad aims of Napoleon III in 1852? **(1)**

2. Describe the political powers of the Emperor after 1852. **(2)**

3. Give an account of the domestic policies of Napoleon III. **(3–5)**

4. Why was the Empire at its peak in 1860? **(6)**

5. Account for the opposition to the Second Empire. **(7)**

6. Describe the various stages by which the Second Empire was transformed into a parliamentary democracy. **(8–10)**

7. What did Napoleon III achieve in foreign affairs before 1861? **(11)**

8. Why did the Mexican venture take place? **(14)**

9. Explain in what way the Austro-Prussian War of 1866 was a humiliation for France. **(16)**

10. Discuss Napoleon's policy of trying to secure a revision of the French north-west boundary. **(12(a), 16(a), 17)**

11. Why did Spain cause a crisis in Franco-German relations in 1870? **(19)**

12. In what way was Bismarck responsible for the war in 1870? **(20–21)**

13. Explain the isolation of France in 1870.   (18, 22)

14. Illustrate why France was militarily unprepared for war in 1870.   (25)

15. Give the main reasons for the German victory.   (23–25)

16. Did Napoleon's domestic and foreign policies conflict in any way? Why did he have difficulty in realising his aims?   (26)

CHAPTER VII

The Third Republic, 1871–1914

CIVIL WAR IN FRANCE

1. Election of a royalist Assembly. Before peace could be concluded, the Germans insisted in the armistice that France be represented by a government that could speak for the whole country. Thus elections were held for a representative Assembly to determine whether or not the war should be continued.

Elections took place on 8th February 1871. Most of the provinces were tired of war. As the monarchist parties strongly opposed its continuation, while some extreme republicans wanted to carry on to the bitter end, it was not surprising therefore that the new National Assembly, meeting in Bordeaux on 13th February, contained over 400 monarchist deputies and only about 200 republican supporters.

The Assembly elected Adolphe Thiers chief executive of the provisional government and he negotiated with Bismarck. The Assembly had to accept severe peace terms.

2. The peace terms. The Treaty of Frankfurt was signed in May 1871. This confirmed the peace preliminaries signed at Versailles on 26th February.

France agreed to the following terms:

(*a*) She was to surrender Alsace (except Belfort) and much of Lorraine, including Metz and Strasbourg.

(*b*) She was to pay a war indemnity of 5 milliards of francs (£200 million). This was to be paid over three years. During this period German troops were to occupy French soil.

3. Causes of the civil war. Not all France wanted to accept defeat. Provincial risings were soon quelled, but the revolt in Paris in March was more serious. The causes of the civil war were as follows.

(*a*) *Refusal to accept defeat and the peace terms.* Some Frenchmen did not want to accept defeat, including Gambetta, who campaigned for a continuation of the war. This refusal was in part a protest of civic pride in Paris against the humiliation of defeat. Also, many Frenchmen disliked the fact that the Prussians were to be permitted to make an official entry into France, though this meant in return that France retained Belfort.

(*b*) *The royalist government and its measures.* Parisians feared a possible royalist restoration and disliked the decision to move the Assembly to Versailles, as this seemed to them to have a distinctly royalist flavour. They had suffered terrible privations, including severe hunger, during the siege. To add to their economic troubles and deteriorating morale, Thiers's government decided to take the following unpopular measures.

(*i*) All back rents and debts had to be paid in full with interest to landlords. This was difficult for the poorer classes at a time of widespread unemployment.

(*ii*) The Paris National Guard was to have its wartime pay stopped and to be disarmed. Thiers ordered troops into Paris to carry out this measure.

4. The Paris Commune. On 18th March radical socialists led by Delescluze declared the Acts of the Versailles Parliament null and void, proclaimed the Commune and ran up the red flag.

(*a*) *Objectives of the rebellion.* The diverse collection of Marxist, socialist, anarchist and Jacobin revolutionaries had no clear-cut programme. However, the aim of the Commune, according to a declaration on 19th April, was that France would become a voluntary and spontaneous Federation of Communes. Each one would control its own budget, policy and National Guard. This federal scheme reflected the Parisian yearning for decentralisation and municipal autonomy.

(*b*) *Rebellion suppressed.* To Thiers there seemed only one course open – forcible suppression. This led to the second siege of Paris. After a savage civil war the government forces broke the resistance of the rebels by 28th May. Many of the rebels were imprisoned, exiled or put to death.

5. Results of the civil war. The important effects of the war were as follows.

(*a*) It lowered French prestige abroad. European powers became suspicious of republican France, which had been established only after bitter domestic upheaval.

(b) It increased the bitterness between social classes. When left-wing radicalism increased in the 1880s the workers were less inclined than formerly to support republicanism, which to them had become associated with rule by the middle class, the group which had taken such heavy revenge on the Commune in 1871.

(c) It led to a firmer foundation for the Republic. Left-wing radicalism was eradicated as a force for nearly a decade, since many of the extremists had been either exiled or executed. Thus many potential monarchist supporters were won over to republicanism for the following reasons.

(i) It had been under a republican government that a movement for the suppression of private property had been subdued.

(ii) Moderation became the keynote of future government. Thiers ensured that France would · be a middle-class parliamentary state.

(d) Paris ceased to exert the political influence that it had previously. The dying flicker of the tradition of the barricades of 1789 and 1848 had been shown in the activities of the Commune.

(e) The temporary expulsion of socialist and Communist movements from France contributed to the growth of socialism elsewhere in Europe.

6. Results of the German victory.

(a) *Germany and Italy achieved final unification.*

(i) On 18th January 1871, at the Palace of Versailles, the Prussian king was made German emperor by the princes of Germany.

(ii) After Sedan, Piedmontese troops marched into Rome, which the French had evacuated at the start of the war. Rome was declared the capital of Italy.

(b) *Permanent Franco-German hostility was created.* This was due to the loss of Alsace-Lorraine. Alsace, seized by Louis XIV at the end of the seventeenth century, was racially German. Lorraine and the town of Metz were mostly French. Certainly both Alsace and Lorraine had been French in spirit for many years, and they remained unreconciled to their absorption into Germany.

(c) *A major alteration had taken place in the European balance of power*. Victor Hugo commented: "Henceforth there are in Europe two nations which will be formidable, the one because it is victorious, the other because it is vanquished." Summarising this turning-point in European history, the English diplomat

Henry Bulwer said: "Europe has lost a mistress and found a master."

(*i*) France ceased to hold the dominant place it had occupied in European affairs since 1856.

(*ii*) Germany became the most powerful nation in Europe. NOTE: During the war Russia took the opportunity, with Bismarck's approval, to denounce the Black Sea clauses of the Treaty of Paris of 1856 (*see* XV, **19**). At a subsequent London conference in March 1871 the European powers agreed not to attempt to enforce the neutrality of the Black Sea.

CONSOLIDATION OF THE REPUBLIC

7. National recovery. It took time for the French to accustom themselves to the loss of Alsace and Lorraine. Many emigrated to France from these provinces rather than accept German rule.

However, French commerce and industry soon prospered as they had before the war. A great programme of national reconstruction was started, and buildings and railways were restored. Two important steps in the programme of national recovery were as follows.

(*a*) *New army law of 1872.* The French army was reorganised on the Prussian model. A compulsory five-year military term was introduced, to be followed by a reserve period.

(*b*) *Rapid repayment of indemnity.* Owing chiefly to the energy of Thiers and to popular support, the enormous war indemnity was collected by September 1873. Thus the German occupation army was withdrawn.

8. Monarchist parties. The three monarchical parties in the Assembly were the following.

(*a*) *Legitimist Bourbons.* About 100 delegates supported the grandson of Charles X. This was the comte de Chambord, who was childless, unambitious and uncompromising.

(*b*) *Orleanists.* About 300 delegates supported the comte de Paris, the grandson of Louis-Philippe.

(*c*) *Bonapartists.* About thirty delegates supported the Prince Imperial, the son of Napoleon III.

9. Monarchy or republic? Though the French people had co-operated in the general economic recovery, it was not as easy to obtain agreement over the form of government. The royalist delegates formed the majority in the National Assembly in 1871. This was because they had been elected on the issue of peace or war. They obviously wanted a restoration of the monarchy but it was not clear at the time what the French people wanted. In addition, the monarchists disagreed as to the choice of king (*see* 8). The National Assembly established a republic until agreement could be reached. The monarchists aimed not to dissolve the Assembly until France had been given a monarchical constitution.

In 1873 the monarchists dismissed Thiers, annoyed at his acceptance of republicanism, and appointed Marshal MacMahon as president. MacMahon was given a term of seven years, and the monarchists hoped that, before his term of office expired, they would be able to choose a king. In fact they decided shortly that the comte de Chambord should, as Henry V, be the King of France. This was on condition that he appointed as successor the rival claimant, the comte de Paris.

10. The Third Republic. The following stages led to the consolidation of republican government.

(*a*) *Failure of restoration plan.* In 1873 it seemed that France would soon have a new king. However, the comte de Chambord insisted on replacing the tricolour with the white fleur-de-lis flag of the Bourbons. This was opposed and the royalists were unable to decide on any alternative ruler.

(*b*) *Growth of republicanism.* By 1875 many people were tired of the continued failure to find a ruler. Some former monarchists became convinced that a restoration was impracticable. The fiery Gambetta campaigned for republicanism in the country, and the republicans gained a small majority in the Chamber of Deputies, owing to the divisions in the ranks of the monarchists.

(*c*) *Provisional constitution.* It was decided that France could no longer continue without an organised government. The so-called "organic laws" were passed, which were regarded as provisional at the time.

(*i*) These laws formed the basis of a constitution. They provided the foundations for parliamentary rule and universal suffrage which would fit either a republic or a constitutional monarchy.

(*ii*) By a majority of one vote the head of state was called "President of the Republic".

(*d*) *Principle of ministerial responsibility established.* The first open crisis occurred on 16th May 1877. MacMahon provoked the resignation of the moderate republican Premier Jules Simon, as he had disliked Simon's inadequate opposition to the anti-clerical Left. Eventually the Chamber's authority triumphed over the personal rule of the presidency. The details were as follows.

(*i*) The Chamber of Deputies refused to approve the President's choice of Premier, the Orleanist duc de Broglie.

(*ii*) MacMahon, with the consent of the Senate, dissolved the Chamber and called a new election.

(*iii*) Eventually in December the President was forced to accept a ministry which the deputies wanted.

11. Republican legislation. In 1879 the republicans gained a majority in the Senate. MacMahon resigned and Jules Grévy became president. Having secured a majority in both legislative assemblies, the republicans decided to embark on the following legislative programme to lessen the chances of internal threats to the Republic.

(*a*) *Middle and lower classes.* Measures to gain support among the middle and lower classes were as follows.

(*i*) Remaining exiled veterans of the Commune were allowed to return (1880).

(*ii*) Full rights of public meeting and of the press were allowed (1881). Trade unions were legalised (1884).

(*iii*) All municipal councils except that of Paris were allowed to elect their own mayors (1883).

(*iv*) Entry into the Civil Service was to be determined by open competition and not by patronage (1884).

(*b*) *The Church.* Measures were taken to restrict the influence of the clericals, who were still sympathetic to the royalist cause. The aim was to destroy the political power of the Church and to subordinate its non-spiritual functions to the State.

(*i*) The Jesuits and other teaching orders were expelled.

(*ii*) Teachers in religious schools were made subject to state examinations.

(*iii*) In 1882 the government took over from the Catholic Church responsibility for primary education, which was made free and compulsory between the ages of six and thirteen. There was to be no religious training.

(*iv*) The government took over responsibility for charities and hospitals.

(*v*) Civil marriages and divorces were permitted.

(c) *The Republic*. In 1884 laws were passed which stated that:

(i) the republican form of government would never be subject to revision;

(ii) members of royal families should not be eligible for the presidency.

INTERNAL THREATS TO THE REPUBLIC

12. Summary of the threats. After 1879 France settled down to constitutional and republican rule. France was the sole republican state among the European great powers, and it was questionable in the 1880s whether the Third Republic had the "staying power" to survive. Before 1914 there were certain periods when it appeared that the system of government would collapse and be replaced by a monarchist restoration or a non-royalist dictatorship.

(a) *Hostile groups*. French society contained two irreconcilable groups on the Right and Left. Both groups nursed memories of past glories, whether they had been before or after 1789, or whether they had been connected with the 1830 or 1848 revolutions.

(i) On the Right the monarchists, clericals and nobility mourned their lost privileges. The nationalist opposition was allied to the Right. It was composed of all those who believed France's main aim should be to gain revenge on Germany for the 1870 defeat. The most forceful group was Paul Deroulède's League of Patriots.

(ii) On the Left the radical socialists demanded recognition and better living conditions. Whether they could be considered enemies or supporters of the middle-class Republic in the 1880s was problematical. However, in time they became influenced by a mixture of Marxist, syndicalist and anarchist ideas. However, they did not pose much of a threat to the government until the 1890s (*see* **18**).

(b) *Periods of crisis*. Notable crises were:

(i) the Boulanger affair in 1886–9 (*see* **13**);

(ii) the Panama scandal in 1889–92 (*see* **14**);

(iii) the Dreyfus case in 1894–1906 (*see* **15**);

(iv) a period of industrial unrest in 1906–11 (*see* **17**).

13. The Boulanger affair. Between late 1886 and early 1889 there seemed a distinct possibility that Boulanger would overthrow the government and establish a personal dictatorship with mass support. The following were the important details of the affair.

(a) *Background.* After the deaths of the Prince Imperial in Zululand (1879) and the comte de Chambord (1883), the monarchists did not immediately support the Orleanist heir. Both the clericals (clergy and lay Catholics) and the monarchists (nobles and aristocratic army officers) were united in opposition to parliamentary rule. They looked to ways of harming the Republic and wanted a "strong" leader to articulate their demands.

Many left-wing workers suffered from the effects of economic depression in the mid 1880s. They were dissatisfied with the measures of the conservative republican government.

(b) *Boulanger's popularity.* The 1885 elections were a victory for right-wing forces. General Georges Boulanger, who had been the military governor in Tunis, was made Minister of War in 1886. He managed to gain considerable support among the people and to unite clericals, monarchists and socialists behind him on a common anti-government platform. This was as a result of:

(i) his frequent and impressive appearances in public;

(ii) his advocacy of the recovery of Alsace-Lorraine;

(iii) his measures to improve army living conditions.

(c) *Boulanger's fall from power.* In 1887 Boulanger left office when the government fell. Though ineligible for the Chamber of Deputies, Boulanger permitted his candidacy to be put forward as a test of his popularity. The government grew alarmed and placed him on the retired list. However, he was promptly elected to the Chamber. In 1889 the government ordered his arrest. At this crucial moment Boulanger lost his nerve and fled to Belgium. In 1891 he committed suicide on the grave of his mistress in Brussels.

(d) *The significance of the affair abroad.* During the period 1881–4 Jules Ferry, the Prime Minister, had co-operated with Bismarck in colonial matters. The fall of Ferry in 1885 ended the temporary *entente* between France and Germany. Boulanger revived the nationalist and revenge sentiment against Germany, and this coincided with pro-French and anti-German agitation by Russian nationalists and a crisis in the Near East (*see* XVI, **18**). For a time there was a prospect of a war between France, perhaps aided by Russia, and Germany. The arrest for a week of

Schnaebelé, a French frontier official, by the Germans on the grounds of espionage aroused great popular excitement in France in April 1887.

14. The Panama scandal. De Lesseps floated a company in 1889 for the construction of a great canal in Panama. It failed owing to difficulties of construction in hilly areas infested with malaria, to the opposition of the United States and to financial mismanagement.

It was not until 1892 that legal action was taken. It was found, in the course of a parliamentary investigation and two trials, that one-third of the capital raised for the company had been spent by two German Jewish financiers in bribes to gain support among politicians and journalists. The government had also been involved. The scandal brought about considerable adverse publicity for the Republic, which was increased when the people learned that the government had tried to silence the whole affair.

15. The Dreyfus case. In 1894 Captain Alfred Dreyfus, who was a young Alsatian army officer, a Jew and a supporter of the Republic, was court-martialled and found guilty of selling military documents to Germany. He was sentenced to life imprisonment on Devil's Island. In 1896 Colonel Picquart, chief of the French Intelligence Department, discovered that a document, presumed to have been written by Dreyfus, had been forged by a Major Esterhazy. The Colonel was removed from his post. In 1898 Esterhazy was tried and acquitted.

The anti-Dreyfusards, who included monarchists, senior army officers, nationalists and anti-Semitics, were anxious to use the Dreyfus case as a means of discrediting the Republic and refused to accept any new evidence that Dreyfus was innocent. As a result the novelist Emile Zola published in Clémenceau's newspaper *L'Aurore* a letter, *J'accuse*, which was addressed to the President denouncing certain members of the general staff. Esterhazy confessed his guilt and in 1899 Dreyfus was pardoned. However, it was not until 1906 that he was fully rehabilitated, being declared innocent and reinstated in the army with the rank of major.

The affair divided France as it became in a larger context a struggle between supporters and opponents of the Republic, but it ended in a victory for the republicans. Army reforms were initiated to curb the influence of monarchists.

16. Church and State. Anti-clerical legislation in the early 1880s increased the hostility of the Roman Catholic Church towards the secular Republic. However, a move towards reconciliation was taken by Pope Leo XIII, who had been disappointed by the failures of the monarchists in France and tried to dissociate the Catholic Church from its royalist ties. As a result of his influence Cardinal Lavigerie, Archbishop of Algiers, said in a famous toast in 1890 that it was the duty of all citizens to "rally" to the support of the existing form of government. Clericals became increasingly willing to support the Republic, as it appeared to represent a stable rather than a radical force.

This so-called *ralliement* was wrecked by the Dreyfus case. In every crisis after 1870 the Church had supported the enemies of the Republic. The Dreyfus affair demonstrated that many clericals were still deeply hostile to the Republic. The following anti-clerical legislation was therefore passed.

(*a*) *Association Law* (1901). This stated that no religious association could exist without specific government permission. Many monastic orders were expelled, including the Assumptionist Order, whose superior had been an implacable foe of Dreyfus.

(*b*) *State monopoly of education introduced* (1904). It was stipulated that all teaching by religious orders must be ended within ten years.

(*c*) *Concordat of 1801 abrogated* (1905).

(*i*) The State's right to make appointments and its obligation to pay salaries were declared ended.

(*ii*) Church property was to remain at the disposal of the clergy but was to be administered in future by elected parish religious corporations.

The Pope refused to allow churchmen to obey the 1905 law. Eventually, however, tension abated between the Church and the government. Measures taken against monastic orders were relaxed, and Catholic schools were reopened.

17. Social issues and unrest. Prolonged struggles by republican parties to secure the Republic from threats from the Right delayed any attempt to tackle social problems before 1900. Many politicians seemed primarily interested in preserving the *status quo* in the interests of the propertied middle class.

Even after 1900 it was still difficult to secure rapid reforms through Parliament. In 1906 Georges Clémenceau formed a ministry with a seventeen-point programme which included various proposals for workers' welfare. It came to little. Immobilism and cynicism characterised the attitudes of many politicians towards reform. Workers were not satisfied and violence increased. From 1906 to 1911 French industry was regularly disturbed by riots and strikes. The government retaliated with ruthless measures. During a rail strike in 1910 the socialist Premier Briand called up the reserves, thus mobilising most of the strikers as soldiers.

Major reform measures were as follows.

(*a*) *Workmen's Compensation Act* (1898).

(*b*) *Ten Hours Factory Act* (1906).

(*c*) *Old Age Pensions Law* (1910).

18. Radicalism. During the last part of the nineteenth century many workers became disillusioned with the politicians. The latter seemed primarily interested in their own struggles for power with rival political factions rather than in the needs of the country. By 1900 workers' organisations constituted a considerable force in the country. Their effectiveness, however, was dissipated by divergences of view and mutual antagonisms.

In time supporters of socialist radicals could be divided into the following two main groups.

(*a*) *Revisionary socialists.* The socialist parliamentary party was created by Jules Guesde in 1880. For a time there were many rival groups and the movement remained weak and divided. Then in 1905 the socialist groups joined forces under Jaurès in pressuring the government for more sweeping reforms. They were prepared to collaborate with the government in securing socialist aims, and some of their leaders took office. For example, Briand and Viviani joined the government in 1906.

(*b*) *Revolutionaries.* Some socialists, Marxists and members of the main trade-union body, the C.G.T., stayed aloof from participation in government. They became imbued with syndicalist-anarchist or Communist ideas for destroying the existing economic system by use of the strike and boycott and by sabotage.

Syndicalism developed into a positive force through the impetus of the ideas of Georges Sorel. In *Reflexions sur la violence* (1908) he advocated the use of the general strike for bringing about a system of federated trade-unionism to replace the existing parliamentary system.

19. The survival of the Republic. Despite the humiliations of 1870–1 and subsequent crises, many French people regarded the years before 1914 as *la belle époque* – the good old days. Factors contributing to the success of the Republic were as follows.

(*a*) *Government leadership.* The government was resolute in taking action and passing legislation to curb agitation and unrest (*see* **17**).

(*b*) *Support of the people.* When threats to the Republic appeared from the Right or Left, the French in general were prepared to support the government in its actions. Moderate socialists were prepared eventually to support the government. For example, Alexandre Millerand was prepared in 1900 to take office in the same government as General Gallifet, who had so savagely suppressed the Commune in 1871.

(*c*) *Successful policies included the following.*

(*i*) Foreign and colonial affairs (*see* **20**).

(*ii*) Economic affairs: after the long depression of 1882–97 France enjoyed a period of remarkable prosperity.

(*iii*) Social affairs: Jules Ferry was active in the 1880s in piloting extensive educational legislation through Parliament.

FOREIGN AFFAIRS

20. Chief objectives. During the period 1871–1914 the main aims of the Third Republic in foreign policy were as follows.

(*a*) *Recovery of the lost provinces.* In 1871 the French regarded the surrender of Alsace-Lorraine as "war in perpetuity". Henceforth it was a chief aim abroad to retrieve these provinces from Germany. This meant that little harmony existed in Franco-German relations. Until 1914 Germany feared French "revanchism" and France feared a possible German "preventive war".

Incidents in Alsace-Lorraine caused deep suspicion between both countries and partially contributed to the war scares of 1875 and 1887 (*see* **13** and X, **12**). The last incident to embitter relations was the Zabern affair of December 1913, when a German officer wounded a lame cobbler with his sword and insulted Alsatian recruits.

After France allied with Russia in 1894, the Alsace-Lorraine issue was the barrier to any effective co-operation between France, Russia and Germany in European affairs. Though these countries worked together in Far Eastern problems in the 1890s (*see* XX, **22, 27**), France resolutely refused to join any Continental combination of the three countries, for this would have implied acceptance of territorial boundaries in Europe. Therefore the Kaiser's proposals in 1900, 1904 and 1905 for some arrangement with Russia, which France would join, broke down as a result of French hostility.

The French were concerned about the rapidly increasing German population. In 1870 both countries were about equal, but by 1911 France had about 40 million inhabitants while Germany had nearly 65 million.

(*b*) *Escape from isolation.* After 1871 Bismarck was determined to keep France isolated from any possible allies. He succeeded in this by allying Germany with Russia and Austria. French relations with Britain remained poor owing to colonial rivalry, while relations with Italy were also sensitive. However, after 1890, France at last managed to gain friends through the following alliances.

(*i*) Alliance with Russia in 1894 (*see* **22**).

(*ii*) Secret alliance with Italy in 1902 (*see* XIII, **53**(*d*)).

(*iii*) *Entente* with Britain in 1904 (*see* **23**).

(*c*) *Colonial expansion.* In compensation for her defeat in 1871 France soon developed a large empire in Indo-China and North and West Africa. From 1870 to 1914 the empire grew from 3 million to 60 million people, the second largest in the world.

21. Reasons for the Franco-Russian alliance. During the Bulgarian and Boulanger crises in 1886–7 private pressure groups in France and Russia urged the need for an alliance, for both countries were anti-German at the time. However, the Tsar, the enemy of republican and secular France, preferred to keep the link open to Germany in a special Reinsurance Treaty. When Germany refused to renew this in March 1890, the prospects of a Franco-Russian alliance grew. The following factors made an alliance more likely.

(*a*) *Economic.* Bismarck's decree in 1887 forbade the Reichsbank to accept Russian securities as collateral for loans. The Russians, who needed loan capital to purchase arms and develop the country, turned to France. The French made loans to help Russia with famine relief (1891) and to build the Trans-Siberian railway (1895).

(*b*) *Political.* France was keener than Russia on securing a firm alliance. However, both countries were without allies, and felt threatened by the following.

(*i*) The Triple Alliance of Austria, Germany and Italy (*see* XIII, 51).

(*ii*) The Mediterranean agreements of Britain, Austria and Italy.

(*iii*) The prospect that Britain might join the Triple Alliance. Both France and Russia were also colonial rivals of Britain.

22. Details of the Franco-Russian alliance. France took the initiative in opening negotiations for an alliance by sending the chief of staff, General Boisdeffre, to Russia in 1890. Eventually the alliance was cemented by the following two agreements.

(*a*) *Entente cordiale* (1891). This was a diplomatic agreement for joint consultation in the event of any "threat to peace".

(*b*) *Military alliance* (1894).

(*i*) Each power would come to the aid of the other if either were attacked by Germany, whether alone or in league with Austria or Italy.

(*ii*) The alliance was to have the same duration as the Triple Alliance.

23. The Franco-British entente. After a lengthy period of hostility and rivalry, Britain and France settled their differences in April 1904.

(*a*) *Causes.* Both governments were anxious to settle outstanding colonial grievances, and to give more attention to European affairs. They were alarmed by the growth in power of the German navy since 1898.

Delcassé, the French Foreign Minister since 1898, would have liked a close alliance, but Britain was not prepared to be deeply committed. The new King of Britain, Edward VII, helped to dispel French hostility to his country by an official visit to Paris in 1903. Britain was anxious to end her isolation in Europe, especially as negotiations for a German alliance had collapsed in 1901.

(*b*) *Details.* Though there was no military pact, there was an unwritten friendly understanding that each country would support the other if assistance was necessary. The following points were agreed.

(*i*) Egypt and Morocco would be respectively British and

French spheres of influence, though the principle of the open door was to be maintained.

(*ii*) In secret articles France and Britain planned for a protectorate to be set up if the policy in (*i*) above broke down. Morocco was to be shared with Spain, the coast opposite Gibraltar being Spanish on the condition that it was not fortified. German interests were to be implicitly excluded.

(*iii*) Disputes regarding Newfoundland, Madagascar and spheres of influence on the frontiers of Siam were settled.

PROGRESS TEST 7

1. Why did France elect a royalist Assembly in 1871 ?   **(1)**

2. Account for the civil war of 1871.   **(3)**

3. What did the Paris Commune hope to achieve ?   **(4)**

4. In what way was 1870–1 a turning-point in European history ?   **(6)**

5. Why did the monarchists fail to restore the Bourbons after 1871 ?   **(8–10)**

6. What measures did the republicans take between 1879 and 1884 to stabilise France ?   **(11)**

7. Discuss the major domestic problems which the government faced between 1880 and 1914.   **(12)**

8. Account for the popularity of General Boulanger.   **(13)**

9. Why was the government discredited by the Panama scandal ?   **(14)**

10. Discuss relations between the Church and government during the period 1880–1910.   **(16)**

11. Account for the growth of unrest in France between 1890 and 1910.   **(17–18)**

12. Why was the Third Republic able to survive ?   **(19)**

13. What were the chief French foreign-policy objectives after 1870 ?   **(20)**

14. Why did France form an *entente* with Britain in 1904 ?   **(23)**

CHAPTER VIII

Early attempts at German unification, 1815–63

THE GERMAN CONFEDERATION

1. Formation of the Confederation. The hopes of German and Prussian nationalists were disappointed by the Vienna settlement of 1815. In view of the conflicting interests of Austria, Prussia and the other German states, the diplomats feared that chaos and war would ensue if attempts were made to unite Germany (*see* **4**(*a*)).

The German Confederation (or *Bund*) was formed instead. Germany had by then been reduced to thirty-nine sovereign states which all became members of the new organisation. Its aim was to guarantee the external and internal peace of Germany and the independence of the member states. The states agreed not to declare war on one another, and had the obligation of helping one another in need.

2. Dominance of Austria. After the Napoleonic Wars Metternich opposed liberal and national aspirations in Central Europe, in Germany and in the Austrian Empire (for his reasons *see* XI, **5**). After 1819 he forced the Diet, the main organ of the Confederation at Frankfurt, to follow reactionary policies similar to those being pursued in the Austrian Empire (*see* **6**).

The Diet provided some basis for the building of the German nation. It became a focal point for the development of co-operation and consultation among German states. However, Metternich had ensured that its powers were few, rendering it an ineffective organisation. It was composed of two assemblies, over both of which the Austrian delegate presided. This meant its decisions were influenced by Austria.

Metternich intervened when he felt it was necessary. When the people of Hesse appealed against the arbitrary acts of their Elector, the Diet condemned the Elector, who refused to accept its jurisdiction. Metternich intervened and rebuked the Austrian

135

president for upholding the Diet's right to intervene between a sovereign and his subjects.

3. Weakness of the Federal Diet. The Diet was weak for the following reasons.

(a) It had limited legal powers and a complicated voting system.

(i) No law was binding on any member state unless that particular state accepted it.

(ii) Unanimity was necessary for any change in the constitution of the Confederation, and a two-thirds majority was required on matters of importance.

(b) It was a diplomatic congress and not a parliament. Its members were ambassadors, the instructed delegates of the German princes. They were not representatives of the states. The Confederation was viewed by Metternich and some of the German princes as a league of states (*Staatenbund*) to protect them against foreign foes and liberalism. It was not a federal state (*Bundesstaat*).

(c) It lacked means of enforcing its wishes. The federal army existed mainly on paper, since the states persistently refused to pay contributions for its upkeep.

(d) It had a mixed composition. The following foreign monarchs were represented because of their interests in certain German states.

(i) The British king ruled in Hanover until the death of William IV in 1837, when Queen Victoria became the monarch in Britain. However, under German Salic Law, a woman could not be sovereign, and Ernest Augustus, Duke of Cumberland, son of George III, then became King of Hanover.

(ii) The King of Denmark was represented owing to the inclusion of Holstein in the Confederation (*see* 15).

(iii) The King of the Netherlands was represented owing to his position as Grand Duke of Luxembourg.

4. Reasons for continued German disunity. Between 1815 and 1848 the following factors mitigated against the forming of a united German state.

(a) *Difficulty in finding an agreed method of unity.* This was illustrated in 1848 when the Frankfurt Assembly tried to solve the question. For the various suggestions put forward to achieve unity, *see* **16**. Basically the problem was one of the conflicting interests of the various German states.

(*i*) Austria opposed measures to promote greater unity lest it encouraged the spirit of nationalism. This would probably result in the collapse of her multinational empire. Further, it would produce a strong rival power if Austria were excluded from Germany. On the other hand, it would pose special problems in terms of her non-German possessions if she were included.

(*ii*) Prussia supported the Austrian policy of maintaining the *status quo*. In 1815 the King had promised liberal reforms and on four occasions pledged himself to grant a constitution. However, he was dissuaded by his nobility and Metternich from taking any steps to promote German unity or to carry out liberal reforms.

(*iii*) The rulers of the smaller German states opposed attempts at greater unity as it would mean the loss of their powers. Considerable rivalry and jealousy existed among them.

(*b*) *Differences and divisions among the German people.* Inhabitants of the sovereign states clung to parochial and particularistic ideas. This made attempts at standardising methods of organisation and administration difficult. Countless parties existed with a variety of aims, but people lacked political experience in self-government.

Differences in outlook were symptomatic of the following fundamental differences in religion and politics.

(*i*) In the north, people were mainly Protestant and inclined to support conservatism and absolutism in government.

(*ii*) In the south, apart from Austria, Bavaria was the chief state. People were generally Roman Catholic and inclined towards liberal ideas.

(*c*) *An ineffectual Federal Diet* (*see* **3**).

(*d*) *Opposition of France.* France recovered her power after 1815. She had some influence among the South German states, which tended to be jealous of Austrian power. Any serious attempts to create a unified German state would have been resolutely opposed by France.

5. Growth of agitation. After 1815, intellectuals, university staff and students, and business groups grew discontented with the reactionary policies of many German states, and the tardiness of rulers in granting constitutions or implementing liberal reforms.

Metternich gradually grew concerned about German affairs as a result of the following developments.

(*a*) *The growth of student societies.* Student societies, called *Burschenschaften*, were formed, gradually spreading from Jena to other universities. Students in large numbers became devoted to the regeneration of Germany and the cause of national unity.

(*b*) *The creation of limited constitutional government.* Article 13 of the federal constitution stipulated that all member states should have constitutions providing for assemblies. Some states, for example Bavaria, Württemberg and Baden in the south, implemented this. Though their franchises were extremely narrow and the elected assemblies almost powerless, Metternich disliked the precedent which had been set.

(*c*) *The Wartburg festival.* In October 1817 students gathered to celebrate the anniversary of the battle of Leipzig and the tercentenary of the Reformation. They aimed to form a closer union among university students. Bonfires were made and selected "guys" and various emblems of militarism were burnt.

(*d*) *The murder of Kotzebue.* In March 1819 August Kotzebue, a Russian dramatist, secret agent and writer of reactionary propaganda, was murdered by a German student.

6. The Metternich system of repression. The Kotzebue murder gave Metternich the opportunity to persuade the German rulers to adopt the reactionary police system enforced in Austria. Examples of his repressive system were as follows.

(*a*) *The Carlsbad Decrees.* At a meeting at Teplitz, Metternich persuaded the Prussian king of the need for forceful measures. Representatives of the eight largest states were called to a meeting at Carlsbad in August 1819. They adopted measures, later approved by the Federal Diet, which involved stricter government control of political agitation by the following methods.

(*i*) Closer supervision of political activities at universities. Commissioners were appointed with powers of dismissal of both students and professors. Student political clubs and meetings were banned.

(*ii*) Censorship of the press, literature and pamphlets.

(*iii*) Establishment of a central commission at Mainz. This commission was given the role of investigating secret societies suspected of harbouring subversive ideas, and was instructed to collect evidence for judicial tribunals. It proved to be ineffective and was disbanded in 1828.

The Carlsbad Decrees were a considerable setback to the hopes of European liberals. However, they were not universally approved by the minor states and Metternich conceded a little. In 1820, when the decrees were renewed, the independence of the minor states was specially guaranteed.

(b) *The Final Act of Vienna.* In May 1820 the Diet agreed:

(i) that it would limit the subjects that might be discussed in elected assemblies; and

(ii) that it had the power to intervene in individual German states where necessary.

7. Revival of agitation. In the short run Metternich succeeded in bringing relative stability to Germany. There were no disturbances in Germany when other parts of Europe were affected in 1820–1.

In the long run, however, Metternich failed to realise that powerful forces were working to undermine the authority of the sovereign rulers on which he attached so much importance. In 1827 radical movements revived through a reorganised university movement and secret clubs. The 1830 revolution in France not unnaturally had some repercussions in Germany. Rulers were forced to abdicate in Brunswick, Saxony and Hesse-Kassel, and new constitutions were introduced in these states, and in Hanover in 1833.

At the Hambrach festival in May 1832 a gathering of 25,000 people, composed of students, professors, journalists and exiled Poles, etc., denounced the Holy Alliance and demanded a republic and German unity. The immediate results of this were as follows.

(a) *The Six Acts.* Metternich had no solution to the agitation except further repression. In July 1832, with the support of Prussia, he enticed the Diet to pass measures banning popular meetings and suppressing liberal ideas generally. Every German ruler was required to reject any requests which limited his own sovereignty.

(b) *An attempt to seize Frankfurt.* In April 1833 there was a plot by international conspirators to capture Frankfurt, dissolve the Diet and unify Germany.

(c) *The creation of a central commission.* The Diet's reply in June 1833 was to appoint, at Metternich's request, a central commission to co-ordinate repressive measures in the various states.

8. Factors contributing to greater unity, 1834–48. Despite the efforts of Metternich and the German princes to preserve the *status quo*, agitation for change continued. Intellectuals (musicians, poets, historians and philosophers) and students continued to foster the spirit underlying the Romantic, liberal and national movements, all forces contributing to greater unity. In summary the important factors were as follows.

(a) *Creation of the Zollverein (see 9).* This promoted economic co-operation, thus furthering the cause of unity.

(b) *Growth of awareness of common nationality.* It has already been noted that German nationalism became a powerful sentiment after 1806 (*see* II, **21**). The German people gradually realised they constituted a single nationality in terms of language, race, historic past, customs and traditions.

An illustration of the growth in the feeling for nationalism was the war scare in 1840 when it seemed France might attack Germany to compensate for her isolation in the Near East (*see* XIV, **29**(*d*)–(*e*)). The historian Treitschke wrote later that Germans at this time seemed as one despite political divisions. This atmosphere produced a flow of patriotic songs, two famous ones being "Watch on the Rhine" by Max Scheckenburger and "*Deutschland über alles*" by Fallersleben.

(c) *Growth of liberalism.* Many liberals looked forward to the creation of a free Germany with constitutional democratic rule. Areas that received notable publicity for the struggle for liberalism were the following.

(i) Southern Germany: all the states here, Bavaria, Baden and Württemberg, had constitutions and representative assemblies. Their parliamentary orators, such as Karl von Rotteck, received a national hearing.

(ii) Hanover: in 1837 the new king, Ernest Augustus, set aside the liberal constitution granted by William IV in 1833. This action was vigorously opposed by the Hanoverian people, who received support from Bavaria and others in the Federal Diet. However, Metternich forced the Diet to approve the King's action. Seven university professors, including the brothers Grimm, were expelled from Göttingen for refusing to acknowledge the action of the King. They became heroes in the eyes of German liberals.

(iii) Prussia: the new king, Frederick William IV, was a romantic, imbued with mystical conceptions, who also aimed at greater political freedom and stronger national unity. He released many political prisoners, moderated the press censorship, gave greater power to provincial Diets and included liberals in his government. However, he was an autocrat at heart and passed a number of reactionary measures after 1843. When the United Diet met in 1847 he refused demands for a constitution and parliamentary rule. In turn the Diet refused to vote funds for the building of a new railway. Deadlock resulted and the Diet was dissolved.

9. Formation of the Zollverein. An obstacle to economic growth in Germany was the existence of customs barriers. Each state had the right to charge dues and tolls on goods passing through its territory. This made goods expensive and discouraged trade. It was estimated that Prussia had sixty-seven different tariff areas within its borders after 1815.

Free trade developed in Germany gradually. The stages of development were as follows.

(a) *Lead taken by Prussia*. Prussia adopted the following measures.

(i) In May 1818 a uniform tariff was imposed on all her territories. Duties on trade between her own lands were abolished.

(ii) In October 1819 she signed an initial tariff treaty with the small neighbouring German state of Schwarzburg-Sonderhausen.

(b) *Rival unions formed*. The Prussian scheme was so successful that other states adopted similar measures. Fearing Prussian power, however, they formed rival unions.

(c) *Other states joined Prussia*. In 1829 the league of Bavaria and Württemberg joined Prussia. Gradually other states followed, so that when the Prussian Customs Union (Zollverein) was formed in 1834 it included most German states. By 1844 practically all Germany was in the Zollverein except Austria, Hanover, Oldenburg, Mecklenburg and three Hansa towns.

10. Importance of the Zollverein. The Zollverein represented a serious threat to the hegemony of Austria in Germany. The development of freer trade had the following significant effects.

(a) *Prussia became economically supreme in Germany*. The tariff law of 1818 and trade agreements afterwards stimulated Prussian trade and led to rapid economic development. A treaty with Holland in 1831 opened the lower Rhine to Prussian goods.

(b) *Economic unity formed the basis for later political unity*.

(i) As Germany achieved fiscal unity, this increased commercial co-operation in improving means of communication (railways and roads), banking, etc.

(*ii*) Prussian economic power was a contributory cause of her later military and political supremacy in Germany. German states became accustomed to the leadership of Prussia.

(*c*) *Austria began to lose influence in German affairs.* As Austria did not become a member, this accustomed people to think of a unified Germany which excluded her. Though Metternich was no economist he appreciated that the Zollverein might well be the first nail in the coffin of the Federal Diet. However, he ignored it at first. Then after 1834, when it was too late, he campaigned unsuccessfully firstly for the lowering of Austrian tariffs as a prelude for admission to the Zollverein, and then for the organisation of resistance to it.

REVOLUTION IN GERMANY, 1848–9

11. Uprising in Germany. In 1848 the February revolution in Paris led to widespread discontent in Germany. First in the south and west, then in the central states, there were popular demonstrations for constitutional changes, reform and national unity. In the first few days, the German rulers, taken off guard, yielded everywhere. Ministries were reorganised along liberal lines and promises of reform were made.

12. The Vorparlament. On 5th March leading liberals, chiefly from South Germany, discussed plans for summoning a preliminary parliament.

The *Vorparlament* met at Frankfurt on 31st March. It had no legal standing and representation was erratic: little Baden was heavily represented with seventy-two members, while only two came from Austria. Despite this, it persuaded the Diet to invite the governments of all German states to elect delegates to a National Assembly. Austria and Prussia were unable to impede developments as they were engulfed in revolution.

13. The Berlin rising. On 16th March unrest occurred in Berlin, capital of Prussia, and troops were called in to restore order. When he heard of Metternich's fall from power in Austria (*see* XI, **14**), the King of Prussia agreed on the 18th to reconvene the United Diet, to grant a constitution and to consider the reorganisation of the German Confederation. The press censorship was abolished. Then an unhappy accident led to renewed fighting in Berlin. The troops were soon demoralised, and their commander urged the King to authorise their withdrawal so that they could bombard the city from outside. The King, sick at the sight of bloodshed and aghast at the idea of his city being levelled by artillery, made more concessions on the 19th. Eventually the troops were withdrawn and the King put his trust in his "dear Berliners". A liberal ministry was formed which included men from the business and professional classes. On the 21st the King issued a proclamation stating that "henceforth Prussia is merged in Germany".

14. Problems of the National Assembly. On 18th May the first National Assembly in Germany was convened in Frankfurt. It suspended the Federal Diet and appointed Archduke John of Austria, the imperial regent, as head of a provisional government. The following factors contributed to the general weakness of the Assembly, as a result of which its influence, and that of German liberals generally, was seriously undermined.

(a) *The difficulty of finding an agreed method of unification* (*see* 16). Much time was spent in tortuous academic debates on drafting the *Fundamental Rights of the German People*. It was obviously necessary to establish the basis for future constitutional and democratic rule. However, before the document was finished, the Austrian government and most German rulers had recovered their authority. This meant that many of its conclusions were opposed by the returning reactionary forces (*see* 19).

(b) *The Danish problem.* A prolonged period was spent on this, which delayed consideration of important German issues (*see* 15).

(c) *The lack of the means to enforce decisions.* The provisional government had no army to help in its task and had to rely on the forces of the separate individual states (*see* 15). It also lacked money or any real moral authority for any of its actions.

(d) *The Polish problem.* After a Polish uprising in Posen, consideration was given to granting the Polish territories of Prussia independence or autonomy. However, the Germans in Posen raised an outcry against being abandoned to the Poles. Disagreement soon occurred over territorial boundaries and as a result nothing was done. The Prussian army eventually crushed the uprising without difficulty.

(e) *The lack of general support.* The Assembly undermined its position by denying the vote to those people who did not pay taxes. The lower bourgeoisie, the artisans and the working classes were thus alienated from it (*see* **21**(*e*)). It also ignored popular petitions for security and social reform.

(*f*) *Its unbalanced composition.* The 800-odd delegates were predominantly from the upper middle classes. There were some 200 lawyers, 100 professors, 140 businessmen, many judges and only four artisans and one peasant.

15. The Danish Question. The King of Denmark ruled over the duchies of Schleswig and Holstein as their duke. Holstein was largely German, was a member of the German Confederation and disliked the Danish connection. Danish nationalists wanted to incorporate the two duchies into the Danish kingdom, while keen Germans wanted to bring them into a united Germany.

After the Paris revolution, the Germans in the duchies of Schleswig and Holstein declared their independence from Denmark and appealed to the Frankfurt Assembly. When the Danish army occupied the duchies, the Assembly decided to support the national claims of the Germans and opposed the historic claims of the Danish king. Prussia was authorised to send troops to aid the Germans, supported by contingents from Hanover and Bavaria. However, the Prussian troops suffered defeat, and Frederick William decided to withdraw after pressure had been exercised by Britain and Russia. He concluded a truce with the Danish king, without reference to the Assembly, at Malmö on 26th August.

Lacking any forces of its own, the Assembly was forced to recognise this armistice. The masses regarded this as a betrayal and attacked members of the Assembly. Prussian and Austrian troops had to be called in to restore order in September. As the Assembly had been obliged to call in troops against its own constituents, it lost a great deal of support and suffered grave humiliation.

16. The problem of German unification. The president of the Assembly, Heinrich von Gagern, echoed the thoughts of all Germans when he asked: "What unity must we seek?" Two basic considerations concerning the new Germany were the following.

(*a*) *Territorial limits.* The exact composition of Germany and the role of Austria in it was the subject of long debate. There were two schools of thought.

(*i*) *The* "Great German" (*Grossdeutsch*) party favoured the inclusion of the German-speaking provinces of Austria, together with Bohemia.

(*ii*) *The* "Small German" (*Kleindeutsch*) party insisted that all of Austria should be excluded.

(*b*) *Basic government structure.* Here again there was a divergence of views.

(*i*) The Right advocated a decentralised monarchy acting in harmony with the separate state governments.

(*ii*) The Right Centre wanted a constitutional monarchy.

(*iii*) The Left Centre wanted a centralised monarchy.

(*iv*) The Left wanted a centralised republic.

17. The decision of the Frankfurt Assembly. Despite waning interest in its activities, the National Assembly continued throughout 1848 to work out a definite constitution. On 28th October it was decided that the new Germany would comprise the same territory as the old Confederation. There was a proviso that no part of the new state should be connected with non-German territory. This meant the exclusion of the non-German territories of the Hapsburg Empire, and in effect the victory of the *Kleindeutsch* group. However, Austria was still in the throes of revolution. There appeared every likelihood that her non-Germanic possessions would break away, leaving her free to join the new Germany.

18. Austrian opposition. By December, Austria regained control in her empire. Schwarzenberg, the Austrian Prime Minister, insisted that Austria and her non-German parts would in future be one single, organic, centralised state and as such must enter the new arrangement made in Germany. He proposed the revival of the old Confederation with a stronger executive.

On 4th March 1849 news arrived that the Emperor Francis Joseph had dissolved the Kremsier Reichstag and that a new Austrian constitution had been proclaimed which was to weld together both the German and the non-German territories. In the Frankfurt Assembly, the majority opinion had been, until this moment, in favour of the inclusion of Austria in Germany. However it was then decided on 28th March to offer the crown of German emperor to the Prussian king.

19. Recovery of the Prussian king. In March 1848 the Prussian king, having withdrawn his troops from Berlin, had been at the mercy of his people, and he had acquiesced in the appointment of a liberal ministry. Stages in his recovery were as follows.

(a) He opposed any basic reform of the Prussian state. A Prussian National Assembly, elected by universal manhood suffrage in May, debated incessantly without taking any firm decision.

(b) Mob violence took place in Berlin on 14th June, frightening respectable burghers.

(c) In November the King felt the moment was opportune to suspend the meetings of the Assembly and to recall the army to the capital. This effectively ended the revolution in Prussia.

(d) In December the King unpredictably issued a written constitution of his own. This laid down safeguards of the liberties of his subjects and provided for a bicameral legislature. Power was to remain firmly in the hands of the nobility and the wealthy under the final authority of the King.

20. Rejection of the German crown by Prussia. On 3rd April the King said he could accept the invitation to become German emperor only after the German princes had accepted the constitution. Later, on 21st April, he virtually declined the crown. Being a king by "divine right" he declared he could not take the "crown of shame" from the hands of a popular assembly. He said it would have to be offered by his equals, the crowned heads, the princes. Perhaps he was conscious of his deficiencies as a statesman and was reluctant to assume leadership. There were other factors, such as the following, which no doubt contributed to his hesitancy to accept the crown.

(a) *Nature of the constitution.* The King would have only a suspensory veto, not an absolute one, on legislation. The ministry would also be responsible to the Reichstag. The King disliked this erosion of his powers.

(b) *Opposition of Austria.* Austrian deputies were withdrawn after the new constitution had been passed and Archduke John abdicated his post of imperial regent on 28th March. Frederick William had moral scruples about supplanting the legitimate claimant to the throne. He was not prepared to run the risk of war with Austria, who was by then rapidly recovering from her own revolt, and would perhaps be supported by Russia.

(c) *Prussian pride.* The King had been successful in restoring his own power in November 1848. He feared that Prussia might lose her separate identity and be merged with the rest of Germany.

He no doubt entertained ideas of Prussia leading Germany to eventual unity.

21. Reasons for the failure of the German revolution. The following factors contributed to the collapse of the revolution in Germany.

(a) *Ineffectiveness* of the Frankfurt and Prussian Assemblies (*see* **14** and **19**).

(b) *Opposition of Austria and some German states* to proposed territorial limits of Germany. In March 1849 Bavaria, Saxony, Hanover and Württemberg opposed the exclusion of Austria from Germany.

(c) *Lack of good leaders.* The imperial regent, Archduke John of Austria, head of the provisional government, lacked both the will and the power to make the Frankfurt Assembly effective. Germany was renowned at the time for numerous differences of opinion and the absence of any forceful personality to unify the people behind any one solution.

(d) *Opposition of the Prussian king*, Frederick William IV, to the revolution.

(i) His lack of co-operation contributed to the failure of the Prussian Assembly.

(ii) His refusal to accept the crown of Germany contributed to the final collapse of the Frankfurt Assembly.

(iii) His activities led to the final collapse of the revolution elsewhere. After recovering his authority in Prussia, he was in no mood to tolerate unrest in neighbouring areas. Troops were dispatched to Dresden in May to suppress a rebellion and restore the King of Saxony to his throne.

(e) *Internal divisions within Germany* (*see also* (b) above). The Frankfurt Assembly did not gain widespread support. Many working-class people were either indifferent to the revolution or formed rival organisations. A deputy called Hecker even tried to form a republic, but his forces were defeated by Baden troops.

AUSTRO-GERMAN RELATIONS, 1849–63

22. Initial Austrian supremacy. Austrian influence in German affairs had been lost as a result of the revolutionary upheavals in her empire. She was able to gain the initiative again when in April 1849 the Prussian king refused the crown of a Germany which virtually excluded Austria. However, in 1850, Austria was suddenly faced with a serious challenge from Prussia for primacy in German affairs. Austria managed to retain her supremacy owing to the following factors.

(a) *Diplomacy of Schwarzenberg.* For example, he secured military alliances with Bavaria and Württemberg in October 1850.

(b) *Support of Russia.* In May 1850 at a meeting at Teplitz the Tsar insisted that good relations should persist between Austria and Prussia. In June he warned Frederick William not to challenge Austrian leadership in Germany.

(c) *Support of South Germany.* The South German states preferred Austrian supremacy in Germany to that of Prussia for the following two reasons.

(i) It would prevent the hegemony of Protestant northern Germany.

(ii) Any Austrian plan for Germany allowed a greater degree of autonomy for the various states or provinces.

23. The Hesse-Kassel affair. The liberals of Hesse-Kassel wanted to retain some of the political gains of 1848. The Elector appealed to the Diet for help against his subjects and Austria sent in troops. Prussia had a strategic interest as Hessian territory divided Prussian territory and Prussia had the right to use certain military roads. Hesse-Kassel had formerly promised to be a member of the Erfurt Union (*see* **24**(*a*)).

A clash appeared likely in mid 1850 between Austro-Bavarian and Prussian forces, as Schwarzenberg did not want Prussia to gain prestige by restoring order in Hesse-Kassel. He sent an ultimatum insisting that intervention could come only from forces of the old German Diet. At the last moment the Prussian king backed down and withdrew his troops.

24. Diplomatic defeat of Prussia. The following events culminated in a humiliating defeat for Prussia in Germany.

(a) *Radowitz's federal plan.* The Prussian Foreign Minister, Radowitz, planned in 1850 a North German union under the presidency of the Prussian king. This appealed to Frederick William, since it did not involve the merging of Prussia in Germany according to the liberal *Kleindeutsch* idea. Rather it meant Prussian hegemony in North Germany. A number of states agreed to send representatives to a meeting at Erfurt in March to ratify a draft constitution.

(b) *Austrian counter-proposal.* Schwarzenberg now suggested a

Grossdeutsch plan. All the Hapsburg lands were to be brought into the German Confederation. Germany was to be under a directory of delegates from Austria, Prussia and the larger states.

(*c*) *Failure of Erfurt meeting.* Schwarzenberg persuaded the larger states to oppose the Prussian plan before the Erfurt meeting, promising that the Diet would be reformed. Thus the Erfurt meeting failed, only Hanover and Saxony supporting Prussia. Radowitz resigned.

(*d*) *Olmütz settlement.* By the autumn, future arrangements in Germany had still not been settled. The South German states favoured the Austrian proposal of a loose German Confederation, and the Tsar was threatening to take the side of Austria. The Prussian king decided to negotiate a strategic withdrawal. At Olmütz in November Prussia agreed to dissolve the Erfurt Union, and to accept the re-establishing of the German Confederation under Austrian presidency.

25. Setback to Austrian diplomacy. Schwarzenberg had succeeded temporarily in maintaining Austrian primacy in Germany. However, Austria soon received two rebuffs which marked the start of her declining influence in German affairs. The specific issue was the relationship between the Austrian Empire and the German Confederation.

(*a*) *Political rebuff.* Schwarzenberg, in a Note to the Federal Diet, demanded the admission of the Austrian non-German possessions to the Confederation. However, at Dresden in 1851, Austria had to accept the revival of the Confederation as it stood before 1848. She received no support for her plan from the following states:

(*i*) Prussia, who was now able to pose as the defender of the *status quo*;

(*ii*) the small German states who believed their survival depended on maintaining a balance of power between Prussia and Austria. The new plan would have given Austria considerable power, and it would also have enabled her to involve German states if necessary in defence of the Austrian Empire.

(*b*) *Economic rebuff.* Bruck, the Austrian Commerce Minister, failed to gain support from many German states for the following proposals.

(*i*) A large economic unit in Central Europe under Austrian leadership. This would link the Zollverein with the Austrian sphere in the Danube basin.

(*ii*) Austrian admission to the Zollverein. This was a back-door method for establishing a closer link between the German states and the Austrian Empire. In 1853 Austria was refused admission and had to be content with a commercial treaty with Prussia which involved mutual tariff concessions.

26. Decline in Austrian power, 1852–63. Austria failed during the early 1850s to gain favourable changes in Germany. Gradually her power position, relative to Prussia, weakened in German affairs. Contributory factors were as follows.

(*a*) *Poor diplomacy* (*see* **27**).

(*b*) *Loss of Russian support.* Russia was severely weakened militarily as a result of the Crimean War. Since Austria had not supported her in the war Russia was less inclined to help Austria in future German affairs.

(*c*) *Financial difficulties.* Austrian finances were crippled as a result of expenses involved in the following military commitments:

(*i*) The control of internal unrest, particularly in Hungary.

(*ii*) The Italian War of 1859. In addition Austria lost the rich province of Lombardy.

(*iii*) The prolonged mobilisation of Austrian forces during the Crimean War.

(*d*) *Domestic unrest* (*see* XI, **31**).

(*e*) *Growth of Prussian power.* During the 1850s Prussia increased her power in both economic and military terms. She soon acquired strong leaders. Prince William became regent in 1858 as a result of the insanity of King Frederick William IV, and he became king himself in 1861. He had the gift of choosing strong, able leaders. Key appointments were as follows.

(*i*) Helmuth von Moltke as Chief of Staff in 1859.

(*ii*) Albrecht von Roon as Minister of War in 1859. Army reforms included the strict enforcement of universal liability for military service and the adoption of the breech-loading needle-gun.

(*iii*) Otto von Bismarck as Premier in 1862 (*see* IX, **2**).

27. Poor Austrian diplomacy. In 1852 Schwarzenberg died suddenly. No Austrian statesman of a comparable stature came to the fore afterwards, and Austrian affairs floundered under the personal direction of the Emperor.

Austria had considerable problems both at home and abroad.

Austria herself was torn between loyalty to Germany (through cultural and national ties) and to her empire (through religious ties). Her failure to resolve her problems as a result of inflexible diplomacy contributed to her decline. Options open to Austria after 1856 were as follows.

(a) *Retention of present position.* This meant the preservation of the boundaries of the Austrian Empire and her position in Germany. This was the policy followed by Austria and resulted eventually in her being forced to withdraw from both German and Italian affairs (*see* IX, **19**).

(b) *Withdrawal from Italy.* This would have avoided the disastrous war in 1859 and the depletion of resources to the Italian front in 1866 when Austria was fighting Prussia. The following were two reasons why Austria might have adopted this policy between 1858 and 1866.

(*i*) She might thus have been able to retain her political influence in Germany.

(*ii*) She would have received monetary compensation for the peaceful exchange of Lombardy and Venetia. Instead she received no compensation at all and became engaged in two humiliating and costly wars.

(c) *Grant of political concessions to Prussia in Germany.* There would have been two advantages in adopting this policy. First, Austria might have secured admission to the Zollverein. In fact in 1860 she again failed to secure admission for herself and her empire owing to Prussian opposition. Secondly, Prussian aid might have been given to help Austria retain her Italian possessions.

Opportunities for Austria to adopt a more flexible policy towards German affairs were presented on the following three occasions but ignored each time.

(*i*) The mission of Prince Albrecht to Prussia (1859). He went to secure aid against France and Italy. Austria, however, offered no benefits to induce Prussia to help.

(*ii*) The Teplitz meeting (1860). Though the Emperor Francis Joseph and the Prussian king agreed on common action to be taken against French designs on western Germany, nothing else was achieved. Francis Joseph would not consider the Prussian suggestion for any alternation in the presidency of the Frankfurt Diet.

(*iii*) The Bernstorff plan (1861). The new Prussian Foreign

Minister, Bernstorff, suggested the union policy of Radowitz. This envisaged a federal state under Prussia, in alliance with Austria. Austria opposed this.

(*d*) *Concentration on domestic issues*. This would have been distasteful to Austria in 1858, but it was the policy she was forced to adopt after 1866. If it had been adopted earlier, Austria might still have retained some influence in Italy and Germany if she had been prepared to give considerable concessions.

NOTE: It is easy to be wise after the event. Austria's problems were considerable, and some might say insurmountable, in the age of nationalism.

28. The Frankfurt Congress. The last opportunity to find a peaceful solution to German unification came in 1863. Francis Joseph called a meeting of German princes at Frankfurt.

(*a*) *Origins*. In 1859 the German National Association had been founded by the northern and central states, which looked to a liberal Prussia to lead in the formation of a "lesser" Germany.

In 1862 the southern states formed a Reform Association at Munich. This favoured a "greater" Germany under a liberal Austria. Francis Joseph was persuaded to exploit this movement in the interests of Austria.

(*b*) *Austrian plan*. The most interesting feature was the proposal for an executive directory of six states. This was to include Austria, Prussia and Bavaria and three others chosen in rotation, and was to be set up under Austrian presidency. The plan made no real concessions to Prussia.

(*c*) *Failure of the Congress*. Bismarck distrusted Austria and persuaded William I not to attend as this would have meant acceptance of continued Austrian leadership in German affairs. The meeting failed as a result of Prussian non-participation.

PROGRESS TEST 8

1. Why was the German Confederation formed? Who were its members?   **(1)**

2. Account for the weakness of the Federal Diet.   **(2–3)**

3. What factors tended to perpetuate German disunity after 1815?   **(4)**

4. Why were the Carlsbad Decrees imposed in Germany? What were the provisions?   **(5–6)**

5. Discuss the impact of liberal and radical movements during the period 1815–47 on the course of events. **(5–8)**

6. What were the chief factors contributing to greater unity during the period 1834–48? **(8)**

7. Trace the growth of economic co-operation among German states before 1848. **(8–9)**

8. Why was the Zollverein important and why was Austria excluded? **(10)**

9. How did the Prussian king deal with the Berlin uprising in 1848? **(13, 19)**

10. What problems faced the German National Assembly in 1848? **(14–16)**

11. Why was the Prussian king hesitant to accept the crown as emperor of a united Germany in 1849? **(20)**

12. Account for the failure of the German revolution in 1848–9. **(21)**

13. Explain why Austria managed to gain the ascendancy in German affairs for a few years after 1849. **(22–24)**

14. Account for the decline of Austrian influence in Germany from 1851 to 1863. **(25–27)**

15. Did Francis Joseph seriously consider the liberal plan for a united Germany in 1863? Why did the Frankfurt Congress of princes fail? **(28(*b*)–(*c*))**

CHAPTER IX

German unification under Prussia, 1863–71

POLICIES AND EARLY CAREER OF BISMARCK

1. Bismarck's rise to power. Bismarck was a *Junker*, one of the aristocratic landowners from east of the river Elbe. In his youth he had a reputation for being tough, outspoken and rather wild. Bismarck's early career can be divided into the following three stages.

(*a*) *Pro-Austrian period.* In 1847 Bismarck served in the Prussian Diet as a conservative and attacked the liberals. In 1849 he opposed the proposed Frankfurt constitution and in 1850 welcomed the defeat of Radowitz's plan for Germany.

In 1851 he became Prussian representative at the Federal Diet. He was appointed to this post as a supporter of the policy of Prussian co-operation with Austria and the preservation of the German Confederation as it then existed.

(*b*) *More radical period.* The arrogance and assumption of superiority of the Austrian president of the Diet, Thun, annoyed Bismarck. He did not hesitate to take up privileges which had been the Austrian delegate's by right. Illustrations of his anti-Austrian attitude were the following.

(*i*) In foreign affairs: in 1855 he recommended Prussia's neutrality instead of involvement with Austria during the Crimean War. Later in 1859 he actively advocated an aggressive Prussian policy towards Austria.

(*ii*) In Germany: he blocked all attempts of the new Austrian president, Prokesch, to strengthen the Diet, as this was likely to secure Austrian ascendancy.

In 1859 Bismarck was removed from the Diet by the new liberal government in Prussia, since he had laboured for so long to make it ineffective. He became ambassador first at St. Petersburg and then in Paris.

(*c*) *Securing of German unification.* The circumstances in which Bismarck became Prime Minister of Prussia and secured the unification of Germany are described below.

2. Constitutional crisis. In 1862 the King was involved in a struggle for power with the liberals in Parliament. They refused to authorise the budget which would have ratified the money he had spent on creating new regiments. They did not object to a large army but disliked the fact that money had been spent on an item for which it had not been voted. They wanted to assert parliamentary control over the King and his ministers.

The King was about to abdicate when von Roon persuaded him to summon Bismarck. On receipt of a telegram, Bismarck hastened to Berlin, and became Minister-President. He ignored the liberals, and continued to collect money for the new army despite parliamentary opposition.

3. Bismarck's aims. Bismarck was a Prussian patriot rather than a German nationalist. He wanted to enhance the prestige and power of Prussia. He did not have any clear-cut long-term plans but concerned himself primarily with immediate problems. His chief objectives in 1862 were the following.

(*a*) *To secure Prussian predominance in North Germany.* This meant control of the German states north of the river Main. Bismarck disliked the predominant Austrian influence in German affairs.

(*i*) In July 1863 he persuaded the Prussian king not to attend the congress of princes summoned by Francis Joseph (*see* **VIII, 28**).

(*ii*) He renewed the convention between the Zollverein and Austria, but refused to allow Austria to become a member.

(*b*) *To oppose liberalism and democracy.* Though Bismarck was a radical thinker in many ways, he had only contempt for liberal notions and took measures to restrict the freedom of the press. As German unity was one of the aims of the liberals, he hoped to win their support by realising at least this part of their programme.

NOTE: By 1866 Bismarck favoured Radowitz's scheme for a Prussian-dominated *Kleindeutschland* as the best solution for Germany. Germany was too small for both Prussia and Austria, he said, as "both plough the same contested ground".

4. Bismarck's methods. Bismarck was basically an improviser who utilised events as they occurred to secure his aims. For example, he used the Danish issue as an opportunity to quarrel with Austria. His tactics were as follows.

(*a*) *To isolate his opponents.* Through the use of diplomatic skill Bismarck made sure that Austria in 1866 and France in 1870 had no allies. Bismarck felt that Prussia was strong enough not to have allies, but he was determined to remain friendly with any potential allies of his opponents. For example, he retained the friendship of Russia after 1863 owing to his action over Poland and his support of the Tsar's desire to revise the Black Sea clauses.

(b) *To use military power effectively*. Bismarck relied on the success of Prussian arms in war to achieve his aims. The following two remarks illustrate his outlook and methods.

(i) "Germany has its eyes not on Prussian liberalism but on its power."

(ii) "The great questions of the day will not be decided by speeches and majority votes," since that was the mistake of 1848, but by "blood and iron".

5. Steps to German unification. It has been said that Bismarck united Germany as the result of three successful wars. However, it must be noted that much groundwork for eventual unification had been achieved before Bismarck came to power.

In summary the major steps towards German unification in the nineteenth century were as follows.

(a) Creation of the German Confederation in 1815.

(b) Formation of the Zollverein in 1834.

(c) The decline of Austrian influence during the period 1852–63 (*see* VIII, **26**).

(i) When Austria failed to gain support for her economic or political plans for Germany this simplified the process of German unity.

(ii) Prussian power in economic and military terms increased. This made it possible for her to implement her own variant of the *Kleindeutsch* plan for Germany – the forceful Prussianisation of Germany on the autocratic model.

(d) Danish War in 1864 (*see* **7–9**).

(e) Austrian War in 1866 (*see* **13–20**).

(f) Establishment of the North German Confederation in 1867 (*see* **21**).

(g) French War in 1870–1 (*see* VI, **23–25**).

(h) Creation of the German Empire in 1871 (*see* **24**).

When reading the following sections on the final steps towards German unification, reference may be made to the accompanying map.

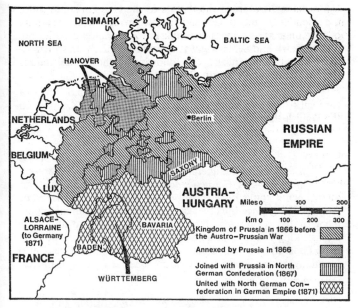

The unification of Germany under Bismarck, 1866–71

SCHLESWIG-HOLSTEIN AND THE AUSTRO-PRUSSIAN WAR, 1863–6

6. The London Protocol, 1852. After the war between Denmark and the German states in 1848 (*see* VIII, **15**) the Schleswig-Holstein problem had been only temporarily solved by the London Protocol. It was agreed by the European powers that Christian, the heir to the Danish throne, would on his succession inherit the two territories. It was also decided that the duchies would remain as they were, part of the Danish kingdom, but would not be subject to its laws. Thus the aspirations of neither the Danes nor the Germans were satisfied.

7. Revival of the Danish Question. In March 1863 the Danish government made plans to incorporate Schleswig into Denmark. Protests were made by Austria, Prussia, the Federal Diet and the German people in the duchies.

Denmark disregarded the threats of the German states, since the essential disunity of Germany seemed evident from the failure of the congress of princes at Frankfurt. A common constitution for Denmark and Schleswig was approved by the Danish Parliament on 13th November. The following further complications then arose, resulting eventually in war.

(a) *Disputed succession to the duchies.* King Frederick VII of Denmark died suddenly. His successor, Christian IX, inherited the Danish throne through the female line. However, the law of the duchies recognised succession only through the direct male line.

The major parties in Germany favoured the claim of the Prince of Augustenburg to the duchies.

(b) *Intervention by German states.* The Prussian and Austrian governments could not recognise the claims of the Prince of Augustenburg since they had been parties to the London agreement of 1852. However, they were not prepared to allow the Danish king to incorporate Schleswig into Denmark. The German Federal Diet had dreams of incorporating Holstein into Germany. It decided on 1st October 1863 that Saxony, Hanover, Austria and Prussia should be entrusted with the task of intervention on its behalf.

(c) *Danish defiance encouraged by Britain.* Britain supported the Danes, despite the violation of the London agreement, since it appeared in 1863 that the German states were about to commit a greater violation. Relations between Britain and Denmark were close at the time since a marriage had taken place between the Prince of Wales and Princess Alexandra of Denmark.

Palmerston, the British Prime Minister, hinted that in case of war Denmark would not stand alone. This encouraged the Danes to rely on British help in resisting the German states. However, British naval power would be of little value to Denmark if war occurred, and Britain was not prepared to risk a land war with Prussia.

8. Prelude to the Danish War. The preliminaries to war were as follows.

(a) In December 1863 Saxo-Hanoverian contingents of the federal troops crossed into Holstein. The Diet was still supporting the Duke of Augustenburg.

(b) In January 1864 Prussia secured an alliance with Austria. Neither power had much interest in the issue. Bismarck, however, wanted to dissociate himself from the action of the Diet and knew that the German liberals would support him if he opposed Denmark. He was not prepared to act, however, without involving Austria. Austria agreed to co-operate, partly to keep a watch on Prussia and partly under the mistaken idea that Prussia had reverted to her former conservative policy of co-operation with her.

Holstein was of strategic importance to Prussia, and Schleswig, in the hands of a hostile power, could be used for naval operations against her.

(c) Austria and Prussia sent an ultimatum to Denmark, asking her to withdraw the common constitution and submit the matter to a European congress. Encouraged by Britain, Denmark refused to comply.

9. The defeat of Denmark. On 1st February 1864 Austrian and Prussian troops invaded Schleswig. Bismarck assured the European powers that they were intervening only to prevent the violation of the London agreement by Christian IX. By 18th April the Germans were invading Denmark. Britain called a conference at London (April–June) to save the Danes. It failed owing to the obstinacy of the Danes and the cleverness of Bismarck. The last chance for the Federal Diet to regain the initiative from Austria and Prussia was then lost. Denmark was defeated and by the Treaty of Vienna (October 1864) the King had unconditionally to sign away to his opponents his rights over the duchies.

10. Uneasy Austro-Prussian collaboration. Neither Austria nor Prussia had plans for the future of the duchies. Bismarck hoped that eventually an excuse would arise for war with Austria. At first Prussia and Austria jointly administered the duchies, ignoring the opinions of the German Diet and the claims of the Prince of Augustenburg. In August 1865 Bismarck manoeuvred Austria into agreeing to the Gastein Convention. Austria was to administer Holstein, while Prussia administered Schleswig. In Bismarck's view this "papered over the cracks" in Austro-Prussian relations, and only prolonged the day of reckoning.

11. Great-power diplomacy, 1863–6. Note must be taken of the relations between the major powers during this period. The various arrangements made were contributory factors to the

Austro-Prussian War and to the military success of Prussia, since Austria was skilfully isolated from possible allies by Bismarck.

(a) *Convention of Alvensleben, February 1863.* A revolt had broken out in the Polish territories of Russia. Prussia also contained discontented Poles, and Bismarck did not want the revolt to spread. Bismarck sent troops to the frontier, and refused asylum to Polish refugees from Russia. This action made it possible for Russia to resist the attempted intervention by Austria, Britain and France on behalf of the Poles. Bismarck won the Tsar's trust and friendship.

(b) *Biarritz meeting, October 1865 (see VI, 16(a)).*

(c) *Austro-Italian relations.* In January 1866 Italy offered to buy Venetia from Austria. If Austria had accepted, this would no doubt have secured Italian neutrality in a war with Prussia. However, this offer was rejected. (*See also* XIII, 41.)

(d) *Prusso-Italian alliance, April 1866.* Bismarck feared that Austria might still surrender Venetia to Italy and that France might reach an agreement with Austria. He managed to secure an Italian alliance. Italy was to help Prussia if Prussia engineered a war with Austria within three months. The reward for Italy would be Venetia.

(e) *Austro-French agreement, June 1866 (see VI, 16(b)).*

12. Austrian diplomacy and the powers. Austrian diplomacy was in a deplorable state at the time. Austria was pressured by demands from the Prussians in the north, the Italians in the south and the Magyars in the east, and she was in financial difficulties at home: her ministers had no clear plans. Austria, as well as most other European powers, expected that she would be victorious in any war with Prussia. This encouraged her not to yield on any front and to ignore any proposals for changes in the present "balance of power". Her War Minister, Belcredi, believed that, if successful in war, Austria would be able to put off concessions to the Hungarians.

In April 1866 Bismarck introduced a motion for federal reform in the Frankfurt Diet, hoping that Austria would reject it and precipitate a conflict. Austria was still not prepared to recognise Prussia as an equal in the German Confederation and rejected any idea of change. In May Austria also rejected the plans of the brothers Gablenz that Prince Albert of Prussia should be made sovereign of Schleswig-Holstein.

Austria, Italy and Prussia had started mobilisation in April.

In May Britain, France and Russia suggested a European congress to deal with the questions of Schleswig-Holstein, Venetia and federal reform, all of which involved the treaties of 1815 and other conventions. Prussia and Italy accepted this suggestion, but on 1st June Austria said she was prepared to accept only on the condition that the congress did not envisage any alteration in the territories of the invited powers. This was tantamount to a refusal.

13. The immediate pretext for war. The issues of control of the duchies and federal reform became the grounds for war. Austrian rule in Holstein had been mild and conciliatory, while Prussian rule in Schleswig had been harsh. Complaints reached Prussia that Austria received refugees from Holstein. Austria decided to refer the question of the duchies to the Diet and on 5th June instructed the Holstein Assembly to debate its own future. By this action Austria had clearly violated her secret agreement with Prussia (January 1864) and the Gastein Convention (August 1865), because in these arrangements Austria had agreed to settle the future status of the duchies only in agreement with Prussia.

Bismarck ordered Prussian troops to invade Holstein. This action did not adequately provoke Austria. On 10th June Bismarck proposed a reform of the Confederation which would exclude Austria entirely. Austria objected and on 14th June the Diet censured Prussia as the aggressor. Bismarck retaliated by declaring that the Diet was dissolved, and the Prussians invaded Hanover, Saxony and Hesse-Kassel on 15th–16th June. On 17th June Austria replied by declaring war on Prussia.

14. Defeat of the Bund. The German states, apart from Hanover, were slow to organise their forces. The Prussians defeated the Hanoverians at Langensalza on 28th June. Contingents of the Federal Diet (*Bund*) from Bavaria, Württemberg, Baden and Nassau were slowly being organised under Prince Charles of Bavaria. He intended to link with the Austrian forces, but Prussian troop movements took him by surprise. In a series of encounters ending with that of Rossbrunn on 26th July the forces of the *Bund* were defeated.

15. Austro-French negotiations. On 2nd July Austria offered to give Venetia to Napoleon if the Emperor would be prepared to act as mediator in Germany and Italy. Austria's aim was to arrange an armistice and to transfer to Bohemia the southern army which would be released by the withdrawal of Italy from the conflict. She could then resume the war, possibly with the help of France. Napoleon, however, was unable to make up his mind.

16. Prussian victory at Sadowa. The only major encounter between Austro-Bavarian forces and the Prussians was a decisive victory for the latter at Sadowa (Königgrätz) on 3rd July. Factors contributing to this decisive victory were as follows.

(a) *Weapons.* The Prussian Dreyse breech-loading needle-gun proved to be superior to the muzzle-loading Lorenz rifle on which the Austrians relied. It fired farther and more rapidly.

(b) *Staff work.* Moltke, chief of the German staff since 1857, had built up a central H.Q. which became the brains of the army. It proved invaluable in:

(i) planning the rapid movement by rail of the troops (*see* (d));

(ii) co-ordinating the operations of all armies with the aid of the telegraph.

(c) *Tactics.* Prussian fighting tactics with the emphasis on mobility were superior to the Austrian, which placed too much reliance on close formations and the use of the bayonet.

(d) *Rail communications.* The highly developed Prussian railway network enabled Moltke to deploy his troops along an arc about 950 kilometres wide to overrun the German states. It enabled three separate Prussian armies to then converge on the main concentration of Austrian troops. In contrast Austria's deficiency in railways made it difficult to move troops from the Italian front after 24th June or for her forces to link up with German allies.

17. Termination of the war by Bismarck. At Sadowa the Austrians lost 44,000 men, almost five times as many as the Prussian casualties. However, Benedek had been able to withdraw a large part of his forces. The war might well have been a protracted one as many European powers expected. It was Bismarck who planned to bring the war to a rapid conclusion. His reasons were as follows.

(a) *He believed that a long war would benefit Austria.*

(i) Prussia had a population only half the size of Austria's. She had few reserves and there had been difficulties in calling up reservists in the Rhineland.

(*ii*) Austria could be reinforced by her southern Italian army and by General Albrecht's army on the Danube. When better organised she might also receive further assistance from the North German princes.

(*b*) *He had limited aims.* Bismarck wanted only to unite Germany around Prussia. After Sadowa it seemed futile to continue the war, for the following two reasons.

(*i*) Austria might be permanently alienated. At a later date she might prove to be a useful ally.

(*ii*) Little further could be achieved. The fighting would take place between armies that were mainly German.

(*c*) *He wanted to prevent French intervention.* Some French troops were in the process of returning from Mexico. Napoleon, anxious to be accepted as a mediator, had after Sadowa sent Benedetti, the French ambassador, to the Prussian H.Q. at Nikolsburg. This visit made Bismarck proceed cautiously and to moderate the terms to be offered to Austria. At all costs he wanted to avoid decisive French intervention on the side of Austria.

18. Austria's reasons for peace. Austria was also receptive to overtures after Bismarck had made appeals to Czech and Magyar nationalists. There was also the prospect of moderate peace terms. Austrian financial resources were weak and her forces were spread over three fronts. There seemed little prospect of finding an ally if she continued the war. Her southern army, which would have been invaluable at Sadowa, defeated the Italians at Custozza on 24th June, and her fleet defeated the Italians at Lizza. However, despite these successes, all she could look forward to on this front was territorial loss. Napoleon eventually advised the terribly disillusioned Austrians to accept Bismarck's conditions.

19. The Peace of Prague. The Prussian king and his generals were keen to continue the war, and to march on to Vienna. With the assistance of the Crown Prince, Bismarck dissuaded them from this course.

The peace preliminaries were signed at Nikolsburg on 26th July, to be followed by the final settlement at Prague on 23rd August. The provisions were as follows.

(*a*) *Austria was excluded from German affairs.* This in itself was a considerable blow to Austria. She had to acknowledge the dissolution of the German Confederation as hitherto constituted and to pay an indemnity.

(b) *Prussia secured increased territory.* She absorbed Schleswig-Holstein as well as Hanover, Hesse-Kassel, Nassau and Frankfurt.

(c) *A new North German Confederation* was to be formed under Prussian leadership. Austria actually agreed to recognise any federal relations which the Prussian king established north of the Main. The new union included Saxony, whose autonomy Austria managed to preserve.

(d) *Southern German states* were to retain a separate existence. They were to form a vague union of their own and to have "an independent international existence".

(e) *Venetia was to be surrendered* indirectly through France to Italy. This was the only territorial loss that Austria suffered.

20. Results of the war. The Prussian victory resulted in considerable domestic changes in Germany and the Austrian Empire. It was also a landmark in French and Italian affairs.

Consequences of the war for the various powers were as follows.

(a) *Prussia.*

(i) Prussia gained a considerable increase in prestige. Single-handed, she had defeated the armies of the other German states and Austria.

(ii) Prussia achieved the predominant influence in German affairs. The way was open for German unity on the *Kleindeutschland* model which Austria had previously resisted.

(iii) Bismarck won the support of the liberals at home (*see* **22(b)**).

(iv) Prussian autocratic methods triumphed over German liberalism (*see* **22(c)**).

(b) *Austria.* Driven from Germany, Austria reorganised her empire in the *Ausgleich* (*see* XI, **38**).

(c) *France.* A severe diplomatic setback was suffered by the French. "It is France that is beaten at Sadowa," said Marshal Randon. Bismarck evaded all attempts by Napoleon to profit from the war (*see* VI, **16(d)**). The collapse of the Second Empire was brought closer.

(d) *Italy.* Unity was brought a stage nearer (*see* XIII, **41**).

THE NORTH GERMAN CONFEDERATION
AND THE CREATION OF THE GERMAN EMPIRE

21. The North German Confederation. The plans for a North German Confederation had been put forward in the Prussian reform proposal to the old Diet on 10th June 1866. Austria eventually accepted them in the Treaty of Prague. After lengthy consultation between the various German states, the constitution was approved and came into force on 1st July 1867.

22. Germany after the Austro-Prussian War. For Germany, the domestic effects of the Austro-Prussian War were as follows.

(*a*) *Bismarck gained popular support.* Many influential Prussians, particularly conservatives, had disliked the war with Austria. The victory of Sadowa won many converts to Bismarck's policies, including the liberals.

In September 1866 Bismarck asked for and obtained a Bill of Indemnity. This was passed by 230 votes to 75 and excused the government for ruling without a constitutional budget since 1862.

(*b*) *German liberals supported Bismarck's policy.* The moderates and liberals, pleased to see a part of their programme – national unity – being achieved, as well as the growth in power and prestige of Germany, abandoned their former opposition.

The Hanoverian Bennigsen headed the newly formed National Liberal Party which faithfully supported Bismarck in his foreign policies until 1878 while working towards the long-term aim of parliamentary government.

(*c*) *Prussian autocracy triumphed over German liberalism.* The North German Confederation had no precedent in Europe. It was not a proper confederation since it was not a league of states. It was a collection of constituent parts forming a new state in which Prussia was supreme. The autocratic constitution remained in its essentials the form of government in Germany until 1914.

Liberal feeling in Germany was strong in 1866. Liberals were prepared to accept an autocratic constitution in 1867, since it was a step towards unity and had a "democratic" content. It included direct male universal suffrage for elections for the Diet. However, though the liberals had great influence in the new Diet, they had little real power. The Diet did not have much authority and the liberal leaders never became members of the government. The latter continued to consist of life-long bureaucrats and conservative nominees of Bismarck. In 1869 the liberals passed a law to establish ministerial responsibility in the constitution of the North German Confederation. Bismarck ignored this.

23. The final stage to unity. North of the Main, Prussia exercised the dominating influence in the North German Confederation. South of the Main remained the three Catholic states of Bavaria, Württemberg and Baden, partly susceptible to French or Austrian influences, where liberal sentiment was strong. The problem remained as to how final union would be achieved. Would it be a voluntary drawing together of the two parts, or a forced union as a result of Prussian power? If the latter, then the final state would inevitably be autocratic along the lines of the confederal constitution. Hopes of the liberals for democratic government would then be vanquished.

Austria had hoped that the states south of the Main would form a union of their own. However, before the Treaty of Prague was signed, Prussia was quick to sign in August 1866 secret treaties of alliance with Bavaria, Württemberg and Baden. Then, when a plan for a South German union was put forward, it failed. It was not "particularist" enough for Bavaria and Württemberg. If the union had been formed, it would have been able to prevent the whole union in 1871 from being a disguised Prussian union.

King Ludwig II of Bavaria and King Karl of Württemberg were averse to any German union which would make them subordinate to the Prussian king. In 1869 the movement towards German unity was further slowed by the victory in the Bavarian elections of the Clerical Party. It was Ultramontane and therefore anti-Prussian and pro-Austrian. In 1871 Bavaria, Württemberg and Baden ironically had to give up their independence almost entirely.

In time, German unity would have come without war as a result of the pressure of national feeling. However, Bismarck, impatient of delay, hastened the process by precipitating war with France in 1870. For details *see* VI, **20–21**.

24. Creation of the German Empire. At the onset of the Franco-Prussian War in 1870 the South German states honoured their obligations to Prussia under the 1866 military treaties and took part. After the war, at the height of national enthusiasm at victory, unity seemed very likely.

There were, however, problems to be settled. German states put forward territorial claims at the expense of each other and

France. Bismarck was being pressed by North German liberals to agree to ministerial responsibility and an upper house or senate. He was determined, however, to keep to his system of a Bundesrat of nominated bureaucrats.

Liberal leaders went on a propaganda publicity tour of southern Germany. The main problem was Bavaria. Bismarck was prepared to make various "prestige concessions" to this state. For example, in the event of Prussia's absence, which was not likely, Bavaria was to have the presidency of the Bundesrat. The last problem was fixing on the title of the executive head of Germany. King William did not want to be called "emperor" or to receive any imperial title from a representative assembly. Eventually the Bavarian king came out of his temporary seclusion and proposed the title of "*Deutscher Kaiser*". The princes agreed, and on 18th January 1871, in a splendid gathering at Versailles, William accepted officially the imperial title.

The imperial constitution dated from 16th April 1871. It differed little from that of the North German Confederation, except for amendments necessary for the admission of the South German states and the adoption of the new title.

25. Did Bismarck deliberately plan war? Viewing German history between 1864 and 1870 it is hard to believe that the wars fought during this period were not planned as part of some great logical design, each stage fitting its preappointed place. Prussia was able to eliminate one by one the possible opponents to any form of German union around herself. Bismarck even took care ahead of the time to isolate his enemies from likely allies. It has even been said that in 1862 he confided his future plans for Germany to Disraeli over a dinner.

The evidence suggests, however, that the wars were not planned in advance. On the other hand, neither were they accidental and the various crises were capable of solution by peaceful means. Bismarck was impatient for results. He realised that success in arms would be a sure and swift method for stirring national enthusiasm, winning the support of the liberals at home and achieving his aims. A shrewd and skilful diplomat, he made use of favourable circumstances to outmanoeuvre and force his opponent into a position when the only alternative which appeared open was war.

PROGRESS TEST 9

1. Describe the early career of Bismarck before 1863 and give some account of his political views.   (1, 2)

2. What were the aims of Bismarck regarding Germany and how did he propose to achieve them?   (3, 4)

3. What steps towards German unity had been taken before 1863?   (5)

4. Give details of the London agreement on Schleswig-Holstein in 1852. Why did a crisis occur in 1863?   (6, 7)

5. Discuss Austro-Prussian relations regarding Schleswig-Holstein between 1863 and 1866.   (8–10, 12, 13)

6. How did Bismarck help the Tsar in 1863?   (11(a))

7. Why did Italy ally with Prussia in 1866?   (11(d))

8. Did Austria cause the war with Prussia in 1866?   (12)

9. Account for the rapid Austrian defeat in 1866.   (14–18)

10. List the provisions of the Peace of Prague. What were the important results of the Austro-Prussian War?   (19, 20)

11. How did Bismarck benefit from the Austro-Prussian War?   (22)

12. What were the hopes of Austria after 1866 regarding Germany? Explain why they were not realised.   (23)

13. Did Bismarck plan the various wars fought by Prussia before 1871?   (25)

CHAPTER X

The German Empire, 1871–1914

DOMESTIC POLICY OF BISMARCK, 1871–90

1. Structure of the new German Empire. After 1871 the German Empire included Prussia, the kingdoms of Bavaria, Saxony and Württemberg, eighteen lesser states, three free cities and the *Reichslande* (Alsace-Lorraine). The following features of the imperial political system should be noted.

(*a*) *A federal system.* Sovereignty was vested by the constitution in the Reich. Most of the matters that affected the German citizens were reserved to the individual states. The imperial government had administrative departments only for naval and foreign affairs, posts and telegraphs, customs and later for colonies. It was not a true federation since Prussia had seventeen out of fifty-eight votes in the upper chamber.

(*b*) *A parliamentary system.* The Reichstag was elected by direct, secret and almost universal male suffrage. It had the power to delay the introduction of new laws and new taxes.

(*c*) *The monarchy.* The hereditary leadership of the Empire was vested in the King of Prussia, with the title of German Emperor.

(*d*) *The Bundesrat.* This was an important institution. It represented the rights of the princes and of the individual states and was the upper house of Parliament. The representatives were nominees of the various governments, not of the German people. It controlled legislation, and possessed the following important powers.

(*i*) It had the right, subject to the Emperor's assent, to declare war and settle constitutional questions and difficulties arising between the states.

(*ii*) It could dissolve the Reichstag.

(*e*) *Autocracy.* Despite the features of federalism and parliamentarianism in the new Germany, the system of government was profoundly undemocratic.

(*i*) Each of the states did not have equal powers in the upper house.

(*ii*) The Reichstag had little control over the appointment or policies of government ministers. The Chancellor was not answerable to the Assembly but dependent on the support of the Emperor.

(*iii*) The Emperor directed foreign affairs, and made all government appointments. Through his Chancellor, he took the initiative in domestic affairs.

2. The main political groups. In 1871 these were as follows.

(*a*) *The Conservative Party*. This was a Protestant party with strong support in Prussia and among the aristocracy, the owners of landed property and eventually the protectionists.

An offshoot was the *Reichspartei*, which had its main support among landlords and industrialists. It supported Bismarck's policies without question and many of its members went into Bismarck's government.

(*b*) *The Catholic Centre Party*. This was founded in 1870 (*see* **5**). It soon acquired a mass following, though its main strength was in Bavaria and the Rhineland. It protected minority groups, resisted centralisation, and supported social reform and constitutional government.

(*c*) *Liberal groups*. There were two liberal groups.

(*i*) The National Liberals represented the educated and wealthy middle class. They supported centralisation policies, constitutional government and free trade. This was the largest party in 1871 but it declined considerably after 1877 (*see* **8**(*d*)).

(*ii*) The Left Liberals shared some of the views of the National Liberals and Social Democrats but were profoundly anti-militarist and anti-state in outlook.

(*d*) *The Social Democratic Party*. This party, formed in 1869, achieved a remarkable growth in the 1870s, and before 1914 became the strongest party in Germany.

(*e*) *Various splinter groups*. Among these were the discontented foreign minority groups whose representatives occupied nearly 10 per cent of the seats in the Reichstag. Bismarck tried to subdue them by means of pacification or pressure. Despite persecution, the minority groups resisted Germanisation. These groups were as follows.

(*i*) Polish (3½ million): there were many Poles in Prussia, especially in Posen, as a result of earlier partitions.

(*ii*) French (2 million): the provinces captured in 1871, Alsace-Lorraine, remained loyal to the French connection.

Their representatives in the Reichstag kept up a continuous agitation.

(*iii*) Danish (150,000): in North Schleswig particularly, many people preferred Denmark and resented the German link.

3. Consolidation of the new Germany. After 1871 Bismarck wanted to complete the unification process by giving Germany the institutions to make it a homogeneous and effective nation. He wanted to reduce diversity and parochialism, and to build a strong centralised authority under Prussian leadership. Since this involved legislation, he co-operated with the National Liberal Party, which commanded a majority in the Reichstag.

The army and Civil Service, and the railway, postal and legal systems, were unified, and a common coinage established. German laws, language and customs were imposed on all foreign minority groups.

4. Opposition to Bismarck. Bismarck was concerned because many groups opposed his policy of centralisation of authority and compulsory Germanisation. Those Germans who wished to preserve a degree of independence for the individual German states received no satisfaction. For example, Bismarck refused to make concessions to the Guelph Party in Hanover, which demanded the restoration of the Hanoverian king.

Bismarck devoted much of his attention to finding ways of crushing discontented elements who appeared to have loyalties conflicting with German nationalism. His methods, however, resulted only in strengthening the opposition. His chief opponents were:

(*a*) the hostile foreign minorities (*see* 2);
(*b*) the Catholic Centre Party (*see* 5);
(*c*) the Social Democratic Party (*see* 9).

5. The Catholic Centre Party. Large sections of South Germany had supported a *Grossdeutsch* policy. They disliked the loss of Austria and the replacement of Hapsburg influence by a Protestant dynasty. The German Roman Catholics were weakened politically by the exclusion of Austria from a united Germany as this meant they formed a minority rather than a majority in the new state.

A small group of Catholics in the universities objected to the doctrine of Papal infallibility pronounced by the Pope in 1870 (*see* XIII, **59**). The Church retaliated by demanding their dismissal.

Bismarck supported the rebellious Catholics, but the majority of Catholics supported the Pope. They also opposed Bismarck for making Protestant Prussia dominant in the Empire and for increasing the powers of the central government at the expense of the states. Fearing religious and political discrimination, they formed a special political party in 1870, the Catholic Centre Party.

This party soon became influential and was supported by many disgruntled elements to which it lent support. For example, it encouraged the demands of the Poles in Prussia for their own language to be taught in the schools. It was supported by a large section of the Rhineland and by the Guelphic nobility in Hanover.

6. Reasons for the Kulturkampf. Bismarck considered that the Catholic Centre Party was seriously challenging his policy of consolidating the new empire. He decided it was necessary to restrict the influence and power of Catholics and the Papacy in German politics. His decision to attack the Catholics was taken therefore on political rather than religious grounds.

He saw the following advantages in the *Kulturkampf*, or "struggle for civilisation", upon which he then embarked.

(*a*) *Strengthening Germany's position abroad.*

(*i*) Closer ties might be established with Russia, a state which was in general hostile to Rome and Roman Catholicism.

(*ii*) It was an indirect way of attacking France, the leading champion of the Catholic Church.

(*iii*) It might help fortify the anti-clerical tendencies of the new Italy, and prevent her linking up with France.

(*b*) *Strengthening internal unity within the German Empire.* The Catholic Centre Party represented an anti-national body which looked outside the State to the Vatican for part of its authority. Bismarck wanted no divided loyalties within the new Germany. He hoped that the Centre Party would be forced to abandon their opposition to his policies, and that various discontented minorities would also fall into line as a result of his anti-clerical measures.

(*c*) *Support of the National Liberals.* The political party on which Bismarck relied for support in the Reichstag were predominantly Protestant and favoured anti-Catholic measures.

7. The anti-clerical period. In 1872 Germany severed diplomatic relations with the Vatican, and the Jesuits were expelled from the country. The *Kulturkampf* was associated particularly with the series of May Laws which were strictly enforced from 1873 until 1879. Important points to note are as follows.

(*a*) *Content of the May Laws.*

(*i*) In 1873 education, appointments and activities of priests were brought under state control. Priests were forbidden to coerce individuals on threat of public excommunication. Lay inspectors of schools were appointed.

(*ii*) In 1875 civil marriage was made compulsory. Religious orders were dissolved.

(*b*) *Effectiveness of the laws.* The Pope declared the laws null and void, and forbade Roman Catholics to obey them. From 1871 to 1877 the Catholic Centre Party increased its number of seats in the Reichstag. The influence of the Catholics increased rather than diminished.

(*c*) *Reasons for relaxation of the laws.* Gradually Bismarck realised he had made a grave political miscalculation and was hopelessly antagonising a third of the German people. A more tolerant attitude on the part of the new Pope, Leo XIII (1878–1903), made conciliation easier. In 1879, in return for a promise that the government would be notified of all impending papal appointments and that German clergy would desist from opposing the government, Bismarck began to revoke anti-clerical legislation.

Other factors influencing Bismarck to make a change in policy were as follows.

(*i*) In foreign affairs the prospects of an alliance with Catholic Austria were increasing.

(*ii*) Bismarck had decided to support economic protection for Germany (*see* 8). This was losing Bismarck the support of the National Liberals. In 1877 he had offered their leader, Bennigsen, a place in the Prussian ministry if they supported his measures, but they refused. In contrast, the Centre Party was sympathetic towards policies of protectionism.

(*iii*) Bismarck had decided to oppose the Social Democratic Party and the socialist ideas which it propounded (*see* 9). This party, which had gained nearly half a million supporters in 1877, now appeared the chief internal threat to Bismarck's policies. The Centre Party would support him in any measures which were taken against the socialists, while the National Liberals would not.

8. Economic protection. In Germany before 1870 agriculture had been the chief occupation. However, payment by France of the war in indemnity resulted in a fever of speculation in new industrial projects, and gradually the economy became more diversified. The agricultural community was soon affected by increased imports of cheap food products from abroad, notably wheat from the United States and Austria and rye from Russia.

In 1879 Bismarck abandoned a free-trade policy and imposed a tariff on foreign corn and other commodities. Factors influencing his decision were as follows.

(*a*) *Popular demand for protection.*

(*b*) *Arguments for nationalism and self-sufficiency.* German economists contended that a country was weak if it did not possess well-developed industries, which could develop under the shelter of tariffs. Other countries, too, particularly Russia, Austria-Hungary and France, were restricting foreign goods on an increasing scale.

(*c*) *Methods of collecting revenue.* Under a free-trade system revenue had to be collected primarily from taxation. This gave the Reichstag important power. Under a protection system revenue could be raised independently of the Reichstag through customs duties.

(*d*) *Political factors.* Supporting protective measures gave Bismarck an excuse to abandon the liberals and turn to the Catholics, who were more likely to be his allies in his coming struggle with the Social Democratic Party. Bismarck had also disliked the demand of the National Liberals in 1877 for some control over the formulation of policy.

9. Bismarck and socialism. To Bismarck the Social Democratic Party represented a threat to the military, monarchical and autocratic nature of the State. He disliked, as a Prussian aristocrat, their demands for the abolition of the private ownership of land and property and for a general sharing of wealth. In addition he felt they could not be true German patriots since they had ties with the international socialist movement.

Bismarck used two recent attempts to assassinate the Emperor, in which the socialists were in no way involved, as an excuse to take measures to undermine their influence. His policies took the following two forms.

(*a*) *Anti-socialist laws.* In 1879 the Exceptional Law was passed which outlawed the Social Democratic Party. All societies, meetings and publications concerned with spreading socialist principles were banned, and the police were authorised to deport any suspected persons. Trade unions were declared illegal.

(b) *Welfare measures.* Bismarck hoped that by introducing small doses of state socialism he could also crush the socialist movement. In this field Germany was generally the pioneer.

(i) The compulsory insurance of workmen was introduced. This was provided in 1883 against sickness, and in 1884 against accident.

(ii) A pension plan for the aged and permanently disabled was initiated in 1889.

These policies failed. Socialist discontent was only driven underground. Secret societies were formed, and meetings were held abroad. In 1890 the Social Democratic Party gained some 1½ million votes.

FOREIGN POLICY OF BISMARCK, 1871-90

10. General principles. Bismarck reasoned that there were five great powers, Britain, Austria, France, Russia and Germany. Italy and Turkey made very weak sixth and seventh powers respectively. He viewed the European scene rather as a chessboard. His basic formula was that Germany should "try to be *à trois* in a world governed by five powers".

Bismarck's aims were as follows.

(a) *Preservation of European peace.* Bismarck believed that Germany was now a satiated power and that her best interests lay in supporting the *status quo.* He was particularly concerned that the rivalry between Austria and Russia in the Near East should not result in a war in which Germany would have to make a choice as to which power to support. Much of his efforts were devoted to solving the Eastern Question. German policy in the Near East is given detailed treatment in XVI, 6, 15(d) and 20.

(b) *Concentration on European issues.* Bismarck believed that Germany's main interests lay in Europe, not in the Balkans, the Near East or Africa. He did not want a colonial empire and remarked: "My map of Africa lies in Europe." He was forced, however, under popular pressure, to seek colonial expansion (*see* XVIII, 5-7 and 10).

(c) *Isolation of France.* Bismarck saw the chief threat to Germany coming in the future from the west. He feared that

France might start a war of revenge to recover Alsace and Lorraine.

(*d*) *Prevention of anti-German coalition.* Since France was unlikely to start a war, except with the support of an ally, Bismarck made it his policy to keep on good terms with Austria, Russia and Britain. In time this led to the policy of forming alliances. Important ones were the *Dreikaiserbund* and the Dual Alliance.

(*e*) *Diversion of other powers to non-European activities.* Bismarck felt that the best way to prevent other powers from taking an active interest in altering European affairs at Germany's expense was to divert them to clashes with each other in areas where German interests were not involved. For example, he encouraged:

(*i*) France in her ambitions in Africa, particularly in Tunis, so that she might forget the Rhine (*see* XIX, 25(*e*));

(*ii*) Britain in Egypt (*see* XIX, 11(*b*)(*ii*));

(*iii*) Italy in North Africa.

11. The Dreikaiserbund. After 1871 Bismarck worked to re-establish the old triple alignment of the "three northern Courts", St. Petersburg, Vienna and Berlin, which had first appeared in 1815 as the Holy Alliance. If this proved to be a workable and durable link it would realise his aims. It would stand for the preservation of conservative principles, and help to maintain peace by the diplomatic isolation of France in the west and its contribution to better Austro-Russian relations in the Near East. Germany would be able to act as a third party. Her security would be endangered if either Russia or Austria was severely weakened or allied with France.

The sequence of events was as follows.

(*a*) An informal alliance was concluded in 1872 between the three emperors. They met in Berlin and agreed to maintain the *status quo* in the Balkans.

(*b*) A series of bilateral military agreements were signed in 1873. Austria, Russia and Germany each promised aid to one another in the event of an unprovoked attack on any of them.

(*c*) More formal arrangements were made in 1881 (*see* 16(*a*)).

(*d*) The arrangements of 1881 were renewed in 1884 (*see* 16(*a*)).

(*e*) The agreement lapsed in 1887. Bismarck made a Reinsurance Treaty with Russia instead (*see* 17).

12. The war scare of 1875. A series of minor incidents accumulated in a diplomatic crisis in May 1875. It was important in illustrating the poor relations which existed between France and Germany after 1870 and which were to persist until 1914.

Relevant details were as follows.

(*a*) *Rapid recovery of France.* Germany was alarmed at the speed at which France was recovering from the Franco-Prussian War. The French army was being rapidly strengthened by the laws of 1872 and further reorganisation was planned in January 1875. Some German officers, influenced by the "preventive war" argument, believed it would be better to fight France then before she became too strong.

Bismarck suspected a monarchist revival in France, and hence an end to her isolation through her reaching an understanding with the clerical powers, Austria and Italy.

(*b*) *Domestic considerations in Germany.*

(*i*) Bismarck was having difficulty in obtaining approval for a new Army Bill by the Reichstag.

(*ii*) The *Kulturkampf* was attacked by clericals in Belgium and France, and incurred increased opposition at home.

(*c*) *Bismarck's provocative measures.* It is not clear whether Bismarck genuinely feared the growth of an international coalition against Germany or whether he just wanted to intimidate France. He certainly encouraged Germans to think in terms of a possible war with France. He was responsible for the following developments.

(*i*) In February 1875 a special envoy was sent to Russia to defend the idea of preventive war.

(*ii*) The export of horses to Belgium was suddenly forbidden.

(*iii*) In April an article entitled "Is War in Sight?" was published in the German press.

By raising the cry "The Fatherland in danger!" Bismarck rallied enough support to enable the new Army Bill to be passed and to divert attention from the *Kulturkampf*.

(*d*) *Decazes and the intervention of Britain and Russia.* The French Foreign Minister, Decazes, planned to bait Bismarck into making indiscretions which might turn Europe, especially Britain, against him. In May he told the British newspaper *The Times* that Germany intended to "bleed France white".

On request from France, Britain and Russia jointly intervened in Berlin to enquire as to the reason for the heightened tension between France and Germany. Queen Victoria wrote to the Kaiser. The Tsar and his Foreign Minister, Gorchakov, visited Berlin. Bismarck protested that Germany's intentions were entirely peaceful and that the crisis was imaginary. The "storm in a teacup" subsided. Bismarck had suffered a setback, since the incident showed that France was no longer isolated in Europe.

13. Reasons for the Dual Alliance. In 1879 Bismarck finally chose Austria as an alliance partner for Germany. The motives which prompted him were complex, but the following were some of the factors.

(*a*) *Worsened Russo-German relations.* The Near Eastern crisis of 1877–8 (*see* XVI, 9) convinced Bismarck that Germany could no longer remain neutral in South-east European affairs and that an alliance might help German influence there.

The Tsar, irritated by the partisan support Bismarck had given Austria during the Berlin Conference, described the alliance as a "European coalition against Russia under Bismarck". He felt Germany owed Russia a favour for the help Russia had given towards the achieving of German unity. Russian troops were concentrated in Poland and Bismarck even feared a possible Russian attack.

On a personal level Bismarck and Gorchakov had disliked each other since the "war scare" of 1875.

(*b*) *Desire for a subordinate partner.* Bismarck in 1879 contemplated and then decided against a Russian alliance. He argued that the Russian character was unpredictable, and her policies too dependent on court rivalries, while on the other hand Germany could control Austria.

(*c*) *Domestic events.* Bismarck was in the process of abandoning the National Liberal Party and turning to the German clericals and the conservatives for support. He wanted a comprehensive alliance with Austria which would form perhaps the basis for a greater Germany. He would thus gain the support of the pro-Austrian elements in Germany, particularly in South Germany. It has also been observed that Germany could not afford to let the Hapsburg monarchy collapse. Austria would have returned to Germany, and so would Catholic preponderance in German affairs.

(*d*) *Fear that Austria might reach an understanding with Russia.* Bismarck also feared lest the successor to the Austrian Foreign Minister, Count Andrássy, might be pro-French or pro-Russian.

The new Austrian ministry of Taaffe was being formed at the time, backed by the Slavs and clerical supporters in Austria. (In actual fact Andrássy's successor was also anti-Russian.)

(*e*) *Belief that ties with Russia could be maintained without a formal commitment.* The German historian Erich Eyck has argued that Bismarck made a choice in 1879 not so much between Austria and Russia as between Russia and Britain, in favour of Russia. If he avoided a formal tie with Russia he would not antagonise Britain. Thus he tried to achieve the best of all possible worlds.

14. Details of the Dual Alliance. The Austrian Foreign Minister, Andrássy, secured a high price for the alliance. He knew Bismarck feared a Franco-Russian combination and had hopes of Austrian aid against France. In the end Bismarck had to accept the Austrian conditions for an alliance, which was directed against the eventuality of Russian aggression.

The alliance was signed on 7th October, the clauses being kept secret.

(*a*) By Article I each power agreed to assist the other if attacked by Russia.

(*b*) By Article II each power agreed to observe "benevolent neutrality" if her ally was attacked by a power other than Russia, i.e. France.

15. Weakness of the alliance to Germany. The chief advantage of the alliance was that, if a choice was necessary, Austria was the logical one in view of past history. The question will remain whether a choice had to be made. The Dual Alliance, even with the addition of Italy in 1882 and Romania in 1883, was not a satisfactory substitute for a German–Austrian–Russian combination. The Emperor, too, had been keen on reconciliation with the Tsar in 1879.

Defects of the agreement were as follows.

(*a*) It tied Germany to defending Austria against Russia without committing Austria to defending Germany against France. The Emperor William soon noticed this and exclaimed that this was "*partie inégale*".

(*b*) Germany received no additional security against Russia or France. Russian interests did not directly conflict with those of Germany, and Russia had indicated in September 1879 that she would remain neutral in a Franco-German war. However, after the signing of the Dual Alliance the prospects of a Franco-Russian alliance were increased, not diminished.

(c) Germany was tied to an unprogressive and disintegrating power which had almost insoluble problems in the Balkans. The alliance drew Germany into an area which Bismarck had previously avoided, and into supporting Austrian interests against Russia.

(d) The secret military agreement created an unfortunate precedent for the future. It led to increased tension in Europe and in time resulted in counter-combinations. This only diminished rather than increased the security of Germany.

16. Network of other alliances. Germany was soon involved in the following network of alliances which contributed to the isolation of France in Europe.

(a) *Alliance of the Three Emperors* (June 1881). More formal arrangements were made regarding the *Dreikaiserbund*.

(i) The emperors committed themselves to consultation and joint action if any change in the *status quo* in Turkey or the Balkans occurred.

(ii) Each power would be a friendly neutral and try to localise war if hostilities occurred between one of them and a fourth.

The Russians had been anxious for this treaty as protection against Austria in the Balkans, and to gain support should Russia wish to take action in the Straits against Britain. It was to last three years, and was renewed in 1884.

(b) *Triple Alliance* (May 1882). Italy joined Germany and Austria in an alliance (*see* XIII, **51**).

(c) *Link with Romania* (October 1882). Romania was dissatisfied with the settlement of 1878 in the Balkans (*see* XVI, **13**) and allied to Austria. Germany adhered to this.

NOTE: Austria also made a secret treaty with Serbia in 1881. This meant that for the time being Serbia would not be hostile towards German interests (*see* XVI, **15**(*e*)).

17. The Reinsurance Treaty. The *Dreikaiserbund* was not renewed in 1887, owing to Austro-Russian antagonism over Balkan affairs (*see* XVI, **20**). To hold the ring between Russia and Austria, Bismarck decided to continue the link with Russia by a separate arrangement. At the time the Russian press was actively anti-German and articles were advocating a Franco-Russian alliance.

The details of the treaty signed by Germany and Russia on 18th June were as follows.

(*a*) If either power was at war with a third party, the other would maintain benevolent neutrality and try to localise the conflict.

(*b*) Germany recognised the preponderant influence of Russia in Bulgaria, and agreed to prevent the restoration of Prince Alexander.

It was agreed that the treaty would not become operative if Germany attacked France or if Russia attacked Austria-Hungary. Bismarck had no intention of attacking France and hoped the treaty would prevent Russia from attacking Austria. The treaty did not improve Russo-German relations, which continued to remain poor. In 1888 Balkan problems forced Bismarck to publish the terms of the 1879 treaty which had pledged him to support Austria.

18. Observations on the Reinsurance Treaty. It might be wondered as to the extent to which the Dual Alliance of 1879 conflicted with the Reinsurance Treaty of 1887.

Much depended on the decision Germany made, in the event of conflict between Austria and Russia, as to which of them was the aggressor. If Austria attacked Russia, Germany could then be neutral in terms of the 1887 agreement. If Russia attacked Austria, Bismarck could help Austria in accordance with the 1879 treaty. The two agreements did not strictly conflict, but the Reinsurance Treaty was a dubious transaction. It meant that the ultimate decision rested with Germany, who was in a position to weight the scales as she thought fit. In October 1896 Bismarck revealed to the world the secret Reinsurance Treaty.

The Reinsurance Treaty not only was unethical from a moral standpoint but also did not improve relations between Germany and Russia. Bismarck at first had to keep it secret from his allies and the Tsar had to keep it secret from his people. It gave to international diplomacy an example of double-dealing. When Italy and France concluded a reinsurance treaty in 1902, in spite of their partnership in the Triple Alliance, they cited Bismarck's treaty of 1887 as a welcome precedent.

19. Critique of Bismarck's foreign policy. Bismarck tried to operate like a skilful juggler, keeping the lines of communication open to all, and making the other powers dependent on Germany. He was never as successful after 1871 as he had been in the period 1862–71, although it is true that he managed to dominate European politics, and even events outside Europe. For example, Berlin acted as the host city for the gathering to settle African problems in 1885.

Bismarck failed to gain security against France, or to solve the problem of Austro-Russian rivalry and thus how to remain on good terms with both these countries at the same time. Perhaps his best course would have been to avoid definite commitments so that he could act as a genuine arbitrator. He abandoned one tenet of his policies when he succumbed to the public desire for colonies in the 1880s. This inevitably led to conflicts with Britain.

20. General comment on Bismarck's policies. Bismarck's policies can be appreciated only if it is realised that the links between his personal political beliefs, his domestic policies and his actions abroad were very close.

(*a*) Philosophical and ideological considerations were important in framing Bismarck's foreign policy. Bismarck tended to view the future conflict in the world as one between the forces of order and stability (represented by the autocratic monarchies of Europe) and the forces of socialism and revolution (inspired by republican France). He believed, wrongly, that France was not likely to find an ally abroad so long as she remained a republic.

As a result of his outlook Bismarck looked for allies chiefly among states with a political system similar to that of Germany. He disliked the idea of having as main allies parliamentary states such as Britain or Italy, as he thought that such agreements were not likely to be either permanent or stable.

(*i*) It was not surprising that Bismarck's first agreement after 1870 was a revived Holy Alliance of the three rulers of Germany, Austria and Russia in defence of conservative principles.

(*ii*) In 1887 Bismarck warned the Tsar that if France ever defeated Germany there would be the likelihood of revolution and republicanism occurring in the latter country. The same would result if the Austrian Empire collapsed. This argument helped persuade the Tsar to sign the Reinsurance Treaty with Germany, rather than to look to France for support.

(b) Bismarck's foreign and domestic policies were closely related.

(i) Domestic affairs influenced Bismarck's decision to form the Dual Alliance with Austria in 1879. He wanted a comprehensive alliance with Austria which would help him secure increased support at home after his abandoning of anti-clerical measures.

(ii) During the war scares of 1875 and 1887, Bismarck encouraged "revanchist" agitation in France to justify the cry "The Fatherland in danger!" and the need for new military laws to be approved by the reluctant Reichstag.

21. Events leading to Bismarck's resignation. In March 1888 the Emperor, aged ninety-two, died. The long alliance which had been preserved between sovereign and minister for more than twenty-five years now ended. The Emperor's son, Frederick III, was liberal and pro-British but died in June, having reigned only ninety-nine days. His son, William II, was aged twenty-one. He was ambitious, self-willed, imaginative and determined to rule in Germany.

Differences of opinion between the Emperor and Bismarck forced the latter to resign in March 1890. At last "the pilot had been dropped". Specific points in dispute were as follows.

(a) *Foreign affairs.* The Emperor wanted to drop the Russian link, and to form friendly relations with Britain. He also wanted to accelerate colonial expansion and to start a naval programme.

(b) *Domestic affairs.* The Emperor favoured measures to conciliate the working classes and wanted the anti-socialist laws to lapse.

(c) *Personal.* In the past Bismarck had claimed a right to supervise the political actions of the Emperor. William II was determined to be an absolute ruler and considered that Bismarck was in the way.

GERMANY, 1890–1914

22. The new course. In 1890 the international position of Germany was strong, and her relations with other countries were good. Germany had close links with Austria and a network of other alliances, she was still on friendly terms with Russia and there was the prospect of an alliance with Britain (*see* **28**).

Bismarck had believed in limited aims in foreign affairs, in increasing German security against attack and in focusing his attention primarily in Europe. In contrast the new Kaiser was interested in events everywhere, and in his *Weltpolitik* he adopted a policy of unlimited goals. Though Germany increased her power after 1890, she did not succeed in increasing her security, since the following policies resulted in antagonising other states, particularly Britain and Russia.

(*a*) *The naval programme* (*see* **31**).

(*b*) *Colonialism.* During the 1890s European colonialism reached its peak. German policies in this field soon aroused the suspicions of France, Britain and Russia for the following two reasons.

(*i*) Germany's unlimited aims: the Kaiser thought Germany was a nation capable of infinite expansion. He hoped the vigorous German Teutonic stock would prove itself the dominating race of the world. Germany soon became involved in events in the Far East, Africa, the Ottoman Empire and Persia, and the Pacific.

(*ii*) Germany's methods: the government sometimes used threats and a form of blackmail to achieve Germany's aims. The various inconsistencies of policy, the suddenness with which Germany interested herself in new regions, and the character of the Kaiser, who loved display and the use of violent gestures, proved an unsettling influence in Europe. For example, the peremptory manner of Germany's intervention in Morocco in 1906 and 1911 caused other powers to unite against her.

(*c*) *Abandonment of Russian link.* In 1890 the Kaiser refused to renew the Reinsurance Treaty when pressed by the Tsar. It has been argued that this step was a logical outcome of the Bismarckian system, of which the Austrian alliance was the cornerstone. Bismarck had feared France far more than Russia. However, by refusing to make any arrangement with Russia, Germany only encouraged Russia to form an alliance with France in 1894.

After 1894 important groups in both Germany and Russia hoped that ties would be restored. The Tsar and the Kaiser remained close friends. However, Baron Fritz von Holstein, influential at the German Foreign Office from 1890 to 1906, advised against renewal of the Reinsurance Treaty, while Russia was alienated by:

(*i*) the German tariffs against Russian grain in 1902 (*see* **24**(*b*));

(*ii*) German activities in the Ottoman Empire and Persian Gulf (*see* XVI, **24**);

(*iii*) Germany's humiliation of Isvolsky during the Bosnian crisis in 1909 (*see* XVI, **32**).

(*d*) *Economic expansion* (*see* XVI, **24** and XXII, **5**).

23. Fragmented government. In theory the political system seemed strong since absolute power was with the Kaiser and his appointed officers. Germany was not a democratic country, and the franchise was restricted to favour the wealthy. Under Bismarck government was effective. After 1890 it floundered since the new ruler, Kaiser William, was weak and indecisive. He refused to delegate any extensive power to capable subordinates, and this proved disastrous. The Chancellor, Foreign Minister and General Staff were answerable only to the Kaiser and to no one else. As no serious attempt was made to guide and co-ordinate their activities, they evolved their own policies, which at times clashed seriously.

The various separate elements of the political system were as follows.

(*a*) *The Kaiser*. In addition to the normal channels of government, the Kaiser relied on a large number of personal adjutants and advisers and headed numerous unofficial civil and military cabinets and other secret bodies.

He was sincere in wanting peace, but he could not forget he was the supreme war-lord. The intemperance of his language, the unaccountability of his actions and his rash and unmeasured ambitions helped to raise the temperature of Europe. For example, without consulting anyone, the Emperor in a *Daily Telegraph* interview (28th October 1908) spoke of the strained relations between Britain and Germany. This irresponsible action caused a serious outcry in Germany.

(*b*) *Parliament*. The Prussian Landtag and the German Reichstag (formed in 1866) had been accustomed under Bismarck to leaving foreign affairs in the hands of the Chancellor, but after 1890 many government policies were criticised. However, the Parliament was not prepared to take any active responsibility for initiating alternative courses of action and had little influence in government. The majority of the people were content with the *status quo* and generally supported the government, which appeared to be realising their hopes for fresh glories through the creation of an empire and a navy.

(*c*) *The armed forces* (*see* **25**).

(*d*) *The pressure groups.* There were a number of powerful private organisations which championed various interests. Notable ones were the following.

(*i*) The Agrarian League (1894): *see* **24**(*a*).

(*ii*) The German Colonial League (1882).

(*iii*) The Pan-German League (1893). This campaigned for the incorporation of Austria, German Switzerland and the Netherlands into the Reich.

(*iv*) The Navy League (1898).

24. Domestic affairs, 1890–1914. The following policies may be noted.

(*a*) *The pseudo-liberal phase* (*1890–4*). The new Chancellor, Count Caprivi, a Prussian soldier, was moderate and conciliatory in politics.

(*i*) Tariff policies: Germany signed a series of commercial treaties with Austria, Italy, Switzerland, Spain, Romania and Russia (1892–4). These reduced import duties and therefore the price of food. Opposition came from the landowners, and the Agrarian League was formed to protect their interests.

(*ii*) Social policies: the Kaiser hoped that the workers would cease to support socialism if social measures were introduced. Anti-socialist laws were repealed and an industrial court was established in 1890 to deal with wage disputes. In 1891 factory inspection was improved, and workers were given the right to negotiate with employers on employment conditions.

(*b*) *Period of reaction* (*1894–1914*). In 1894 Prince Hohenlohe was appointed Chancellor, to be followed by Count von Bülow in 1900.

(*i*) Tariff policies: gradually the "alliance of rye and steel" was formed. Protectionists supported those industrialists who favoured increased arms expenditure in return for support for higher tariffs. In 1902 a new tariff law restored the previous high duties on foreign grains, and this alienated Russia.

(*ii*) Social policies: social benefits were gradually increased. In 1903, for example, a sickness insurance law provided for more generous help to sick workers.

(*iii*) Minorities: after 1900, more repressive measures were taken against minorities in the Polish provinces and against Alsace-Lorraine.

(*c*) *Growth of opposition and unrest.* Germany made considerable social, industrial and scientific progress after 1890 but this did not stop the growth of discontent. In the 1912 elections the Social Democrats became the largest political party in the Reichstag. By 1914 divisions between various social and income groups had become marked.

25. Militarism. The atmosphere of the Kaiser's Germany was steeped in militarism. German arms had been so successful during the period 1864–71 that victory in any future war was regarded as almost inevitable. Many writers, such as Friedrich von Bernhardi in *Germany and the Next War* (1911), encouraged the idea that war was not a crime but a test of the fitness of the individual and the State. Many aggressive acts had public support since they seemed to enhance German power and prestige.

A large officer caste exercised considerable influence at Court and in the government. This group often made decisions that reversed the policy of the Chancellor and Foreign Office or committed them to a course of action that would normally have been rejected.

(*a*) *War plans*. Until 1892 the German General Staff planned their strategy on the assumption that war would occur in the east, and that Germany might have to fight Russia in co-operation with Austria.

In 1892 Count Schlieffen became Chief of Staff. He then assumed that France was so closely tied to Russia that any war in the east would involve France too. The Schlieffen-Moltke plan contemplated a "knock-out blow" in the west against France before fighting Russia.

(*b*) *Austrian alliance*. In 1909 the General Staff, on its own authority, promised aid to Austria in virtually any contingency. This changed the fundamental character of the Austrian alliance, which was purportedly a defensive one.

The Kaiser also, without consulting the government, encouraged Austria to believe in 1908 and 1912 that "whatever came from the Vienna Foreign Office was a command for him".

ANGLO-GERMAN RELATIONS, 1870–1914

26. Introduction. When Germany became a united nation there were influential circles in Britain and Germany who hoped these countries would form closer links, being regarded as "natural allies". There seemed to be a number of ties. For example, there were linguistic and racial (Teutonic) affinities. In addition Britain had a German dynasty and had been the traditional ally of Prussia in the eighteenth century.

Anglo-German relations after 1870 form an interesting subject for study. The failure of these powers to reach a permanent accord was part cause and part effect of the growing economic, colonial and naval rivalry which grew between them. It was also a subordinate cause of the First World War.

Details of the efforts made to form an alliance are covered in 27-29 below.

27. Bismarck and Britain. During the 1870s, when Disraeli was British Premier, and in the 1880s, when Salisbury was Premier, Bismarck suggested that Britain and Germany should come to an arrangement combined with Austria. He argued rather illogically that Britain belonged with Austria and Germany to the satisfied peace-loving powers, who were being menaced by France and Russia.

However, all attempts to form an alliance failed, for the following reasons.

(a) *Differing policies towards Russia.* Russia and Britain were colonial rivals while Germany was friendly to Russia. The unwillingness of Germany to break with Russia contributed to the failure of negotiations with Britain.

On 28th September 1879 Saburov, the Russian Foreign Minister, suggested a Russo-German alliance in which Germany would be neutral in a war between Britain and Russia. Bismarck knew that such an arrangement would be compatible with an Austro-German alliance which was being planned and of which the Russians had some knowledge. It would be incompatible with an Anglo-German alliance. At this point Bismarck called off negotiations with Britain. He considered there was little to fear from Britain, since she was embroiled in colonial rivalry with both France and Russia.

(b) *Differing attitudes to France.* While Britain and France were colonial rivals there were no permanent causes for antagonism between these countries. In contrast, Bismarck found it difficult to work with the French, who vowed to regain Alsace-Lorraine. Britain, under Salisbury, was not prepared to enter into an alliance against France, only against Russia. Bismarck, on the other hand, hoped that traditional Anglo-French colonial rivalry would induce Britain to join an anti-French alliance.

(c) *Reluctance to be committed.* Both countries considered they could remain friendly with each other without the need for formal commitment. Britain was not yet ready to abandon her policy of "splendid isolation". Salisbury pleaded Britain's world interests and the necessity for every government being "dependent upon the wind of popular favour" as reasons against an alliance.

(d) *Differing political systems.* Britain had a liberal, constitutional and democratic form of government. Germany had an autocratic system with certain "democratic" features added. This would have been no barrier to an alliance had Bismarck not been inclined to view foreign affairs in philosophical terms. He liked alliances with states which were monarchical, conservative and autocratic. He disliked republicanism and democracy, particularly as it was personified by France. Britain occupied an ambiguous position.

28. Anglo-German relations, 1890–1914. The new Kaiser, William II, was the grandson of Queen Victoria. Germany in the 1890s soon became a good customer for British goods. It seemed that reasons making for closer relations were becoming stronger. In fact in 1890 an Anglo-German treaty settled many outstanding differences.

Germany dropped the Reinsurance Treaty with Russia, and it was now thought in some circles that Britain might join the Triple Alliance.

However, the German attitude towards Britain remained ambivalent. For example, while the Kaiser liked Britain and wanted to co-operate occasionally, he was also motivated by a desire to compete with Britain, and to show that Germany was a great power. Misunderstanding or dissension occurred over the following.

(a) *Asia.* In 1893 Britain asked for German support in the quarrel with France over Siam. Germany remained neutral. When Britain reached agreement with France, this was interpreted by Germany as an indication that Britain was weak and had capitulated. As a result Germany sought to work more closely with Russia and France, particularly in the Far East.

(b) *Africa.*

(i) South Africa: in January 1896 the Kaiser sent a telegram to President Kruger of the Transvaal, congratulating him on the defeat of the Jameson Raid. This caused considerable annoyance in Britain.

(*ii*) **North Africa**: it is doubtful whether Germany had any serious colonial designs here. However, her policy united France and Britain against her.

(*c*) *The Ottoman Empire and Persia.* Salisbury started his third ministry as Premier in 1896 and sought closer relations with the Triple Alliance. At a meeting during the Cowes yacht races he hinted to the Kaiser a possible partition of the Ottoman Empire. This suggestion was misinterpreted by the Kaiser and led to further misunderstanding between the two countries. It was perhaps an unfortunate remark since the Kaiser soon became a leading champion of the Ottoman Empire. German policies in the Ottoman Empire and Persia after 1896 were disliked by Britain (*see* XVI, **24**). The growth of German economic influence in the Middle East was a factor leading to the co-operation of Britain and Russia after 1907, since they saw their own interests threatened.

(*d*) *Naval affairs* (*see* **31**).

(*e*) *Trade* (*see* **24**(*b*)).

(*f*) *The* "*Daily Telegraph*" *episode* (*see* **23**(*a*)).

29. Alliance proposals. At the end of the 1890s Britain felt isolated in Europe and started to look round for allies (*see* XXI, **7**). On three occasions Britain made definite suggestions for a German alliance.

(*a*) *1898.* In March the British Colonial Minister, Joseph Chamberlain, suggested an alliance. The Kaiser tactlessly informed the Tsar of this, who in turn mentioned the earlier British overtures to Russia.

(*b*) *1899.* In November the Kaiser and his Foreign Minister, Bülow, visited Britain. Chamberlain, in a public speech at Leicester, spoke of the community of German and British interests and proposed an alliance. This raised a storm of protest, which was greater in Germany than in Britain. As a result Bülow made no effort to raise the matter in the German Reichstag in December but used the revival of hostility towards Britain to secure support for the new Naval Bill.

(*c*) *1901.* In January, when the Kaiser visited his grandmother Queen Victoria at Osborne, Chamberlain again suggested a defensive alliance.

30. Reasons for failure of alliance negotiations. Basically German statesmen were not keen on an alliance, and Holstein particularly exercised a decisive influence in ruining the alliance attempts of

Britain. Germany based much of her policy on false assumptions. Her statesmen felt that the rivalry between Britain on the one hand and France and Russia on the other would continue. They felt that Germany controlled the balance of power in Europe as arbiter between Britain and the Continental powers. Little consideration was given to the thought that the division would eventually be between the Triple Alliance and the Dual Entente, with Britain joining the latter combination of Russia and France. Negotiations were eventually dropped in December 1901 after Germany suggested that any alliance should include the Triple Alliance and be approved by the British Parliament.

The negotiations between Germany and Britain failed since it was realised there were few mutual political interests. In contrast it was found that there were many areas where their views could not be reconciled.

(a) *Europe.*

(i) Germany wanted a military ally to help her in the Balkans or against a possible attack from France or Russia.

(ii) Britain was not primarily interested in European questions, nor easily able to perform the role in Europe that Germany wanted. As Salisbury aptly remarked, her navy did not "run on wheels". In any case, Britain was not prepared to guarantee German retention of Alsace-Lorraine or support the declining Hapsburg Empire.

(b) *Far East.*

(i) Britain wanted an ally against her naval rivals Japan and the United States, and to support her to check the expansion of Russia in Asia.

(ii) Germany had been working closely with France and Russia in the Far East, and was not perturbed by the prospect of these powers quarrelling with Britain in this region. Germany was prepared to promise neutrality only if an Anglo-Russian war occurred.

(c) *South Africa.* The Kaiser gave no help to the Boers during their war with Britain from 1899 to 1902. However, German public opinion was strongly anti-British during this war. This provided an additional reason why German statesmen did not press too strongly for a British alliance.

(d) *Naval matters* (*see* 31).

31. Naval rivalry. Early after 1890 the Kaiser said that Germany's future lay on the sea. In 1895 the Kiel Canal was completed, connecting the Baltic and North Sea, a vital development for future naval power. Soon naval rivalry became the main source of contention in Anglo-German relations.

(a) *Germany starts a naval programme*. It was argued by Admiral Tirpitz that German world economic, colonial and political interests justified a large navy. German inability to exert any influence over the events of the Boer War, had she so desired, owing to British sea power, was an argument which won public support for the naval programme.

Important navy laws were passed in the Reichstag in 1898, 1900, 1906, 1908 and 1912.

(b) *Britain begins to rearm*. In 1903 British statesmen feared that Germany sought world domination. Germany not only had a powerful army but also was determined to build a navy so strong that, according to Admiral Tirpitz, even the greatest naval power, i.e. Britain, would hesitate before attacking it. The British Parliament approved the formation of a North Sea fleet based on Rosyth. For the first time naval strategists made plans in the event of the outbreak of war with Germany rather than with Russia or France.

(c) *Mutual suspicion and arms race*. In 1904 some Germans feared that Britain planned to "Copenhagen" the new German fleet. In 1904 Britain started to build a new powerful battleship, the *Dreadnought*. Germany soon followed and a competitive race took place. During 1907–9 Britain tried to slow down the arms race. However, public opinion began to panic at the spectre of a German invasion of Britain and it was feared that Germany was building "Dreadnoughts" in excess of their published figures. In 1909 economists proposed the building of four new "Dreadnoughts", the Admiralty six. However, a press campaign on the slogan of "We want eight and we won't wait" and a public outcry resulted in the government's decision to build eight.

(d) *Joint conversations in 1912*. An Anglo-German conference took place with the aim of reducing the size and number of new battleships built. The British were represented by Lord Grey and Lord Haldane. The meeting failed for the following reasons.

(i) The navy party in Germany were determined that Germany should equal or surpass British naval power. They refused to consider any suggestions for slowing down the arms race.

(ii) Germany disliked the fact that Britain and France were

co-operating closely. After the passage of the German Naval Law of 1912, Britain and France agreed to so arrange their fleets that Britain would defend the English Channel and North Sea while France would safeguard the Mediterranean. This would facilitate the passage of reinforcements from North Africa to France in the event of war.

PROGRESS TEST 10

1. Why was Prussian influence supreme in the new German Empire? **(1)**

2. Which political groups opposed Bismarck after 1870? **(2, 4)**

3. What was the chief objective of Bismarck in domestic affairs? **(3)**

4. Give reasons for the *Kulturkampf*. **(6)**

5. Give reasons for the abandonment of free trade by Germany in 1879. **(8)**

6. How did Bismarck try to undermine the influence of socialism? **(9)**

7. What general principles guided Bismarck's foreign policy? **(10)**

8. Describe the provisions of the various arrangements made by Austria, Prussia and Russia jointly between 1872 and 1881. **(11(a)–(c))**

9. Why did Germany form the Dual Alliance? What were its drawbacks? **(13, 15)**

10. In what way was the Reinsurance Treaty of 1887 a dubious transaction? **(17–18)**

11. Explain what is meant by "the new course" in German foreign policy after 1890. **(22)**

12. What problems faced Germany in home affairs after 1890? **(24)**

13. Why did Bismarck not form an alliance with Britain during the period 1870–90. **(27)**

14. Describe the various causes for dissension between Britain and Germany after 1890. **(28)**

CHAPTER XI

The Austrian Empire, 1815–1914

THE AUSTRIAN EMPIRE IN 1815

1. Unifying influences in the Empire. Cohesive forces in the multinational Hapsburg Empire were the following.

(a) *Hapsburg monarchy*. In 1520 Charles I had been elected Holy Roman Emperor. He came from one of the great European families, the Hapsburgs. By the nineteenth century their role was recognised as being as follows.

(i) The supreme bond of union: the most important link between the various parts of the Empire was the common allegiance of the people to the Hapsburgs. The Empire appeared as a large dynastic family estate, in contrast to the political unit, the modern state, which began to emerge in Europe in the sixteenth century.

Metternich recorded in his *Memoirs* that, on a visit by the Emperor Francis to Cologne Cathedral in 1818, "the people, who had forced the doors to see the Emperor, all fell on their knees instantly", while the Prussian king stood among his subjects looking "very uncomfortable". This instinctive loyalty to the Austrian House was described by Bismarck as "a garnish of medievalism".

(ii) The custodian of the imperial tradition: as a result of past marriages the dominions of the Hapsburgs covered at one time Spain, the Netherlands, Naples and parts of Germany. In the process of consolidation the crowns of Bohemia and Hungary became joined to the Hapsburgs.

The Hapsburgs had been the rallying bulwark of Christendom against the Turkish Islamic invasions.

(b) *Roman Catholic Church*. The throne kept close ties with this Church, which had as members some three-quarters of the population. Its influence among the masses was aimed to instil in them a spirit of unquestioning semi-religious loyalty to the Emperor.

(c) *Aristocracy*. The nobility had a monopoly on social,

political and economic leadership, which helped hold the Empire together. Its members came from numerous national groups. Many of the nobility were descendants of warriors who had come to Central Europe to help the Hapsburg Catholic cause during the Thirty Years War in the seventeenth century. They were cosmopolitan in outlook and their loyalty to the dynasty outweighed other loyalties.

(*d*) *Centralised bureaucracy.* During the eighteenth century government became centred on Vienna. Most of the Civil Servants believed it their purpose to fight forces of decentralisation, local patriotism and aristocratic privilege.

(*e*) *Armed forces.* Members were drawn from all nationalities.

(*f*) *Economic links.* Examples were trade and communications.

(*i*) The industrial districts of the German and Bohemian provinces exchanged their manufactured goods for foods and raw materials from Hungary and Galicia.

(*ii*) Most of the Empire was linked by the Danube and eventually by a railway network reaching out from Vienna.

2. The Empire's heterogeneous character. Russia and Prussia had alien peoples, but they were mostly in the border regions. In contrast the Central European plains had been subject to the constant movements of peoples since the decline of the Roman Empire. When they had settled, the tribal groups became interwoven. However, there was never a general process of assimilation.

The Vienna settlement of 1815 made the Austrian Empire more compact by giving her Italian territory to replace the Austrian Netherlands (Belgium). However, this did not make for greater internal unity. Her 30 million people differed in racial origins, historic background, customs and language.

The Austrian Empire constituted a collection of peoples, an association of eleven nationalities. In 1815 the territorial sections and the nationality of the people were as follows.

(*a*) *Austria* – entirely German (accounting for 23 per cent of the population of the Empire in 1910).

(*b*) *Hungary* – Magyar (20 per cent), with minorities of Slovaks, Ruthenes and Germans.

(*c*) *Bohemia and Moravia* – chiefly inhabited by Czechs (12 per cent) with minorities of Germans and Slovaks.

(*d*) *Galicia* – mainly Poles (10 per cent) and Ruthenes.

(*e*) *Transylvania* – Romanians.

(*f*) *Illyria and Dalmatia* – Serbs, Slovenes and Croats.

(*g*) *Lombardy and Venetia* in northern Italy – Italians.

3. The chief nationalities. In terms of population and power the Germans and Hungarians were the most important groups in the Empire.

(*a*) *German dominance.* The Hapsburgs were a German dynasty. German was the official language, and the chief one in business and the cities (not only in Vienna but also in Budapest and Prague). Germans filled most of the positions in the imperial bureaucracy and were influential in most large towns.

(*b*) *Special position of Hungary.* The privileged position of the German race was challenged in time by the strongest of the subject nationalities. The Magyars had always insisted that they recognised the Hapsburgs as their kings, never as their emperors. In 1791 the Hungarian Diet forced Leopold II to acknowledge the special position of Hungary. The Diet was dominated by the nobility and Latin was used as the only acceptable lingua franca.

DOMESTIC AND FOREIGN AFFAIRS, 1815–48

4. The Austrian problem in 1815. Austria's greatest concern was one of adjusting and balancing the desires of her diverse peoples in such a way as to preserve the unity of the Empire. Austria was more vulnerable than other countries (Turkey excepted) to the impact of the ideas of the French Revolution. Claims for autonomy or independence from Viennese control on grounds of nationalism, liberalism or democracy created manifold problems. Emperor Francis once remarked that his realm resembled a "worm-eaten house" and that "if one part is removed, one can never tell how much will fall".

Metternich's friend Gentz commented that "the end of the Turkish Empire could be survived by the Austrian but for a short time". Metternich believed revolution would come soon enough but that his role was to delay it as long as possible.

Complications to the Austrian problem were as follows.

(*a*) *The struggle between the dominant nationalities and races.* Magyars and Czechs wanted more recognition of their rights at the expense of the Germans.

(*b*) *Conflicting allegiances.* German minorities in Bohemia felt the pull of allegiances both towards the Austrian Empire and towards Germany.

Many Slavs (Croats, Serbs and Poles) and Latins (Romanians and Italians) wanted to join members of their race or nationality who formed an entity outside the Empire.

5. The philosophy of Metternich. Prince Metternich, a man of high rank, was by upbringing a Rhinelander. He was educated at the universities of Strasbourg and Mainz. He was wealthy and had abundant self-confidence. In 1809 he became Chancellor or Chief Minister. This post carried special responsibility for foreign affairs. Metternich was the leading personality of Europe during the period 1815–48, and was described as the "Prince of Diplomats". It was perhaps understandable that his views were representative of the nobility and autocratic monarchs of the day. The following were the main tenets of his beliefs.

(*a*) *Monarchy*. The prime duty of government, he believed, was the preservation of law and order. This was best achieved under a monarch who united his subjects by a common bond of loyalty.

(*b*) *Conservatism*. He regarded progressive ideas as presumptuous, unsound and selfish, only likely to change "daylight into darkest night".

(*c*) *Autocracy*. He disliked liberalism, nationalism and democracy, ideas popularised during the French Revolution. He believed in absolute rule and disliked any thoughts of social equality. The only form of equality he believed in was equality before the law.

(*d*) *Cosmopolitanism*. He regarded himself as belonging to a class rather than a country. He carried out his daily work in six languages. In 1824 he told the Duke of Wellington that Europe had long been his fatherland.

6. Foreign policy. With the decline of the Ottoman Empire, and therefore of the Turkish threat to Europe, in the eighteenth century and the rise of nationalism in the nineteenth, another role became necessary for the Hapsburgs.

Austria was vitally interested in events in Central and Eastern Europe because of the size, character and geographical position of her empire. The supreme mission or aim of Metternich became the preservation of order and the *status quo* in Central Europe, which was conceived as the best method of maintaining the survival of the Austrian Empire. He sought to achieve this in the following two ways.

(*a*) *By co-operation with other European powers*. Metternich believed in joint consultation to solve European problems. With

Castlereagh he was a prime mover in the origination of the Conference System and the Quadruple Alliance (*see* III, 13).

This policy was successful so long as there were common interests. During the 1820s Britain ceased working closely with Austria. A further complication was the interest of the Tsar Alexander I in liberalism and his desire to support the subject nationalities in the Ottoman Empire.

(*b*) *By the alliance of the three eastern powers.* When the European concept began to collapse after 1818, Metternich relied on his powers of influence to wean the Tsar and the Prussian king away from liberalism.

Metternich made use of the Holy Alliance agreement concluded between the three eastern monarchs of Austria, Russia and Prussia to achieve his aims. He was able to convert it to a reactionary, conservative coalition to oppose threats to the established autocratic monarchical order in Central Europe and for joint co-operation elsewhere. Examples of this co-operation were:

(*i*) the support of the French action in Spain in 1823;

(*ii*) the prevention of intervention by the western powers in Italy in 1830;

(*iii*) the suppression of the Polish revolt in 1830;

(*iv*) the preservation of the *status quo* in the Ottoman Empire after 1833. At Münchengrätz the three monarchs reaffirmed their belief that a sovereign threatened with revolution had the right to call on them for help.

NOTE: Metternich's policies towards Germany, Italy and the Ottoman Empire are covered in detail elsewhere (*see* VIII, 6; XIII, 3; XIV, 20(*b*) and 27(*b*)).

7. Methods used by Metternich. Metternich relied on his own personal diplomatic skill and charm and the resources of the Austrian Empire to implement his policies.

He was backed by a loyal bureaucracy, the Roman Catholic Church and the secret police. He set up a special office in Vienna for opening, decoding and researching all correspondence to help in censoring all progressive political ideas. Metternich was not averse to the use of troops if other methods failed. Thus Austrian troops were used to suppress the Naples revolt of 1821 and to aid the Pope in 1832. He also applied the time-honoured Hapsburg principle of keeping control, namely divide and rule (*see* 8).

8. Policy of divide and rule. The Hapsburgs preserved their authority by diverting the attention of particular groups who were agitating against Vienna to other groups who were making conflicting demands. This policy was designed to keep the nationalities together by inciting them against each other. In the general confusion the Emperor and his government would maintain control as mediators. The policy proved successful during the events of 1848–9. It was also applied to the German Confederation (*Bund*) after 1815 and to the Galician revolt in 1846 (*see* **11**(*c*)).

(*a*) Demands by dominant aristocratic groups (Germans, Magyars or Poles) for independence could be checked by Vienna's reliance on the support of the following.

(*i*) The peasants who preferred remote and benevolent Hapsburg rule to the absolute control of local landlords.

(*ii*) Minority national groups such as Czechs and Slovaks in the German area, Ruthenes in the Polish area, and Croats and Romanians in Hungary.

(*b*) Liberal and democratic movements from below implied a direct challenge to the order of society. Vienna could then rely on the support of the dominant aristocratic groups.

(*c*) Non-German movements for liberalism or national independence united the Germans against them. The latter feared the loss of aristocratic privileges or the influential positions they had.

(*d*) National groups were used to check each other by being sent, when in the army or government, to administer or garrison other territories.

9. Domestic administration. Until 1805 Francis II had been assisted by a minister who had direct control over the various departments of government. After this, Francis ran domestic affairs directly himself, while allowing Metternich wide powers in foreign affairs.

(*a*) *Government was inefficient.* Hartig once remarked that "administration has taken the place of government".

(*i*) There was no co-ordinating body over the various elements of government.

(*ii*) Government machinery was extremely complicated. Adherence to protocol resulted in excessive delays in decision-making and volumes of paper work.

(*iii*) Few reforms were permitted. The motto of Francis was

"Rule, and change nothing". Useful suggestions on fiscal and tariff reform, etc., were pigeon-holed.

(b) *Metternich failed to achieve reforms.* If the Empire was to survive, Metternich believed some changes were necessary. However, few of his constructive ideas were accepted. He once said that he had "sometimes governed Europe, but never governed Austria".

Count Kolowrat, a Czech, became Minister of State in 1826. He hated Metternich and succeeded in undermining his influence in home affairs. In 1832 the Emperor combated Metternich's suggestion for a new constitution. Metternich urged on Francis for more than twenty years the need for a Reichsrat and suggested that provincial Diets should send delegates to one. In 1834 Francis agreed at last to call a central Reichsrat to consider the budget and laws, but he died in 1835 before this could be done. Unable to get reforms from his successor Ferdinand, who was epileptic and morally weak, Metternich went back resignedly to "propping up mouldering edifices".

10. Assessment of Metternich's policies. He succeeded in securing peace during the period 1815–48, and in making Austria ascendant in European affairs. He also taught European statesmen the importance of international co-operation. The problems of the "ramshackle" Austrian Empire were all too obvious, the answers none too clear. However, Metternich made little effort to find alternatives to undiluted absolutism in foreign affairs. He had a consuming fear of France, revolution and progressive ideas. He was cynical and resigned to what he regarded as the inevitable, the collapse of the old order. His ideas were consequently unoriginal and negative, his policies aiming at achieving short-run stability and ignoring the prospect of long-term ruin.

He made little effort to formulate new paths, or to utilise his abilities to see if a heterogeneous state such as Austria could possibly benefit by the new "winds of change", liberalism and nationalism. Napoleon once aptly remarked that "he mistook intrigue for statesmanship".

11. Reasons for unrest in the Empire, 1815–48. The nobility held the monopoly of the higher official posts in government. They were exempt from taxation and owned most of the land. Provincial estates, representing the privileged groups, rarely met. They were jealous of their rights, and resented advice from Vienna and resisted demands for change from the people. The basis of the economy was agriculture. A large proportion of the people were peasants, living under conditions similar to those of the serfs in Russia, forced to pay onerous dues and labour services to their local lords.

One basic problem was the opposition of the emperors to any attempt to reform the administration and government structure. Thus little attempt was made to cope with the problems which have already been outlined (*see* 4). As a result agitation soon increased in various parts of the Empire. Important areas were the following.

(*a*) *Hungary, Italy and Austria.*

(*b*) *Bohemia.* A Czech literary movement revived. In the 1840s attention was turned to the demand for constitutional rights. The Czech movement was weakened by the existence of a strong German minority in Bohemia.

(*c*) *Galicia.* Polish inhabitants wanted independence but displayed intolerance towards the Ruthenian minority.

In 1847 Polish landlords demanded greater rights. The Austrian government replied by encouraging the Ruthenian peasants to massacre their landlords, promising them freedom from *robot*, or statutory labour.

12. Growth of unrest in Hungary. After 1815 the Emperor Francis tried to rule in Hungary without summoning the Diet. Resistance on the part of the nobles to certain tax and recruiting decrees issued by Vienna forced the Emperor to summon the Diet in 1825. He agreed that in future he would not levy taxes without its consent, and that it was to meet once every three years. Soon the following liberal and national movements developed.

(*a*) *Magyar movements.* In 1840 the Diet managed to get Magyar substituted for Latin as the official Hungarian language. Various groups formed in the Diet, composed of the nobility. They all favoured the maintenance of the dominant position of the Magyars over the minorities in Hungary. The groups in the Diet were as follows.

(*i*) The moderates, under Count Stephen Széchenyi, who aimed at a cultural renaissance, the economic development of the country, a closer union with Austria and the abolition of some of the privileges of the nobles to help the peasants. His plans received little support from Vienna or from the lesser nobles. However, they did result in some economic improvements after 1825.

(*ii*) **The extremists, under Louis Kossuth:** in 1832 the lesser nobles found a leader in Kossuth, a journalist. He soon divided the nobility into two camps by his radical views. He advocated parliamentary rule and autonomous institutions for Hungary, which would have involved almost complete separation from Austria.

(*iii*) **The liberals, under Francis Deák:** in 1847 the liberals returned a large majority to the lower house of the Diet. They agreed on a compromise programme of ten points (later known as the March Laws). This demanded liberal and constitutional concessions from Vienna and recognition of Hungary's rightful position of autonomy within the Empire. Deák undertook negotiations with Vienna, but deadlock resulted.

(*b*) *Minorities' movements.* An independent Illyrian and Slavonic movement developed, centred on Agram. These minorities, owing to Hungarian oppression, supported Austria.

13. Growth of Austrian liberalism. Though publications in Austria were subject to a strict censorship after 1815, liberal publications were secretly introduced from abroad. University professors were allowed a fair degree of intellectual freedom. In Lower Austria and particularly Vienna the educated classes began to agitate for constitutional changes before 1848. This movement was strengthened by the growth of a middle class and an industrial working class anxious to take part in politics.

Some of the more radical liberals considered that the Austrian Empire would survive only if a decentralised federal system was introduced, with democratic rights and autonomous rule for the various provinces. This was the hope particularly of Dr. Fischhof, of the University of Vienna, who played an important role in the first and second Viennese revolts in 1848 (*see* **14** and **20**(*b*)).

THE REVOLUTIONS OF 1848–9

14. Turmoil in Vienna. The February revolution in Paris and the speech of Kossuth in Hungary on 3rd March (*see* **16**) encouraged the opponents of Metternich's regime in Vienna to press for reforms. Business and professional groups combined with workers, peasants and students in demonstrations, and petitions were made to the Emperor. The 76-year-old Metternich was abused by reformers outside his home, and clashes with troops occurred. To avoid the outbreak of violence, the Emperor

Ferdinand asked Metternich to resign on 13th March. Metternich fled to Britain, and by 15th April Ferdinand had granted a number of concessions. These included a free press and a liberal constitution. A volunteer National Guard was also permitted.

In May the government tried to reassert its authority but was faced by a demand for universal suffrage from the students. On 15th May the National Guard refused to intervene on the government's behalf, and the Emperor fled secretly to Innsbruck on 17th May, afraid to trust his own troops.

15. The Prague revolt. On 11th March some moderate Czechs and Germans met in Prague to urge liberal reforms, such as linguistic equality and the abolition of *robot*. The movement was harmed by extremists of both groups, which resulted in internal divisions.

(*a*) *Some Czechs* called for a responsible ministry, a parliament and all the lands that had belonged to St. Wenceslas, which included Bohemia, Moravia and Silesia.

(*b*) *Some Germans* supported the *Grossdeutsch* idea. The Germans of Bohemia sent deputies to the German Parliament at Frankfurt.

(*c*) *The Bohemian leaders*, in retaliation, on 2nd June, opened a Slav congress at which allegiance to the Hapsburg dynasty was reaffirmed. To them the *Grossdeutsch* movement seemed a greater menace than the Hapsburgs. The Czech Palacký commented that, "if the Austrian Empire did not exist, it would be necessary to create it".

The flight of the Emperor led to a rising by the Czechs on 13th June. Windischgrätz, the Austrian commander, bombarded Prague and forced it to surrender on 17th June.

16. Events in Hungary. On 3rd March, in the Hungarian Diet at Pressburg, Louis Kossuth demanded the abolition of serfdom and a constitution making Hungary entirely independent, save only for the link of a common king-emperor. These demands resulted in what became known as the March Laws.

On 11th April Ferdinand confirmed Hungary as a separate state. Kossuth abolished feudalism and gave land to the peasants, but he made it clear that no racial privileges would be given to the Serbs, Croats or Romanians. He demanded a ruthless Magyarisation policy. The Diets of Croatia and Transylvania were summoned to vote their own dissolution. This senseless action only created allies for Vienna.

17. Austrian aid to Croatian resistance. Hungary rejected requests for autonomy from the Croatians, who retaliated by electing Jellačić to lead the resistance. When the Emperor's advisers heard that Hungary would not provide troops for the Italian campaigns, they decided to recognise Jellačić as Ban (Governor) of Croatia.

The Hungarians persuaded Ferdinand to dimiss Jellačić in May, but the Austrians continued to follow the policy of divide and rule. Though Jellačić was officially dismissed, the Court privately backed him when he ignored the imperial dismissal. In June Count Latour, the Minister of War, sent secret aid from Vienna to Croatia for use in a future war against Hungary.

18. Divisions in the Austrian Assembly. In July the Constituent Assembly of the western provinces met in Vienna. Its object was to draw up a constitution based on universal suffrage. On 7th September it abolished feudal obligations and *robot*. On the important issue of future territorial boundaries, no agreement could be found. The two broad divisions were as follows.

(*a*) *The radical Germans who proposed the Grossdeutsch solution.* They urged support for the Frankfurt Assembly and recognition of autonomy. This would enable Austria to sever connections with her outer provinces and to join a greater Germany when unified.

(*b*) *The opponents of the German radicals.* These included:

(*i*) Czech, Slovene and Ruthenian minorities, hostile to both Germans and Magyars;

(*ii*) German liberals;

(*iii*) the aristocracy and upper bourgeoisie, whose economic and social interests lay in a united Empire.

19. Kossuth's appeal rejected. On 11th September Jellačić invaded Hungary. Though he was driven back, the situation remained critical for the Hungarians for a time, since the Croats were supported by the Serbs, Slovaks and Romanians. Kossuth appealed to the Constituent Assembly for help, assuming that it would contain a German majority and that the two "master races" would stand together. However, the Slavs and the German liberals combined and managed to secure a majority for the rejection of any idea of aid for Hungary. This suited the Austrian government, which was likely to regain control if the various groups demanding concessions quarrelled amongst themselves.

20. Events in Austria. The Austrian government was gradually gaining the upper hand, since the Czech rising had been suppressed and Radetzky had been victorious in Italy, reoccupying Milan on 6th August. The Emperor had felt it safe to return to Vienna on 12th August.

Subsequent events were as follows.

(a) *Aid to Jellačić against Hungary.* The government felt that after the victory of the opposition in the Assembly it would not be hampered by any pro-Hungarian movement in Vienna. Count Latour ordered grenadiers to assist Jellačić against Kossuth. Austria declared war on Hungary on 3rd October.

(b) *Second Viennese rising.* The action of the government precipitated another mass rising in Vienna, led by the liberals, radicals, students, artisans and unemployed. They supported the idea of both a national Germany and a strong, autonomous Hungary. In the riots the Minister of War was lynched. The Court fled once again, this time to Olmütz, on 7th October. It was followed by the Czechs and moderate Germans. The Assembly adjourned to the Moravian town of Kremsier on 22nd October.

(c) *Surrender of Vienna.* In early October, Jellačić and his forces were driven from Hungary. He advanced into Austria and on 31st October helped Windischgrätz bombard Vienna into submission.

(d) *New ministry.* In November a new ministry under Felix Schwarzenberg, the brother-in-law of Windischgrätz, was formed. He had been adviser to Radetzky in Italy.

(e) *New emperor.* The Emperor Ferdinand had been compromised by his acceptance of an autonomous Hungary in the March Laws of 1848. In December he was persuaded to abdicate in favour of his nephew, the eighteen-year-old Francis Joseph. At his accession, the new emperor issued a manifesto stating his aim as being to unify the Empire.

(f) *Kremsier constitution.* The Austrian Reichstag completed its work on 1st March 1849. The Kremsier constitution provided for a decentralised federal form of government. It was regarded by many as offering the last chance for a healthy reorganisation of the monarchy.

(g) *New compromise constitution.* Schwarzenberg dissolved the

Reichstag and allowed Count Stadion, Minister of the Interior, to issue, on 4th March 1849, a new constitution. It included liberal features, so that German princes who might be attracted by the *Kleindeutsch* solution for Germany (*see* VIII, **16**) would believe Austria was seriously liberalising her system. It was an interim measure to rally Czech and German support until the Hungarians had been defeated.

21. Features of the constitution. Notable points were as follows.

(*a*) *Centralism.* There was to be one citizenship, one law and one administration throughout the "single and undivided Empire of Austria".

(*b*) *Liberalism.* There was to be a parliament at Vienna, based on universal suffrage. The government, though chosen by the Emperor, was to act under a Prime Minister and be responsible to Parliament.

(*c*) *Organisation.* All areas were to be governed from Vienna. Thus the special position of the Magyars was not recognised.

(*i*) Certain areas such as Hungary were permitted a degree of communal autonomy and the recognition of linguistic and national rights.

(*ii*) Areas containing mixed populations such as Galicia were divided into crown lands. German language and law became the basis of all official transactions.

22. Hungarian Republic proclaimed. During the winter of 1848–9, Hungary owed its safety to the slow tactics of Windischgrätz. Jealousy between Görgei and Kossuth prevented the former from establishing control over the Hungarian army until March 1849. The proclamation of the new Austrian constitution drove Hungary into open rebellion. The Hungarian Republic was declared on 14th April with Kossuth as president.

In April Görgei moved swiftly upon Windischgrätz and defeated him at Isaszeg on the 6th. Jellačić was also forced back. In May Görgei recaptured Budapest. Hungary then failed to take decisive action, being undecided as to the best course to take.

23. Russian intervention. Austria began to look for allies. As French troops were involved in an expedition to Rome, on 21st April Austria appealed for help to the Tsar. The Tsar answered this appeal for the following reasons.

(*a*) To prevent revolution in his Polish territories. Russia wished to intervene before revolution spread to its Polish territories. Already close relations had been established between the Poles and the Magyars since:

(*i*) Poles were fighting in the Hungarian army and many were prominent as generals;

(*ii*) Hungarian divisions had been stationed near the Galician frontier to encourage the Poles to revolt against Austria.

(*b*) To preserve the principles of autocracy and monarchy that Austria represented.

24. Results of Russian intervention. These were as follows.

(*a*) *Defeat of Hungary.* Hungary was pressed on three fronts, by Haynau, the new Austrian commander who had relieved Windischgrätz, Jellačić from the direction of Zagreb, and the Russians. Görgei decided to surrender to the latter at Vilagos on 13th August. Kossuth fled to Turkey, burying the Hungarian crown near the frontier, and then to the United States.

(*b*) *Defeat of the revolution.* Austrian recovery from the throes of revolution and internal upheaval was accelerated. She was able to resist further reforms. Haynau earned himself the nickname of "Hyena" for his policy of repression in Hungary. At the end of 1851 the constitution which had been given in April 1848 was rescinded.

25. Reasons for the failure of the revolutions. At one time the Austrian Empire was on the verge of total collapse. It survived owing to the following factors.

(*a*) *Loyalty of Austrian armies.* In Galicia Count Stadion prevented any Polish uprising, while Radetzky was successful in Italy and Windischgrätz, the imperial commander, checked the Prague and Vienna risings.

(*b*) *Lack of concerted action among the nationalities.* The rebels had no clear plan of action and did not co-ordinate their actions in different parts of the Empire. It was difficult to get any agreed definition of territorial boundaries. There were divisions in all the areas of revolt.

(*i*) Vienna (*see* **18**).

(*ii*) Prague (*see* **15**): differences between Germans and Czechs prevented joint action.

(*iii*) Budapest (*see* **22**): in proclaiming Hungary's own independence, the Magyars were not willing to concede autonomy to their own subject races. Thus the various Slav nationalities decided to remain loyal to the Hapsburgs. In May 1848, at Blas in Transylvania, the Romanian nation decided always to remain faithful to the Emperor.

(*iv*) *Galicia*: among the Slavs, the Poles did not want equal rights with the Ruthenes.

(*c*) *Policy of divide and rule*. Until Hungary was defeated, Austria was prepared to make concessions elsewhere. The Hapsburgs were able to survive by juggling successfully with the component parts of the Empire.

To divert pressure from Vienna, Austria exploited the following differences.

(*i*) Between the nationalities: Austria encouraged resistance by the Czechs to the Germans and by the Slovaks and Croats to the Magyars.

(*ii*) Between the classes: there were two groups which gave little support to the second Viennese rising. Middle-class liberals feared for the safety of property, and Bruck's plan for a wider German Zollverein was aimed to attract their support. Concessions to the peasants through the abolition of *robot* (7th September 1848) secured their loyalty.

THE YEARS OF INTERNAL
REORGANISATION, 1849–67

26. Domestic alternatives. Various choices were open to the Hapsburg monarchy in planning the reorganisation of the Empire after the upheavals of 1848–9, and each of the possible policies had influential advocates. The alternatives were as follows.

(*a*) *Return to status quo ante*. This meant a return to the situation prior to March 1848, when the feudal aristocracy had played the dominant role in the provincial Diets and the traditional conservatives had held power at Court. This was never seriously considered.

(*b*) *Liberalism*. German and Czech liberals favoured the idea of a limited regional autonomy, though there would be a single central parliament (Reichsrat), a single citizenship and a unified administration. German financiers also wanted real democratic concessions in the form of parliamentary control over policy.

(*c*) *Federalism*. This would involve the separation of the nationalities, which would be united under the personal authority of the Hapsburg Crown. There would be common institutions for defence, foreign policy, finance, etc. The Kremsier Assembly had advocated in March 1849 a form of federalism. Though popular among nationalists in Bohemia, Hungary, etc., there was the problem of mixed areas. For example, in 1848, the Magyars had disliked giving rights to minority groups.

(*d*) *Centralised equality.* This was advocated by the bureaucracy and powerful monarchists such as Schwarzenberg and Alexander Bach. This method was tried to some extent during the period 1848–59.

27. A mixture of alternatives. Unfortunately the new emperor, Francis Joseph, disliked abstract principles and long-range plans. He was not prepared to support any one idea wholeheartedly and sought to reach a compromise which embraced some of the advantages of the various alternatives without being committed to any of them. The object was to find the solution which would provide maximum peace and security for the Austrian Empire with the minimum concessions from the government.

Since these compromise solutions invoked opposition from various quarters, Francis Joseph never stayed with one arrangement for very long before embarking on another. Eventually, after experimenting with various constitutions, the Dual Monarchy became the final pattern (*see* **38**).

28. Liberal measures revoked. The revolutions produced two positive results in the abolition of the feudal privileges of the nobility and of the serfdom of the peasantry.

Soon Francis Joseph felt that his power had been sufficiently consolidated to enable him to pursue reactionary policies. In December 1851 he officially opposed any plan for constitutional government and assumed absolute control, though he accepted an Imperial Council, the function of which was to offer advice. When Schwarzenberg died in April 1852, no successor was appointed. Francis Joseph acted as his own Prime Minister for the remainder of his reign.

29. The Bach system. Alexander Bach, the Minister of the Interior, believed that the modernisation of the Empire could best be achieved by the standardisation of all administrative procedures, without regard for national or linguistic differences, backed by the effective use of government power. No devolution of power was allowed. The Bach system was a continuation of the policies planned by Schwarzenberg of centralised authority shorn of the liberal trimmings of Stadion. It was based on the army, the bureaucracy and the Catholic Church.

Official communications had to be in German. Though reforms were made in education, this was soon subject to increased religious control. A new Concordat of 1855 allowed the Roman Catholic Church greater influence in education and the daily life of the community. A stringent press censorship was introduced in 1852.

30. Repression in Hungary. Hungary was reduced virtually to the status of an "Austrian province". It was administered by state officials, many of them Czechs, who became known as "Bach Hussars". Bach was unsympathetic towards Magyar patriotism, which had left Hungary one of the most backward countries in Europe. He was determined to enforce his ideas ruthlessly and had no qualms about backing up officials with soldiers and gendarmes. The Diet was abolished. When the tariff barrier was removed between Austria and Hungary, the Empire became the greatest trade area in Europe outside Russia.

31. Growth of unrest. The policies of Bach resulted in apathy in intellectual circles as a result of restrictions on all political activity. The national minorities became increasingly embittered about the curbs on freedom and about the government's policies of centralisation and enforced Germanisation.

Many Germans complained about the increased taxation necessary for the vast administrative expenditure of the government. Though the early 1850s had been a period of economic progress and prosperity, the Austrian economy was weakened by the military cost of the occupation of the Danubian principalities during the Crimean War in 1856 and by the economic recession of 1857.

32. Change in policy. In 1859 Francis Joseph decided to abandon centralised absolutism and Bach was dismissed.

(a) *The Laxenburg Manifesto.* On 23rd August this manifesto set out the government's new programme. It promised that:

(i) government expenditure would be submitted in future to effective control;

(ii) non-Catholic religions would be allowed autonomy and freedom of worship;

(*iii*) many duties of the Austrian government would be transferred to autonomous bodies.

(*b*) *Enlargement of the Imperial Council.* In March 1860 thirty-eight members were added to the Imperial Council from the various *Landtags*, though it was to remain only advisory.

(*c*) *The Majority Report.* Some of the new members, drawn largely from the aristocracy, representing the leading nationalities, Hungarians, Bohemians and Poles, supported by the Croats, made a recommendation known as the Majority Report. It was suggested that the monarchy should take into account "the historic-political individualities of its various components". This report was opposed by the Slavs such as the Serbs and Ruthenes, and also by the Romanians.

33. The October Diploma. The Emperor was assured by the aristocracy that the nationalities would remain loyal if the Imperial Council and the old provincial Diets were restored. Count Szeczen, leader of the Hungarian contingent on the enlarged Imperial Council, was commissioned to draft a constitution. This was issued on 20th October 1860 and closely followed the recommendations of the Majority Report. Its provisions were as follows.

(*a*) The Crown was to exercise its legislative powers with the co-operation of the *Landtags* or Diets in provincial matters and the Imperial Council in general matters.

(*b*) Organs of local self-government were to be restored in Hungary, and analogous institutions were to be created in other "historic provinces" such as Transylvania and Croatia.

(*c*) Communal elections were to be held.

34. Rejection of the Diploma. The scheme of Szeczen satisfied nobody, though he had hoped it would be accepted by Hungarian nationalists as a basis for bargaining.

(*a*) The Slovaks, Serbs and Romanians resented being sacrificed again to the Magyars.

(*b*) The Diploma disappointed the aristocrats who had recommended the Majority Report, since the central Austrian government insisted on retaining power through the bureaucratic machinery.

(*c*) The bureaucrats attacked the revival of archaic aristocratic institutions.

(*d*) The Germans and Hungarians objected to the concessions made to the other nationalities. Also, both groups opposed the Diploma for the following reasons.

(*i*) The Germans disliked the preferential treatment accorded to Hungary. If the latter could be regarded as a single constitutional entity, why not Austria?

(*ii*) The Hungarians demanded restoration of their own constitution.

35. The February Patent of 1861. Francis Joseph then turned to the bureaucrats and appointed Anton von Schmerling to provide a constitution. The result of his work was a compromise between bureaucracy and liberalism.

(*a*) The Imperial Council became an elected parliament or Reichsrat. Its powers were weak. Taxes could be levied without its consent and it had little control over ministers.

(*b*) The provincial Diets lost their legislative powers. Their main function was to act as electoral colleges to send representatives to the Reichsrat.

(*c*) German ascendancy in the Diets and Reichsrat was assured by four grades of electors in the voting system which gave greater weight to the towns.

(*d*) Francis Joseph retained control over the army, the executive and the finance departments. The bureaucracy remained the effective agent of government.

36. Rejection of the Patent. The Germans and Czechs generally supported the Patent, though the old conservative aristocracy disliked their loss of influence. The non-German elements vehemently rejected it, the main opponents being the following.

(*a*) *The Magyars.* The new Hungarian leader, Francis Deák, pointed out that Hungary had always been a separate nation, united with Austria simply in the person of the sovereign. It was entitled to a constitution of its own and not to a "granted" one. Hungary refused to send any delegates to the Reichsrat until the March Laws of 1848 were restored. Schmerling dissolved their Diet and sent the "Bach Hussars" once more to Hungary, putting the country again under bureaucratic rule.

(*b*) *The Croats.* The Croats were dissatisfied since they had never been rewarded for their help in 1848 by having Dalmatia added to Croatia as Jellačić had hoped. Their Diet was also dissolved.

37. Austro-Hungarian relations. By 1865 Austria was on the verge of serious conflict with Prussia over the question of German leadership. Criticism from the Reichsrat convinced the Emperor that he must never become fully associated with German liberalism. In July he dismissed Schmerling and appointed a government under Count Belcredi as Chancellor. The latter was keen on a federal scheme which would include negotiations with Hungary. Deák was persuaded to remain loyal to Austria during the Austro-Prussian War and not to exploit the situation to the advantage of Hungary.

When Austria was defeated at Sadowa, Hungarian extremists hankered after independence. This was resisted by Deák, who believed that Hungary had grown great only through her link with Austria. He was supported by Count Gyula Andrássy, who believed that Hungary could remain great only if the Magyars predominated over the Slavs and were allied with an Austria which the Germans dominated. Only by retaining a connection with Austria could Hungary stand up to the Slav elements within her portion of the Empire, the Serbs, Croats and Slovaks, and also the Romanians.

THE DUAL MONARCHY

38. The Ausgleich. In 1867 arrangements were completed for transforming the Hapsburg monarchy into a dual monarchy. This settlement (*Ausgleich*) represented a compromise between federalism, centralisation and liberalism.

(*a*) *Unifying links.* Austria and Hungary were to be completely independent, but were to be united in the following ways.

(*i*) The two territories were to have the same ruler. Francis Joseph remained as emperor in Austria and the northern provinces, including Bohemia. He was for the first time formally crowned King of Hungary.

(*ii*) Joint ministries were to be established for foreign affairs and military and naval matters.

(*iii*) Annual delegations from the two parliaments were to be empowered to decide on matters of common interest.

(*iv*) A decennial treaty was to regulate tariffs, currency, military matters, etc.

(*b*) *Constitutions.*

(*i*) Austria: the Germans were to dominate the other

peoples through a constitution based on the February Patent. Equality of rights in linguistic matters was granted to the other nationalities.

(*ii*) Hungary: the March Laws of 1848 were restored and these permitted the Magyars to dominate the other nationalities. Magyar jurisdiction now covered the South Slav states and Transylvania.

39. Czech agitation. In 1868 the Bohemian Czechs demanded the same rights as the Magyars. They wanted the Kingdom of Bohemia restored and Francis Joseph crowned in Prague. Thus the Emperor was soon seriously considering federal ideas, and the possibility of a triple monarchy.

In September 1871 Francis Joseph was on the point of conceding the wishes of the Czechs. However, he was dissuaded by the Austrian Germans and the Magyars, who feared that concessions would stir up demands from Slavs in Hungary. The Czechs, the third-largest ethnic group in the Empire, had by this time replaced the Magyars as the most vocal and discontented section. They retaliated by boycotting the imperial and provincial parliaments until 1878.

40. Consequences of the Ausgleich. For a time renewed strength was given to the ailing Empire through the strengthening of the links of the two strongest elements, the Germans and the Magyars.

In the long run the Dual Monarchy contained the seeds of decay. Austria had relinquished all rights to control the non-Austrian sections of her empire. The Magyars were not prepared to recognise the rights of subject nationalities within their sphere, and increased agitation from Slavs within and without the Empire as a result of severe Magyarisation policies involved the European powers in Balkan affairs. After the Franco-Prussian War of 1870, Austria abandoned any hope of recovering her position in Germany. She became increasingly entangled in supporting Hungarian policies in South-east Europe. The resultant clashes with Russia, protector of the Slavs, were a contributory factor to war in 1914.

41. Magyarisation policies. Francis Deák took measures, as he had promised, to reconcile the non-Magyars to the political changes. The Croats were given a large measure of autonomy in 1868 and the Croatian language was encouraged. Only foreign affairs remained the concern of the Hungarian Diet. By the Law of Nationalities of 1868 Magyar became the official language in government and parliamentary proceedings for the sake of unity, but in the county assemblies, courts of law and schools the use of other languages was permitted.

However, as the influence of Deák in politics waned, the above legislation remained largely a dead letter. The Magyars attempted to break down the individual differences of subject nationalities, for example, by the following means.

(a) An electoral law of 1874 concentrated the vote almost entirely in Magyar hands.

(b) Slovak cultural organisations were dissolved in 1875.

(c) By about 1905, the number of Slovak schools had been reduced from over 2,000 to 241.

42. Downfall of the liberals. In the Austrian section of the Empire the German liberals were in power. They passed a number of progressive measures such as those reforming court procedures, abolishing church control of schools and establishing compulsory elementary education.

The Emperor was annoyed with the liberals, since they opposed the Austrian occupation of Bosnia and Herzegovina (see XVI, 13(a)). He therefore decided to appease the subject nationalities in order to gain their support against the German liberals. Count Edward Taaffe, the master of political improvisation and compromise, became Premier in 1879. He persuaded the Czechs and other nationalities to join with the German conservatives and clericals in a parliamentary bloc known as the "Iron Ring".

43. Concessions to minorities. Taaffe rewarded the Czechs and Slavs for their support by making a number of concessions during his ministry of 1879–93. Naturally these were opposed by the Germans and Magyars.

(a) *Concessions to Czechs.* The Czechs disliked the fact that in Austria the electoral arrangements ensured the predominance of the Germans in Parliament and political life. Gradually their grievances were met by the following measures.

(i) An electoral law was passed which assured them a majority in the Bohemian Diet and the Bohemian delegation to the Reichsrat.

(ii) The University of Prague was divided into two institutions – one German and one Czech.

(*iii*) German ceased to be the sole official language, Czech also being permitted.

(*b*) *Concessions to Poles.* In Galicia the Poles, though a minority, obtained control of the Diet. They continued to oppress the Ruthenes.

44. Growth of further agitation. Owing to Taaffe's political skill the Empire had a period of relative calm. However, he could not stifle the nationalist strivings of the subject peoples. After his fall in 1893 agitation increased and more aggressive organisations were formed, such as the Young Czechs. The Pan-Slav movement, which advocated a union of all Slavic peoples, gained in strength.

Soon increased opposition also came from the Germans and Magyars. The Germans were not very satisfied with the political arrangements in any case. Since 1867 they had lost their overriding authority in the Empire, and they could not gain full control over their own affairs, owing to the continuation of strong executive power in Vienna. Some Germans began to look increasingly to the new united Germany for leadership. Two leaders of German agitation were the following.

(*a*) *Georg von Schöner.* He preached doctrines of German racial superiority, anti-Semitism and Pan-Germanism, and he advocated that the Prussian monarchy should be the leader of all Germans.

(*b*) *Karl Lueger.* He was mayor of Vienna from 1897 to 1907 and made his city a showpiece of municipal socialism. He formed the Christian Socialist Party, which combined the aims of clericalism, anti-capitalism and anti-Semitism. He drew wide support from the urban shopkeepers and artisans, who felt threatened by big business and suspicious of Jewish activities. Among those attracted to his ideas was Adolf Hitler.

45. The road to universal suffrage in Austria. The one point on which all political parties were agreed was the need for the extension of the franchise. In 1897 the new Premier made suffrage reforms and in 1901 further concessions were made to the Czechs. It was stated that all state officials had to know both German and Czech.

Unrest still continued. Soon heated debates took place in the Austrian Reichsrat, and disturbances made it difficult for business to be carried on. When the Emperor dissolved the Reichsrat a period of crisis in government took place. Realising that changes were necessary, the Emperor in January 1907 introduced universal manhood suffrage for those over the age of twenty-four, and he ensured that national minorities had adequate representation. However, the Reichsrat still had little control over administration.

46. Austro-Hungarian relations, 1867–1906. After 1867 Hungary gained the better terms in negotiations with Vienna. This reflected the Emperor's determination to keep on friendly relations with the Magyars. It was thus difficult for the Austrian government to adopt positive measures of reconciliation with its own minority nationalities, for this would have resulted in the minorities in the Hungarian sphere also demanding a fairer deal and would have made relations between the two halves of the Empire worse than ever.

Sources of contention between Austria and Hungary were the following.

(a) *Economic.* The Magyars wanted greater economic independence. Both Hungary and Austria wished to retain the tariff between the two countries. However, Hungary gained advantageous terms for her agricultural exports to Austria. She was not prepared to allow Austrian manufactured goods an equivalent advantage in Hungary.

(b) *Joint services.* The Austrians disliked the fact that Hungary contributed less than a third to the cost of the jointly provided services such as those providing for defence and the diplomatic corps. The Magyars wanted:

(i) control over their foreign relations;
(ii) a separate Hungarian army.

(c) *Language.* The Magyars wanted the use of their language in the Hungarian part of the Dual Monaichy. This was firmly opposed by the Emperor as he believed the safety of the Empire depended on the use of only one language in the army.

47. Unrest in Hungary, 1906–14. In Hungary, as in Austria, though to a lesser extent, the forces of nationalism developed. At the same time Magyar demands for concessions from Austria increased the general atmosphere of unrest.

(a) *Breakdown in relations with Austria.* Opposition to Francis Joseph grew after the defeat of Istvan Tisza, leader of the moderate Liberal Party, in the Hungarian elections of 1905. This led to a constitutional crisis.

In 1906 the Hungarian Parliament was overthrown by the troops. The country was governed for a short while by Viennese government officials aided by the Croats. To restore normal Austro-Hungarian relations Francis Joseph had to subdue the Magyar nobles by threatening to:

    (*i*) encourage Croatian independence;

    (*ii*) close Austrian markets to Hungarian corn;

    (*iii*) introduce universal suffrage in Hungary.

These threats eventually broke down the resistance of the magnates in April 1906. The old partnership was resumed. Hungary continued to contribute contingents to the common army, and in return the magnates were allowed to preserve their supremacy.

(*b*) *Opposition of the minorities to Magyar rule.* The Emperor did not force the Magyars to introduce universal suffrage in Hungary after 1907. This only increased resentment among the subject nationalities, particularly in the following areas.

    (*i*) Croatia: serious unrest had already occurred in 1902. The government tried to break the Croats' resistance by encouraging the Serbs against them.

    (*ii*) Transylvania: there was a serious irredentist movement among the Romanians. The Magyars tried to suppress it, which resulted in ill-feeling in Romania proper.

Count Tisza, who became Prime Minister in Hungary in 1913, was eager to reach an understanding with the minorities. However, he rejected any proposal for universal suffrage, for this would have given the subject nationalities a voice in politics (the Magyars numbered only 6 million out of a population of 15 million). It would also have enabled the lower classes to challenge the domination of the Magyar aristocracy.

48. Foreign affairs. The foreign policies of the Austrian government after 1867 are covered elsewhere. In particular note the following:

(*a*) *Foreign relations generally.* The relations between Austria and the following countries were particularly important:

    (*i*) Germany (*see* X, **13**);

    (*ii*) Russia (*see* XVI, **8, 25** and **29–30**);

    (*iii*) Serbia (*see* XVI, **26**(*c*) and **27**).

(*b*) *Austria's interests in the Balkans* (*see* XVI, **26**). Note that, in addition to the Triple Alliance, Austria was involved in the Mediterranean agreements (*see* XVI, **20**(*d*)).

PROGRESS TEST 11

1. Mention the chief unifying influences in the Austrian Empire. **(1)**

2. List the various nationalities in the Empire. Which were the major groups? **(2, 3)**

3. What was the main domestic problem in 1815? **(4)**

4. Discuss the policies and outlook of Metternich in foreign affairs. **(5–7, 10)**

5. Explain the policy of "divide and rule". **(8)**

6. Why did Metternich fail to secure domestic reforms? **(9)**

7. Trace the growth of unrest in the Austrian Empire in the 1840s. Where were the important centres? **(11–13)**

8. Why was the Czech revolt ineffective in 1848? **(15)**

9. What were the March Laws? Assess the role of Kossuth in Hungarian affairs between 1832 and 1849. **(12(a), 16, 19, 22)**

10. Why was it difficult for the Assembly which met in Vienna in 1848 to secure agreement among its members? **(18)**

11. Why did the second Viennese rising occur? Why was the Emperor Ferdinand urged to abdicate? **(20(b), (e))**

12. Account for the defeat of the Hungarians in 1849. **(22–24)**

13. Were the revolutionaries responsible for their own lack of success during 1848–9? **(15–19, 25)**

14. Which political system probably had the best chance of general acceptance among the nationalities in 1849? **(20(f), 26(c))**

15. What solutions were put forward to solve Austria's domestic problems? **(26–27)**

16. Why was Francis Joseph in 1859 forced to abandon the policy of undiluted repression in home affairs? **(29–31)**

17. Describe the attempts of the Emperor to secure constitutional reform during the period 1859–62. **(32–35)**

18. Why did the *Ausgleich* in 1867 fail to solve the problem of securing unity within the Empire? **(38–40)**

19. Account for the persistence of unrest within the Austrian Empire after 1893. **(44–47)**

CHAPTER XII

Russia, 1801–1914

DOMESTIC AFFAIRS, 1801–56

1. The character of Alexander I. Alexander I became Tsar in 1801 after the murder of Tsar Paul. In his youth he had been influenced by the liberal ideas of his Swiss tutor, César Laharpe, a disciple of Rousseau.

Alexander had a paradoxical character, and was given to fits of sudden enthusiasm which soon waned. He was self-willed, also indecisive, unstable, impressionable and changeable in behaviour. He was torn between liberalism and the traditions of Russian autocracy. In Russia the Romanovs were absolute in every sense of the word: power was rarely delegated to ministers to the extent practised in other countries. Alexander therefore vacillated between the desire to make the world free and the natural instinct to acquire as much personal power as possible. His influence in foreign affairs has already been discussed (*see*, for example, III, 3(*c*) and 15).

One of his advisers, Speransky, confessed that Alexander was "too weak to rule and too strong to be ruled".

2. Tentative liberalism. Alexander began his reign by granting an amnesty to all political prisoners and exiles. He abolished torture and repealed the prohibition of foreign books.

In 1803 the first step was taken to abolish serfdom when landowners were empowered to free their serfs. This was largely ignored, though serfdom was abolished in Estonia and a few other non-Russian provinces. The sale of serfs as a substitute for army recruits was abolished. Alexander also founded several schools and three universities.

In 1807 Alexander asked Speransky to draw up a comprehensive system of constitutional government. However, the only one of Speransky's suggestions which was enacted in 1810 was that of the Council of State. This was composed of ministers appointed by the Tsar to draft new laws and watch over the legality of administration. Speransky's proposal for representative

central and local assemblies was not adopted partly owing to the
opposition of the nobles, who had also disliked the 1809 proposal
for an examination test for higher promotion in government.
Alexander did not want to antagonise the nobles as he needed
their support for his wars, for example, the Third Russo-Turkish
War (*see* XIV, **14**). As a result, consideration of reforms was
shelved in 1809.

3. Reaction. After 1815 Alexander continued to consider the
possibility of liberal reforms but in practice he became increasingly conservative. Metternich did his best to frighten the Tsar
out of any liberal notions (*see*, for example, IV, **11**(*a*)).

Alexander never carried out a proposed codification of the law
and became apathetic about other reforms. Secret societies began
to form after 1817. Disturbances at home and abroad led
Alexander to pursue reactionary policies. Russians were no
longer allowed to study abroad and a strict censorship was
imposed. Secret societies were suppressed, and restrictions
imposed in Poland and Finland.

4. Disputed succession. Alexander died on 13th December 1825.
There was misunderstanding as to the succession, for in 1822
Alexander's brother Constantine had renounced his claims in
favour of his younger brother Nicholas. This arrangement had
been kept secret. Nicholas refused to accept the throne in 1825
until he had received further confirmation from Constantine.

5. The Decembrist conspiracy. During the interval of general
uncertainty revolts occurred. They were half-hearted, ill-planned
and easily suppressed by Nicholas on 26th December. Harsh
reprisals against the rebels followed.

The two groups of army officers and liberals involved were as
follows.

(*a*) *The northern group*, under Colonel Muraviev, aimed at a
federal constitutional monarchy. About 3,000 troops mutinied
and called for "Constantine and a constitution".

(*b*) *The southern group*, under Pestel, aimed to establish a
democratic, centralised Jacobin republic and to call for the
freeing of the serfs and land reform.

6. Policy of Nicholas I. Nicholas was conscientious and devoutly
religious. He had previously been an army commander. His

domestic policies included both reactionary and progressive measures.

(a) *Repressive measures.* Nicholas's basis of government was the three principles of orthodoxy, autocracy and nationalism. This meant adherence to the state religion, unquestioned obedience to the Tsar and loyalty to the government. He was the enemy of liberalism at home and abroad.

The major bulwark of Nicholas's system was the army, the bureaucracy and the notorious Third Section. This secret police force had been re-established in 1826, having been previously abolished by Alexander. A rigid censorship was imposed on all writings. Suppression moved a stage further with the creation of the Buturlin Committee in 1848 to censor the censors.

(b) *Mild reforms.* Some changes were made which would have been useful if they had been strictly enforced. Some technical institutes were founded, the currency was improved, the first Factory Acts were passed, and punishment by the knout was abolished. A summary of Russian laws was compiled but no attempt was made to modernise them.

Nicholas was aware of the need to abolish serfdom to curb unrest, but nothing effective was done as he was afraid to weaken the privileges of the nobles who were the basis of his power. However, the following points may be noted.

(i) In 1841 the callous practice of the auctioning of serfs was forbidden.

(ii) The conditions of the state serfs were improved.

(iii) The future Alexander II was given the task of presiding over committees to consider the serf problem.

The government gradually came increasingly into debt as a result of numerous wars. In 1853 the National Debt was nearly £144 million. New loans had to be floated.

7. Growth of unrest. Gradually there developed numerous opponents to Tsarism. The rigid censorship displeased the intellectuals and nobles who had seen the growth of liberalism and democracy in the West. Returning to Russia, many of the younger elements became dissatisfied with the regime. Numerous conspiratorial societies started which had varied aims. Some people wanted to abolish serfdom, and to have a free press and a constitutional monarchy. Others favoured more radical steps such as the assassination of the royal family and the creation of a republican dictatorship. Socialism of a peculiarly Russian kind was preached by Alexander Herzen.

The serfs were subject to harsh punishments and long working hours, both on the farms and in the factories. Various outbreaks of violence occurred.

The following two opposing cultural schools of thought developed among those people who desired change.

(a) *The Westernisers.* They argued that Russia should follow as much as possible the heritage of the West in political, social and intellectual matters.

(b) *The Slavophiles.* They argued that Russian culture was superior to that of the West. They wanted to follow a road independent of western influences.

ALEXANDER II AND DOMESTIC REFORMS, 1856–81

8. Reasons for reform. Nicholas died in December 1855. The new Tsar, Alexander II, was by nature conservative like his father. However, he succeeded to the throne in the midst of the Crimean War, when Russia was burdened with financial debt and faced unrest at home and defeat abroad.

The Crimean War showed up the weakness of Russia, and Alexander quickly realised that fundamental reforms were needed. Out of a total population of 60 million, 46 million were serfs. Industry was little developed. There were only about half a million industrial workers, and most of them went back to the land at harvest time. Ninety per cent of the export trade was in foreign hands. There were only three railways and none near the Crimea. Government officials were badly paid and often corrupt.

9. Reforms of Alexander. Alexander II was known as "the Liberator" for the changes which were made as a result of his encouragement. At the time of his coronation in September 1856, a manifesto was issued granting pardon to political prisoners. Unpaid taxes were cancelled, and recruitment to the army was suspended for three years. Subsequent reforms had effects in the following fields.

(a) *Education.* A new university code restored autonomy to the universities, which were expanded and liberalised. In 1864 improvements were made in secondary education, which was made available for all who passed the necessary examinations

Books which had previously been censored were allowed to be published. Scholars were given grants to travel abroad.

(b) *Industry.* Some progress was made. Railways were greatly extended and grain exports trebled. Industrial development took place.

(c) *Agriculture.* This involved the Edict of Emancipation of Serfdom (*see* 10).

(d) *Local government* (*see* 12).

(e) *The law and the army* (*see* 13).

10. Abolition of serfdom. On 30th March 1856 Alexander said to the Moscow nobility that it was "better to abolish serfdom from above than to await the time when its abolition would begin from below without action on our part". The only group of nobles which accepted the Tsar's invitation to propose measures of reform, the Lithuanians, suggested that serfs could be allowed to buy land. Most of the nobles refused to co-operate at all, though some were prepared to give the serfs their freedom but not to allow them to have land. The Tsar was aware that radicals and socialists insisted that the land belonged to the serfs who worked it.

Reform might have failed but for the determination of the Tsar, and for the efforts of many members of the Court and the Civil Service. After many years of intensive work a compromise arrangement was made between the two extreme viewpoints. The provisions of the Edict of Emancipation of February 1861 were as follows.

(a) *The serfs were to be freed.* Serfs were to be free to marry, to own property and to engage in business. They were to be free from all services, payments and obligations to their former masters. These reforms were not put into effect immediately.

(i) The 22 million peasants in private ownership were to be freed after a period of two years had elapsed.

(ii) The 18 million state serfs were to be freed after five years had elapsed. Thus they had to wait until 1866 to benefit by the measure.

(b) *The serfs had to pay for their land.* The details were as follows.

(i) The government gave the landowners financial compensation for the land sold to the peasants. This was in the form of bonds bearing 5 per cent interest.

(ii) To reimburse the Treasury the government allowed the

peasants to buy the land from the nobles by a series of redemption payments over forty-nine years.

(c) *The serfs were to be placed under the control of village communes.* It was believed that the freed serfs would not be able to run their own lives at first. Thus their personal freedom was restricted by the rules of the commune which held title to the redeemed land. The commune distributed land among the peasants according to the size of their families.

11. Consequences of emancipation. The following important results should be noted.

(a) *Emancipation led to increased agitation (see* **14–15**).

(b) *The position of the peasantry was not greatly improved.* The serfs had believed that the land belonged to them. They felt it was unfair to have to pay the landowners for it. The Edict, rather than alleviating the poor conditions of all the serfs, actually increased the poverty of some of them.

(i) Many peasants were soon in debt as a result of the need for heavy payments. Their condition was not improved by high taxation and frequent famines.

(ii) Many peasants actually had less land than before the Edict was passed. Land was distributed according to the size of the family. Further, those peasants who were poor chose to take an allotment one-fourth of the size of a full holding since it could then be obtained at no cost.

(iii) Many peasants sold their land to the more successful farmers and moved to the towns.

(c) *Complementary changes were made.* As emancipation inevitably involved a complete change in the social and legal system of the country, other reforms were made (*see* **12** and **13**).

12. Local government. In 1864 local government, previously under the control of serf-owners and crown officials, was reorganised. New district and provincial assemblies (*zemstvos*) were created. Members were elected by a system which favoured the land-owning nobles but the townsmen and peasants also had a voice. The *zemstvos* were essentially aristocratic bodies, and could always be overruled by the officials who had to implement the programmes. Their functions concerned primary education, public health and hospitals, outdoor relief, welfare and charities, maintenance of roads and bridges, and the fostering of local industry. They had no control over police.

In 1870 a similar system was introduced into municipal government in the towns. The old patrician system was replaced by self-government under councils elected by the propertied classes.

13. Legal and military reforms. Extensive reforms were carried out in both these areas.

(*a*) *The law.* Legal reform was necessary when nobles could no longer punish serfs. In November 1864 the archaic, corrupt inquisitorial system of justice was replaced by one modelled on western ideas. Special provisions were made, however, in Poland and certain other areas. The following were some of the details.

(*i*) Judicial proceedings were made public.

(*ii*) The emancipated classes obtained equality before the law, uniform procedures being introduced.

(*iii*) Juries were created for the more serious criminal cases.

(*iv*) Judges of the higher courts were declared to be independent of the government and irremovable except by the decision of a court of law.

NOTE: The government continued to imprison "political" prisoners without trial and to put pressure on judges. However, the new system was superior to the old. The only drawback to the spread of the new system was the shortage of trained lawyers, but in time the legal profession attracted many able men.

(*b*) *The army.* Improvements were gradually introduced, of which the following are examples.

(*i*) The more brutal forms of punishment were abolished in 1861.

(*ii*) Military colonies were abolished.

(*iii*) The army ceased to be used as a form of harsh punishment for criminals.

(*iv*) Universal military service was introduced in 1874. In future conscripts were not to come exclusively from the lower classes. The term of active service, which earlier had been reduced from twenty-five to fifteen years, was further cut to six years.

(*v*) Conditions of life in the army were improved and basic education made available.

14. Growth of agitation. Alexander soon found to his surprise that his reforms resulted only in increased unrest. Once reforms had been started, the people wanted more. Agitation grew among the following groups.

(a) *The peasants.* They had hoped that the Edict of Emancipation would be the first stage towards greater economic and social freedom. Thus the shortcomings of the Edict and the incompleteness of the reforms led to increased discontent. In time this took the form of rioting and revolutionary agitation.

(b) *The liberals.* They wanted a parliament. However, Alexander was determined to maintain autocratic rule. He thus denied the educated Russians the reform most urgently desired.

(c) *Former political opponents.* As a result of Alexander's reforms political enemies emerged from Siberia or secret hideouts. They encouraged reckless and sometimes unjust criticism of the government. Educational improvements and relaxation of the censorship supplied disgruntled elements with means to agitate against the government.

15. Return of reaction. The position of the Tsar seemed to be imperilled by the criticism and agitation. He was also shaken by the Polish rebellion of 1863 and the attempt on his life by the fanatic Karakosov in 1866. These developments frightened him into abandoning further liberalisation measures and embarking on reactionary policies.

Censorship of the press was restored, and many privileges granted to educational and local government institutions were modified. Government control of the universities was restored to stop the spread of socialist ideas, and science was dropped from the syllabuses to prevent the spread of atheism. In 1868 the powers of the *zemstvos* over taxation were reduced, and local Tsarist agents took over control of their activities.

As terrorism increased, so reactionary measures became more stringent. In February 1878 a woman shot unsuccessfully at the Prefect of Police in St. Petersburg. At her trial she was acquitted by the jury. After this trials of political offenders were transferred to a court martial without a jury.

16. Opposition movements. Movements which drew substantial support were as follows.

(a) *Populism.* A characteristic Russian form of socialism, called Populism, gained support at the end of the 1860s. Its advocates wanted to solve the land question to the satisfaction of the peasants. It was argued that the adoption of the communes and other peculiarly Russian institutions would enable Russia to advance into socialism without having to go through a stage of capitalism as in the West.

In 1874 the Populists donned peasant garb and went to the country to convert the peasantry to their ideas. They were unsuccessful. Under the leadership of Michael Bakunin, Peter Lavrov and Nicholas Chernyshevsky they organised the "Land and Liberty" secret society in 1876. The government took alarm and suppressed the movement, treating it as revolution.

(b) *Nihilism.* After the collapse of Populism many radicals adopted Nihilism, a peculiar Russian form of anarchism. Inspired by Bakunin, it rejected all traditional values and institutions. He wanted to organise a conspiracy in Russia and abroad to overthrow the State, and started a campaign of terror and violence. In 1879 the society "Will of the People" was formed, which hoped that by assassinating government leaders it would produce chaos or frighten the government into making concessions.

(c) *Liberalism.* The liberals wanted the adoption of a constitution. They were further estranged from the government when a constitution was granted to the new Bulgarian state in 1879 (*see* XVI, 16).

(d) *Pan-Slavism.* The unsatisfactory outcome of the war with Turkey in 1878–9 broadened the base of popular discontent. The Pan-Slavists in particular became extremely critical of the government for its failure to complete the work of liberating the Balkan Slavs from Turkey (*see* XVI, 13–14).

17. Moves towards conciliation. Several attempts were made to kill the Tsar. In 1880 Alexander appointed General Loris Melikov to solve the problem of domestic unrest. Melikov was popular, since he was renowned for the capture of Kars from Turkey in 1878. In February 1880 he was made head of a commission to combat Nihilism, and in August he was made Minister of the Interior. He released hundreds of prisoners and in many cases commuted the death sentence.

Melikov urged the Tsar to grant the people some share in government. He believed that this would kill Nihilism or at least gain the support of the liberals. On the morning of 31st March 1881 the Tsar finally agreed to call a committee to consider reform. This was to be composed of representatives of the *zemstvos* who would co-operate with the Council of State in discussing new laws and the question of a constitution. Before anything could be achieved Alexander was killed on the afternoon of the same day by a bomb thrown by a terrorist.

THE ERA OF REACTION AND REVOLUTIONARY ACTIVITY, 1881–1906

18. Continuation of repression. Alexander III (1881–94) and Nicholas II (1894–1917), the son and grandson of Alexander II, were narrow-minded and of limited intelligence. Nicholas II was religious and did not have the strength or determination of his father. Under both Tsars, policies of repression were strictly enforced and increased the agitation of the people for reforms and freedom.

Alexander III submitted himself to the political guidance of his former tutor and jurist, Constantine Pobyedonostsev, who was a reactionary Slavophile and a chief lay official of the Russian Orthodox Church. Melikov was forced to resign and no efforts were made to carry out the late Tsar's promise of a constitution.

The Russian people as a whole suffered from heavy political restrictions, but the following groups were affected more than others by the repressive policies.

(*a*) *Non-Orthodox religious groups.* Pobyedonostsev was the main inspiration behind the new militant religious policy of Alexander III. Loyalty to the State was identified with loyalty to the Orthodox Church, and attempts were made to crush other religions. Two of the groups which suffered from religious persecution were the following.

(*i*) The Jews, after centuries of harsh treatment, gained concessions from Alexander II. They were prominent in business, education and the professions. Under Alexander III the government began to curb their political and social rights. It tolerated and sometimes promoted anti-Jewish riots, known as *pogroms*. In 1891 thousands of Jews were evicted from Moscow and hustled into ghettos in the interior.

In 1903 the system hardened, encouraged by the police. The aim was to distract the fury of the peasants from Tsarism to the Jews. The police benefited through their ability to elicit "protection money" from Jews in their districts.

(*ii*) The Roman Catholics in certain areas were unable to hold government posts.

(b) *National minority groups.* In the 1890s a deliberate policy of Russification of the 40 million non-Russian peoples was embarked upon. No Poles, Finns, Ukrainians or Armenians could hold government posts. Two of the areas which had their political rights curtailed were the following.

(i) Finland had its own parliament and constitution which the Tsar as grand duke was supposed to uphold. Alexander III attacked their liberties and in 1899 Nicholas II issued a manifesto which abrogated the constitution. The Finns protested but a petition signed by some half a million of them was simply ignored. After 1905 Finland recovered her autonomy, and though she lost it again before 1914, she retained some vestiges of her independence.

(ii) Estonia and Livonia had their local liberties suspended.

19. Economic progress. Russia had immense resources but remained a poor country for many years as they were not developed. The government was uninterested in industrial development, and feared it as a disruptive force.

A change occurred when Sergei de Witte was made Minister of Finance and Commerce in 1892. He argued that Russia could not remain a great power unless the government sponsored and guided economic progress. The government was soon persuaded to adopt policies which increased industrial production.

Some of de Witte's achievements were connected with the following.

(a) *Foreign loans.* Loans came particularly from France to pay for necessary imported equipment. To pay the interest on its debts the government imposed indirect taxes which fell heavily on the peasantry.

(b) *Railway expansion.* Before 1892 the rate of Russian rail-building had been less than 400 miles per year. For the next few years it increased to about 1,400 miles per year. The most important line was the Trans-Siberian Railway, begun in 1891 and completed in 1902. It reduced the time and cost of travel to the Far East by half.

(c) *Industrial advance.* De Witte argued that if Russia remained chiefly agricultural she would be dependent on other states. He felt she ought to be self-sufficient and advocated extensive protection and concentration on development in the oil, cotton, iron, steel and machine industries. Coal production doubled in ten years.

De Witte was responsible for nationalising the liquor traffic, establishing the gold standard and implementing a number of Factory Acts.

20. Growth of political groups. The government's repressive measures incurred the anger of a large body of intellectuals, students and non-Russian or non-Orthodox groups such as the Jews. Industrial progress led to the rise of a wealthy middle class which wanted to share in government. The Industrial Revolution in Russia led to overcrowding and appalling slum conditions in towns and factories. Workers had long hours and poor wages, and soon joined the ranks of the discontented.

The main groups which developed in opposition to Tsarism were as follows.

(*a*) *The Social Democratic Party.* Marxism attracted those disgruntled revolutionaries and reformers who were disenchanted with Populism. Marx claimed that a socialist revolution had to base itself on the industrial workers, and not on the peasantry. A society had to pass through a capitalist stage before socialism could be reached.

In 1898 nine representatives of Marxist groups met at Minsk. Under George Plekhanov they formed the Social Democratic Party, which was the forerunner of the Communist Party. In 1903 the party split into the following two groups:

(*i*) the Bolsheviks ("Majority" men), led by Nikolai Lenin, who favoured a dedicated élite with tight discipline to lead the way to revolution;

(*ii*) the Mensheviks ("Minority" men), who acquired this name since they failed to win support for the idea of looser party control and for a transitional period of co-operation between liberals and socialists.

(*b*) *The Social Revolutionary Party.* This was formed in 1901 and was inspired by the earlier Populist movement. It included many students and was mainly concerned with the peasant problem, advocating the nationalisation of the land. Its methods were those of terrorism.

(*c*) *The Union of Liberation Party.* This was formed in 1903. It was composed largely of intellectuals, members of the liberal professions and *zemstvo* workers. Its aim was to establish a liberal constitution.

21. Period of unrest. Plehve, the able but reactionary Minister of the Interior, was murdered in July 1904. Defeats inflicted by

Japan on Russia during the war of 1904–5 showed the inefficiency of the Tsarist regime and made change inevitable. In November 1904 Prince Mirski, Minister of Home Affairs, said that the *zemstvos* "might be given greater freedom of action". This encouraged the liberals to demand a number of fundamental rights.

In January 1905 a peaceful procession of some 200,000 people, led by the priest Father Gapon, went to the Winter Palace Square in St. Petersburg to present a petition to the Tsar. When the demonstrators refused to disperse and knelt in the snow, the soldiers were ordered to fire and many in the procession were killed. The incident became known as "Bloody Sunday".

Strikes and general unrest followed, culminating in October in wholesale agitation and stoppage of work. The crew of the battleship *Potemkin* mutinied, ostensibly because of a load of maggot-ridden meat. The sailors scuttled the ship in a Romanian harbour.

22. Political concessions. The outbreak of general unrest induced the government to attempt a policy of conciliation. Nicholas realised that, until he could recall his best troops from Manchuria, concessions would have to be made or he would lose his throne.

A manifesto was issued in October 1905 which promised a constitution, and an elected parliament (*Duma*) with real legislative power. Freedom of the press and speech was granted, and also religious toleration. This led to the following developments.

(*a*) *Increased opposition by the Social Democrats*, who rejected the concessions. They tried to organise another strike. This failed and further unrest in December was suppressed by the army.

(*b*) *A split in the liberal group.*

(*i*) The moderates who accepted the concessions became known as the Octobrist Party.

(*ii*) The progressives became known as the Constitutional Democratic Party, or "Cadets". They wanted further reforms.

RUSSIA AND THE DUMAS, 1906–14

23. The Fundamental Laws. Before the First Duma met, the government passed the Fundamental Laws in May 1906. Much of the value of the political concessions was lost as a result of the provisions of these laws.

(*a*) The Tsar was to retain most of his autocratic powers. For example, he would control the executive, the armed forces and foreign policy.

(b) The legislative power was to be divided between the following bodies.

(i) The Duma.

(ii) An upper house, the "Council of Empire". Its consent was necessary before laws could be passed. Half the members were to be appointed by the Tsar.

(c) The government could legislate by decree when the Duma was not in session.

24. The Dumas. Certain points should be noted concerning the history of the Dumas.

(a) *The First Duma*. This met in May 1906. The "Cadets" were the largest group. They were disappointed by the Fundamental Laws and they demanded that ministers should be made responsible to the Duma, that the upper house should be reformed and that the crown lands should be given to the peasantry. The government disagreed. Eventually the deadlock was ended by the dissolution of the Duma in July.

(b) *Viborg Manifesto*. Some of the "Cadets" left for Finland and issued a manifesto urging people to pay no taxes until some reforms had been achieved. However, this found little support in Russia. The "Cadets" in Finland were forbidden to seek re-election.

(c) *The Second Duma*. The government used pressure at the elections to prevent radicals being elected. Despite this, when the new Duma met in March 1907, at least a quarter of the members of the lower house were revolutionary agitators. This was due to the participation for the first time in the elections of the revolutionary parties. The "Cadets" were reduced from 150 to 123 members. The Social Democrats had fifty-four members and the Social Revolutionaries thirty-five. The reactionary groups at Court forced the dissolution of the Second Duma within three months.

(d) *New electoral law*. The franchise was then altered to increase the representation of the propertied classes. This worked to the detriment of the peasants and workers and the national minorities.

(e) *The "Loyal" Dumas*. New elections for the Duma returned a conservative majority composed largely of landowners and industrialists. The strongest party was the "Octobrists", who had accepted the Tsar's manifesto of October 1905. Only fifty-four "Cadets" and a handful of socialists remained of the once large government opposition. In 1913 the Third Duma was replaced by the Fourth Duma.

25. Domestic reform. The Duma co-operated with Peter Stolypin, Premier from 1906 until his assassination in September 1911, in various reform measures which gave Russia a period of relative tranquillity. He was a conservative who hoped Russia would cease revolutionary agitation if well-planned reforms were made. Reforms were therefore carried out in the following areas.

(a) *Land-ownership.* An agrarian law ended the communal (*mir*) system of landholding, provided that the majority of the members of each commune wanted this. Each peasant could then receive his own share of the land in private ownership. By 1914 one in four peasants had their own land.

(b) *Welfare.* In 1912 schemes of accident and health insurance were introduced.

(c) *Miscellaneous.* These included the improvement of educational facilities and *zemstvo* reform.

Stolypin's successor, Kokovtsev, was unable to overcome the opposition of the Tsar to political reform and was dismissed in January 1914 for protesting against the baneful influence in politics of the dissolute monk, Gregory Rasputin, a friend of the Tsarina.

RUSSIA AND POLAND

26. The new Polish political system. In 1815 the Tsar permitted Poland freer institutions than existed in Prussia and Austria at the time. Alexander I considered his Polish experiment to be the prelude to the introduction of similar reforms in Russia, but the latter were never realised.

(a) *Poland was to be an independent kingdom*, in permanent union with the Russian Empire. The main political link was to be in the person of the ruler. The Tsar was to be the King of Poland.

(b) *Poland was granted a constitution*. This provided for:

(i) a parliament elected on a franchise wider than that which existed in Britain or France;

(ii) liberty of the press and religion;

(iii) Polish to be the official language;

(iv) a separate administration and army.

27. Polish rebellion of 1830. The relevant details were as follows.

(*a*) *Causes*. Russian rule had been mild. However, Russo-Polish relations had deteriorated after 1820, when Alexander had been unwilling to abide by the constitution and summon the Parliament. Alexander had also disliked the claims of Polish nationalists to White Russia, Lithuania and the Western Ukraine.

More immediate factors were the following.

(*i*) Policies of Nicholas II, who showed no willingness to redeem Alexander's promise to include Lithuania in the Polish kingdom. He withdrew Polish officials from Lithuania and substituted Russians. He also applied a censorship which was contrary to the constitution and postponed calling the Diet until 1830.

(*ii*) The July revolution in France, which further inflamed Polish opinion, particularly when the Tsar proposed to use the Polish army to suppress the new governments in Belgium and France.

(*b*) *Outcome*. The rebellion occurred in November. The Russian governor, the Grand Duke Constantine, was forced to retire with his troops. In January 1831 the Tsar was declared dethroned, and Polish independence and union with Lithuania were proclaimed.

The Poles succeeded at first but soon the Russian forces returned in strength. The Poles were defeated at Ostrolenka in May, and the Russians re-entered Warsaw in September. Most of the Polish leaders escaped to the West.

(*c*) *Consequences*. Nicholas then embarked on a policy of oppression. All elections and the Diet were abolished, leading government posts in Poland were given to Russians, and the Russian language was made compulsory for official purposes.

28. Reasons for failure. In a general appeal issued in April 1831 the Polish government pointed out that Poland had far more right to national independence than either Belgium or Greece. However, the rebellion soon collapsed for two basic reasons.

(*a*) *Lack of foreign support*. The new French king, Louis-Philippe, was cautious and wanted to secure his throne and avoid ambitious ventures abroad. Britain considered she was too far removed to contribute any direct aid. Both powers were interested at the time in the fate of Belgium and Greece, which lay geographically within areas of more direct concern to them. This explained the comparative ease with which both Belgium and Greece obtained their independence (*see* IV, **25**, and XIV, **21**).

(*b*) *Internal divisions.* The rebellion was not a popular movement. To divide the Poles further. Nicholas improved peasant conditions on all estates captured by Russian armies. The rebels were not united among themselves.

(*i*) The moderates had little enthusiasm for social change. This group included the leaders, the aristocracy and gentry. They had no concern for the welfare of the peasants and desired only to regain the eastern provinces which Russia had taken in 1772.

(*ii*) The radicals wanted agrarian reforms and national independence.

29. Causes of the 1863 revolt. After 1856 Alexander II made certain political concessions. For example, Warsaw University was reopened and Polish was made the official language again. However, while this placated the moderates, it only encouraged the extremists to work for complete independence.

Immediate causes of fresh uprisings were:

(*a*) the attempts of the Tsar to press suspected Polish nationalists into the army;

(*b*) the dissolution of the Agricultural Society, which had aimed to improve peasant conditions.

30. Reasons for failure. The revolt in January 1863 rapidly spread to Lithuania and White Russia. Eventually in May 1864 Russia was able ruthlessly to suppress the revolt. Her success was due to the following factors.

(*a*) *Support of Prussia.* Bismarck had wanted to secure Russian co-operation for his own national policies, and he was concerned about possible trouble from the Poles in Prussia. In February 1863 he concluded the Alvensleben Convention with Russia in order to help in suppressing the uprisings.

(*b*) *Division of the other powers.* Since autonomy had been granted to Poland by the Vienna settlement of 1815, the great powers claimed the right to be consulted regarding that country's future. Notes from Britain, France and Austria contained proposals which would give the moderate Polish party many of their demands. However, the powers failed to work together to bring pressure on Russia for the following reasons.

(*i*) Austria distrusted Napoleon III, who was sympathetic

towards the submerged European national groups. Austria thus refused the offer of a French alliance.

(*ii*) Britain suspected Napoleon's aims on the Rhine. This suspicion was strengthened in the autumn of 1863 when Napoleon reinforced his proposal for a European Congress with the public statement that the treaties of 1815 were no longer in effect. The British government made it clear that this was not their view.

(*iii*) Britain was also partly distracted by the economic and maritime complications of the American Civil War.

31. Significance of the Polish revolt. The failure of the great powers to agree regarding the nature of intervention had been a factor contributing to the success of the Italian movement for freedom (*see* XIII, **38**). In contrast, a similar lack of agreement over Poland had ruined the cause of freedom in that country. Specific points to note are the following.

(*a*) *Napoleon III lost the friendship of the Tsar.*

(*b*) *Austria remained isolated in Europe.* Austria repeated the blunder of the Crimean War. She antagonised the Tsar through failing to support him, and like France she had done nothing positive to help Poland. Also she failed to secure another ally to compensate for the loss of Russian friendship. An alliance with France might have prevented her defeat in 1866 by Prussia (*see* IX, **11**).

(*c*) *The Russification of Poland was started.* The Polish rebellion gave the Tsar additional grounds for abandoning liberalism. The Tsar took the following measures.

(*i*) Poland lost her recently recovered autonomy. The name "Poland" was obliterated, and the country administered as a Russian province.

(*ii*) The power of the Polish nobility was broken. Further, the peasants were rewarded for not supporting the gentry by being given more land than the emancipated Russian serfs.

PROGRESS TEST 12

1. Give some account of the reforms enacted during the reigns of Alexander I and Nicholas I. (**2, 6**)

2. Why did the Decembrist conspiracy occur? (**4, 5**)

3. Why was Alexander II convinced in 1866 that radical reforms were necessary? (**7, 8**)

4. What were the provisions of the Edict of Emancipation in 1861? Discuss its consequences. **(10)**

5. Is there any justification for calling Alexander II "the Liberator"? **(9–15)**

6. Give some account of opposition movements to Tsarism before 1881. **(5, 7, 14, 16)**

7. Which groups suffered particularly from the repressive policies of Alexander III and Nicholas II? **(18)**

8. Describe some of the economic measures of Sergei de Witte after 1892. **(19)**

9. Account for the 1905 revolution. **(20, 21)**

10. Did the Dumas of 1906–14 manage to achieve any worthwhile reforms? **(24, 25)**

11. What were the causes and results of the Polish rebellion in 1830? **(27)**

12. Why did the Polish rebellion of 1863 fail? **(30)**

CHAPTER XIII

Italy, 1815–1914

ITALIAN AFFAIRS, 1815–48

1. Political composition in 1815. After the collapse of the Napoleonic Empire, the great powers considered that Italy was not sufficiently strong or self-supporting to stand alone. They made arrangements which perpetuated the division and foreign rule which had existed previously. The only important territorial changes compared to the situation before 1789 was the annexation of the Venetian Republic by Austria and of the former Genoese Republic by Piedmont. Metternich regarded Italy as merely a "geographical expression": Austrian influence in the peninsula was increased to act as a barrier to any new French invasion, and as compensation for the loss of the Austrian Netherlands.

The various units in Italy were as follows.

(*a*) *Lombardy and Venetia.* Both were placed under direct Austrian rule.

(*b*) *The Kingdom of Naples and Sicily* (the Two Sicilies). Austrian arms were responsible for restoring the tyrant Bourbon ruler King Ferdinand. He immediately concluded an offensive and defensive treaty with Austria.

(*c*) *The Papal States.*

(*d*) *The duchies of Parma, Modena and Tuscany.* Austrian princes or persons friendly to Austria or related to the House of Hapsburg were made rulers.

(*e*) *Piedmont.* This included Savoy, Nice, Genoa and the island of Sardinia. This was the only Italian state under Italian rule.

2. Barriers to Italian unity. No great demand existed among Italians for unity after 1815. They were not encouraged to see Italy as a whole entity, and considerable apathy existed. Some factors accounting for the lack of feeling for unity were as follows.

(*a*) *Tradition of localism and separatism.* The "way of life" differed greatly between southern and northern Italy. Feuds and general dissension seemed more characteristic of Italian life than united activity. There was no national flag. Thus the consciousness of a common nationality was little developed. In his *Memoirs* Metternich wrote: "In Italy provinces are against provinces, towns against towns, families against families, and – men against men."

Examples of the divisions were as follows.

(*i*) Numerous sovereign states (*see* **1**): there had been little co-operation between Italian states in the past. Often local rulers had sacrificed national aspirations for self-interest and had sought foreign aid to help win their domestic quarrels. The states were used to a separate existence and had differing interests, organisation and loyalties.

(*ii*) Geography: though Italy formed a unity on the map, there were many natural barriers, particularly mountain ranges, and too few roads. This hindered concerted action.

(*iii*) Administration: there were different customs houses for the various states, and there was no uniformity in the currencies, weights and measures, and other necessary aspects of organisation.

(*b*) *Autocratic rule.* Italy was a backward area, especially in the Papal States and the Two Sicilies. After 1815 there was a universal reaction among the rulers against all the ideas of the French Revolution. No state had a parliament, and there was no semblance of popular participation in government. Restored princes abolished all constitutions and many laws and institutions of French origin. Vaccination and gas illumination were forbidden for the simple reason that the French had introduced them.

Local rulers, with the exception of those of Piedmont, opposed any plans for unity since they were likely to result in the loss of their powers and privileges. Even in Piedmont the aristocracy continued to exercise feudal rights over the peasantry.

(*c*) *Different schools of thought.* Italy represented several myths based on past traditions. Italians were aware that Italy represented to some the glories of the Roman Republic or Empire, to others the medieval free city-states or the power of the Pope. In the period 1815–48 there were three main schools of thought on how to achieve unity, but all three groups disliked each other and had no wish to co-operate.

(*i*) Democratic republicans: Mazzini wanted to abolish monarchies and to establish a democratic republic (*see* 5).

(*ii*) Papal federalists: the idea that the Papacy was the best instrument for uniting Italy and modernising her political institutions had had support in Italy since the Middle Ages. It was known as the Neo-Guelf movement and received renewed impetus when Vincenzo Gioberti suggested in his *Primato* (1843) that Italy should be a federal state under a reformed Papacy.

(*iii*) Liberal monarchists: there were hopes among intellectuals and businessmen in Piedmont that Charles Albert would liberalise the institutions and lead Italy to unity. Piedmont had the best chance of defeating foreign powers, if only her monarch, from the House of Savoy, would take the lead.

The sentiments of this school were expressed in Balbo's pamphlet *On the Hopes of Italy* (1844) and the writings of d'Azeglio.

(*d*) *The Roman Question.* The Pope had temporal power over central Italy. He was supported not only by loyal Catholics in Italy but by France and Austria. He opposed any movement in Italy likely to threaten his authority in the Papal States, and his territory constituted a wedge between the northern and southern parts of Italy.

(*e*) *Presence of Austria.* Austria was an important conservative Catholic power. This state had considerable influence in Italy after 1815, except in Piedmont, and was the chief barrier to the aspirations of Italian nationalists.

3. Early Italian revolts. Numerous revolts occurred during 1820–1, but the tradition of separatism prevented any co-ordination between them. For example, the rising in Naples collapsed before the one in Piedmont started.

After 1820 the King of Piedmont tried to arrange some concerted organisation among Piedmont, Bavaria, Naples and the Papal States to oppose Austria. This failed owing to the opposition of the last two states.

The revolts in the following states were easily suppressed by Austrian forces.

(*a*) *Naples.* In July 1820 General Pepe marched on the capital and extracted a democratic constitution from the King. This was based on the Spanish constitution of 1812. Eventually the King was able to gain the support of Austria. Her army, with the moral support of Prussia and Russia at the Troppau meeting, intervened in Naples and punished the rebels. The constitution was abolished. Austrian troops remained garrisoned there until 1828 to defend the King in case his subjects tried to force him to grant a constitution again.

(b) *Piedmont.* In March 1821 a mutiny occurred in the Piedmontese army, with demands for a constitution. Victor Emmanuel abdicated in favour of his brother Charles Felix The young Charles Albert, known for his liberal sympathies, became regent. Felix appealed to Austria, and Austrian troops put down the rising at Novara.

(c) *Papal States.* At the end of 1830 disorders spread throughout central Italy in a chain reaction from Modena to Parma and from there to the Papal States. Provisional governments were formed and new charters granted. In 1831 rebels in the Papal States demanded lay government, but Pope Gregory XVI was not prepared to remove priests from political, administrative and judicial posts. He appealed to Austria, and the rebellion was crushed. The rebels had expected aid from France, but Louis-Philippe was not willing to help.

Austrian forces were withdrawn in July 1831 but had to be recalled to Bologna in January 1832. This provoked the French into sending a force to occupy Ancona.

4. Factors promoting unity. Despite the causes of disunity, Italy constituted an entity from the racial, linguistic and cultural standpoints. Factors making for eventual political unity were as follows.

(a) *Growth of national feeling.* Among the intelligentsia and the progressive middle classes there was a growing interest in the prospects of unity after 1815. It was partly inspired by the following.

(i) An increased hatred of Austria, whose presence in the north served as a perpetual reminder of the humiliating situation of Italy.

(ii) The memories of the efficiency of French administration and the liberalism of French legal codes. This made Italians dissatisfied with the feudal and reactionary practices restored after 1815.

(b) *Economic progress.*

(i) Free trade: internal customs barriers hindered trade both within and among Italian states. Domenico Romagnosi (1761-1835) was one of the school of economists who saw the abolition of customs frontiers in Italy and the adoption of freer trade as a step to unity.

(*ii*) Communications: D'Azeglio remarked that railways, which started with the Lombardo-Venetian line in 1835, would provide stitching for the Italian boot.

(*iii*) Agriculture: numerous societies not only helped the application of modern science to land but also increased the sense of Italian solidarity. Charles Albert, King of Piedmont after 1831, became president of the Piedmontese agricultural association. It drew members from various north Italian states, who in time expressed a desire for greater unity.

(*c*) *Cultural and literary works.* Certain men of letters helped to inspire the people to resist the tyranny of foreign rule. Notable contributors were the following.

(*i*) Vittorio Alfieri (1749–1803), who in his plays created an image of Italy as a place of tragic drama and a passion for liberty.

(*ii*) Giacomo Leopardi (1798–1837) whose literature and poetry on Greece and Rome helped to stir the consciousness of people about Italy's mighty classical past.

(*iii*) Alessandro Manzoni (1785–1873), who in his historical novel *I Promessi Sposi* (1825) encouraged Italians to adopt an optimistic outlook regarding their future.

(*d*) *Activities of secret societies.* The most significant forms of resistance after 1815 were the numerous conspiratorial societies. Their membership was made up partly of the disgruntled elements of society and partly of adventurous youth looking for an exciting and glamorous life. The societies were important in giving Italians training in how to fight for their rights.

Two of the societies were the following.

(*i*) The Carbonari: this was the so-called Society of Charcoal-burners which originated in Naples. At first it was an association for mutual assistance among officers of lower rank. After 1811 its activities became increasingly political. It aimed to expel the Austrians from Italy and played an active part in the revolutions of 1820–1 and 1831.

(*ii*) The Federati: this was an aristocratic society in Piedmont. It supported the 1821 rebellion.

(*e*) *Inspiration of Mazzini* (*see* **5**).

5. Work of Mazzini.

Giuseppe Mazzini (1805–72), the son of a Genoese doctor, was the soul of Italian unification.

(a) *His ideas.* Apart from being a patriot, he was a gifted orator and idealistic writer. He believed that a nation had a moral purpose and that unity, achieved through war, would be a stage towards a free confederation of all Europe influenced by a spirit of Christian brotherhood. He was described by Metternich as the most dangerous man in Europe.

(b) *His activities.* In 1827 he joined the Carbonari. In 1830 he was arrested, imprisoned and then exiled. Charles Albert, who became King of Sardinia in 1831, ignored Mazzini's appeal to assume the leadership of the movement for Italian freedom.

The succession of Italian failures in 1820–1 and 1830 convinced Mazzini of the need to appeal to a wider audience than that reached by the secret societies. He started to publicise the problems of Italy abroad and to impress on people the need for co-ordinated action.

(i) In 1831 he formed at Marseilles the society of "Young Italy". It was designed to be a national rather than a regional movement and soon had a large membership throughout Italy. In 1832 he was exiled from France and in 1833 organised an unsuccessful invasion of Savoy from Switzerland.

(ii) In 1834, working from England, he founded the society "Young Europe".

(c) *His contribution.* He dissipated much of his time in encouraging ill-prepared risings. Examples were the revolt in Cosenza in 1843 and the fruitless Calabrian expedition of two Venetian sailors in 1844.

However, he was invaluable in encouraging many Italians in the cause of unity and in showing them a way to achieve it. He was the first Italian to promote nationalism and to work actively towards a united Italy through political action. He popularised ideas for:

(i) the overthrow of native and foreign tyrants in Italy;

(ii) the unification of Italy on republican and democratic lines;

(iii) the need for Italians to achieve their goal through good organisation and their own united efforts.

6. Reforms of the new Pope. In June 1846 Giovanni Mastai Ferretti (1792–1878) was elected Pope Pius IX. He began with the reputation of being a liberal. He was interested in Gioberti's idea of a confederation of states under his leadership, and his love of Italy, dislike of Austrian domination and moderate political concessions made many liberals see him as a possible leader of Italy. However, there was nothing radical about any of his acts. He firmly believed that representative government and Papal authority were incompatible.

In the first few months of Pius's reign the following developments occurred.

(a) An amnesty was given to exiles and political prisoners, limited freedom of speech was granted and the press censorship was modified.

(b) In June 1847 the Pope agreed to the appointment of a Council of Ministers to help in the governing of the Papal States.

(c) In August 1847 the Pope made the suggestion that a customs union should be formed. Piedmont rejected this, fearing competition for Italian leadership from the Papacy. In the same month Austria sent troops to Ferrara in Romagna in protest against the direction of Papal policy.

THE REVOLUTIONS OF 1848-9

7. Outbreak of revolution. In 1848 a series of events led to either the expulsion of Austrian troops or the granting of political concessions in the following states.

(a) *Lombardy.* In January the citizens of Milan abandoned smoking to annoy the Austrians, who monopolised the tobacco trade. A series of incidents, the "tobacco riots", resulted in Austrian troops using force, and several people died. Later, on 18th March, a desperate five-day battle resulted in the expulsion of the Austrian troops.

(b) *Sicily.* On 12th January rebels in Palermo defeated Ferdinand II's troops. The King was forced to accept the 1812 constitution and to extend it to Naples and grant an amnesty to political prisoners.

(c) *Tuscany.* On 11th February the Grand Duke agreed to allow representative government and the grant of a constitution.

(d) *Piedmont.* On 4th March Charles Albert, anxious to have the support of the liberals for any war with Austria, granted a constitution.

(e) *The Papal States.* On 15th March the Pope reluctantly accepted a new constitution.

(f) *Venetia.* On 22nd March Venice rose and expelled Austrian troops. Under Manin an independent republic was proclaimed.

8. Start of Austro-Piedmontese war. Originally Charles Albert contemplated allying with Austria to gain territory from the French. He was reluctant to attack Austria, a Catholic power. However, when Austria occupied Ferrara in 1847 despite the Pope's protests, this gave him an opportunity to pose as the defender of the Church.

Charles Albert became interested in the possibilities of taking Lombardy from Austria. He was influenced by the aristocratic liberals, led by Balbo and Cavour, who wanted to unite the northern states in one economic unit. On 23rd March he issued a proclamation declaring that his people sympathised with the heroic struggles of Lombardy and Venice. His troops then attacked Austrian forces in Lombardy.

9. The Pope and the war. When the war in Lombardy began, Papal troops were dispatched to the north, presumably to co-operate with the Piedmontese army. However, on 29th April the Pope announced that he opposed offensive war against Austria and refused to permit his troops to fight against fellow Catholics. Therefore, in his desire for peace and legitimacy, the Pope had abandoned the national cause.

The results of the Pope's actions were as follows.

(a) *The Pope lost the opportunity to pose as Italian leader.* Liberals lost faith in the Pope as a potential political leader. Thus Gioberti's solution had little chance of being accepted. People were now keener to turn to Piedmont for a leader in establishing unity.

(b) *The Italian revolt was seriously weakened.*

(i) Popular enthusiasm for the national cause weakened, since the Pope no longer gave it his moral support.

(ii) King Ferdinand was able to use the opportunity to recall General Pepe's army of Neapolitans which had set off for the north. It was to be used to reconquer Sicily and to re-establish his autocratic rule once again.

(iii) Papal troops were withdrawn. Thus Charles Albert received little military support outside Piedmont.

10. The revolt weakened by disunity. Mutual suspicions and jealousies prevented effective co-ordination between the Italian states. Local feelings were strong, and Charles Albert was not popular in the rest of Italy.

Outside Piedmont there was little organisation to the revolts, and there was a diversity of aims. Numerous groups, royalists, republicans and autonomists, pursued different objectives, which made concerted action difficult.

(a) *Lombardy and Venetia.* Friction existed between Venice and Milan. When the two states had asserted their independence from Austria they were reluctant at first to surrender it to a new North Italian kingdom based on Turin in Piedmont.

There were further complications. In Milan the upper bourgeoisie supported Charles Albert, while the lower bourgeoisie under Cattaneo were republican-minded and wanted autonomy within a federation. It was not until the beginning of July that they agreed on union with Piedmont. By then the fortunes of war were turning against the Italians.

(b) *Southern Italy.* Before they were actually withdrawn from the north, the Neapolitan and Papal troops had been instructed not to cross the Po into Austrian territory. In the south there was rivalry between Messina and Palermo. Class rivalry also undermined the struggle. The aristocratic liberals were not prepared to implement agrarian reforms which the farmers wanted.

Disorders occurred in Naples owing to the liberal government's lack of experience. Ferdinand took advantage of this to dismiss the short-lived parliament and recover complete power. Sicily, which had declared its independence, was then forced by an intensive bombardment to surrender in May 1849.

(c) *Tuscany.* Leopold, the Grand Duke, approved of the idea of calling an Italian Constituent Assembly for settling the conditions of union among the states. The scheme failed owing to the opposition of Piedmont and the Pope. Leopold thereupon abandoned the national cause.

11. Defeat of Piedmont. Despite the lack of support from other Italian states, it seemed at first that Piedmont might succeed against Austria, who had serious domestic troubles at home.

Unfortunately Piedmont had no great statesman capable of welding the various groups who were hostile to Austria into one united body. Charles Albert was courageous and determined, but possessed little military skill and had no distinguished generals on whom he could rely. Initially his forces were successful, capturing the fortress of Peschiera and winning the battle of Goito. However, he failed to pursue his advantage, which gave the Austrians time to consolidate their position and to gain reinforcements.

Austria defeated Piedmont decisively on the following two occasions.

(a) *Custozza* (25th July 1848). While attacking one wing of the Quadrilateral (*see* 13(a)), Piedmontese forces were defeated by a counter-attack of Radetzky's forces. In August Piedmont withdrew from the struggle.

(b) *Novara* (23rd March 1849). Following a renewed outbreak of violence in Vienna in March 1849, Charles Albert again marched his troops into Lombardy. The King was heartbroken when his troops were defeated again and abdicated in favour of his son Victor Emmanuel II.

Piedmont suffered no territorial loss since Austria was anxious not to annoy Britain or France. She had to pay an indemnity of 75 million lire, but the new king refused to abrogate the constitution as the Austrians demanded.

12. Events in Rome. For a time there was hope that something fruitful could still come from the Papacy. In September the Pope appointed as Prime Minister a liberal, Count Rossi, who explored the possibilities of Gioberti's scheme of federation. On 15th November 1848 he was murdered by some Lombard volunteers. Events then took the following course.

(a) *Flight of the Pope.* Pius IX fled to Naples on 24th November, disguised as a simple priest.

(b) *Declaration of a republic.* A provisional government administered the city until a Constituent Assembly could be elected. In February 1849 this latter body proclaimed Rome a republic.

Mazzini became the head of government and carried out a series of reforms. However, his doctrines were little understood and his appeals to duty and self-sacrifice did not attract the support of the labourers and peasants.

(c) *Papal authority restored.* The Pope appealed to European powers to help him, and the governments of Spain, Naples and Austria indicated their intentions of rendering aid. However, France intervened first, the new leader Louis Napoleon seeing an opportunity to win glory.

(i) In March 1849 the Constituent Assembly voted funds for a military expedition. Its object was to mediate between the Pope and his rebellious subjects.

(ii) A French army under General Oudinot landed in April

but was repulsed at first by Garibaldi when it advanced on Rome.

(*iii*) Oudinot waited for reinforcements and then on authority from Napoleon began a full-scale military operation. The Neapolitans gave some assistance and Rome surrendered to the French on 30th June.

13. Reasons for the failure of the uprisings. The various contributing factors were as follows.

(*a*) *Austrian military power.* The Austrians held the famous "Quadrilateral" of Verona, Peschiera, Legnago and Mantua, all places of great strength. This gave their army a link with Austria so that they could receive reinforcements. The discipline of their troops and the military skill of their commander, Radetzky, could not be equalled by the Piedmontese.

The Venetians were the last to surrender. However, long-range artillery bombardment, cholera and starvation eventually forced Manin in Venice to admit defeat on 24th August 1849.

(*b*) *Lack of external aid.* Charles Albert was determined to fight Austria without foreign support, believing in the maxim "*Italia fara da se*". The Lombards had been anxious to enlist the help of the French, but France was discouraged by Britain from playing any active part in the rebellion.

(*c*) *Lack of unity and organisation* (*see* **10**).

(*d*) *Lack of outstanding statesmen or generals* (*see* **11**).

(*e*) *Opposition of the Pope* (*see* **9**).

(*f*) *Intervention of the French in Rome* (*see* **12**(*c*)).

CAVOUR AND PIEDMONT

14. Factors aiding Italian unification after 1848. After the setbacks received during 1848–9, the following factors contributed to the creation of the Italian nation during the period 1849–71.

(*a*) *Diplomatic skill of Cavour.*

(*b*) *Fighting qualities of Garibaldi* (*see* **34–36**). Early in life Garibaldi was a faithful follower of Mazzini and joined the "Young Italy" movement. He entered the Piedmontese navy to induce it to mutiny in favour of Mazzini's plot of 1833. He escaped, was condemned to death in his absence and disappeared to South America. He played an important role from 1848 onwards, for example, as regards the following.

(*i*) In the troubled times of 1848 he fought for the Lombards against the Austrians and in 1849 defended Rome in vain against the French.

(*ii*) Cavour was able to gain his support for Italian unity built around Piedmont and its monarchy.

(*iii*) He had the capacity to instil confidence into people and to draw followers for his cause, whatever it was. It was his influence in Sicily and Naples during 1860 which was decisive in winning converts to Italian unity (*see* **34–36**).

(*c*) *Agitative activities of Mazzini.* It must be noted that Mazzini became increasingly an embarrassment to the cause of Italian unity after 1848. His occupation and defence of Rome in 1848–9 proved to be abortive. He disapproved of Piedmont's participation in the Crimean War and her use of France as an ally in 1859. He believed that Italians should achieve unity through their own efforts and that a democratic republic should be the aim. This conflicted with the aims of Piedmont. After another Mazzini-sponsored rising had failed in 1857 many of his followers deserted him.

Mazzini disliked the diplomatic methods used by Cavour to secure the south in 1860–1. However, his continued efforts kept alive the spark of resistance in Italy, as outlined in **5**(*c*) above.

(*d*) *Use of foreign aid.*

(*i*) France helped gain Lombardy in 1859 and Parma, Modena, Tuscany and Romagna for the new Italian state in 1860.

(*ii*) Britain lent moral support (*see* **38**(*a*)).

(*iii*) Prussia helped gain Venetia in 1866 (*see* **41**).

(*e*) *Leadership of the Piedmontese state* (*see* **15**).

15. Piedmontese leadership. After 1848 Piedmont was recognised as the hope of liberal Italy, for the following reasons.

(*a*) It alone possessed an army capable of fighting Austria.

(*b*) It had a constitution and a liberal government.

(*c*) In contrast to the other states it alone had taken the lead in 1848 in the cause of national unity.

(*d*) In Victor Emmanuel II it possessed a ruler determined to continue the struggle against Austria.

(*e*) It provided a base for the fostering of political groups. An important one later proved to be the National Society (*see* **23**).

(*f*) The ideas of Gioberti, Mazzini and republicans in general no longer seemed feasible.

16. Rise to power of Cavour. Camillo di Cavour (1810–61), a Piedmontese aristocrat, had travelled widely and had studied the political life in Britain and France. In 1847 he founded the liberal newspaper *Il Risorgimento*. In 1848 he was elected to the first Piedmontese Parliament. He played an important role in planning and retaining the *statuto* (constitution) of 1848 with its bicameral legislature and responsible cabinet. In 1850 he became Minister of Agriculture and Commerce, and in 1852 he succeeded Massimo d'Azeglio as Prime Minister.

17. Cavour's domestic measures. Cavour aimed to make Piedmont economically progressive, politically liberal and financially stable. In this way he hoped that Piedmont would be strong enough to assume the leadership of Italy in the event of another war with Austria.

Examples of areas in which Cavour's measures were effective were the following.

(*a*) *Administration.* He encouraged reforms in the army, state administration and legal systems.

(*b*) *Trade and industry.* He pioneered scientific agriculture, negotiated trade treaties and introduced new industries. He encouraged overseas investors and advisers to help in the economic development of Piedmont.

(*c*) *Religion.*

(*i*) In 1850 he drafted the Siccardi Laws which curbed the powers of the Church by abolishing ecclesiastical courts.

(*ii*) In 1855 religious orders were abolished, except those concerned with teaching, preaching and helping the sick.

(*d*) *Communications.* He worked to make Piedmont part of an international network. Schemes were initiated for the piercing of Mont Cenis by a rail tunnel and for turning Genoa into a great commercial port.

18. French aid sought. The Italian failures of 1848–9 convinced Cavour that Italy could not achieve unity without foreign help. Britain was sympathetic to the Italian cause, but was not likely to render material assistance. Her diplomats believed that Austrian power in Central Europe was necessary to preserve the balance of power between France and Russia.

Cavour wanted to prevent any chance of Austria consolidating her power in Italian affairs. Napoleon III, the champion of nationality, seemed a likely ally to help Piedmont overturn the *status quo*.

19. Reasons for Napoleon's interest. For different reasons Napoleon was interested in the affairs of northern, central and southern Italy.

(*a*) *Northern Italy*. Napoleon's family origins had been Italian and he was a former member of the Carbonari. He wanted to help Piedmont free Italy from Austrian rule, but his motives were far from altruistic. French nationalists did not want a strong power rising on their south-east border. Napoleon hoped that French influence would replace that of Austria in northern Italy, and also that France's Alpine frontier might be restored by the acquisition of Nice and Savoy.

(*b*) *Central and southern Italy*. Napoleon had no wish to unite Italy as many liberals hoped. He wanted to keep Italy weak and divided, and, except as far as the north was concerned, was a supporter of the *status quo*.

(*i*) Napoleon relied on the support of the clericals at home. He therefore supported the Pope's position in central Italy even though this presented an obstacle to Italian unity after 1848.

(*ii*) King Ferdinand of the Two Sicilies was supported by the Tsar, with whom Napoleon wanted to remain on good terms. Napoleon therefore opposed any action likely to harm the position of the Bourbon monarch.

20. Piedmont in the Crimean War. Cavour hoped European powers might be interested in Italian problems if Piedmont played an active role abroad. In December 1855 France and Britain invited Piedmont to join them in the Crimean War. The Piedmontese cabinet opposed the idea, but Cavour eventually brought Piedmont into the war.

In 1856 a Piedmontese force under La Marmora did well at the battle of the Tchernaya. This helped to extinguish the stigma of earlier defeats at the hands of Austria, and Piedmont staked a claim to Italian leadership.

At the Paris peace conference Italian affairs were debated and Napoleon continued to express interest. However, Cavour was unable to gain French support for any changes in Italy.

FRENCH AID AND THE AUSTRIAN WAR OF 1859

21. The Orsini incident. Cavour despaired of help from France. Napoleon appeared to have forgotten about the Italian cause. However, it was soon brought to his attention in a forcible manner. In January 1858 Felice Orsini, an Italian patriot, tried to assassinate the Emperor in front of the Paris Opera House.

Orsini, together with his accomplices, was arrested. He later appealed to the Emperor to assist Italian liberty, charging him with being a traitor to the cause of Italian freedom. This appeal was read out at his trial. Napoleon was sufficiently impressed to have it published and sent a copy to Cavour.

France protested strongly to Britain, where the bombs used had been manufactured, and to Piedmont. Victor Emmanuel gave a firm reply, while Cavour took measures against the Mazzini press. This mollified the anger of Napoleon, who then decided to assist Cavour in earnest.

22. Franco-Italian negotiations. The following steps were taken to form closer liaison between Piedmont and France.

(*a*) *Plombières meeting.* Napoleon invited Cavour to a meeting on 20th July 1858. He suggested that a northern Italian state under Victor Emmanuel and a central Italian federation under the presidency of the Pope should be formed.

Cavour was cautious and nothing definite was signed. The meeting was novel in that it was a deliberate attempt to manufacture a war.

(*i*) Napoleon agreed to help Piedmont if she were involved in war with Austria.

(*ii*) Nice and Savoy were to be ceded to France in return for her assistance.

(*b*) *Marriage arrangement.* It had been agreed at Plombières that a marriage would first be arranged between the daughter of King Victor Emmanuel, the fifteen-year-old Princess Clotilde, and Jerome, a cousin of Napoleon III. This took place in September 1858 and cleared the way for tightening the arrangements between the two countries.

(*c*) *Military alliance.* France and Piedmont signed a formal military alliance in January 1859. This time no mention was made of a federation or of any specific state boundaries. Napoleon hoped these would be based on his Plombières proposals. The details were as follows.

(*i*) France would defend Piedmont from attack if Cavour was able to engineer hostilities so that Austria appeared the aggressor.

(*ii*) France would supply 200,000 troops and Piedmont 100,000.

(*iii*) A northern kingdom would be created, and Papal sovereignty maintained. Piedmont would gain Lombardy and Venetia in the event of the Austrian defeat.

23. Formation of the National Society. In 1857 Mazzini, working from England, organised insurrections in Genoa and Livorno. They failed and a similar fate befell a landing at Sapri on the Calabrian coast. Many Italian nationalists then realised the futility of isolated risings. A new organisation, the National Society, was formed which united many of the groups of the early *risorgimento*. Its leaders were Pallavicino, La Farina, Garibaldi and Daniele Manin. They believed that Cavour would be a valuable ally to co-ordinate the activities of the Italian national movement. The motto of the society became "Independence, unity and constitutional liberty under the Savoy dynasty."

24. Austria provoked by Cavour. In 1857 the liberal Archduke Maximilian had been made viceroy in Lombardy and had tried to enforce a conciliatory Austrian policy. However, relations with Piedmont had been poor. In February Cavour had broken off diplomatic relations with Vienna over the expulsion of a Sardinian senator from Lombardy.

After the Plombières meeting in mid 1858 Cavour planned to bring about war with Austria. He tried to avoid placing Piedmont and France too clearly in the wrong.

Austria disliked the following.

(*a*) *Piedmont's refusal to extradite draft evaders.* At the end of 1858 Austria imposed military conscription in Lombardy and Venetia. To evade the draft, many fled to Piedmont, and when Austria demanded their return this was refused.

(*b*) *Cavour's negotiations with the National Society.* Cavour saw the value of encouraging the conspiratorial activities of the secret societies, which many Italians supported. These societies advertised the problems of Italy abroad and contributed to the raising of the political temperature at home.

Publicly Cavour disowned any activities which would be viewed with alarm in London and Paris. Privately he opened negotiations with the National Society. He informed La Farina in October 1858 of his aims to bring about risings in the northern and central states. The Society played a valuable part in preparing the public mood for war. Garibaldi was asked to form a volunteer force, and many of the recruits for this were Lombards. The Society prepared arms depots and circulated pamphlets supporting Piedmontese leadership.

(c) *A provocative speech by Victor Emmanuel.* In January 1859, on a suggestion of Napoleon, the King spoke of the "cries of grief" that were reaching Piedmont from the rest of Italy.

(d) *Piedmont's efforts to raise war loans.* Austrian war preparations gave Cavour an excuse to take similar action. La Marmora, the Finance Minister, was told to raise the necessary loans for a war in February 1859.

25. Intervention of other European powers. Both Piedmont and Austria started to mobilise their forces. Cavour aimed at a defensive mobilisation to force Austria to issue an ultimatum.

In February 1859 Britain sent a mission to Vienna to urge demobilisation. However, in March a secret Franco-Russian Treaty provided for Russian neutrality in the event of a Franco-Austrian war and for Russian troop movements to threaten Austria in the east, on condition that France supported Russia's policy of revising the Black Sea clauses.

Gorchakov, the Russian Foreign Minister, proposed a congress to solve the question. This was accepted by Britain and Napoleon, but Austria demanded Piedmont's exclusion from the congress and demanded the disarmament of Piedmont before the congress met. Napoleon, pressured by the other European states, and disheartened by the lack of enthusiasm at home, forced Cavour to agree to the Austrian demand on 19th April.

26. The Austrian ultimatum. Because of the wish to protect her security, Austria had made the initial mistake of mobilising her large army too soon. To keep the Austrian army mobilised indefinitely was an expensive procedure if peace negotiations were prolonged. Buol, the Austrian Chief Minister, was impatient of delay. He ignored the warning of his more cautious colleagues to avoid precipitate action until the French position had been clarified. This was sound advice, for there was the possibility that the Franco-Piedmontese alliance would collapse, given time for diplomatic pressure to be exerted on the wavering Napoleon.

Piedmont was on the point of disarming when Buol, on 19th April, sent a fatal ultimatum giving Cavour the alternative between unconditional demobilisation "within three days" or war. This was a blunder as it supplied Cavour with the provocation he needed. Piedmont refused, and Austria declared war, thereby appearing the aggressor.

27. Defeat of Austria. The military weakness of Austria was soon revealed. Important factors contributing to her defeat were as follows.

(*a*) *Poor commanders.* The Emperor Francis Joseph took personal charge of the army. He relied for advice on the courtier-soldier Count Grunne, who had no combat experience. The incompetent Gyulai was appointed to the Italian command. Inadequate use was made of the abilities of Benedek or the strategist Hess.

(*b*) *Poor strategy.* Austria delayed invading Piedmont in force until 29th April. This gave Napoleon time to move troops into Italy, making maximum use of the recently completed railway system. The Austrians were confident of victory, and neglected to organise an adequate supply system (there was no railway between Trieste and Venice) and to acquire accurate knowledge of enemy strength and capabilities.

(*c*) *Insufficient forces.* Austria was not able to utilise all her available forces. It was necessary to retain German and Czech troops in Hungary to prevent a possible rising there. Troops were also kept in reserve in case France attacked through South Germany. Austria thus sent only 90,000 men to Italy.

(*d*) *Poor morale.* The loyalty of many to the Austrian cause was slender. The different national elements of the army had no interest in the issue of the campaign. Italians, Hungarians and even the trusted Croats deserted in large numbers.

Gyulai's lack of decisiveness allowed the French and Italian forces to combine. After preliminary skirmishes, two bloody battles were fought at Magenta (4th June) and Solferino (24th June). Losses were heavy on both sides but they were narrow victories for the French and Italians, who then conquered the whole of Lombardy. The Austrians retreated into the Quadrilateral (*see* 13).

28. Reasons for the end of the war. The war might have been prolonged as the Austrian defeats had not been decisive. However, the chief contestants were by then anxious for peace. Napoleon was shocked by the terrible toll which the war had taken of human life and the lack of adequate medical facilities for the wounded. He decided, without consulting Cavour, to negotiate directly with Francis Joseph for a peace settlement. He found the Emperor as eager to abandon the war as he had been previously to enter into it. The following factors contributed to the premature peace.

(a) *Prussian mobilisation and offer of mediation.* Britain had stated that she would remain neutral if the war was confined to Italy. It was hinted that Prussia should adopt the same approach but that Britain would not object if Prussia mobilised on the Rhine.

Prussia offered to mediate and backed up the offer with the mobilisation of six army corps in the Rhineland on 24th June. This did not please the French or the Austrians.

(i) Napoleon felt that a prolonged war would tempt Prussia to cause trouble.

(ii) The Prussian mobilisation indirectly threatened Austria. The war had revealed the weak state of the Austrian army. If more reinforcements were sent to Lombardy, this would have made Austria utterly dependent on the Prussian army to defend Germany. Thus Austria wanted to avoid Prussian involvement in the war, which would have meant the granting of political concessions to Prussia in German affairs.

(b) *Unstable conditions in Austrian Empire.* Owing to an economic slump Austria had difficulty in raising loans to finance the war. Civil war threatened in Hungary and troops had to be stationed there to keep order and to collect the taxes, which the government officials had been unable to do. The Hungarian leader Kossuth visited Napoleon's headquarters, and Austria feared the possibility of open revolt breaking out in Hungary.

(c) *Developments in Italy.* The tremendous upsurge of popular enthusiasm for the national cause which had followed the battles surprised both the French and the Austrians. Austria disliked the prospect of losing all influence in Italy, and Napoleon feared that France would lose all opportunity of exerting influence herself. Instead of a weak, loose federation being formed in the north the nucleus of a strong, unified state was appearing, as shown by the following developments.

(i) The duchies: the hereditary rulers of Tuscany, Parma and

Modena fled to the Austrian camp after Magenta. National risings took place in Tuscany and Parma. Cavour sent agents to organise pro-Piedmontese governments, and he had plans for incorporating Tuscany, which Napoleon had envisaged would form part of a central Italian federation under the Pope.

(*ii*) The Papal States: the withdrawal of the Austrian garrison from Bologna (Romagna) paved the way for risings in the Papal States and the spread of the influence of Piedmont to the south. The French clericals had vehemently opposed the war in the first place. If the war continued it seemed likely that the Italians might try to capture Rome. Napoleon wanted to avoid any unnecessary complications which would be involved in sending troops to aid the Pope.

29. The Peace of Villafranca. Preliminary peace terms were settled by Napoleon and Francis Joseph on 11th July at Villafranca near Verona. Cavour was not consulted.

(*a*) *Peace conditions.* These were as follows.

(*i*) Lombardy, except for the fortresses of Mantua and Peschiera, was to be transferred to Piedmont. Napoleon was to be the intermediary in this arrangement. Parma was tacitly conceded as well.

(*ii*) All Italy was to be included in a new confederation. This was to be under the titular presidency of the Pope.

(*iii*) The hereditary rulers of Tuscany and Modena were to be restored.

(*iv*) Austria was to retain Venetia. This state was to form part of the new confederation.

(*b*) *Short-term results.* Provisions listed as (*a*)(*iii*) and (*iv*) above seemed to negate the purposes of the war, for the following reasons.

(*i*) Austria was still in a dominant position in Italy. She was still militarily strong, controlling the Quadrilateral without having to defend the awkward Plain of Lombardy.

(*ii*) France had achieved nothing. She had incurred considerable military expense and her troops had suffered heavy losses, but she received no thanks for her help and made no territorial gains. The war had provoked much hostile criticism at home, and Piedmont considered Napoleon a traitor to the Italian cause for abruptly terminating hostilities.

(*iii*) Piedmont had gained only Lombardy. Cavour resigned in disgust.

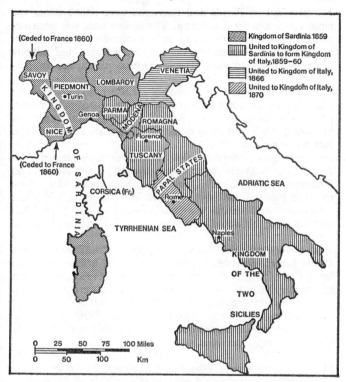

The unification of Italy, 1859–70

Reference may be made to the accompanying map, which shows how Italian unity was achieved between 1859 and 1870.

30. Failure of the settlement. Events in Italy took a surprising turn which was to help the Italian cause. The Villafranca terms were unenforceable, for the following reasons.

(*a*) *The duchies refused to accept the return of their rulers.* After successful revolutions the duchies were not prepared to accept the restoration of their rulers. The royal commissioners (agents of Cavour) refused to stand down. They were helped by the National Society.

    (*i*) Modena, Parma and Romagna were united under the name of Emilia by La Farina. The government was then organised to petition for annexation by Piedmont.

    (*ii*) Tuscany wanted to unite with Piedmont, but initially distrusted her. However, Baron Ricasoli triumphed in persuading the Assembly to vote for union.

    (*b*) *The Pope refused to co-operate.* He was not keen to see the formation of any confederation, fearing the loss of his temporal power. A pamphlet had been issued in France with the approval of Napoleon which suggested that the Papal territories should be reduced to a minimum.

    (*c*) *Napoleon refused to allow force to be used to implement Villafranca.* In August the representatives of France, Austria and Piedmont met at Zürich. Napoleon opposed the idea of an enlarged Piedmontese union. He also rejected the use of force. This meant that Austria was unable to restore the rulers in the duchies, since this would have been impossible without the use of force.

    (*d*) *Britain gave moral support to Italy.* In the 1859 elections a strong Liberal government came to power in Britain under the leadership of Palmerston and Russell, who favoured the creation of a unitary Italian state. In January 1860 they urged France and Austria to abstain from intervention in Italian affairs.

    Russell suggested to Napoleon four points which would allow the duchies to vote on the question of annexation to Piedmont through elected assemblies.

31. Agreement between Cavour and Napoleon. Piedmont was as powerless as Austria to act without the consent of the powers. However, events were by then favourable to the Italian cause and Cavour returned to office in January 1860. He resolved to break the deadlock and bluntly asked Napoleon for his price for annexation. Napoleon III was only prepared for Piedmont to annex Tuscany and Emilia if France was compensated for the creation of a powerful state on her south-eastern flank. Cavour agreed to cede Savoy and Nice.

    It was agreed in the Treaty of Turin of 24th March that plebiscites would be held in all the areas concerned. Austria was prepared to acquiesce in these arrangements, and Cavour was ready to abandon his belief in elected assemblies in favour of this rather false method of testing popular approval. The plebiscites were carried out in the presence of French and Piedmontese troops. They resulted in an overwhelming majority in favour of annexation by Piedmont of the central Italian states, and for annexation by France of Nice and Savoy.

UNIFICATION OF SOUTHERN ITALY WITH THE NORTH

32. Re-emergence of Garibaldi. Only a little over half the peninsula had been won for the new Italy. Venetia, Rome and the Kingdom of Naples were not included.

In 1859 Garibaldi had returned from his home on the island of Caprera to lead a guerrilla band for Piedmont in the Austrian War. In 1860 he commanded part of the forces of the revolutionary governments in central Italy. He proved to be somewhat unreliable, temperamental and impatient. There were fears that he might use a personal army he had been building to attack Venetia or Rome. He was infuriated at the cession of his native Nice to France and contemplated a raid on the ballot boxes to stop the plebiscite.

33. Unrest in southern Italy. The success of national movements in central Italy encouraged similar movements in the south. Francis II had become King of Naples in 1859 and contemplated reforms to retain control. The danger-spot from his point of view was Sicily.

It was not clear, however, what interpretation Sicilian rebel leaders would give to liberty and unity. In March 1860 Sicilian autonomists approached Cavour for his terms should they succeed in a revolt in the south, but Cavour gave no encouragement to them. Since the south was temperamentally so different from the north, Cavour wanted to avoid complications in the former area until the work of union had been consolidated in the latter.

Crispi, a subtle republican conspirator, incited the Sicilians to revolt on 4th April. It was clear that this revolt needed external aid for its success.

34. Expedition of the Thousand. The rapidity of events forced Cavour to take advantage of movements already beyond his control. He had no particular sympathy for the south and distrusted Garibaldi. However, he knew that Mazzini's agents were active in the south and that unless he tried to mould events to his advantage republican and separatist ideas might succeed there.

He managed to divert the energies of Garibaldi to Sicily without officially encouraging him.

Garibaldi gathered a thousand picked volunteers at Genoa. Cavour refused to give public support, wanting to avoid a clash with Austria, and Garibaldi was prevented from getting recruits from the Piedmontese army or rifle supplies. The expedition, aboard two leaky steamers, made a successful landing at Marsala in Sicily on 11th May. The Neapolitan garrison realised too late that Garibaldi's Red-shirt army had no connection with the British navy, which had turned up at the same time to enforce respect for British property.

35. Conquest of Sicily. Garibaldi's ill-equipped army defeated the Neapolitans at Calatafini and he negotiated for their withdrawal to Naples. He gained thousands of recruits for his army and was helped by a rising in Palermo. By mid July he controlled the whole island. Cavour worried in case a republic was established, thus provoking intervention by the European powers. Though Garibaldi adopted the watchword of "Italy and Victor Emmanuel", Cavour had no faith as to the genuineness of Garibaldi's monarchical feelings or in his precipitate tactics.

36. Annexation of Naples and Sicily. On 18th August Garibaldi crossed the Straits of Messina. His progress on the mainland was triumphant, and resistance to him was negligible. King Francis was betrayed by many of his ministers and soldiers, and left Naples for Gaeta on 6th September. Garibaldi entered the city the next day.

The future was uncertain and Cavour decided it was time for Piedmont to take an official part in the drama. On 12th September he informed the powers that he was sending troops to the Papal States to re-establish order. He had the approval of Napoleon. His troops defeated the Papal army at Castelfidardo on the 18th and then pushed on into the Neapolitan kingdom. Cavour secured the consent of the Piedmontese Parliament for the annexation of southern Italy if this was approved by plebiscites. Garibaldi's forces had become involved in various engagements along the river Volturno. The Piedmontese invasion led to victory on 1st October. In February 1861 Gaeta fell and Francis II fled to Rome. Plebiscites held in the south in late 1860 registered large majorities for annexation by Piedmont. However, much pressure was put on voters to vote in this way and many southerners voted "yes" as signifying a return to settled government. Garibaldi handed over authority to King Victor Emmanuel and returned to Caprera.

37. Reasons for the Piedmontese invasion. Numerous factors prompted Cavour in his decision to send the army into the Papal States. His purpose was as follows.

(*a*) *To regain the initiative for Piedmont.* Cavour's political position was precarious since the cession of Nice and Savoy had been unpopular. Victor Emmanuel was also secretly working with Garibaldi. At the same time Garibaldi was gaining all the prestige and glory, and Cavour thought it politically unwise that his fame should completely overshadow that of the King.

(*b*) *To prevent the occupation of Rome.* It seemed that Garibaldi had no intention of handing over his command until he had conquered Rome, which would have provoked French or Austrian intervention. Cavour knew that Piedmontese troops could capture the Papal States while avoiding the occupation of Rome.

(*c*) *To prevent the creation of a republic.* Mazzini was in Naples and there was a strong party in favour of giving Naples and Sicily a separate and independent standing in a free and united Italy. Cavour had failed previously through his own agents to influence events there, and Garibaldi had refused to declare Sicily annexed to Piedmont. Cavour had no confidence in Garibaldi's ability to cope with the situation. There was even a faint possibility of a recovery by the supporters of the Bourbon monarchy.

(*d*) *To forestall Austrian intervention.* Cavour was anxious to achieve the *fait accompli* of annexation in the south before Austria was able to gain allies. He knew that Austria might well intervene if the Warsaw talks in October with Russia and Prussia were successful.

38. Non-intervention of the powers. The cause of Italian unity was helped by the rivalry of the powers, which prevented effective collaboration between them.

(*a*) *Anglo-French rivalry.* Both Britain and France suspected each other of trying to gain from the unrest in southern Italy.

(*i*) Napoleon, fearing a possible attack on Rome, proposed that a joint Anglo-French force should prevent Garibaldi crossing from Sicily to the mainland.

(*ii*) Cavour officially requested these powers to stop Garibaldi. He then sent a private envoy to Russell asking for no action to be taken.

(*iii*) Britain then said that the presence of French ships in the Straits of Messina would be resented. As the British navy was in the vicinity this indirectly helped Garibaldi to cross to Sicily without incident.

(*b*) *October dispatch of Russell.* British moral support for the Italian cause discouraged concerted action by the three eastern powers in Italy. In October, after plebiscites had been held in Naples and Sicily, Russell sent a famous dispatch to the European powers, which:

(*i*) stated that all states had the right to start revolutions similar to the 1688 revolution dethroning James II;

(*ii*) noted "the gratifying spectacle of a people building up the edifice of their liberties and consolidating the work of their independence".

(*c*) *Austro-Prussian rivalry.* Austria feared Piedmont might attack Venetia. She wanted to intervene in Italy but was anxious to reach an agreement with Prussia and Russia to protect her rear. Russia was prepared to give some moral assistance. However, Austria was not prepared to give concessions to Prussia in Germany to gain her support in Italy. Thus Prussia saw little to gain. Moreover, she wanted to remain on good terms with Britain over Schleswig-Holstein and with France.

Thus the meetings of the three eastern powers at Teplitz (July) and Warsaw (October) proved abortive on the Italian Question.

FINAL UNIFICATION, 1861–70

39. New Kingdom of Italy. After Villafranca Cavour had been determined to work for a unitary state. He opposed the federal concept of France and Austria. He gave Neapolitan and Sicilian leaders some hope that annexation would be followed by a large measure of autonomy for the south.

However, the Piedmontese began to impose a ruthless centralisation, ignoring many local customs and codes in the south. As a result the popularity which Victor Emmanuel had gained in Naples in November 1860 had almost disappeared by January 1861.

On 17th March 1861 the first Italian Parliament met in Turin and proclaimed Victor Emmanuel II King of Italy. The government was to be a limited constitutional monarchy based on the *statuto* of 1848 and a highly centralised one.

40. Death of Cavour. In June 1861 Cavour died, exhausted by his exertions, embittered by the attacks of Garibaldi and alarmed by his reports of unrest in the south. Cavour was himself partly responsible for the resurgence of trouble there, since he refused to adopt any administrative policy to allow for the acute differences between the south and the north. However, his death was a great blow to the new Italy. No future politician seemed capable of devising suitable policies for the centre and south, and Cavour might have prevented much of the chaos which was to follow in subsequent years.

41. Annexation of Venetia. The primary objective of Italian leaders became the acquisition of Venetia, but even the most skilful diplomacy could not get Austria to part with it voluntarily. In January 1866 Italy offered to purchase Venetia for 1,000 million lire. Francis Joseph appeared willing, but the military group at Court dissuaded him from a course which was considered contrary to Austria's honour.

In 1866 Italy allied with Prussia against Austria. Her army was defeated at Custozza and her navy at Lissa. However, Prussia was victorious, and Italy was rewarded for participating in the conflict by being granted Venetia.

42. Occupation of Rome. Cavour's last political act had been the securing of a parliamentary declaration that Rome should be the capital of Italy. As a result most Italians regarded unification as incomplete as long as the city was not under their control.

Events culminating in the occupation of Rome were as follows.

(*a*) In 1862 Garibaldi landed in Sicily without government support. He marched on Rome with his volunteers, but his forces were checked at Aspromonte by Piedmontese troops and dispersed. Napoleon told the Italians that it was impossible to withdraw French troops from Rome.

(*b*) A convention was settled in September 1864. Napoleon wanted to divert the Italians from Rome. It was agreed that French troops would be withdrawn if Italy guaranteed Papal territory and moved her capital to Florence within six months.

(*c*) The French garrison left Rome in December 1866. It got as far as Marseilles when news came in January that Garibaldi was making another attempt on Rome. It re-embarked and reached

Italy in time to join the Papal troops to defeat Garibaldi at Mentana.

(d) On the outbreak of the Franco-Prussian War the French troops garrisoned in Rome left. Italian troops then occupied the city.

DOMESTIC PROBLEMS, 1861–1914

43. Introduction. The new Italian state was formed in 1861, but serious internal problems remained, and new ones developed. The main problems, some of which were resolved successfully, were concerned with:

(a) relations between the north and south (*see* **44**);

(b) finance (*see* **45**);

(c) the creation of a stable political system (*see* **44** and **46**);

(d) the preservation of law and order (*see* **47**);

(e) the growth of socialism (*see* **47**);

(f) the Roman Question. For relations between the government and the Vatican, *see* **60**.

44. Differences between north and south. After political unification the problem of effective integration remained. D'Azeglio remarked: "We have made Italy; now we have to make Italians." Important social, economic, political and psychological differences continued to divide the people, and the south looked to the north with some degree of envy and dislike. The various problems were as follows.

(a) *Economic.* The north had the major share of the raw materials and industries, and a better soil and climate than the south. Consequently it had a higher standard of living. In the south there were virtually no industries, agricultural methods were old-fashioned, and the soil was poor and the climate dry.

(b) *Political.* Many southerners who had hoped for a degree of autonomy for the south were unreconciled to control from Piedmont. This included the aristocracy, who largely retired from active political life to the feudal isolation of their estates, many remaining loyal to the Pope and the Bourbons.

Many of the Neapolitan peasants who voted in the plebiscites of 1860 were voting, not only for the first time in their lives, but also for the last time. Property and literacy qualifications for the vote excluded far more southerners after 1861 than Piedmontese. It was not until 1912 that universal manhood suffrage was adopted for those aged over thirty.

(c) *Social*. Italians in the south adopted different attitudes to those in the north and were content with a slower pace of life. Interests were primarily political (in a conspiratorial and manipulative sense). Vast industrial projects linked to a competitive economic system, though likely to help their problems, evoked little enthusiasm.

(d) *Educational*. Owing to the higher degree of poverty in the south, illiteracy was common. There was a higher standard of elementary education in the north. Not until 1877 was any provision made for public education, and then it was not enforced owing to the expense.

(e) *Preservation of order*. After the death of Cavour no politician seemed able to devise suitable social and economic programmes to meet the needs of the centre and the south Free trade hardly seemed the answer, since it would depress the already struggling industries in the south. A combination of economic, social and political grievances soon led to a revival of brigandage and violence. The southerners hated taxation and conscription. Soon sixty battalions of troops were needed to quell civil war. In Sicily prolonged agitation led to a general revolt in 1866, when political forces of the Right and Left combined to defy the government. Secret societies, such as the Mafia, developed to terrorise the countryside.

45. Financial difficulties. Debts of the different states taken over by the new Italian kingdom were large. The nation also had to spend large sums on the army and navy and on public works, especially on the building of railways. In 1862 government receipts were found to meet only half of government expenditure. For several years there were large annual deficits, involving the need for new loans and increased taxation. In 1868 an excise duty was levied on corn passing through the mill. The high price of bread reduced many in the south to starvation level. Not until 1879 was financial stability achieved, with receipts exceeding expenditure.

46. Political instability and corruption. During the period 1871–1914 there were frequent changes of government. Weak leadership and numerous opposition factions gave little cohesiveness to the political system.

Loose coalitions of Right and Left existed, the former being strong in the industrial north and the latter in the south. However, ideological or sectional affiliations were of less significance than the desire of deputies to gain office and retain it by any means possible. Many politicians nurtured on corruption in the south carried their methods into Parliament. Bribery and corruption, notably the buying of the votes of one or more factions (known as *transformismo* – opportunism), was freely engaged in by the political leaders. It was justified on the grounds of the impossibility of forming a government by any other means.

Generally Italians despised their parliamentarians as greedy hypocrites who seemed more concerned with local issues, petty intrigues and special interests than with important major economic and social issues. Depretis, Crispi and Giolitti, the outstanding names of the period 1871–1914, all practised the manipulation of votes and the rigging of elections.

47. Socialism and violence. During the 1890s socialist and anarchist sentiment grew among the workers and poorer groups. In 1893 there were serious peasant troubles in Sicily. In 1898 the army was called out to deal with widespread violence. In 1900 King Humbert was assassinated. During 1901–4 there was a series of strikes, riots and bomb-throwing incidents.

(*a*) *Reasons for the growth of discontent.*

(*i*) Disgust of the people with the political corruption practised by their leaders.

(*ii*) Lack of concern of the government with poverty and poor social conditions.

(*iii*) Lack of machinery for the airing of grievances in a legitimate fashion. Trade unions were not permitted. After 1894 severe laws were passed against anarchist and socialist organisations.

(*iv*) Colonial failures.

(*v*) Restricted franchise. It was not until 1912 that all men aged over thirty were allowed to vote.

(*b*) *Reasons for the decrease in discontent.* Socialist agitation and violence diminished after 1904, though people still disliked parliamentarianism as it was practised. Factors contributing to the decline of discontent were as follows.

(*i*) Social reforms: old-age pensions were introduced in 1898. Giovanni Giolitti, the left-wing Premier during most of the period 1901–14, introduced a number of social reforms. These included measures which improved factory conditions and public health, established national insurance and abolished child labour.

(*ii*) Harsh treatment of agitators: the government took forceful measures against all offenders against law and order. In 1898 martial law was proclaimed and heavy sentences were given by courts-martial. In 1902 the railway strikers were called up as reservists.

(*iii*) Influence of Pope Pius X: after 1903 he permitted Catholics to take part in political struggles involving the safety of the political order.

ITALIAN FOREIGN POLICY, 1870–1914

48. Great-power policy. Italy was basically a poor country with grave internal problems. The illiteracy rate was considerable and high taxes and low wages encouraged emigration. The country lacked essential raw materials such as coal and iron.

However, Italy's large population entitled her to rank as one of the smaller of the great European powers, and her political leaders wanted her to play an important international role. Exploits abroad were convenient, too, for distracting popular attention from ills at home. However, her military capability was weak. Bismarck once remarked that Italy had "poor teeth and such a large appetite".

Evidence of her desire for great-power status was shown in the following.

(*a*) Irredentist agitation (*see* **49**).

(*b*) Colonial activities (*see* **50**).

(*c*) The creation of a network of alliances (*see* **51–54**).

(*d*) The building of a large army and navy.

49. Irredentism. After 1870 the Italian government maintained a constant agitation for the following territories which were still under Austrian rule.

(*a*) *The Trentino.* In 1866 Venetia had been interpreted in a narrow sense. The Trentino (South Tyrol) contained 370,000 Italians under Austrian control. Austria had in effect a military outpost thrust deep into the heart of Italy. The region's industrial products were excluded from the Italian market. Clashes frequently occurred between Italian workers and Austrian officials in Trieste and the Trentino.

(*b*) *Istria.* In 1903 the Austrian authorities refused Italian

subjects a separate university, and an anti-Austrian demonstration occurred in Fiume.

50. Colonialism. Italy was the one power whose European policy
was largely dominated by colonial considerations. Italy had an
expanding population, but many migrated to North and South
America to improve their economic conditions. Italy desired to
find her own territories abroad which would provide outlets for
emigration, satisfy the rising ambitions of big business for
markets and of the leaders for great-power status, and boost
the nationalistic spirit. She had thoughts of reviving the glories
of the ancient Roman Empire and of establishing an African
colony on that "fourth shore".

Her activities were concerned with the following areas:

(a) *Tunis.* At first Italy had her eyes on this North African
possession of Turkey. Her designs were thwarted by France in
1881 (*see* XIX, 25).

(b) *Ethiopia and the Red Sea* (*see* XIX, 27).

(c) *Tripoli.* Eventually, in 1911, Italy achieved her aim at
founding a North African empire in Tripoli (*see* XIX, 26).

51. The Triple Alliance. In 1882 Italy joined the Dual Alliance
of Austria and Germany, thus converting it into the Triple
Alliance.

(a) *Italy* wanted an alliance for the following reasons.

(i) Fear of isolation: the Italians resented the French protectorate over Tunis (1881) and wanted allies to support her
colonial ventures.

(ii) Desire to strengthen the position of the government
against the Papacy: some Roman Catholics had been plotting
with Austria to restore the Papacy's former power or for Austria
to regain Venetia.

(iii) Need to fortify the monarchical principle: the King was
alarmed at the continued evidence of republicanism in the
country.

(b) *Austria and Germany* hoped that the alliance would
prevent Italy from:

(i) attacking Austria in the rear if that power was involved
in war with Russia;

(ii) forming an alliance with France or Britain. In actual
fact Italy was to reach understandings with other powers which

virtually made null and void her obligations in the Triple Alliance (*see* **52–54**).

52. Friendship with Britain. Rudini, the Italian Premier in the 1890s, stated that Britain formed the cornerstone of Italy's other alliances. Economic considerations necessitated close links, since Britain provided valuable iron and coal to Italy. Evidence of Italian concern to maintain friendly relations with Britain can be seen from the following.

(*a*) *The special reservations made in the Triple Alliance.* When Italy joined the Triple Alliance in 1882, a protocol was added stating that that alliance was not directed against Britain. Though this was left out in the renewal treaties of 1887 and 1890, in the latter year provision was made to include Britain in the alliance if necessary. Italy made it clear that she would not support her allies against Britain.

(*b*) *The Mediterranean agreement of 1887 with Britain and Austria.* The three powers agreed to maintain the *status quo* in the Near East, the Turkish Straits and the Balkans. Italy was also promised the same sort of help in Tripoli as she might give Britain in Egypt. The agreement was aimed against France.

53. Co-operation with France. At first there was acute tension between the two countries. This was due to Italy's claims on Tunis, the Italian refusal to divulge the contents of the Triple Alliance, the tariff wars and French support of the Vatican.

However, France wished to detach Italy from her existing alliances and to break up the Mediterranean coalition. Relations improved gradually as a result of the following developments.

(*a*) *Franco-Italian convention* (1896). Italy recognised the French protectorate over Tunis in return for certain political and commercial privileges.

(*b*) *Commercial treaty* (1898). This ended the tariff war.

(*c*) *Secret agreement* (1900). Italy agreed to recognise French aspirations in Morocco in return for French recognition of Italian aims in Tripoli.

(*d*) *Secret agreement* (1902). Italy promised that she would remain neutral in any war in which France was involved. This meant that Italy would no longer help Germany in the event of a French attack, one of the original purposes of the Triple Alliance.

(*e*) *Exchange visits.* In 1903 Victor Emmanuel visited Paris, and in 1904 President Loubet visited Rome, where he received a great welcome.

54. Arrangements with Russia and Austria. In 1909 Italy made the following agreements with Russia and Austria which partly conflicted.

(*a*) *The Racconigi agreement with Russia.* In October, after the Bosnian crisis, Russia and Italy made an arrangement by which they agreed on the following points.

(*i*) As far as possible, they would both preserve the *status quo* in the Balkans and would not make agreements about that area with a third power without the participation of the other.

(*ii*) Russia would observe "benevolent neutrality" towards Italian designs in Tripoli and Cyrenaica.

(*iii*) Italy would support Russia in her plans to open the Turkish Straits to her ships.

(*b*) *The agreement with Austria.* The provision in (*a*)(*i*) above was aimed against Austria and hence was contrary to Italian commitments in the Triple Alliance. A few days later Italy balanced it with an agreement with Austria. This stipulated that neither would make agreements with a third party without the knowledge of the other.

55. Observations on Italian foreign policy. As Italy was not quite a great power, she tried to occupy an indeterminate position between the powers. The following points can be made for and against her policy.

(*a*) The secret and inconsistent promises in Italy's alliance arrangements made nonsense of the whole system. Italy found the obligations to various countries difficult to reconcile.

(*b*) Italy failed to give consistent support to her allies.

(*i*) In 1906 at Algeciras she supported France and Britain against Germany.

(*ii*) She made it clear to Germany that in any war between France or Britain and Germany she would not consider herself bound.

(*c*) Italy acted as a restraining influence to prevent major war. This was illustrated in her policy during the Algeciras Conference of 1906, and during the Balkan crises of 1906, 1909 and 1912–13 when she worked to hold back the warlike pretensions of Austria.

THE PAPACY

56. The eclipse of the Papacy after the French Revolution. In 1796 French armies invaded Papal territories, and in 1798 the French created the Roman Republic. The Pope, Pius VI, was taken to southern France. In 1801 a new Pope, Pius VII, concluded a Concordat with France and was given back most of his former territories. This, however, was not the end of the conflict between France and the Papacy. As a result of Pius's refusal to join the Continental System, the Papal States were declared incorporated into France in 1809. The Pope replied by excommunicating Napoleon, whereupon he was arrested by the Emperor.

57. Restoration of Catholic power. After 1815 the Papacy recaptured much of the ground lost during the period 1789–1815. The Papal territories were restored and there was a revival of Catholicism in Europe. In Protestant states, specially among the governing classes, sympathy grew for the Catholic Church as a mainstay against the disruptive tendencies of liberalism and nationalism.

The Pope's position was strengthened by influential writings which glorified the Catholic Church. An example of such works was Joseph de Maistre's *Du Pape* (1817).

After 1848 the middle classes in Europe also became acutely aware of the rising influence of socialist ideas among the working classes. Men of property saw priests of the Catholic Church as the "spiritual gendarmes" who might guard the populace against the infection of "social heresies". Pope Pius IX, threatened with the loss of temporal sovereignty, sought compensation by strengthening the influence of the Papacy. He concluded advantageous Concordats with Spain in 1851 and Austria in 1855. Roman Catholic hierarchies were re-established in Britain in 1850 and Holland in 1853.

58. Opposition of the Vatican to contemporary ideas. The growth of nationalism, in particular in Italy, threatened the Pope's temporal power. In addition, many nineteenth-century developments appeared to threaten the spiritual power of the Pope. As a result the Vatican steadily opposed all modern ideas.

(*a*) *Nationalism.* Catholics tended to support the nationalist cause in the Polish and Belgian rebellions of 1830 and they animated much of the Irish resistance to Britain. However,

Pope Gregory XVI ordered the clergy to support the established governments. For the role of the Pope in the Italian risings of 1830 and 1848, *see* 3(*c*), **6** and **9**.

(*b*) *Liberalism*. In 1830 a French priest, Félicité de Lamennais, founded a paper called *L'Avenir* and campaigned for freedom of education, the press and worship. In 1832 the Pope issued an encyclical, the Bull *Mirari Vos*, which condemned liberty of conscience and the press, and stated that revolt for any reason against established governments was intolerable.

(*c*) *General progress*. An example of modern trends disliked by the Church was the theories propounded by Charles Darwin in his *Origin of Species* (1859). His account of the descent of man from the lowest animals seemed to render untenable the Biblical account of life and to deprive man of the immortal soul bestowed on the race of Adam.

In the *Syllabus of Error* (1864) the Pope reaffirmed his opposition to nationalism and liberalism, and to many of the current ideas and movements in science and politics. He declared that it was an error to assume that the Pope ought to agree with the trends of "modern civilisation".

59. Doctrine of Papal infallibility. In July 1870, at the time of the impending downfall of the Pope's temporal authority, the Vatican Council stated that, when pronouncing *ex cathedra* on matters of faith and morals, the Pope speaks with final and supernatural authority. Catholic bishops were empowered to punish those who refused compliance with such pronouncements by excommunication, expulsion or refusal to perform the marriage ceremony.

This was an attempt to exalt the Papacy above all secular states and to extend "faith and morals" to the political sphere. It resulted in the following.

(*a*) Considerable dissension within the Catholic Church.

(*b*) An outbreak of a feud between the Vatican and many European governments. In particular Austria annulled the Concordat of 1855 in 1867 and Bismarck pursued the *Kulturkampf* in Germany (*see* X, **6**).

60. Relations between Italy and the Vatican. In 1861 Cavour failed to induce Pope Pius IX to abandon his claims to temporal power. After the Piedmontese invasion, the Papal States became part of the new Italy. In September 1870 the Italian troops entered Rome on the withdrawal of the French.

Relations between the Italian government and the Vatican were fixed for many years by the policies adopted by each during the period 1871–4.

(a) *Policy of the Italian government.* The government tried to carry out Cavour's idea of "a free Church in a free State". In 1871 the Italian Parliament passed the "Law of Guarantees". Its provisions were:

(i) the recognition of the Pope as an independent sovereign of the Vatican state within the city of Rome, and in possession of the Vatican and Lateran Palaces;

(ii) the offer of an annual income of £129,000 in compensation for the loss of his possessions, and the grant of exemption from tax to his state.

(b) *Policy of the Vatican.* The Pope refused to accept the Law of Guarantees and regarded himself a "prisoner" of the government. He refused to recognise the new Italy, and this created religious disunity. In the Bull *Non Expedit* (1874) he ordered Catholics not to vote in general elections. This was generally ignored, but it meant that for many years devout Catholics were prevented from contributing to political life.

61. Policies of Pope Leo XIII. Pope Leo XIII (1878–1903) opposed liberal and national ideas alike. He made little change to the political principles of Pius IX, and insisted that the Church should superintend every form of secular life. However, he was more tolerant than his predecessor and he perceived that democracy might prove as useful as monarchy for preserving Catholic principles, though he did not want to advocate any particular form of government.

(a) *Relations with Germany and France.*

(i) After 1878 relations were improved with Germany, where the anti-clerical legislation was gradually repealed.

(ii) As relations between the Vatican and the Italian government remained poor, the Pope wanted to secure French aid for the solution of the Roman Question. After 1870 the French government had steadfastly supported the Vatican in its domestic struggle with the government but had also passed a number of anti-clerical measures at home. In 1890 Leo made a deliberate effort to improve his relations with France by instructing French Catholics to break with monarchical principles and support the Republic. He encouraged the policy of the *Ralliement* of 1890. The Tsar, contemplating a Russo-French alliance, accepted the Pope's judgment that the French Third Republic was permanent.

(*b*) *Encyclical Rerum Novarum* (1891). This was an attempt to apply Christian principles to the relations between capital and labour. It stated that a worker had the right to a just wage sufficient to allow him and his family to live properly and that employers had important moral duties to perform.

62. Pope Pius X. This Pope was less prone to compromise with the forces of secularism than his predecessor. Relations between the Vatican and the Italian state improved but Vatican-French relations became worse.

(*a*) *France.*

(*i*) The Pope quarrelled with the French government over the appointment of bishops.

(*ii*) The Pope denounced the visit of President Loubet of France to the Italian King in 1904 as "a grave offence to a sovereign pontiff". As a result, the French government increased the severity of the anti-clerical laws and ended the Condordat (*see* VII, 16(*c*)).

(*iii*) The anti-clerical laws were condemned by the Pope in the encyclical *Vehementer*. Modernism was denounced as a heresy and in 1908 the French Catholic priest, Alfred Loisy, a scholar, was excommunicated. Many of his works were already on the Index of Prohibited Books.

(*b*) *Italy.* In 1904 the Pope was asked by some laymen if they could take part in the elections to keep out the socialists. He replied, "Do as your conscience dictates." As a result, two clerical members were elected to the Italian legislature and the socialists lost six seats.

NOTE: Relations between the Vatican and the Italian government were not regularised until the Lateran Treaty of 1929.

PROGRESS TEST 13

1. What were the main political units in Italy after 1815? **(1)**
2. Why was no attempt made in 1815 to promote Italian unity? **(1, 2)**

3. Discuss the various suggestions made as to the future Italian state. (2(c))

4. Estimate the influence of Austria in Italian affairs before 1833. (1, 3)

5. Mention the factors which contributed to greater Italian unity between 1815 and 1848. (4, 5)

6. Estimate the importance of Mazzini in stimulating Italian nationalism before 1848. (5)

7. Was Pope Pius IX a liberal? (6)

8. What were the areas of revolt in 1848? (7)

9. Account for the collapse of the 1848 revolts. (9–13)

10. Why did Piedmont become the hope of the Italian liberals after 1848? (15)

11. Explain how Cavour planned to promote Italian unity. Illustrate your answer with events from the period 1850–6. (16–18, 20)

12. Describe Napoleon III's interests in Italy. (19)

13. What arrangements were made by Cavour and Napoleon during 1858–9? (22)

14. Did Cavour provoke Austria into war in 1860? (24–26)

15. Why did Napoleon decide to make peace with Austria without consulting Cavour? What were the provisions of the Peace of Villafranca? Why were they unenforceable? (28–30)

16. Discuss the role of Britain in assisting Italian unity in the years 1859–61. (30(d), 38(a)–(b))

17. What contribution did Garibaldi make towards aiding Italian unity? (32, 34–36, 42)

18. Why did Piedmont invade the Papal States in 1860? (37)

19. What problems concerning Italian unity remained after Cavour's death? (39, 41–44, 49)

20. Account for the political instability in Italy after 1870. (44–47)

21. What did Italy hope to achieve in foreign affairs after 1870? To what extent was she successful? (48–55)

22. Discuss the influence of the Vatican in European affairs between 1815 and 1905. (57–59, 61)

23. Why were relations between the Italian government and the Vatican poor after 1871? (60)

CHAPTER XIV

Turkey and Europe, 1768–1841

THE EMERGENCE OF THE EASTERN QUESTION

1. Introduction. At the beginning of the nineteenth century the Ottoman Empire stretched from Asia Minor to North Africa. It was still substantially intact and in South-east Europe bordered Austria and Russia. In Europe the Sultan still ruled over some 238,000 square miles and some 8 million people, mostly Christians. By 1908, as the map on p. 282 shows, Turkish territory in Europe had been greatly reduced in extent.

2. The Eastern Question. This term covered the problems caused in the nineteenth century through the decline in power of the Ottoman Empire. Lord Morley summed up the Eastern Question as "that intractable and interwoven tangle of conflicting interests, rival peoples, and antagonistic faiths".

The specific problems were as follows.

(*a*) Turkey was an Asiatic (Oriental) power ruling European territory. As the Turks differed in race, creed and social customs, they had never been accorded an equal place among the European Christian powers. This was changed in 1856 (*see* XV, **19**(*b*)).

(*b*) Turkey misgoverned millions of Christians. As the vast administrative machine based on Constantinople decayed, her subjects were governed with greater inefficiency and harshness.

(*c*) Periodic outbreaks of revolt occurred against the inept and unjust rule. Gradually small subject Christian nationalities organised themselves to fight for independence. The first serious revolt was by the Serbs in 1804 (*see* **15**).

(*d*) Turkey had no effective answer to the problems of her empire.

(*i*) The Sultans either had difficulty in implementing reforms owing to the opposition of vested interests or refused to consider them. Suggestions of the European powers were ignored or implemented only when force was threatened.

(*ii*) Turkey's response to rebellion was massacre and murder.

The government had no constructive ideas. Again, it was prepared to make concessions only if the European powers threatened the use of superior force.

(e) The relationship which should exist between European powers, Turkey and her empire was never certain. The position first became serious when Russia contemplated partitioning the Ottoman Empire, first with Austria in 1781, and then with France in March 1801 (see **10** and **13**).

3. European powers and Turkey. No agreement was ever reached for long among European powers as to the most appropriate policy to adopt towards Turkey. Their conflicting interests complicated the problem of how best order and stability could be maintained in the "power vacuum" created in Europe as Turkey declined.

The basic alternatives were as follows.

(a) *Preservation of Turkey.* Britain and Austria once hoped that Turkey might reform her administration and act as a bulwark against Russian expansion. Towards the end of the 1870s both abandoned this policy for different reasons (see (b)(iii) and (iv)).

(b) *Dismemberment of Turkey.* This policy came to be followed by four of the powers.

(i) Except for temporary policies of supporting the *status quo* after 1833 and 1897, Russia pursued expansionist policies at Turkey's expense. These policies were carried out from the direction of the Black Sea coast, the eastern flank as Persia declined, and later from the Balkans.

(ii) Before 1840 and after 1871, France had designs on the African territories of the Sultan.

(iii) In the 1870s Austria embarked on an active expansionist policy to compete with Russia and as compensation for the loss of influence in Germany.

(iv) In the 1870s Britain decided that independent Balkan states might stabilise the area better than tyrannical Turkish rule.

4. Conflicting interests of the European powers. The powers involved, Russia, France, Britain and Austria, had various interests with regard to the Ottoman Empire.

(a) *Russia.* Her interests were as follows.

(i) Political and strategic. Russia was a land-locked state

in winter when the sea froze and blocked her ports. Hence she was anxious to extend her power along the Black Sea and gain access to the Mediterranean.

(*ii*) Religious. Since 1774 the Tsar had had rights as protector of the Greek Orthodox Christians (*see* **20**(*a*)).

(*iii*) Racial. The Tsar considered himself the natural protector of fellow Slavs in the Ottoman Empire (*see* XVI, **1**).

(*b*) *France*. This country had two important interests.

(*i*) Politico-economic. Since Napoleon Bonaparte's time France had entertained hopes of extending her power in North Africa and Asia Minor. She therefore supported dependencies of Turkey in these parts in their resistance to the Sultan. In 1840 her policy of supporting Egypt against Turkey received a severe setback (*see* **30**).

(*ii*) Religious. France had treaty rights as protector of Roman Catholic interests in the Ottoman Empire.

(*c*) *Britain*. This country had developing interests in the Mediterranean for commercial and strategic reasons. Britain was determined to:

(*i*) protect the route to India;

(*ii*) oppose the intention of France and Russia to dismember Turkey. Britain preferred to see the weak power of Turkey in control of the vital seas to the development of Russian and French influence in Asia Minor and the Persian Gulf.

(*d*) *Austria*. Her interests in the Ottoman Empire were until the 1870s of a defensive nature. They were as follows.

(*i*) Strategic. Austria was concerned lest a strong power threatened her by controlling part of the Danube.

(*ii*) Racial and political. As a large proportion of her subjects were Slavs they were closely akin to the peoples in the Ottoman Empire. Therefore any demands for independence from Turkish subjects might result in similar demands being made to Austria from her Slav subjects.

5. Reasons for the slow decline of Turkey. Turkey's decline after 1683 until 1914 was only a very gradual process. She managed to survive for a long time owing to the conflicting interests of European powers and of various rebellious groups in her empire. Turkey continued to be a substantial military power. This was illustrated by her defeat of an Austrian force in 1788 and her delay of a Russian advance at Plevna in 1879. However, Turkey's decline became inevitable as the result of the following factors.

(*a*) The growth of the power of Russia and her expansion from the eighteenth century onwards.

(*b*) Turkey's failure to reform her inefficient system of government (*see* **6**).

(*c*) The decline in the military prowess of Turkey's armed forces (*see* **7**(*b*)).

(*d*) The spread of the ideas of nationalism and liberty as a result of the French Revolution. For early outbreaks of revolt in the Ottoman Empire, *see* **15–24**.

6. Turkish government and society. At one time the Turkish Civil Service was unmatched by any in the West. Gradually, however, it became corrupt, lazy, disloyal and inefficient. Also, the social system helped to undermine the fighting spirit of the Turkish forces. The Turks came to rely more and more on slaves and foreigners to do the work for them.

(*a*) *Turkey was a slave society.*

(*i*) Most of the officials from the Grand Vizier downwards were technically slaves of the Sultan. Most of the palace officials were recruited from the tribute of Christian boys levied every few years in the provinces. They were brought up as Moslems and trained for administrative posts or for the Sultan's special body of troops, the Janissaries.

(*ii*) At one time unveiled Turkish women were free and respected companions of their warrior husbands. Then the harem system achieved an importance out of all proportion to its true significance.

(*b*) *Turkey relied on foreigners to help in government.* The Phanariot Greeks (those resident in Constantinople) helped administer the Empire, aided by the Orthodox Christians.

7. Divisions in the Ottoman Empire. The Turks had never been successful in welding together into a political whole their disparate lands. Government was highly decentralised, as can be seen from the existence of the following groups.

(*a*) *Local chieftains* (pashas). When they had been in power a long time they established virtual autonomy from the Sultan's rule. They engaged in continuous intrigue and warfare against each other and ignored many of the Sultan's decrees. Two rebellious subordinates were:

(*i*) Ali Pasha, the "Lion of Janina" (*see* **16**);

(*ii*) Mehemet Ali (*see* **26**).

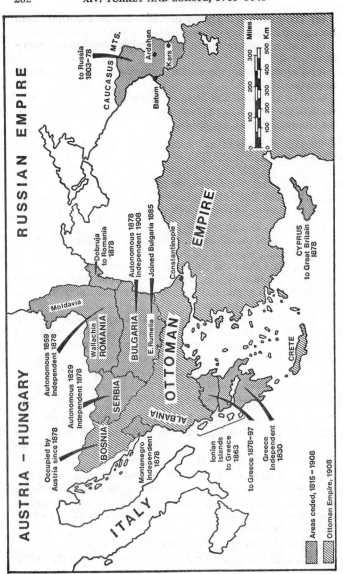

The dismemberment of the Ottoman Empire in Europe, 1815–1908

(*b*) *The Janissaries.* This professional picked corps of shock troops, founded in the fourteenth century, developed in time a "will of its own" and became a closed corporation of some 112,000 guards. They lived in exclusive barracks at the expense of the surrounding countryside. When they ceased to be significant as a fighting force they continued to have a stranglehold on government.

In 1826 Mahmud II established a new military corps loyal to him personally, and, when the Janissaries in Constantinople rebelled, they were destroyed.

(*c*) *Rival factions.* Though the Sultan was in theory autocratic with supreme power, in practice he had to conciliate vested interests and rival factions.

Reforms were difficult to introduce. Selim III (1789–1809) attempted reform but roused opposition in the Central Council, the army and the aristocracy. He was deposed in 1807 by a palace revolution led by the Janissaries. In the following year a counter-revolution led to the murder of Selim and his successor and the accession of Mahmud II.

THE OTTOMAN EMPIRE BEFORE 1812

8. The Ottoman Empire. The House of Osman (Ottoman is a corruption of Osman) ruled the Ottoman Empire from 1288 to 1922. It was the longest-lived dynasty known in history. Osman I (1288–1325) belonged to a warlike Turkish-speaking tribe in the frontier lands of Central Asia which had been converted to Islam.

(*a*) *Expansion of the Turks.* In the fourteenth century the Turks migrated to and overran Anatolia. They gained a footing on the European shore of the Dardanelles owing to dissensions between European peoples. After the defeat of the Serbs and Bosnians at the battle of Kossovo (1389) all of South-east Europe was open to the invaders. In 1453 they overran the Eastern Roman or Byzantine Empire and captured Constantinople.

By 1675 they were in the Ukraine, the Balkans, North Africa and the Persian Gulf. Apart from a few Spanish outposts in North Africa, the entire Mediterranean coastline from Morocco to Dalmatia was under Turkish control.

(*b*) *Their main opponents.* The Christian rallying-point against the Turkish onslaught was the Hapsburg monarchy. One part guarded East and Central Europe and the Danube. The other, based on Spain, the Balearic Isles, the Two Sicilies and Sardinia, opposed the Turks advancing westwards. At various times the Pope organised Holy Leagues against the Turks. The Hapsburgs had numerous allies to help them.

One decisive defeat of the Turkish navy was at the battle of Lepanto by a combined Spanish and Venetian fleet in 1571.

(c) *Withdrawal of the Turks.* In 1683, for the second time, the Turks besieged Vienna. They were routed by a combined German and Polish army under Charles of Lorraine and King John Sobieski of Poland, who came to the rescue of the Hapsburgs.

From this time Turkish power slowly declined.

(*i*) After her defeat by Russia in the war of 1677–81 Turkey had to give up most of the Ukraine, only recently gained from Poland.

(*ii*) In 1699 Hapsburg forces led by Eugene of Savoy drove the Turks out of Hungary. Austria then received Hungary, Transylvania, Croatia and Slavonica.

9. The Russo-Turkish War, 1768–74. In 1768 France urged Turkey to defend the Poles against Russian pressure. However, the Turks were soon defeated, and the Russians occupied the Crimea and the territory bordering Austria, Moldavia and Wallachia. This had the following important results.

(a) *Threat of Austrian intervention* (1771). Austria was alarmed at the sudden growth of Russian power and threatened war.

(b) *First partition of Poland* (1772). To prevent an Austro-Russian war, Frederick the Great of Prussia persuaded the two powers that the partition of Poland might be an acceptable alternative to outbidding each other in the Balkans. Exhausted after four years of civil war, Poland offered no resistance.

(c) *Treaty of Kutchuk-Kainardji* (1774). Catherine the Great of Russia, disturbed by the Pugachev rebellion at home (1773) and now involved in Poland, agreed to peace terms with Turkey. As a result Russia made the following substantial gains at Turkey's expense.

(*i*) Freedom of navigation for Russian ships on the Black Sea. This sea had been closed to all non-Turkish vessels since the end of the sixteenth century.

(*ii*) The right to send merchant ships through the Straits of the Bosphorus and Dardanelles to the Mediterranean.

(*iii*) Special rights in the Moldavian and Wallachian provinces.

(*iv*) The right to build an Orthodox Christian church in Galata (the foreign quarter of Constantinople).

(*v*) The granting of Crimean independence by Turkey.

10. Russo-Austrian co-operation. In 1780 Catherine the Great schemed to drive the Turks out of Europe and restore the Greek Empire with her grandson as emperor. As part of this scheme, which was never put into operation, Austria was to receive the western half of the Balkans.

After 1781 Austria decided to co-operate with Russia in the Near East. Russia then demanded the establishment of a hereditary Russian governor in Moldavia and Wallachia. Turkey had been intriguing with the Crimean Tartars, and in 1783 Russia occupied the Crimea on the pretext of restoring order. Britain and Austria persuaded Turkey to accept the inevitable.

In August 1787 war broke out between Turkey and Russia, joined in 1788 by Austria. At first Austrian forces were defeated by Turkey but they eventually took Belgrade. However, Austria was soon alarmed by unrest at home and the French Revolution, and under pressure from Prussia the Treaty of Sistova was made with Turkey in August 1791. Belgrade was given back to Turkey in return for a strip of northern Bosnia for Austria.

In 1792 Russia gave Turkey favourable peace terms at Jassy, so as to concentrate on her war with Sweden and on Polish affairs.

11. French interest in Egypt. In 1798 France took an active interest in the Near East. France had succeeded in fighting a European coalition, but Britain remained unsubdued. An expedition to attack Britain via Ireland had failed. A direct invasion of Britain seemed risky, and Napoleon concluded that the best way to injure Britain was through her overseas possessions.

Napoleon interested the Directory in a project to attack Egypt. His reasons for the scheme were as follows.

(*a*) It would be a useful "jumping-off point" for establishing alliances with the semi-independent rulers of Syria, Mesopotamia, Arabia and Persia.

(*b*) If a French navy could be established in Red Sea ports, France might recover her former pre-eminence in India and check the growing British power.

(*c*) Egypt would be useful for resources and trade, and as a base for founding a new empire or attacking Turkey if it was decided "to take Europe in the rear".

12. Defeat of Napoleon. In May 1798 Napoleon led a French expedition to Egypt. Malta was captured *en route*. The military caste of the Mamelukes were defeated at the battle of the Pyramids and Napoleon entered Cairo. However, on 1st August, the British fleet under Nelson destroyed the French fleet at Aboukir Bay on the Nile. This meant Napoleon was cut off and could no longer rely on reinforcements from France. While he was confined in Egypt, numerous scientific and archaeological activities were carried out by civilian specialists he had brought with him.

Turkey declared war on France. Napoleon abandoned plans for an overland advance towards India and invaded Syria. He was held up by the English admiral Sir Sidney Smith, who defended Acre. Napoleon was forced to retreat to Egypt in May 1799, his army having suffered heavy losses. He defeated a Turkish army but then European problems forced him to return to France. The remaining French forces surrendered in 1801.

13. Franco-Russian rivalry. Both France and Russia were uncertain as to the best policy to adopt over Turkey. In 1801 each country contemplated partitioning Turkey with the help of the other, at another time of taking unilateral action against Turkey, and at yet another time of aiding Turkey against the rival claims of the other.

Examples of these shifting policies were as follows.

(*a*) *Russian aid to Turkey against France.* In 1799 Russia negotiated with Turkey a secret clause for the right of passage of her ships through the Straits during the duration of the war with France. A joint Russo-Turkish expedition expelled the French from the Ionian Isles.

(*b*) *Russian plan for Turkey's partition.* In 1799 Count Rostophchin, the Tsar's chief adviser, recommended Turkey's partition in conjunction with the French. Austria and Prussia were to receive compensation.

The murder of the Tsar Paul in 1801 led the advisers of his son Alexander I to avoid plans for partition. They considered it would result in Russia having a powerful France as a neighbour instead of a weak Turkey.

(*c*) *French plan to help Turkey against Russia.* France then co-operated with Turkey in the Balkans and in her plan to recover the Crimea. The prospect increased of a French–Persian–Turkish alliance. French influence increased in Egypt, where Mehemet Ali became Pasha in 1805. In 1807 the British made an unsuccessful attempt to exclude French power from Egypt.

14. Third Russo-Turkish War. In 1806 the Russian Tsar renewed old claims to influence in Moldavia and Wallachia. Turkey accused Russia of giving help to the rebellious Serbs (*see* **15**), though Russia had in fact given little help apart from small subsidies. Turkey declared war on Russia but was heavily defeated. In 1812, by the Treaty of Bucharest, Turkey received favourable peace terms owing to the imminent French invasion of Russia. Details of the treaty were as follows.

(*a*) Most of Bessarabia went to Russia.

(*b*) Moldavia and Wallachia remained under Turkish rule.

(*c*) Parts of Serbia which had rebelled in 1804 were to be autonomous.

EARLY REVOLTS IN THE
OTTOMAN EMPIRE, 1804–30

15. Serbian rebellion. In 1804 the first rebellion occurred among the subjects of the Sultan. The Serbs, under the wild chieftain Kara George, rose not against the Sultan's authority but against the cruel rule of the local Janissaries and their oppression of the Christian population. After 1805, however, the Serbs demanded regional autonomy and in March 1807 embarked on a massacre of Turks in Belgrade.

The Sultan had been sympathetic at first to the cause of the rebels but then decided to quell the disturbances. In 1812 the Serbs were crushed and Kara George exiled. However, they rose again in 1815 under Milosh Obrenovich and in 1817 secured substantial concessions. The Serbs were to have some local autonomy under a hereditary prince of the native dynasty.

Subsequent developments are discussed in a later chapter (*see* XVI).

16. A rebellious pasha crushed. By 1817 a powerful Turkish chieftain, Ali, and his son, Veli, controlled the whole of Albania, Thessaly, Western Macedonia and central Greece. In 1821 Ali Pasha attacked the Sultan's forces, promising the people a constitution if they would help him. Ali was defeated and killed in 1822. The significance of the revolt was that it kept Turkish armies occupied throughout 1822, which allowed a national revolt in Greece to develop.

17. Revolt in Moldavia and Wallachia. In 1821 a former Greek general in the Russian army, Prince Alexander Ypsilanti, attempted a revolt against Turkey in the provinces inhabited by Romanians. The object was to invade Greece after these provinces had been liberated. He had been allowed to prepare his filibustering expedition in Russia, but the Tsar, under Metternich's influence, refused to give him the expected support and disowned him at the Laibach Conference of the major powers.

Ypsilanti was defeated by the Turks at Dragashan in June 1821. He fled and was imprisoned by the Austrians.

18. The Greek rising in the Morea. The revolt of Ypsilanti inspired imitation. In the Morea the Greeks rose and started to massacre all available Mohammedans. When a Turkish force surrendered at Tripolitsa 12,000 of them were put to death. The Turks retaliated in kind. The Greek Patriarch and two other bishops were hanged in Constantinople, and in April 1822 most of the Greek islanders of Chios were slaughtered.

In January 1822 a National Assembly at Epidauros proclaimed the independence of Greece. However, this meant little as the Greeks did not combine their forces at this time, being split into rival groups. Yet the Sultan was unable to subdue the rebellion owing to the weakness of the Turkish fleet. The Turks were not natural sailors, and before the revolt the Greeks had supplied most of the recruits for their navy. The Greeks maintained control of the surrounding isles of the Aegean and the mastery at sea.

In 1824 the Pasha of Egypt, Mehemet Ali, was requested by the Sultan to send aid. Mehemet Ali sent his son Ibrahim to the Morea, where he started to exterminate the Christian population. His reward was to be Crete. It soon appeared that Ibrahim intended to resettle the Morea with colonists from North Africa.

19. Cause of the Greek revolt. The revolt in Greece arose, in part like the Serbian revolt, from exasperation over the maladministration of Turkish officials. Other factors were as follows.

(a) *Revival of national self-consciousness*. This was stimulated by the following influences.

(*i*) There was a renewed interest in Greek classics, both in literature and in language. It was associated with the writings of propagandists and scholars such as the martyr poet Rhigas (killed by the Turks in 1798) and Korais.

(*ii*) There was an increase in secret societies, the most famous being the *Philike Hetairia* (Association of Friends), founded at Odessa by four Greek merchants in 1814. It had a membership of 200,000 by 1820 and aimed to expel the Turks from Europe and to re-establish the Greek Empire.

(*iii*) Ideas of liberty and nationalism were spread by the French Revolution. Such ideas were often brought back by Greek merchants trading abroad.

(*iv*) Russian encouragement was important. Catherine the Great's Greek scheme of 1780 has been noted (*see* 10). The *Philike Hetairia* kept in close touch with the Russian government, particularly with Capo d'Istria, a close friend of the Tsar.

(*b*) *Tradition of independence of the Greek community.* In the past the Greeks had occupied a special position in both the Turkish government and the navy. They had secured a degree of independence from Turkey in respect of the following.

(*i*) Trade: Greek merchants were a prosperous and cultured community on the isles of the Aegean. They had trade connections from Marseilles to Odessa. In 1774 they were allowed to carry a growing proportion of the grain trade from Russia to France.

(*ii*) Education: the Greeks had been granted a limited amount of local autonomy. They had established schools, had founded a university at Chios and had developed close ties with intellectual movements in France and other countries.

(*c*) *Knowledge of the weakness of Turkey.* The Ottoman Empire was one in which a small group of Turks ruled a large number of dissatisfied diverse racial and religious groups.

20. Policy of the major powers towards Greece. From 1821 to 1826 European powers took no active part in the Turkish–Greek conflict. It was generally agreed to "hold the ring", to prevent outside interference, and to regard the dispute as a private affair between Turkey and Greece.

However, the individual attitudes of the powers differed markedly in their approach to the problem.

(*a*) *Russia was anxious to aid the Greeks.* In 1821 the Tsar Alexander was anxious to help the Greeks, as he regarded himself the natural protector of the Greek Orthodox Christians. He wanted the Concert of Europe to solve the question by exerting diplomatic pressure on Turkey to grant Greece autonomy.

(b) *Austria firmly opposed any form of intervention.* Metternich disliked any idea that the European powers should try to solve the conflict collectively. He feared, along with the British Foreign Minister, Canning, that any intervention might lead Russia to "gobble Greece at one mouthful and Turkey at the next". Metternich pointed out to the Tsar that he was the founder of the Holy Alliance, and thus the enemy of revolutions against legitimate sovereigns everywhere.

(c) *Britain adopted a policy of non-intervention.* The British government co-operated with Austria in dissuading Russia from intervention. Unofficially many in Britain wanted an independent Greece to be formed, and volunteers went to help the Greek cause.

British merchants traded in the Eastern Mediterranean in the Levant Company, which was friendly to Turkey. They soon demanded legal status for the Greek rebels who were attacking their shipping. Canning submitted to popular pressure and recognised the Greeks as belligerents in March 1823.

(d) *France adopted an independent policy.* France did not intervene but she was sympathetic towards Mehemet Ali. Some French circles believed after 1824 that the Egyptians in the Morea would be a stronger bulwark against the Russians than the Greeks.

21. Intervention by Britain, France and Russia. The Greek revolt in 1826–7 was on the point of collapse owing to Ibrahim's vigorous activities. The new Tsar, Nicholas I, who succeeded Alexander in December 1825, was determined to intervene to help the Greeks. Canning then decided on British intervention to prevent Russia monopolising all the benefits. The powers were also forced to take action as a result of the rapid spread of philhellenism in Germany, Switzerland, France and Britain.

The various events were as follows.

(a) *Russian ultimatum.* In March 1826 the Tsar demanded the withdrawal of Turkish forces from Moldavia and Wallachia.

(b) *Protocol of St. Petersburg.* In April 1826 the Duke of Wellington was sent to Russia. Britain and Russia signed a protocol providing for an autonomous Greek state.

(c) *Convention of Akkerman.* The Sultan, thoroughly alarmed at the turn of events, signed an agreement with Russia, settling the Moldavia–Wallachian dispute.

(d) *Treaty of London.* In July 1827 Canning, by then Prime Minister, called a meeting in London. France joined with Britain and Russia in agreeing that an autonomous Greek state should be established under Turkish suzerainty. The three powers agreed to conclude an alliance, and if the Turks refused an armistice they would work together to secure Greek independence. Prussia and Austria refused to be associated with this.

22. The battle of Navarino and its consequences. The Turks rejected a Note of the three powers in August 1827 demanding an armistice. As a result the Allied navies were instructed to stop all reinforcements and supplies sent from Egypt to Ibrahim in Greece. The Turkish-Egyptian fleets were ordered to return under escort to Egypt. An incident started the battle of Navarino, in which the Turkish and Egyptian fleets were utterly destroyed on 20th October 1827.

The results were as follows.

(a) *Britain withdrew from the dispute.* Wellington became Prime Minister in January 1828. He apologised to the Sultan for the "untoward event" which had occurred without any official declaration of war.

(b) *Ibrahim had to evacuate the Morea.* The region was occupied by the French, who cleared the area of the remaining Turkish forces.

(c) *The Sultan repudiated the Convention of Akkerman.* He then proclaimed a Holy War against the Christian powers.

(d) *Russia declared war on Turkey (see* **23**).

23. War between Russia and Turkey. In April 1828 the Tsar declared war on Turkey. Turkey was defeated, and by the Treaty of Adrianople (14th September 1829) Russia secured the following.

(a) A virtual protectorate in Moldavia and Wallachia. This was due to Turkey's acceptance of:

(i) the stationing there of a Russian garrison pending her payment of a large indemnity;

(ii) the destruction of her fortresses in the area and the expulsion of the Moslems.

(b) Serbian autonomy under Russian protection.

(c) Commercial concessions in Turkey.

(*d*) Demilitarisation of the right bank of the Danube. This meant that Turkey was forced to give up control of the mouth of the Danube.

24. Greek independence. The Treaty of Adrianople had said nothing specific about Greece. It seemed that the Greeks would have considerable autonomy but would still be subject to the overlordship of Turkey. Britain and Austria then felt an independent Greece would be the best solution, to discourage future Russian intrigues.

In February 1830, at the London Conference, the independence of Greece was declared. It was placed under the guarantee of Britain, France and Russia. Capo d'Istria, who had left the service of the Tsar in 1827, was elected President of the Greek Republic, but he was assassinated in 1831. Eventually the boundaries of the new state were agreed. The powers had difficulty in finding a ruler, but finally the crown was accepted by Prince Otto of Bavaria in 1832.

FRENCH AND EGYPTIAN INFLUENCE, 1829–41

25. French designs. Napoleon Bonaparte was the first European to encourage Egypt to modernise in 1799. Since then France had maintained friendly links with Egypt. She sent skilled advisers to help Mehemet Ali, and in 1826 students were sent from Egypt to France.

France had designs on the North African possessions of the Sultan and on Syria.

(*a*) *The Drovetti project.* In 1829 the French consul-general in Egypt, Drovetti, suggested that Mehemet Ali conquer, with French support, Tripoli, Tunis and Algiers. This would wipe out piracy and France could be given part of Tunisia. This scheme broke down owing partly to:

(*i*) the opposition of Britain and Turkey;

(*ii*) the excessive demands of Mehement Ali for French ships and money.

(*b*) *A plan for the partition of Turkey.* Also in 1829 Polignac, the French Chief Minister, had a scheme which included the partition of the Ottoman Empire.

(*c*) *The invasion of Algeria in 1830 (see* XIX, **23**).

26. Increase in Egyptian and Russian power. The Pasha of Egypt was dissatisfied with receiving only Crete for his intervention in the Greek revolt. He had designs on the pashaliks of Syria and Damascus.

(a) *Egypt attacked Turkey.* In November 1831 Mehemet Ali sent his son Ibrahim to invade Palestine. Mahmud II denounced Mehemet Ali as a rebel and sent his troops against Ibrahim. In December 1832 at Koniah Ibrahim routed the last army the Sultan had available.

(b) *Metternich failed to secure European co-operation.* Metternich tried to bring the major powers together to protect the Sultan, but Britain refused to co-operate and France was sympathetic towards Mehemet Ali.

(c) *The Sultan secured Russian aid.* Russia accepted the Sultan's appeal for aid and sent a squadron to the Bosphorus in February 1833. In April 6,000 Russian troops landed on the Asiatic shore opposite Constantinople.

(d) *Egypt made territorial gains.* Britain and France advised Turkey to make concessions to Mehemet Ali. The latter was given Palestine, Syria, Aleppo and Damascus.

(e) *Russia and Turkey signed the Treaty of Unkiar Skelessi.* Before withdrawing her troops Russia concluded an agreement with Turkey in July 1833. Important provisions were:

(i) a mutual assistance agreement in case of attack by other states on either one of them;

(ii) a secret article by which Turkey agreed to close the Dardanelles to all warships as Russian interests dictated.

27. Agreement of the eastern powers. In 1826 Nicholas I of Russia had detached himself from the other Holy Alliance powers to aid Greece against Turkey. However, the Tsar was influenced to support the *status quo* for the time being by the following two factors.

(a) *The report of a secret Russian commission in 1829.* This stated that the advantages offered by the preservation of the Ottoman Empire exceeded its inconveniences. Reasons given were as follows.

(i) Russia would not be so effective in influencing independent Balkan states as in influencing Turkey. Her influence in Turkey could be further increased by economic control and peaceful penetration.

(ii) Russian expansion offered more prospects in the direction of Armenia or Baghdad than towards Constantinople.

(b) *The influence of Metternich.* At Münchengrätz, in September 1833, the three eastern powers confirmed the need to preserve Turkey. The Tsar agreed that if partition became necessary he would consult Austria first.

28. British policy. Initially British policy towards Turkey was indecisive. Britain declined to help Mehemet Ali in 1829 when the latter suggested an alliance after the failure of the negotiations with the French (*see* 25). However, in 1833, Britain was not prepared to support Turkey either.

Eventually Palmerston, the British Foreign Minister, became convinced of the necessity of defending the Ottoman Empire against the designs of both Egypt and Russia. He aided Turkey in the construction of a fleet and concluded a tariff treaty in 1838. Reasons for his policy were as follows.

(a) *Suspicions concerning the ultimate designs of the Holy Alliance powers.* Palmerston believed that:

(i) at Münchengrätz Austria and Russia had planned the partition of Turkey;

(ii) the Treaty of Unkiar Skelessi meant that the Bosphorus was to remain open to Russian warships and that Turkey had become almost a Russian vassal.

(b) *Fear of French designs on Egypt.* Egypt could be a useful French ally since she relied on French officers and experts. Egypt could help French commercial interests in the Levant and act against British interests in the Mediterranean.

(c) *Poor relations with Egypt.* Mehemet Ali had rejected a British proposal for a railway line from Cairo to the Red Sea. By 1838 he had pushed his own conquests as far as the Persian Gulf and the Indian Ocean.

(d) *Need to preserve route to India.* Since 1833 successful experiments had been made with steam navigation on the Red Sea and the Euphrates. This increased the importance of overland routes to India. In 1838 Britain occupied Aden.

In December 1838 Reshid Pasha went to London to secure an offensive and defensive pact against Egypt. However, Palmerston was interested only in a defensive pact and would help Turkey only if Mehemet Ali declared his independence.

29. The Egyptian–Turkish War and Allied intervention. In April 1839 the Sultan's forces attacked Ibrahim in Syria, but they were routed by him at Nezib in June. The Sultan Mahmud died in July and the Turkish fleet sailed off to Alexandria and surrendered to Mehemet Ali, alleging that the Grand Vizier planned to abandon it to Russia.

Turkey was ruled by a boy-Sultan aged sixteen, Abdul Mejid I. Palmerston resolved to break the power of Mehemet Ali, with the aid of naval power and Allied support.

The various stages of the Allied intervention were as follows.

(*a*) *Britain sent a fleet to blockade Alexandria.*

(*b*) *The five powers sent a collective Note to Constantinople* (July 1839). Austria, Prussia, Russia, France and Britain reserved the right to settle matters with Mehemet Ali.

(*c*) *An Anglo-Russian agreement was signed* (September 1839). As France secretly supported Mehemet Ali, and refused to consider measures to coerce him, Britain came to a separate arrangement with Russia in September. Russia was prepared to modify the Treaty of Unkiar Skelessi, and the two powers both aimed to force Mehemet Ali to give up Syria.

(*d*) *The London Convention* (July 1840). This was signed by Britain, Austria, Prussia and Russia. France was not a signatory.

(*i*) Mehemet Ali was to be the hereditary Pasha of Egypt and Pasha of Acre for life.

(*ii*) If he refused to evacuate his other conquests and accept these terms within ten days, he would be confined to Egypt alone.

(*e*) *France threatened war.* France was furious at being excluded from the deliberations of the powers. Thiers, the Prime Minister, threatened war against Britain and even against Prussia, but in October 1840 Thiers fell from office and French passions subsided. Palmerston rightly believed that France would not risk war with Britain.

(*f*) *Mehemet Ali ignored the London Convention.*

(*g*) *Ibrahim was forced to evacuate Syria.* In August 1840 an Austro-British squadron appeared off Beirut and demanded the Egyptian evacuation of Syria. Two events in hastening Ibrahim's departure were:

(*i*) the bombardment of Beirut and Acre by Admiral Stopford, which demonstrated the effective use of sea power;

(*ii*) the revolt of the Syrians, who had previously considered Ibrahim their deliverer.

(*h*) *The Sultan then deposed Mehemet Ali.*

(*i*) *The Sultan and Mehemet Ali were forced to submit.*

(*i*) After a threatened bombardment of Alexandria by

Admiral Napier in November 1840, Mehemet Ali agreed to return the Turkish fleet and to abandon Syria in return for the hereditary rule of Egypt.

(*ii*) The Sultan finally accepted the above terms in February 1841.

30. Final results of the Egyptian–Turkish War. These were as follows:

(*a*) The Straits Convention was signed. In July 1841 the major powers and Turkey agreed that the Straits (the Bosphorus and Dardanelles) were to be closed to all foreign warships while Turkey was at peace.

(*b*) Egypt no longer posed a threat to Turkey. (By 1854 it had become one of the weakest of her provinces.)

(*c*) France was discredited for having schemed with Mehemet Ali.

(*d*) Britain earned Turkey's gratitude for having supported her.

(*e*) Russia began to doubt the value of preserving Turkey, and to consider partition plans again (*see* XV, 3(*e*)).

PROGRESS TEST 14

1. What were the specific problems of the Eastern Question? **(2)**

2. Why did the interests of the European powers conflict over Turkey? **(3, 4)**

3. Account for the decline of Turkey. Why was it only a gradual process? **(5–7)**

4. Give details of the Russo-Turkish wars between 1768 and 1812. **(9–10, 14)**

5. Why was Napoleon interested in Egypt? **(11)**

6. List the causes of the Greek revolt of 1821. **(19)**

7. Why did the European powers intervene in the Turkish-Greek issue in 1826? **(21)**

8. How was the Greek revolt resolved? **(24)**

9. Why did France back Mehemet Ali against the Sultan? **(25, 28(*b*))**

10. What were the important provisions of the Treaty of Unkiar Skelessi? Why was Palmerston alarmed? **(26(*e*), 28(*a*))**

11. Why did the Tsar agree to support the *status quo* at Münchengrätz in 1833? **(27)**

12. Why did Britain support Turkey against Egypt? **(28)**

13. How did the European powers check the threat of Mehemet Ali to Turkey? **(29)**

14. What were the final effects of the Syrian question? Give details of the Straits Convention of 1841. **(29, 30)**

CHAPTER XV

The Crimean War

BACKGROUND TO THE OUTBREAK OF HOSTILITIES

1. General distrust among the powers. During the early 1850s relations between the major European powers were poor. This was evident, for example, from the attitudes to each other of the following states.

(a) *Holy Alliance states.* Austria, Prussia and Russia ceased working closely together after the revolutionary upheavals in Europe of 1848–9.

(i) Austria resented the fact that she had to rely on Russia to retain her empire (*see* XI, **23**).

(ii) Austria and Prussia began to regard each other as rivals for mastery in German affairs (*see* VIII, **22–25**).

(b) *Russia and Britain* (*see* **3**).

(c) *Russia and France.* Tsar Nicholas regarded Napoleon III as an adventurer who had come to power through revolution, and he did not recognise him as a brother sovereign. For example, in correspondence, he addressed Napoleon as "*mon cher ami*" and not in the customary way as "*M. mon frère*". As a result Napoleon disliked the Tsar.

2. Causes of the Crimean War. The weakened international atmosphere influenced events in the Near East, which had been comparatively peaceful between 1841 and 1852. General factors in producing war were as follows.

(a) The deterioration of relations between Britain and Russia (*see* **3**).

(b) The dispute between France and Russia over the Holy Places (*see* **4**).

(c) The aggressive nature of Russian policy in the Balkans. This was illustrated by:

(i) her demand for a protectorate over the Christians in that area (*see* **5**);

(*ii*) her occupation of Moldavia and Wallachia (*see* **6**).

(*d*) The general indecisiveness of European diplomacy (*see* **10**).

3. Deterioration of Anglo-Russian relations. Until the 1840s Anglo-Russian rivalry in the Near East had not been serious, for both countries feared possible French designs in Egypt and the Levant. However, after 1841, France confined her main interests in the Near East to North Africa, and Anglo-Russian rivalry then became acute. Also, it was aggravated by dissension over other issues.

The various factors causing poor relations between Britain and Russia were as follows.

(*a*) *Russian intervention in Central Europe in 1849* (*see* XI, **23**). Britain resented this interference, and feared Russian power.

(*b*) *Different forms of government.* It was argued in Britain that the two countries could have little in common since the one's system of government was liberal and constitutional, while the other's was autocratic.

(*c*) *Imperial rivalries in Asia* (*see* XX).

(*d*) *British blockade of the Piraeus* (the Don Pacifico incident). In 1850 the British fleet had blockaded some Greek isles without giving advance notice to the powers, and this annoyed Russia.

(*e*) *Differing policies regarding Turkey*, "the sick man of Europe". The Tsar made suggestions which created among British statesmen a deep distrust of Russian designs in the Ottoman Empire. As a result misunderstanding developed. Nicholas had no wish to act unilaterally or to threaten Britain in the Mediterranean, but Britain suspected that this was precisely what he intended to do.

(*i*) The Tsar felt the collapse of Turkey was imminent. In 1844 he suggested to his friend Lord Aberdeen, the British Foreign Minister, plans for the partition of Turkey which excluded France. In January 1853 he repeated his ideas to the British ambassador, Sir Hamilton Seymour.

The Tsar hinted that the Balkan states should be independent under Russian protection, that Britain should occupy Egypt and that Russia should occupy Constantinople but not annex it. Britain did not repudiate the Tsar's suggestion and the Tsar thus gained the impression that Britain supported his scheme.

(*ii*) The British hoped to maintain Turkish integrity and to encourage the Sultan to reform. Thus Turkey might become an adequate bulwark against the south-westerly expansion of Russia.

4. The Holy Places. The Holy Places of Palestine in the Ottoman Empire were tended by monks of the Roman Catholic and Greek Orthodox Churches. By the Capitulations of 1740 France had been granted rights of general protection over the Roman monks and also special privileges. Russia had gained similar rights over the Greek monks by the Treaty of Kutchuk-Kainardji of 1774.

After 1789 the interest of France in the quarrels between the Roman and Greek Churches lapsed and the Greek monks gradually encroached upon the rights of their Latin rivals. Napoleon III, to gain popularity in France, particularly among the clericals. demanded from Turkey the restitution of the old Latin privileges. He thus entered the quarrel which had developed between Latin and Greek monks over the guardianship of the Holy Places. The Sultan agreed to the restoration of the rights of the Latin monks in December 1852.

5. The Menshikov mission. The Tsar intervened on behalf of the Greek monks and sent Prince Menshikov to Constantinople as a special envoy in March 1853. The outcome of this mission was as follows.

(a) *The Holy Places.* In April the Sultan agreed to withdraw the concessions which France had demanded and to guarantee the rights of the Greek monks.

(b) *Further Russian demands.* Menshikov also put forward further demands which shifted the issue to a new plane – Russia in effect reopened the Eastern Question. These demands were for:

(i) a Russo-Turkish defensive alliance;

(ii) the recognition of Russia's special right to be the protector of all Orthodox Christians in the Ottoman Empire. This claim was supposed to be based on the treaty of 1774. (If the Sultan had accepted this the Tsar would have had a pretext for constant interference in Turkish affairs.)

(c) *Further Russian demands rejected.* The Sultan, influenced by the British ambassador, Lord Stratford de Redcliffe rejected these Russian demands. In May Menshikov and the staff of the Russian embassy left Constantinople in protest against this decision.

6. Russian occupation of the principalities. In July Russian troops were ordered to cross the river Pruth and occupy Moldavia and Wallachia. The Tsar stated he did not want war but wished to obtain security for the recognition of Russian religious rights.

Russia's action lost her the support of Austria, since it seriously interfered with the navigation of the Danube. Austria massed troops on the Serbian border. Turkey herself, on the advice of Britain, offered no resistance to the Russian invasion.

7. The Vienna Note. Austria joined Britain and France in constructing a Note which aimed to pacify the Tsar. The Treaty of Kutchuk-Kainardji was confirmed. Turkey was to be asked to guarantee that there would be no change in her rule over her Christian subjects "without previous understanding with the governments of France and Russia".

The Note was accepted at first by the Tsar. However, the Sultan proposed an amendment, making it clear that the protection of the Christians should depend on the Sultan, not on the "active solicitude" of the Tsar. In September Nesselrode, the Russian Foreign Minister, tried to maintain in a "violent interpretation" of the Note that all Russia's demands had been recognised. The Tsar rejected Nesselrode's interpretation. However, the Tsar, pressured by the Pan-Slav group at Court, was not prepared to accept a modified version recognising the Sultan's amendment. He tried unsuccessfully at a meeting at Olmütz to gain the support of Francis Joseph of Austria and the Prussian king.

8. Outbreak of Russo-Turkish hostilities. Affairs drifted until October. Then Russia refused to comply with a Turkish ultimatum to withdraw from the principalities, and Turkey declared war on the 5th. The British and French governments undertook to keep their fleets out of the Black Sea if Russia remained on the defensive north of the Danube and refrained from attacking Black Sea ports.

Owing partly to Napoleon's influence the French and British fleets passed the Dardanelles on 22nd October. On 30th November a Turkish fleet was utterly destroyed at Sinope by a Russian fleet. This shocked the western powers. The Russian action was described in the British press as an unwarranted massacre. Demand for active British intervention grew, supported by *The Times*.

9. The war entered by France and Britain. In January 1854, at Napoleon's suggestion, the French and British fleets entered the Black Sea to protect the Turkish coasts and transport. This amounted to an act of war. In February the Tsar submitted a draft of terms for a peaceful settlement to the representatives of the powers at Vienna. It was not given careful consideration and was rejected.

Russia refused an ultimatum from Britain and France to withdraw from the principalities. The western powers made a treaty of alliance with Turkey on 12th March and on the 28th declared war on Russia.

10. Indecisiveness of European diplomacy. No country, with the possible exception of France, expected that the outcome of the dispute over the Holy Places would be a major war. A series of events created a situation in which neither side was prepared to back down for fear of "losing face". As the western governments wavered, the influence of public opinion became decisive. British and French opinion seemed eager for war and the governments allowed their states to drift into open conflict with Russia.

The policies of the European powers involved were as follows.

(a) *Britain.* Since 1853 there had been a coalition government. Aberdeen, the Prime Minister, and Clarendon, the Foreign Minister, wanted to avert war. However, they were reluctant to take a strong line to deter the Tsar from actions of an aggressive nature. Aberdeen suspected Lord Stratford de Redcliffe, the British ambassador in Turkey, of not acting strictly according to his instructions but took no action. Palmerston, the Home Secretary, favoured a forceful policy to deter the Tsar. Thus there was no unified leadership, and this misled both Russia and Turkey.

(i) The Tsar was misled into believing Britain would not take aggressive action against him.

(ii) Turkey was misled into thinking Britain was on her side. This was due to the attitude of the British ambassador in Constantinople and the movements of the Franco-British fleet in the vicinity of the Dardanelles. For example, in June, the combined fleets had moved to Besika Bay.

(b) *Russia.* The Tsar would have been less inclined to pursue a bellicose policy in the Balkans if he had realised Austria and Prussia would not support him. He learnt this only when it was too late. He hoped for their support since he had rendered invaluable aid to them in the 1848–9 revolutions.

(c) *Austria.* Basically she wanted to deter Russia and to preserve the *status quo* in the Ottoman Empire as the eastern powers had agreed at Münchengrätz in 1833 (*see* XIV, 27(b)). However, if Austria had fully supported one side or the other, this might have averted war. Instead Austria pursued a vacillating policy which misled both sides.

Austria was uncertain of the policy of Prussia in the event of war. Further, she saw little to gain from being militarily involved at the time.

(i) If Austria fought Russia, France stood to gain most. While French territory was far removed from Russia, Austrian territory was vulnerable if the Russians concentrated their attacks against her.

(ii) If Austria supported Russia, this would have involved her fighting in the Balkans. This would have had repercussions in her empire, particularly in Hungary and Transylvania.

(d) *Prussia.* King Frederick William did not want to be involved in an issue which did not actively concern Prussia. He was prepared to back Austria in Germany but objected to an alliance with France and the "infidel" Turks.

COURSE OF THE WAR

11. Start to the war. For six months there was no purposeful military activity between the two sides, and since operations were carried out in the Baltic and the Balkans the term "Crimean War" was not strictly correct. The following developments can be noted.

(a) *Naval activity.* France and Britain found it difficult to fight Russia in the Baltic or Pacific, since the Russian navy was able to retire to port for safety. An ineffectual joint Anglo-French expedition under Napier was sent to the Baltic in August 1854. It was difficult to plan an extensive campaign in the Baltic without the support of Prussia and Sweden.

(b) *Events in the Balkans.* The bulk of the Russian troops did not cross the Danube until March 1854. The delay was due to poor communications and the vast distances it was necessary to travel. The Russians attacked Silistria, south of Wallachia.

The Anglo-French forces failed to make contact with the

Russian forces and hence to aid Turkish troops. After a long delay they arrived at Gallipoli and Scutari to defend Constantinople. When the expected Russian attack did not materialise, they moved to Varna on the Bulgarian coast in May to relieve Silistria. However, by the time they were ready for action the Russians had withdrawn (*see* (*c*)).

(*c*) *Events in the principalities.* In April Austria had formed an alliance with Prussia to protect her territories against revolutionary disturbances. She mobilised her forces on her eastern border to threaten Russia.

(*i*) In June both Austria and Prussia demanded Russian evacuation from the principalities.

(*ii*) On 8th August Russian troops were withdrawn, and, on the 22nd, Austrian forces, with the consent of Turkey, occupied the principalities until the end of the war.

12. The Vienna Four Points. Throughout the summer Britain and France tried to persuade Austria to support them militarily. Encouraged by the failure of Russia's first offensive in the Balkans, the Allies, in collaboration with Buol, the Austrian Foreign Minister, drew up four points which they wanted the Tsar to accept.

These points were as follows:

(*a*) no Russian protectorate in the principalities;

(*b*) free navigation on the Danube;

(*c*) renunciation by Russia of her exclusive patronage over the Sultan's Christian subjects;

(*d*) revision of the Straits Convention of 1841.

13. The Sebastopol expedition. France and Britain then planned an expedition which would in effect demilitarise the Black Sea.

(*a*) *Reasons for the expedition.*

(*i*) Delay of the Tsar in accepting the Four Points: the Tsar hesitated until October and then accepted all the points except the neutrality of the Black Sea implicit in the last one.

(*ii*) Strategic reasons: the Allied forces had failed to make contact with the Russians in the unhealthy Balkan plains. A campaign directly into the heart of Russia, which had been Napoleon's undoing, seemed unattractive. An expedition into the Crimea would utilise the Allies' naval forces and Russia would have untold problems of supplies and transport over land.

(*iii*) Reasons of prestige: the war had been ineffective so far and there seemed no other way to strike at Russia except via her "big toe". If the Russian naval base at Sebastopol was destroyed, this was expected to aid Turkish security and to satisfy public opinion and the national desire for glory.

(b) *Initial fighting.*

(i) The Russians were defeated at Alma in September. However, the British and French forces, commanded by Lord Raglan and St. Arnaud respectively, failed to follow up their victory by attacking Sebastopol at once. Instead they settled down to a lengthy siege.

(ii) Menshikov, allowed time by the Allies to gain reinforcements from Bessarabia, attacked in October in an attempt to raise the siege. He was defeated in the battles of Balaclava and Inkerman in November.

(iii) Because they had failed to realise their objective of reducing Sebastopol, the Allies had to plan to stay in the Crimea throughout the winter. The fortifications of Sebastopol were greatly improved by the engineer Todleben, who was aided in its defence from the sea by Admiral Kornilov.

14. Mismanagement of the war. It was discovered by eager enthusiasts that war was far from glamorous under conditions of prolonged fighting and poor weather. Trench warfare made its first appearance. Notable characteristics of the war were as follows.

(a) *Inadequate provisions.* Neither side appreciated the problems involved in fighting a war far from supply sources. Russia had to transport supplies some thousand miles from the north, while Allied supplies came over lengthy sea-routes.

No plans were made for a lengthy winter campaign. Thus the Allies had no adequate supply of fuel, tents, warm clothing and food in the winter of 1854. Cholera attacked the camps and eventually the hospitals. Owing to the inadequate medical facilities, thousands died for lack of proper treatment and care.

(b) *Weak leadership.* The Allies had no outstanding leaders. Patronage and the practice of purchasing commissions produced aristocratic British officers who had an amateur outlook on war. Rivalry and jealousy existed between commands.

No attempt was made to blockade Sebastopol from the north to prevent the arrival of Russian stores or reinforcements. Instead it was decided to camp on the south. This allowed the Russian engineer Todleben time to construct fortifications which kept the Anglo-French forces at bay from September 1854 until September 1855.

(c) *Great but futile heroism.* Troops on both sides often fought bravely but achievements were minimal.

(i) The futile charge of the Light Brigade at Balaclava took place as a result of misunderstanding, jealousy and the lack of liaison between the British commanders Lord Lucan and Lord Cardigan.

(ii) The Russian defence of Sebastopol was a courageous effort which was to prove of no avail.

(d) *Anglo-French rivalry.* The French and British did not co-ordinate their operations closely. After the battle of Alma, Lord Raglan wanted to attack Sebastopol, but he was opposed by the French commanders, who refused to attack until the siege-guns had arrived. Then at the critical moment they vetoed an assault since it would involve loss of life.

15. Military reforms made. If the supply of goods was defective at the onset of the war, the supply of news was greatly improved by the introduction of the electric telegraph. The first modern war correspondents also appeared. Journalists were able to use the submarine cable from Balaclava to Varna to telegraph their news.

They gave full publicity to the mismanagement of the war. The British public were horrified by the reports of W. H. Russell of *The Times*. As a result, improvements occurred in the following fields.

(a) *Military organisation.* Following demands in Britain for an enquiry into the conduct of the war, Palmerston replaced Aberdeen as Prime Minister in January 1855. Reforms were made in supply and transport, and steps were taken to remove the overlappings in military authority.

(b) *Medical facilities.* Florence Nightingale and a team of nurses improved the hospital services in the Crimea.

16. Austrian neutrality. Since Russia had withdrawn from the principalities, her forces no longer menaced the Austrian Empire. When the Allies failed to defeat Russia decisively in the autumn of 1854, Austria became less anxious to help them.

On 2nd December Austria signed an agreement with France and Britain by which she would declare war if Russia failed to accept the Four Points by the end of the year. This caused rejoicing among the Allies which was soon shown to be premature.

The agreement remained a dead letter since to be operative it had to be accepted by the German Confederation. Bismarck urged the Prussian king to take no active part and to concentrate troops in Silesia as a check to the power of Austria. The German Diet eventually refused the Austrian request for support, and Austria remained neutral.

17. The war during 1855. During 1855 the following important events took place.

(a) *Entry of Piedmont into the war.* In January 1855 Piedmont agreed to contribute 17,000 troops to the Allies in the war (*see* XIII, 20).

(b) *Battle of Eupatoria.* The Russians were defeated by the Turks on 17th February.

(c) *Negotiations at Vienna.* The Tsar, heartbroken at Russian reverses in the war, died in March. His son, Alexander II, was not so keen on continuing the war. However, he refused to agree to the neutrality of the Black Sea. Thus peace negotiations at the congress at Vienna failed and war continued.

(d) *Battle of the Tchernaya.* The French and Sardinians were repulsed by the Russians on 16th August.

(e) *Capture of Sebastopol.* This was eventually achieved on 9th September after a lengthy bombardment and Russian evacuation. The French public were delighted, and Napoleon, having achieved some success, was anxious for peace.

(f) *Russian capture of Kars.* The Turks lost this town to the Russians on 26th November.

(g) *Agreement of Austria to mediate.* It was clear to the Allies that, since Russia had inexhaustible supplies of manpower, the Tsar could be persuaded to yield only through Austrian intervention. The following two factors induced Austria, in December, to start negotiating with Russia again on behalf of the Allies.

(i) There was the prospect that Britain and France might assist Piedmont in Italy. Austria feared the possibility of an attack by Piedmont on Lombardy.

(ii) Austria was alarmed by the knowledge that secret talks had been held between the Tsar and Napoleon. Napoleon wanted moderate peace terms and to repair Franco-Russian relations without losing the British alliance.

18. The end of the war. No worthwhile achievements had been gained as the result of a lengthy war. Both sides wanted peace.

Specific points to note about the termination of the war are as follows.

(*a*) *General factors.*

(*i*) Both sides had suffered severe loss in manpower, and the war had been a financial strain.

(*ii*) By the autumn of 1855 neither side had much idea on how to continue the war, or how to resolve the stalemate that had been reached.

(*iii*) Both sides had achieved some success which helped national self-respect.

(*b*) *Russian problems.* The Tsar was concerned about problems unrelated to Turkey.

(*i*) *Domestic considerations.* The home economy was in a ruinous condition and there was serious internal unrest (*see* XII, 8).

(*ii*) *North-east Europe.* Palmerston was keen to continue the war in this area if it became necessary. The Tsar, already in dispute with Sweden over the Norwegian–Finnish frontier, wanted to avoid any extension of the fighting. He even had fears that Napoleon was scheming to return Finland to Sweden or that he might encourage unrest in Poland.

(*c*) *Diplomacy of Austria.* This eventually resulted in ending hostilities. The stages were as follows.

(*i*) In December Buol sent an ultimatum to Russia. This demanded that the Tsar accept the Allied demands – which had been slightly revised – by 18th January 1856.

(*ii*) The Tsar continued to delay his reply. He disliked a fresh fifth point which Palmerston had added and which would allow the Allies to make such demands additional to the Four Points as the fortunes of war justified.

(*iii*) Austria then proposed to include Prussia in the Allied deliberations on further measures if the Tsar refused the peace terms. On 16th January the Prussian king, Frederick William, a personal friend of the Tsar, made a plea to Alexander to accept the terms, which the Tsar finally agreed to do.

RESULTS OF THE WAR

19. Provisions of the Treaty of Paris. The settlement of the war was based on the Four Points. The following provisions were agreed at the Paris peace conference of February and April 1856.

(a) *The Black Sea was neutralised.* No fortifications were to be permitted on its shores. Though this affected Turkey as much as Russia it was intended to erect a barrier to Russian expansion.

The Straits Convention of 1841 was reaffirmed. (During the Russo-Japanese War (*see* XX, 25), Russia found the closure of the Straits a handicap because her Black Sea Fleet could not be moved.

(b) *Turkish independence and integrity* were recognised and guaranteed by the European powers. Forthwith no power had the right to intervene between the Sultan and his subjects. The Russian claim to a protectorate over the Sultan's Greek Orthodox subjects was denied. Turkey was admitted to the Concert of Europe.

(i) It was agreed that all conflicts between Turkey and another party had to be submitted to the mediation of the powers.

(ii) A recent decree of the Sultan was noted in which he promised to give equal rights to Christians and Moslems to practise their religion and serve the State.

(c) *Free navigation on the Danube was confirmed.*

(d) *The Danubian principalities* were placed outside the Russian sphere of influence. The powers promised them an "independent and national administration" within the Ottoman Empire. (France had favoured their union but this had been opposed by Turkey and Austria.)

(e) *Russian power was reduced.* Checks on Russian expansion were contained in provisions (a), (b) and (d) above. The following provisions further reduced her power.

(i) South Bessarabia was transferred to the principalities.

(ii) Kars was restored to Turkey. Palmerston's demand for an independent Trans-Caucasian state was rejected through the intervention of Napoleon.

(iii) Russia had to accept the neutralisation of the Åland Islands in the Gulf of Finland.

(iv) Britain and France undertook to guarantee Norway and Sweden against Russian aggression.

(f) *Maritime warfare was regulated.* Britain had to accept conditions she had long resisted, including the following points governing commerce during naval warfare.

(i) Privateering was to be abolished.

(ii) Enemy goods on a neutral ship could not be seized unless they were in the category of "contraband of war".

(*iii*) Blockades, to be respected, should be effective. A general blockade of the type Britain had declared against Napoleon could no longer be used.

20. Changed relations between the powers. Considerable changes in the balance of power had taken place.

(*a*) *France* became the most powerful European state. Success abroad buttressed the leadership of Napoleon at home. He embarked on an ambitious foreign policy and refused to make any liberal political reforms in France.

(*b*) *Russia* lost the ascendancy in Europe for the first time since 1815. Her humiliating defeat in the Crimea led to:

(*i*) the diversion of her interests to Central Asia and the Far East (*see* XX, **5**);

(*ii*) radical domestic reforms (*see* XII, **8–13**).

(*c*) *Austria's* prestige was weakened. By remaining neutral in the war Austria lost the respect of both sides.

(*d*) *Britain's* military prestige declined. Europe doubted the capability of the British army. This was due to its initial poor performance in the Crimea.

(*e*) *Piedmont* gained publicity for the Italian cause. Austria was unable to prevent Cavour attending the peace conference. There he highlighted the Italian problem and gained moral encouragement from France and Britain.

21. Breakdown of the Concert of Europe. The Paris Conference reaffirmed the principle of collective responsibility of the powers. However, the 1848–9 revolutions and the Crimean War gravely weakened the commitments of the powers to the existing territorial arrangements in Europe. In future, Austria excepted, they were prepared to be "revisionist" in foreign affairs.

(*a*) *France*, under Napoleon, desired a thorough revision of the Vienna settlement of 1815.

(*b*) *Russia* was transformed from one of the strongest supporters of the treaty structure to having a "revisionist" policy regarding the Black Sea clauses. Close relations were formed with France as the Tsar hoped Napoleon would help him.

(*c*) *Prussia* became discontented with her subordinate position in Europe. She was soon to embark on an aggressive foreign policy.

(*d*) *Britain* became increasingly isolationist in outlook. She was less concerned about preserving the *status quo* in Europe. For example, she lent moral support to the Italian cause in 1859.

NOTE: In the past alliances and diplomatic alignments had been concluded generally for defensive purposes to maintain the *status quo*. In future they were to be formed more frequently for aggressive designs.

22. Final assessment of the war. The war was distinguished as being one of the most futile in modern history. Over half a million people died to secure a treaty which proved completely unstable. The following points should be noted.

(*a*) *The war resulted in reforms.* Britain and Russia soon made reforms in army conditions and organisation, while unrest in Russia finally led to the emancipation of the serfs in 1861. The war also inspired the creation of the International Red Cross in 1861.

(*b*) *Many treaty provisions proved to be only of short-term duration*

(*i*) The Black Sea clauses were denounced by Russia in 1870 (*see* VII, **6**).

(*ii*) The Danubian principalities became united and independent of Turkey in 1862 (*see* VI, **11**(*a*)(*iii*)).

(*iii*) Turkey refused to keep her promise to introduce reforms. Her administration was not overhauled as the powers hoped, and the Christians of Turkey were soon ill-treated again.

(*iv*) The Balkan Wars (1875–9) resulted in further revision of the boundaries of the Ottoman Empire.

PROGRESS TEST 15

1. What were the main causes of the Crimean War? **(2)**

2. Why were relations between Britain and Russia poor after 1841? **(3)**

3. Why did the Tsar send Prince Menshikov to Constantinople? What was the outcome? **(4–6)**

4. Why did the Tsar declare war on Turkey? **(7–8)**

5. Describe the policies of Britain and Austria towards Turkey on the eve of the Crimean War. **(10)**

6. List the Vienna Four Points. **(12)**

7. Why did France and Britain send an expedition to the Crimea? **(13)**

8. Why was Austria neutral during the war?   **(10, 16)**

9. Explain why the war was badly conducted by the British and mention reforms that were made as a result.   **(14, 15)**

10. Why did the Tsar Alexander II want to end the war?   **(18(*a*), (*b*))**

11. Describe the role of Austria in the termination of hostilities.   **(18(*c*))**

12. How was the position of Russia weakened as a result of the war?   **(19)**

13. Which European power benefited most from the Crimean War? Give reasons.   **(20)**

14. Why were many of the provisions of the Paris Conference only of a temporary nature?   **(22)**

CHAPTER XVI

The Balkans and the Eastern Question, 1870–1914

BALKAN UNREST AND THE CONGRESS OF BERLIN

1. Russia and Pan-Slavism. During the latter half of the nineteenth century, Russia progressively justified her expansion and influence in the Balkans in terms of realising Slav national aspirations. Though there is some doubt as to the existence of a distinct Slavonic race, there was a Slavonic group of languages. This included Russian, Czechoslovak, Serbo-Croat and Bulgarian.

Significant events in the development of Pan-Slavism were as follows.

(*a*) *Publicity given to a famous poem.* Jan Kollar, a Slovak, in his poem "*Slavy Dgera*" (1824), proclaimed: "Scattered Slavs, let us be one united whole and no longer be mere fragments."

(*b*) *Revolution in the Austro-Hungarian Empire.* Two important events encouraged Pan-Slav consciousness.

(*i*) The first ethnic and linguistic Slav conference was held at Prague in 1848. The Czechs were anxious to build the foundations of their nationality and to drive German speech and rule from Bohemia.

(*ii*) In 1849, for the first time, Catholic Croats and Orthodox Serbs were prepared to unite as Slavs to fight the Magyars.

(*c*) *Russian encouragement of Slav nationalism.*

(*i*) In 1861 Russia supported the uniting of Moldavia and Wallachia to form one country – Romania.

(*ii*) In 1867 Russia intervened to remove Turkish garrisons from Belgrade and other Serbian fortresses.

(*iii*) In 1867 a great ethnic exhibition was held at St. Petersburg, attended by delegates of all Slav races except the Poles. The Tsar addressed them as "brother Slavs".

2. Creation of a Bulgar (Slav) Church. Until 1870 Christian Slavs of the Balkans, whether Bulgars or Serbs, came under the spiritual jurisdiction of the Greek Patriarch at Constantinople. Russia demanded, through the Bulgars, the creation of a Slav Church with its own religious leader.

The Sultan complied in a *firman* (edict) of 10th March. The Slavs were recognised as a separate religious nation with a Church headed by one of their own people. However, the Turks showed a Machiavellian understanding of the policy of "divide and rule". The head of the new Church was to be a Bulgar, called the Exarch. Quarrels broke out between followers of the Greek Patriarch and the Bulgar Exarch, while the Serbs were furious at the installation of a separate Bulgar Exarch.

3. Growth of Pan-Slav agitation. Romania, Serbia and Montenegro were still nominally under Turkey. The only part of the Ottoman Empire to be completely independent in the Balkans was Greece.

The Slavs in the Ottoman Empire, who were mostly Christians, grew increasingly restive at the misgovernment and oppression which existed. They hoped that soon they would become independent like Greece or largely self-governing like Serbia.

The Bulgar Church became a focal point for nationalistic agitation in Bulgaria. Throughout the Balkans, Pan-Slavism developed in popularity, encouraged by the propaganda of Serbian and Russian Pan-Slav agents. A central Pan-Slavist committee, based on Moscow and Bucharest, also stirred up racial and national consciousness.

4. Rebellion in Bosnia and Herzegovina. In July 1875 a rising occurred in the two Turkish provinces of Bosnia and Herzegovina, which were mostly inhabited by Serbs. The causes of the revolt were as follows.

(*a*) *Pan-Slav agitation.*

(*b*) *Social and economic grievances.*

(*i*) Oppressive feudal restrictions: the peasants were forced to pay taxes to Turkish officials and to native landowners. In 1875 they refused to pay taxes or perform the customary labour services.

(*ii*) Poor economic conditions: in 1874 the harvest had failed, which caused widespread distress and unemployment.

(*c*) *Oppressive Turkish rule.*

(*d*) *Activities of the "Young Turkey" society.* This society had recently been formed. It aimed to reform The Porte (the Ottoman court) and pursue a holy war against the Christians.

5. European powers and the Eastern Question. The policies of the great powers at this time are summarised below.

(*a*) *Austria.* Since losing influence in Germany in 1866, Austria had been interested in extending her influence in the Balkans towards Salonika, on the Macedonian coast. She was no longer so anxious to preserve the *status quo* (*see* **26**).

(*b*) *Russia.* Russia regarded the Slav peoples in the Balkans as a legitimate concern of hers. She feared that Austria might establish prior influence of a political, economic or religious nature. At this time her policy wavered under the influence of the following two factions.

(*i*) Supporters of the *status quo* and of co-operation with Austria, led by Gorchakov.

(*ii*) Supporters of a policy of freeing the Slavs, led by Ignatiev. Russian policy became steadily influenced by this group as the crisis developed in the Balkans in 1877.

(*c*) *Britain.* Disraeli became Prime Minister in 1874. He favoured a policy of "standing up" to Russia and was reluctant to join in any pressure exerted upon Turkey which might incur her in territorial loss. He wanted to preserve Turkish integrity and to influence her to carry out reforms voluntarily.

(*d*) *Germany.* One of the objectives of the *Dreikaiserbund*, formed in 1872, had been to draw the rivals Austria and Russia together to pursue a united policy in the Near East (*see* X, **11** and **16**). Bismarck was anxious to be neutral and said in December 1876 that the Balkan issues contained "no German interest worth the bones of a Pomeranian musketeer". His only concern was to prevent Austria and Russia coming to blows, so that Germany would not have to make a choice between them.

6. Attempts of the powers to stop the Balkan rebellion. The Balkan disturbances immediately caused dissension between Britain, Russia and Austria. They were anxious to localise and stop the disturbances, but could not agree on a common policy. If they had managed to work together, peace could probably have been restored. The course of events was as follows.

(*a*) *The Andrássy Note.* On 30th December 1875 Austria, Germany and Russia proposed in a Note that Turkey should accept an armistice and implement certain reforms. Though this was approved by the British and French governments, Disraeli was annoyed as Britain had not been consulted. Turkey showed no intention of carrying out the proposed reforms.

(b) *The Bulgarian atrocities*. Rebellion spread to Macedonia and Bulgaria, where it was suppressed with unusual efficiency and extreme cruelty. Some 12,000 peasants were massacred, and the French and German consuls were killed in Salonika. Gladstone, the Opposition leader in Britain, wrote a pamphlet which aroused wide sympathy for the struggle.

(c) *The Berlin Memorandum*. In May 1876 Russia, Germany and Austria tried to enforce an armistice. In the Berlin Memorandum, it was suggested that a mixed tribunal of Christians and Moslems be appointed to reform abuses. This was ineffective since:

(i) Britain rejected the clause which threatened armed intervention if the reforms were not carried out;

(ii) the Sultan felt he could ignore the suggestions as the European powers were not united in their policy.

(d) *The Serbian defeat*. Serbia and Montenegro declared war on Turkey on 30th June. The Serbs were routed and appealed to the powers to mediate. Only a Russian ultimatum prevented the Turks taking Belgrade.

(e) *The armistice*. Under threats from Russia and international pressure, Turkey agreed to an armistice and a conference at Constantinople in December.

7. Turkey and the great powers. In 1874 Turkey had been unable to meet its foreign debts. It had to submit to financial control by the great powers, who were acting on behalf of their subjects who were creditors of the Ottoman Empire. In 1876, as a result of internal revolts, it seemed that Turkey was able to create a liberal constitutional government under the new Sultan, Abdul Hamid II.

The great powers recommended certain reform provisions for Turkey. The Sultan, encouraged by Britain, objected to the suggested international commission, and demanded a "free hand" to implement any changes. The conference failed to achieve any results and the Sultan repudiated recent constitutional changes he had made.

8. Austro-Russian collaboration. In 1876 both Austria and Russia had sounded Bismarck as to his reactions if both countries were at war with each other. When Bismarck would not commit himself, the Tsar came to an informal arrangement with Francis Joseph at Reichstadt in June.

In January 1877 the arrangements were made precise in the Budapest Convention.

(*a*) Austria would remain neutral in an eventual Russo-Turkish war.

(*b*) If Turkey was defeated in a future war, it was arranged that:

    (*i*) Austria would be allowed to annex most of Bosnia and Herzegovina;

    (*ii*) Russia would take back the Bessarabian strip which had been ceded to Moldavia in 1856;

    (*iii*) Bulgaria and Rumelia would become autonomous states.

In an additional convention on 18th March, Austria and Russia agreed that no large state should be erected in the Balkans.

9. The Russo-Turkish War. In April 1877 the Tsar, impatient with the Sultan's refusal to implement reforms, yielded to the pressure of Pan-Slav circles and declared war on Turkey. Russia was assisted by irregulars from the various rebellious Balkan states and Romania. Her forces, under General Todleben, met strong resistance by the Turks under Osman Pasha. They were held up at the fortress of Plevna for nearly six months. This ruined the Russian plans of a quick war, and by the time the breakthrough came on 10th December the other European powers had become sympathetic towards the "stout Turks". The Russian advance was then swift and her troops captured Adrianople in January 1878. In the Caucasus, Russian troops overran Armenia and captured Kars.

Britain and Austria then intervened to stop the war.

(*a*) On 15th January Britain reminded Russia that any treaty between Russia and Turkey affecting the 1856 treaties must be a European treaty. In February the British fleet moved towards Constantinople to discourage Russian troops from advancing on the capital.

(*b*) On 28th January Austria proposed a conference and demanded an armistice. Her forces were mobilised.

10. The Treaty of San Stefano. Russia, fearing intervention by Austria and Britain, hurriedly forced the Turks to sign peace terms. The results were the work of the Pan-Slav enthusiast Ignatiev, and not of Gorchakov, who had favoured a moderate settlement. The terms, signed on 3rd March 1878, were as follows.

(a) *Serbia, Montenegro and Romania* were to receive independence and were to be allowed to extend their boundaries.

(b) *Romania* was to acquire the region of Dobruja as compensation for the loss of southern Bessarabia to Russia.

(c) *Russia* was to receive Batum and Kars in the Caucasus.

(d) *Bulgaria* was to become a large autonomous principality under a Christian governor, while paying tribute to Turkey. She was to be administered and garrisoned for an initial period by Russia.

(e) *Bosnia and Herzegovina* were to remain dependent on Austria, but were to receive home rule. Russia was to supervise reforms in Bosnia.

11. Observations on the treaty. The following points can be noted about this treaty.

(a) *Advantages*. The idea of a "big" Bulgaria was one solution to the troubled Balkans, but only provided that its independence was guaranteed by the great powers. It might well tranquillise areas seething with revolt under Turkish rule and provide a bulwark against Russian expansion. Later, on 4th May 1878, Gladstone said in the House of Commons: "Surely the best resistance to be offered to Russia is by the strength and freedom of those countries that will have to resist her."

(b) *Disadvantages*. Apart from Russia and Bulgaria, no state liked the treaty.

(i) It violated the Budapest Convention. No mention was made of Austria's rights in Bosnia and Herzegovina.

(ii) Russia appeared to be gaining substantial influence in the Balkans.

(iii) Romania considered she had been inadequately compensated for her part in the war.

(iv) Serbia, Montenegro and Greece resented the emergence of a large Bulgaria.

12. British diplomacy. British interests were not directly threatened by the Treaty of San Stefano. Russia had made no attempt to take Constantinople. However, as Turkey had hoped, Britain was not prepared to accept the treaty. Disraeli threatened Russia with war unless she agreed to its revision. Jingoism became a word for the eccentric national enthusiasm whipped up in

Britain at the time. A popular music-hall expression was: "We don't want to fight, but by jingo, if we do, we've got the men, we've got the ships, we've got the money too." The reservists were called up and Indian troops sent to Malta.

Bismarck backed up the Austrian demands for a conference. Eventually Russia gave in and Bismarck's offer to preside over the conference at Berlin was accepted. Disraeli took the following preparatory measures before the conference.

(a) *Agreement with Russia.* On 30th May Britain and Russia agreed that the project of a large Bulgaria should be abandoned.

(b) *Anglo-Turkish treaty.* On 4th June Britain agreed to defend Turkish interests in Asia against Russia if she were allowed to purchase Cyprus as a military and naval base. Britain wanted it to counter Russian gains in the Caucasus.

(c) *Agreement with Austria.* On 6th June Britain and Austria agreed to support each other at the forthcoming conference. Britain agreed to acquiesce in an Austrian occupation of Bosnia and Herzegovina.

13. The Congress of Berlin.
Details were settled smoothly and the Congress was a success since most of the principal items had already been agreed. The provisions were as follows.

(a) *Austria-Hungary* was allowed to occupy and administer Bosnia and Herzegovina and the province of Novibazar. These areas were to remain under the nominal suzerainty of the Sultan.

(b) *Turkey* surrendered Cyprus ("the key to Asia" as Disraeli termed it) to Britain.

(c) *The "big" Bulgaria* was divided into the following three parts.

(i) Bulgaria, an independent state.

(ii) Eastern Rumelia, which was to have some autonomy under a Christian governor chosen by the Sultan, though it was to be subject to occupation by Turkish troops. (Russia had pleaded in vain that it should have no Turkish troops and that it should be called "South Bulgaria".)

(iii) Macedonia, which was to be returned to Turkey.

(d) *Serbia, Montenegro and Romania* were slightly enlarged and made entirely independent of Turkey.

(e) *Russia* was allowed to retain Southern Bessarabia, Kars and Batum. Romania had to be content with the barren Dobruja.

(f) *Turkey* promised reforms and full religious liberty to all her subjects.

14. Appraisal of the Treaty of Berlin. Disraeli counted it as one of his greatest achievements that "there is again a Turkey in Europe". After the Congress, he made a triumphant return to Britain, bringing as he thought "peace with honour". At the time, many considered the results of the Congress as a fine diplomatic victory for Britain, and Disraeli was knighted for his services. He had prevented war, checked Russian expansion, safeguarded the navigation of the Straits and secured Cyprus.

Both Disraeli and Andrássy thought that any future Bulgarian state would be under Russian influence. Consequently Bulgaria should be severely limited in size. Hence thousands of Bulgars, Greeks and Serbs were forced to return to Turkish rule. To be wise after the event and view the treaty from events twenty years later, it could be condemned for perpetuating Turkish rule in Macedonia. However, Austria and Britain could not foresee that Russian influence would decline in a future Bulgarian state.

The following points can be noted about the treaty.

(*a*) *Favourable aspects.* It averted major war and allowed many areas to secure independence from Turkey. It was an example of the "Concert of Europe" at work for the first time since 1856 to avert major war or unilateral action by a major power.

(*b*) *Unfavourable aspects.* In the long run, it was realised that the settlement was only a temporary "plastering" arrangement and that the seeds of future turmoil had been laid. In time, its provisions were gradually revised. For example, Austria annexed Bosnia-Herzegovina in 1908. Drawbacks of the treaty were as follows.

(*i*) Disraeli was mistaken in thinking that Turkey was capable of reform and of standing up to Russia. Turkey refused to carry out reforms and thus disturbances increased in Macedonia. Lord Salisbury later remarked that Britain had "backed the wrong horse".

(*ii*) The Balkan states were dissatisfied (*see* **15**).

(*iii*) Russia secured little benefit. It was ironical that, though victorious in war, Russia should suffer humiliation in peace. In July 1886 she fortified Batum, though it had been agreed that this town would only be a commercial port.

15. Significance of the Berlin Congress. The events of 1878 were important in determining future policies and actions of the powers.

(*a*) *European interest in African possessions of Turkey.* European states began to look towards the African territories of Turkey as areas for expansion. For example, France occupied Tunisia in 1881 (*see* XIX, **25**).

(*b*) *Continued unrest in the Balkans.* The Treaty of Berlin sowed the seeds of future conflicts.

(*i*) Montenegro and Serbia disliked the absorption of many Slavs into the Austrian sphere of influence when Austria occupied Bosnia-Herzegovina.

(*ii*) Serbia, Montenegro and Bulgaria found that their hopes of larger territorial boundaries that had been raised by the Treaty of San Stefano were frustrated by the Treaty of Berlin.

(*iii*) Romania was dissatisfied with the marshy Dobruja as recompense for giving Russia Bessarabia.

(*iv*) Greece gained nothing, though she had invaded Thessaly during the Russo-Turkish War.

(*c*) *Stronger rivalry between Russia and Austria.* Both were now about even in strength in the Balkans and felt they had real interests to protect – the one in Bulgaria, the other in Bosnia-Herzegovina.

(*d*) *Sensitive Russo-German relations.* Bismarck considered he had played the role of "honest broker" during the conference. By his refusal, however, to uphold the Russian claims to a large Bulgaria, he had shown that, if forced to decide, Germany would favour Austria-Hungary. The Tsar wrote to the German emperor in April 1879, expressing doubts as to whether peace could be preserved between the two countries (*see also* X, **13**).

(*e*) *Harbinger of European alliance system.* As a result of the deterioration in Russo-German relations, Germany decided to choose Austria as an ally in October 1878 (*see* X, **14**). This was the start of the alliance system which led ultimately to the division of Europe into two blocs. Prince Milan of Serbia, angry at having been deserted by Russia in 1878, allied with Austria in 1881. Romania made an alliance with Austria in 1882.

This alliance grouping eventually stirred France and Russia to form a counter-bloc in the 1890s.

(*f*) *Renewed Russian interest in Asia.* Russia, checked in Europe, now continued her expansion towards India and China (*see* XX, **5**(*c*) and **7**(*a*)).

THE BULGARIAN CRISIS, 1885-7

16. Bulgaria under Russian influence. Russia, chiefly responsible for the creation of the new state, helped in the first years to organise its political and military institutions.

On the basis of a new constitution, the Sobranje (Assembly) was called. In April 1879 this body elected Alexander of Battenberg, nephew of the Tsar, to be their ruler. Gradually increased friction arose between Russian and Bulgarian administrators. The former looked to the Tsar as their superior and not to Alexander, and were inclined to regard Bulgaria as a sort of Russian province. Alexander annoyed Russian officials by giving preference to the interests of the Austrians who wanted a Bulgarian link to complete the projected Orient Railway. In 1883 the Russian ministers were forced to resign.

17. Revolt in Eastern Rumelia. In September 1885 Eastern Rumelia revolted against Turkish rule and demanded union with Bulgaria. This time Russia objected to the enlarging of Bulgaria, having failed to make a satellite out of her. In contrast, Austria and eventually Britain decided that a union would not be a bad idea after all. It would form a more effective barrier against Russia.

Serbia and Romania, however, were not so keen. King Milan of Serbia invaded Bulgaria but his forces were decisively beaten. The overrunning of Serbia was prevented only by the intervention of the Austrians, who compelled the Bulgars to withdraw. Eventually the union of Eastern Rumelia and Bulgaria was accepted by the great powers in the spring of 1886.

18. The war scare of 1886-7. The Tsar, angry at the decline of Russian influence, organised the kidnapping of Alexander in August. Stambulov, the Bulgar leader, demanded his release, annoyed at this insult to his country. Eventually Alexander reappeared in Bulgaria, but this time he found no friends and abdicated his throne in September.

The outbreak of a general war seemed a distinct possibility in the autumn of 1886 and early 1887. This was for the following two reasons.

(a) *Russia* tried to induce Bulgaria to accept a ruler chosen for her. She contemplated the use of force to subdue Bulgaria. As a result, Austria made counter-military preparations against Russia.

(*b*) *In France* General Boulanger made menacing speeches about the necessity of regaining the lost provinces (*see* VII, **13**). It seemed that the Third Republic would soon be replaced by a dictatorial regime under the War Minister. There seemed to be some prospect of a Franco-Russian alliance, which was openly discussed in the Pan-Slav press.

19. Stable rule in Bulgaria. In July 1887 the Bulgars chose Ferdinand as their prince. He was a grandson of Louis-Philippe and had served as an officer in the Hungarian army. This arrangement was acceptable to Austria, but not to Russia. Again intervention by the latter seemed likely.

Russia, uncertain of the support of France, and faced with hostile combinations of the other powers, was eventually content with asking the Sultan to declare the election of Ferdinand illegal.

In time, Bulgaria was able to pursue a policy independent of any major power. This was under the strong leadership of Stambulov, who earned the title of "the Bulgarian Bismarck". His measures led to opposition, however, and he was forced to resign in 1894. He was murdered in the following year.

In February 1896, the new Tsar, Nicholas II, desired to end the feud with Bulgaria and took the initiative in securing the recognition of Ferdinand by the great powers.

20. Measures taken to avert war. The fact that the crisis was solved peacefully owed much to the efforts of Bismarck. Bismarck knew that, if a clash occurred between Austria and Russia, he would be impelled to support Austria. He dared not suggest this to Russia for fear of driving her into a French alliance. He constantly urged an agreement based on the division of the Balkans into an Austrian (western) and a Russian (eastern) sphere of influence, but to no avail.

Bismarck took the following measures to deter France and Russia from taking aggressive action while aiming to stay on good terms with both Austria and Russia.

(*a*) *Increase in the German standing army* (January 1887). When the Reichstag refused to approve the increase in the army, Bismarck dissolved it and conducted an electoral campaign that eventually gave him the majority he wanted. This checked the French enthusiasm for war.

(b) *Renewal of the Triple Alliance with Austria and Italy* (February 1887).

(c) *Reinsurance Treaty with Russia* (June 1887). This was intended to prevent Russia from turning to France for help. He hoped it would placate Russia for his refusal to support her demands for the expulsion of Stambulov.

(d) *Formation of the Mediterranean agreements* between Italy, Austria and Britain. Bismarck encouraged this.

(i) The first agreement in March provided for mutual support in case of differences with a fourth power in the Mediterranean. It was to provide a basis for common action in the event of a disturbance in the area caused by France or Russia.

(ii) The second one in December was a vague agreement to preserve the *status quo* in the Balkans and Ottoman Empire.

(e) *Financial measures* (November 1887). The German government forbade the Reichsbank to accept Russian securities as collateral for loans. The resultant sale of Russian holdings led to a fall in prices. This handicapped Russian financial operations and effective action in the Balkans.

(f) *Publication of the Dual Alliance* (February 1888). Bismarck hoped that this would serve as a warning to both Russia and Austria.

(i) Russia would not want to attack Austria, since the latter could rely on the support of Germany.

(ii) Austria would not be encouraged to attack Russia since the alliance was purely defensive.

(g) *Great Reichstag speech* (6th February 1888). Bismarck said, with Russia in mind, that: "We Germans fear God, and nothing else in the world." The main terms of the Triple Alliance and of the Mediterranean agreements were allowed to leak out. These measures served again as a cold douche on the aspirations of France and Russia.

GROWTH OF RIVALRY IN THE BALKANS

21. The collapse of the Turkish Balkans. During the period 1896–1913, Turkey gradually lost her Balkan possessions. This was caused through her own inept rule, the ambitions of the Balkan states and the rival intrigues of Austria and Russia.

The important developments were as follows.

(a) *The Crete crisis* of 1896–7 (*see* **23**).

(b) *Internal Turkish revolution* in 1908–9 (*see* **28**).

(c) *The Bosnian crisis* of 1908–9 (*see* **31**).

(d) *Unrest in Macedonia.* This Balkan area, still directly under the control of Turkey, contained a mixture of races, religions and languages which defied analysis. It did not contain the nucleus of a possible new state. Consequently Greece, Bulgaria and Serbia were interested in annexing various parts of Macedonia if Turkey ceased to maintain control. Austria and Russia were interested in extending their influence towards Salonika and Constantinople respectively. Turkey fostered divisions among the rival interests to preserve her own authority and remain in possession. The Sultan persistently refused to carry out reforms in his administration of the Macedonian Christians as he had promised the great powers. The continued unrest led to the following developments.

(i) Austro-Russian condominium (1903): eventually the powers gave Austria and Russia the responsibility of handling reforms. An international gendarmerie was established and an international finance committee was set up to supervise the collection of taxes. This arrangement collapsed when Austria, in return for a rail concession from Turkey, practically abandoned attempts at reform.

(ii) Loss of Turkish control as a result of the Balkan Wars in 1912–13 (*see* **34** and **36**).

NOTE: The active concern of the European powers with disturbances in Turkey's Balkan possessions where their interests were involved can be contrasted to their negative response to disturbances in remote Asiatic Armenia.

The Armenian subjects of Turkey were situated between the Caspian and Black Seas. In 1878 the Sultan had promised to reform the Turkish administration. However, no improvements took place and soon revolutionary agitation grew among the Armenians, who demanded autonomous rule. The Sultan decided on a policy of massacre to discourage them in 1894.

In 1896 the Armenians appealed in vain for help from the great powers. (1) Russia was not keen to raise up another "ungrateful Bulgaria" in Armenia. There was no appeal of a common faith, since the Armenians were Gregorian and not Orthodox Christians. Russia also feared the repercussions of

Armenian nationalism within her own Caucasian territories.
(2) Germany, anxious to win Turkey's friendship for her own
schemes, took no action. She was supported by Austria. (3)
Britain protested on behalf of the Armenians but took no
action.

22. Greece's territorial aims. In 1833, when the Greek state was
formed by the great powers, many Greeks in Thessaly, Epirus
and Macedonia were left under Turkish rule. In 1863 Britain
ceded to the Turks the Ionian Isles, which had been under British
protection since 1815. In 1881 the great powers persuaded Turkey
to cede to Greece a third of Epirus and the greater part of
Thessaly.

Greece then wanted the rest of those provinces, part of Macedonia and the island of Crete. A patriot secret society formed in
1894 called the *Ethnike Hetaireia* (National Society) worked to
accomplish these aims.

23. The Crete crisis. In 1896 riots broke out in Crete between
the Moslem Turks and the Christian Greeks. The latter declared
their union with Greece. Greece sent naval aid and invaded
Thessaly. However, her forces were defeated by Turkey, and she
had to cede territory and pay a large indemnity to Turkey in
1897.

Eventually a compromise arrangement was made regarding
Crete which did not satisfy Turkey, Crete or Greece. The events
were as follows.

(*a*) A joint Anglo-French fleet landed troops on the island to
stop the fighting. This was to avert a general Balkan war. When
the Turks murdered the British vice-consul, the British expelled
Turkish officials and troops.

(*b*) Prince George of Greece was invited by Britain, France,
Italy and Russia to govern Crete. Crete remained officially in the
Ottoman Empire and flew the Turkish flag. In practice, however,
Crete was an independent state with a Greek ruler.

24. Turkey and Germany. One result of the Crete crisis was
Turkey's decision to continue close relations with Germany.
Britain was no longer anxious to preserve the *status quo* in the
Ottoman Empire. Her occupation of Egypt and control of the
Suez Canal gave her security against Russian expansion at
Turkey's expense.

Kaiser William II had already paid a ceremonial visit to Turkey in 1889. In 1898 he went on a pilgrimage through the Holy Land. At Damascus he assured the Turks that "the Kaiser will be their friend at all times".

Military contacts had already been established when German officers started reorganising the Turkish army in 1881. Now commercial relations were strengthened. In 1899 Turkish rail concessions were given to a German company which planned to connect Berlin with the Persian Gulf. The company was to be given mining rights and other privileges in the areas which it covered. This would help the expansion of German influence in the Balkans and the Middle East. Soon, many German bankers, traders and financiers were involved in business dealings in the Ottoman Empire (see XX, 9(a)(ii)).

25. Austro-Russian collaboration. Austria and Russia agreed in 1897 to try to maintain peace in the Balkans. This was renewed by the Mürzsteg agreement of October 1903. The reasons for this are summarised in 21(d)(i) and in (a) and (b) below.

(a) *Difficulty of devising a satisfactory Balkan policy.* A number of countries – Greece, Bulgaria and Serbia – coveted Turkey's Balkan possessions. A partition of Turkey's remaining territories thus seemed a complicated and dangerous exercise. Austria and Russia expected that these areas would not long remain Turkish, since the Turkish administration would collapse through its own internal inefficiency and corruption. Thus caution seemed the best policy.

(b) *Russia wanted to concentrate on Far Eastern expansion.* France was not prepared to help Russia in her Balkan interests as Russia would not aid France in her colonial struggles with Britain. Thus for Russia to concentrate on extending her influence in Asia seemed a safer and more fruitful policy.

26. Austria and the Balkans. During the period 1867–1914 Austria's primary interest shifted from German affairs to the Balkans. She was concerned about South-east Europe for strategic and economic reasons and wanted to forestall Russian influence there. Points to note are as follows.

(a) *The Danube.* Austria relied on the Danube as a trade route. This meant she was interested in events in Serbia, Bulgaria and Romania, along whose borders or through whose territory the Danube passed.

(b) *Access to the sea.* The Austrian Empire's direct access to the sea depended upon its continued possession of the Istrian peninsula at the head of the Adriatic, with its three ports of Trieste, Pola and Fiume, and of the Dalmatian coast. This was inhabited by Serbo-Croats in the Hungarian province of Croatia-Slavonia. Trieste was a territorial objective of Italy, since its inhabitants were largely Italian-speaking.

(c) *Relations with Serbia.* Serbia joined the Triple Alliance in 1881 and until 1903 her relations with Austria were friendly, despite territorial differences. Close commercial relations were maintained. Serbia was thankful for Austria's intervention that had prevented the destruction of the Serbian army after the battle of Slivnitza in 1885 (*see* 17).

(d) *Pan-Slavism.* Austria felt compelled to block any Yugoslav (South-Slav) movement which developed in Serbia, and which might ally with the Serbs who inhabited Montenegro. This was because Austria's coastal possessions would be natural objectives of any such policy. In addition, Pan-Slav agitation threatened to dismember the Austrian Empire if her subject Serbs and Croats broke away.

One school of thought in Austria was that the problem could be solved by the union of all Serbs and Croats in Serbia, Montenegro, Dalmatia, Istria, Bosnia, Herzegovina and Croatia-Slavonia within the Hapsburg Empire. This group, the "Trialists", hoped that such a union would form a third section on an equal basis to Austria and Hungary within the Empire. It would resolve the dangerous disaffection among the Empire's Croats and the growing nationalism of Serbia. The scheme was bitterly opposed by the Magyars.

(e) *Macedonia.* Austria worked to obtain rail concessions from Turkey in this area and to extend her influence to the Aegean. If she were ever cut off from the Adriatic, this would become her only maritime outlet.

27. Deterioration of Austro-Serbian relations. In 1903 the Serbian king was murdered. The Obrenovich dynasty was replaced by the Karageorgevitch dynasty. The new King Peter I, supported by his son, Prince Alexander, was pro-Russian and advocated an expansionist policy. Hence Serbian policy soon became actively anti-Austrian.

Sources of dissension were the following.

(a) *Serbian policy of Yugoslavism* (South-Slavism). Serbia, under the illusion that Austrian control of Bosnia and Herzegovina was only temporary, wanted to free these provinces from Austrian control. This was so they could join a new Slav state, together with those Serbs and Croats presently within the Hapsburg Empire in Croatia and the Banat. Austria opposed this policy for reasons already mentioned (*see* **26**(*d*)).

(*b*) *Customs union.* The Serbian government planned a customs union with Bulgaria in 1904. This threatened Austria's "most favoured nation's" rights in Serbia.

(*c*) *Economic policies.* In 1906 Hungarian magnates refused to accept continuance of the common army unless Austria enforced prohibitive tariffs against Serbian agricultural produce, especially pigs. Austria complied and this resulted in the so-called "pig war" which lasted until 1908. Serbia, facing possible economic ruin, eventually found an outlet for her livestock in Turkey and Germany. Other ways by which Serbia asserted her economic independence from Austria were by raising loans in Paris and by the purchase of arms from France instead of from the Skoda works in Bohemia.

(*d*) *Revival of Austrian ambitions in the Balkans.* Aehrenthal became Foreign Minister in 1906. He tried to devise some plan which would revive the declining prestige of the Hapsburg monarchy. In view of the increased Serb agitation, the policy of preserving the *status quo* in the Balkans was abandoned. Austria started to encourage the territorial ambitions of Bulgaria to check Serbia. Aehrenthal's first thought, soon abandoned, was to partition Serbia with Bulgaria.

28. The "Young Turk" revolt. A group of "Young Turks", called the Committee of Union and Progress, led a revolt against the Sultan on 23rd July 1908. It was partly caused by the desire of Turkish patriots to retain Macedonia, which seemed to be passing under the influence of other powers. They forced the Sultan to agree to elections for a national parliament and other constitutional changes.

Reforms were made which the Sultan later rescinded. He was deposed in May 1909. However, liberal reforms did not occur. The new Sultan embarked upon a rigid policy of Turkification.

The revolt had significant effects in Europe. It caused consternation among Austrian and Russian statesmen, who took it as evidence that Turkey might become a reviving power and cease to decline. It seemed to herald a tightening of Turkey's administration in the Empire and a more vigorous assertion of her rights, which would be applied, for example, to Bosnia and Macedonia. The revolt thus set in motion the train of events leading to the Bosnian crisis.

THE BOSNIAN CRISIS, 1908–9

29. The meeting at Buchlau. Aehrenthal and Isvolsky, the Russian Foreign Minister, met in September at Buchlau to discuss the recent Turkish revolt. It threatened to balk any designs the two countries had at Turkey's expense.

Aehrenthal wanted Bosnia, since it would give a hinterland to the Dalmatian coast, linking it to Hungary, and also would bring Austria several miles nearer the Aegean. Austria and Russia came to an informal arrangement. Russia would allow Austria to annex Bosnia and Herzegovina and in return Austria would support Russia's aim of achieving the opening of the Straits of the Bosphorus and Dardanelles to her warships. It was agreed, tacitly, that their announcements to change the *status quo* and infringe treaty obligations would be made simultaneously.

30. The Eastern Question reopened. While Turkey was recovering from the "Young Turk" revolt, Bulgaria and Austria took the opportunity of furthering their own plans, which were as follows.

(*a*) *Declaration of independence by Bulgaria.* On 5th October Prince Ferdinand, encouraged by Austria, threw off all suzerainty to the Sultan and proclaimed himself King of Bulgaria.

(*b*) *Annexation of Bosnia-Herzegovina by Austria.* Aehrenthal was not prepared to wait until a suitable time arrived for a joint Austro-Russian announcement. In a telegram to Isvolsky, he said circumstances necessitated Austria's acting without further delay. On 8th October Austria annexed Bosnia-Herzegovina. This action represented a public affront to Russia and a personal slight to Isvolsky.

31. The Bosnian crisis. Isvolsky had not informed his Russian colleagues about the Buchlau arrangements. He soon made the unpleasant discovery that many Russians cared more for the Slavs than the Straits and resented Austria's annexation of Bosnia. Thus he now denied that he had consented to the annexation and described Austria's action as a flagrant breach of written arrangements. This led immediately to a diplomatic crisis.

(*a*) *Turkey*, supported by Russia, was determined to re-establish her authority in the lost territories.

(*b*) *Russia* demanded compensation. The problem was that Russia stood little chance of obtaining satisfaction. There had been adverse international reaction to Austria's action, and France and Britain opposed any further violation of treaty rights at the Straits.

(*c*) *Serbia* mobilised her forces against Austria. Serbia, infuriated by the loss of the opportunity to have the annexed provinces, was encouraged by Pan-Slav agitation and Isvolsky's lack of moderation into believing that Russia would support her. Thus the Serbian army was alerted for a possible "show-down" with Austria.

32. The Bosnian crisis resolved. Britain worked to pacify Turkey and to restrain Serbia. Supported by Russia, Britain demanded a conference. Austria replied that she would accept one only if it was held to recognise the *fait accompli* of Austrian annexation. This was tantamount to a refusal. Germany supported Austria.

By March 1909 the issue was still unresolved. Germany then came as a "knight in shining armour" to the aid of Austria. Austria was determined, unless Serbia recognised the annexation, to declare war on her. Bülow, the German Chancellor, asked Russia to recognise the Austrian annexation and to advise Serbia to give way. Russia gave an evasive reply and Bülow followed it up by demanding a categorical answer. Russia, unsupported by Britain or France, gave way.

33. Consequences of the Bosnian crisis. It had been a diplomatic victory for Germany and Austria. However, as Bülow admitted later, it was only a Pyrrhic one. Austria did not gain additional security, and her action resulted only in aggravating the Slav problem and rendering her policy suspect throughout Europe.

It brought the First World War a stage nearer since both Russia and Serbia were determined not to be humbled a second time. Britain, Russia and France drew closer together in the Triple Entente. Germany's policy of "brinkmanship" towards Russia gave them the impression that she was more interested in demonstrating her power than in serving the cause of peace.

Isvolsky worked to gain his revenge on Aehrenthal. Russia took the following two important steps:

(a) *the signing of the secret Racconigi agreement with Italy (see* XIII, **54**(*a*));
(b) *the formation of a Balkan League (see* **34**).

THE BALKAN WARS AND THE PRELUDE TO GENERAL WAR

34. The Balkan League and war. In 1909 Russia formed an alliance with Bulgaria. She hoped this would be the start of a League of Serbs and Bulgars which would be anti-Austrian and pro-Russian, in support of Pan-Slavism. When Italy defeated Turkey in a short war (1911–12), this encouraged the territorial ambitions of the Balkan states. In 1912, largely owing to the efforts of the Greek minister, Venizelos, Greece, Serbia and Montenegro joined Bulgaria. The common factor in their unity was hatred of Turkey rather than Austria. This was not the intention of Russia and consequently her influence in the League faded.

As a pretext for war, the League, in October 1912, called for immediate reforms in Macedonia. The European powers attempted to restrain the League by forbidding it to fight.

Montenegro, without consulting her allies, attacked Turkey. The other three Balkan states followed her and soon Turkey was heavily defeated. Macedonia and Albania revolted, and Serbia reached the Adriatic, after overrunning northern Albania. Then the League started to divide the spoils. However, their arrangements were countermanded by the powers, who insisted on the end of the war and a conference in London.

35. The London Conference. In May 1913 Britain and Germany worked together in reaching a peace settlement, but friction occurred between Austria and Russia. Austria wanted to prevent Serbia from gaining access to the sea, but Russia wanted Serbia and Montenegro to gain access. Eventually a settlement was reached concerning the distribution of all Turkish possessions ceded west of the Enos–Midia line.

Details of the Treaty of London were as follows.

(*a*) An independent Albania was created on the Adriatic.

(*b*) Serbia acquired Central Macedonia in compensation for the loss of an Adriatic port.

(*c*) Bulgaria gained Thrace and some of the Aegean coast. However, she considered that most of the fighting had been done by her and was not satisfied. She desired Central Macedonia.

(*d*) Greece received Salonika, Southern Macedonia and Crete. This closed the door on Austria's hopes of reaching the Aegean.

36. The Second Balkan War. Serbia, balked in Albania, insisted on retaining territory to the east. This, though occupied by Serbian troops, was mainly inhabited by Bulgars. Bulgaria refused Serbia's demands for a larger share of territory from her.

In June, Bulgaria suddenly attacked Serbia. Eventually Greece, Montenegro and Romania supported Serbia, while Turkey joined in to recapture some of the territory lost to Bulgaria. Austria was anxious to aid Bulgaria, but Germany dissuaded her from intervention. Three of Bulgaria's enemies had links with Germany: Turkey, Romania (ruled by a Hohenzollern) and Greece (where the Kaiser's brother-in-law was King).

37. Results of the Balkan Wars. Neither Austria nor Russia was satisfied. Austria disliked the growth in power of Serbia and blamed Germany for failing to support her. Russia blamed Britain for the creation of Albania, which blocked Serbia from the sea, and was critical of France for her inactivity during the crisis.

The following points should be noted:

(*a*) Turkey was reduced to areas ethnically Turkish. This meant she retained only a small portion of European territory.

(*b*) Serbia was strengthened territorially and gained new confidence. She renewed her efforts to unite the remaining Serbs of the Balkans under her rule. Pashitch, the Serbian leader, remarked: "The first round is won; now we must prepare for the second, against Austria."

(*c*) Bulgaria was reduced in size. Bulgaria remained friendly with Austria and Germany.

(*d*) World war was brought one stage nearer. This was due to the following reasons.

(*i*) All the Balkan states regarded the peace treaties as only provisional. They looked forward to a renewal of hostilities. The position in Albania remained distinctly unstable.

(*ii*) Britain and Germany became increasingly reluctant to restrain their respective allies, Russia and Austria, from impetuous actions.

(*iii*) The swift, decisive battles encouraged the great powers to assume that the same conditions would apply to future war.

(*e*) The Wars illustrated the influence of the principle of "national self-determination". Once it was accepted as a basis of international organisation, this principle enabled small states to develop. They gained an importance out of proportion to their size and showed themselves unwilling to follow patterns devised for them by the major powers.

PROGRESS TEST 16

1. Describe the development of Pan-Slavism and the increasing influence of Russia. How did Russia contribute to the growth of Slav nationalism? (**1–3**)

2. Give the reasons for the Bosnian uprising in 1875. (**3–4**)

3. Describe the attempts made by the European powers to stop the Balkan rebellion. (**6**)

4. What arrangements did Austria and Russia make in 1876–7 regarding the Balkans? (**8**)

5. Why did Russia end the war with Turkey? What were the provisions of the San Stefano Treaty? (**9–10**)

6. Why did Austria and Britain dislike the San Stefano Treaty? (**11, 14**)

7. Explain why the Berlin Treaty was unsatisfactory. (**14(*b*), 15**)

8. Describe the events leading to the Bulgarian crisis in 1886. (**16–18**)

9. What measures did Bismarck take to avert war between Austria and Russia? (**20**)

10. Why did a crisis occur in Crete in 1896? How was it solved? (**22–23**)

11. Why did Austria and Russia agree to co-operate in the Balkans in 1897? (**25**)

12. Explain the Austrian policy in the Balkans after 1867. (**26**)

13. Describe the course of Austro-Serb relations between 1881 and 1909. (**26(*c*), 27, 31(*c*)**)

14. Explain why the Bosnian crisis occurred. What were the consequences?   (29–31, 33)

15. What role did Germany play during the Bosnian crisis? (32)

16. What arrangements were made in the Balkans as a result of the wars of 1912–13.   (35–37)

CHAPTER XVII

European imperialism

CAUSES OF IMPERIALISM

1. Introduction. Various arguments were used to justify imperialism. The reasons or motives which inspired particular European powers were a combination of some or all of the closely related factors listed below.

2. Political and strategic factors. The rush for possessions and for hegemony in Africa and the Far East after 1870 by European powers was dictated primarily by considerations of European power diplomacy.

After 1871, when Germany and Italy became united countries, European governments ceased to be preoccupied with European problems. There seemed little room for diplomatic manoeuvre. To resolve the deadlock they looked to fresh regions to find scope for their ambitions, thus "projecting European conflicts" elsewhere.

The statesmen were also prompted by considerations of the relative balance-of-power position in Europe and elsewhere rather than by purely colonial interests. Each country looked with envy at any increased power obtained by another. Italy and Germany wanted to prove that, as new states and great powers, they were also entitled to empires. As other powers, jealous of Britain's large empire, began to expand, Britain started on an active colonisation policy to keep ahead.

Britain's major concern was to protect established interests, and safeguard the route to the guaranteed markets of India, China and the Australasian colonies. As a result Britain acquired strategically located possessions *en route* to these areas (*see* XXI, 6).

Another political argument advanced was the need for security. In certain regions savage, nomadic or tribal populations embarked on raids or acts of pillage against their neighbours. The interests of stable government, law and order, and secure trading conditions necessitated their suppression. This argument was advanced by the following powers.

(*a*) *The British*, to extend control in West Africa after numerous conflicts with the Ashanti, and in India.

(*b*) *The Russians*, to extend control in Central Asia.

3. Economic factors. J. A. Hobson, in his book *Imperialism*, stressed economic considerations as being the primary motive for imperialism. Lenin drew upon Hobson to formulate his theory of imperialism as the highest form of capitalism. Though the economic factor has been exaggerated as an underlying cause of imperialism it was still important.

Natural resources (especially iron and coal), accumulated capital from various activities (including the slave trade and plantation system in the colonies), new inventions, and a religious and political environment congenial to economic enterprise resulted in the Industrial Revolution in Britain. During the nineteenth century industrial growth also occurred in other European countries. It was closely connected with imperialism for the following reasons.

(*a*) *It created a demand for colonies.* Rapid industrialisation involved large factories and mass production. This encouraged nations to look for colonies which would provide them with the following.

(*i*) Raw materials: it was discovered that overseas areas possessed cheap supplies of necessary and sometimes valuable commodities. These were in short or non-existent supply at home. Examples were gold, ivory, oil (especially in North and West Africa), rubber (Belgian Congo and Malaysia) and tin (East Indies).

(*ii*) Markets: colonies provided markets for surplus manufactured goods. In exchange they provided agricultural produce. As living standards grew in Europe, some colonies also satisfied the growing demand for exotic tropical products.

After the abandonment of free trade and the revival of high tariffs in Europe during the 1870s, European powers became anxious to obtain key trade areas. They feared that otherwise they would not benefit since their rivals would enclose their own colonies within high tariff barriers.

(*iii*) Investment: in the years 1860–78 many investors, particularly British ones, lost heavily when several Central and

South American states and Turkey and Egypt defaulted. Investors looked for new fields of investment for surplus capital. When Egypt and Tunisia became bankrupt, they were forced to borrow money at high interest rates from European investors. This foreign financial control over their economies preceded their occupation by France and Britain respectively. In other parts of Africa, and in Asia, Europeans invested vast sums of money. As the British government was reluctant to help, the device of the chartered company was used in Britain for overseas expansion. In the 1880s, for example, the Imperial East African Company, the Royal Niger Company and the South Africa Chartered Company were created to conduct operations in Africa.

(b) *It created the means to obtain colonies.* Industrial progress resulted in the following two factors which contributed to effective European occupation.

(i) Superior firepower (*see* 8(c)): if Europeans had not possessed superior military arms they would have been unable to have occupied many areas owing to the opposition of hostile inhabitants.

(ii) Developments in rail communication and medicine: progress in unhealthy tropical regions in Africa and in Asia was impeded before the development of railways in the 1870s. Progress in hygiene and medicine made it possible to deal with conditions found in new regions. For example quinine was discovered as a counter to malaria.

4. Psychological factors. The idea took root in Europe, particularly after 1870, that great states possessed the respect of their neighbours only when they acted like great states. Use was made of the following arguments to justify expansionist policies.

(a) *Power.* It was argued by some writers that a powerful nation was justified in seeking colonies. It illustrated its virility and strength. This argument was advanced by Sir John Seeley in his work *The Expansion of England* (1883) and by the Frenchman Leroy-Beaulieu. The views of the following were also important.

(i) Herbert Spencer (1820–1903) popularised the theory of "the survival of the fittest", an adaptation of the biological theories of Darwin to the struggles of man.

(ii) Friedrich Nietzsche (1844–1900) believed that brute force alone would help the nation in its struggle for life.

(b) *Prestige.* Ventures were sometimes embarked upon to satisfy public demands for the preservation of national prestige as compensation for some failure in domestic or foreign policy in Europe. This factor influenced the colonial policies of the following powers.

(*i*) France (in 1830 and after 1871).

(*ii*) Russia (in 1856 and 1879).

(*iii*) Italy (in the 1880s).

5. Cultural factors. In the past some people had desired to spread a religious faith or bring the benefits of an "advanced civilisation" or way of life to others.

During the nineteenth century missionaries were keen to spread the Christian faith, and also encouraged the philanthropists and humanitarians who wanted to abolish un-Christian customs in Africa and India such as human sacrifices. Britain justified her extension of power in West Africa partly on the grounds of the need to suppress effectively the indigenous slave trade.

6. Racial factors. Support was given to imperial ventures by some nineteenth-century writers who encouraged the notion of the innate superiority of the Teutonic, Anglo-Saxon or European race over others. Though some felt that the "white race" had a mandate to rule the "coloured races" of the world, race in the nineteenth century meant not so much colour as "nation" or group of nations.

"Racist" ideas were particularly popular in Britain and Germany during the late nineteenth century. In 1895 Joseph Chamberlain, Secretary of State for the Colonies, claimed that "the British race is the greatest of governing races that the world has ever seen". During the height of British imperial feeling, in the period 1885–1905, Rudyard Kipling said it was the "white man's burden" to help educate and civilise the less fortunate elsewhere.

7. Demographic factors. Small countries with large populations and a high birth rate, such as Italy, advanced the need to survive as a reason for expansion. Nationalists also argued that, if colonies were possessed, people who wished to migrate could still remain under the home country's flag. Arguments on these grounds were also made in Germany in the late nineteenth century. Though many countries desired a "place in the sun", many overseas areas were to prove unsuitable for large-scale European settlement.

CHARACTERISTICS OF IMPERIALISM

8. Features of European imperialism after 1870. European imperialism during the late nineteenth century was particularly notable for the following features.

(*a*) *Rapidity and extent.* In 1870 European influence was only moderate in Africa, Asia and the Pacific. By 1900 practically all Africa had been successfully partitioned, extensive spheres of influence gained in China and South-east Asia, and available Pacific isles annexed.

By 1914 European powers directly or indirectly influenced the destinies of over 80 per cent of the world's population.

(*b*) *Ruthlessness.* The opposition of tribes was ruthlessly eliminated by the British, French and Germans in Africa. Certain areas, such as the Belgian Congo, were exploited in the interests of a concession company or an imperial power. Natives were ill-treated and the interests of their region disregarded.

(*c*) *Military power and organisation.* Before the nineteenth century many countries contributed to the development of firearms. The cannon and gunpowder were probably Chinese inventions. However, firearms were first used effectively by the Turks and the British.

Technical progress during the Industrial Revolution widened the gap in military terms between Europe on the one hand and Africa and Asia on the other. The growing complexity of weapons led to an emphasis on minimum standards of literacy, so that their users could maintain them properly. Principles of infantry training, developed in Germany, were made virtually into a religion in their application in the British army. During the nineteenth century superior artillery, the mass-produced rifle, the machine gun, and their proper use, combined with discipline and organisation of a high standard, contributed to the European supremacy in India, China and Africa. Non-European peoples either lacked access to these weapons or lacked the organisation and knowledge to utilise them effectively when they were available.

9. Forms of imperialism. These are as follows.

(*a*) *Colony.* The land is annexed and governed by the imperial nation, which exercises full control over the people.

(*b*) *Protectorate.* The native ruler retains his title, but officials of a foreign power maintain control. The "protecting" powers keep out other foreign nations. Examples were the British protectorate over Zanzibar and the French protectorate over Tunis and Morocco.

(c) *Economic concession.* This is the grant of rights and privileges to merchants or industrialists who want to trade, build railways, or develop mines or natural resources. Such concessions were granted to the Russians and Japanese in Manchuria and Korea, and to European powers in North Africa.

(d) *Sphere of influence.* This is a region of a foreign country where other nations recognise that one nation has special economic and political privileges.

(i) Britain was recognised as having such privileges in the central region of China along the Yangtze river.

(ii) Germany was in a similar position in northern China, in the Shantung peninsula.

(e) *Non-alienation rights.* This is an agreement over the disposal of colonial territory if one power is no longer able to exercise authority.

(i) France, in 1884, made an agreement with King Leopold of Belgium to take over his portion of the Congo if he wished to relinquish responsibility.

(ii) Britain and Germany, in 1898, agreed to share Portugal's African possessions if Portugal had to abandon them.

(f) *Extra-territoriality.* In China the European powers insisted that their own nationals should be tried under their own laws for any offences committed, and not under Chinese law.

10. Interested groups. A special feature of early nineteenth-century imperialism was the role of individuals, pressure groups and organisations. Their activities, undertaken without official sanction, frequently led to the government embarking on imperialist ventures.

The major groups, official and unofficial, who participated in the process of imperialism were as follows.

(a) *Explorers and scientists.* Europeans considered Africa the "Dark Continent" since its vast interior was unknown to them. Numerous expeditions under British, French, German or Portuguese leadership made important discoveries about African geography, resources and peoples. They awoke European interest in Africa's economic potentialities, and discovered areas where white men could live.

Perhaps the most famous explorer was Dr. David Livingstone,

who went from Scotland and carried on important medical and missionary work in Central Africa between 1840 and 1871.

(b) *Missionaries.* In particular it can be noted that French and British missionary societies were important in China and Africa. They worked to convert the natives to the Christian religion, and to improve the health and welfare of the poor.

(c) *Traders.* Particularly notorious activities were the slave trade in Africa and the opium trade in China. In time trade in a variety of commodities developed as rich resources were found. The Industrial Revolution resulted in great interest in the economic development of overseas areas on the part of industrialists, investors and bankers.

(d) *The military.* When news arrived that one of the groups (a)–(c) above had been abused by natives, land or naval forces would be sent to protect them.

(e) *Governments.* The European government would decide whether to make the military occupation permanent or temporary. Invariably, unless it had to give way to the prior claim of another European power, it allowed the occupation to become permanent and sent out civil administrators. Cynics made up a formula concerning the arrival of "first the missionary and trader, then the soldier and governor with the flag".

THE COURSE OF
NINETEENTH-CENTURY IMPERIALISM

11. Temporary retreat. Between 1763 and the 1870s few European powers showed much interest in acquiring territory outside Europe. Where new holdings were gained this was not always the result of conscious policy and had little public support. Reasons for this were as follows.

(a) *Colonial defeats.*

(i) French ambitions in India, North America and elsewhere were thwarted by Britain in the eighteenth century and during the Napoleonic Wars.

(ii) Britain, though she gained Canada from the French in 1763, lost much of her colonial empire in North America in 1782.

(iii) Spain and Portugal lost empires in South America when they became independent after 1815.

(b) *Abolition of the slave trade.* European powers, except France and Britain, gradually withdrew from West Africa after the abolition of the slave trade in the early part of the nineteenth century since a major source of revenue had been lost.

(*c*) *Preoccupation with European events*. The French Revolutionary and Napoleonic Wars had been costly for European powers in terms of lives and money. After 1815 they were mainly concerned with:

(*i*) domestic recovery and adaptation to a period of great economic and industrial progress (commonly known as the "Industrial Revolution");

(*ii*) problems caused by the development of liberal and national movements resulting from the French Revolution, which threatened the *status quo*.

(*d*) *Belief that costs of colonies outweighed benefits*. The experience of the revolt of the thirteen American colonies seemed to prove that colonies did not pay. This was the attitude of the British government during the mid-Victorian era.

12. The major colonial powers, 1815–70. The chief colonial powers in 1815 were Spain, Portugal, the Netherlands, Britain, France and Russia.

(*a*) *Government policies*.

(*i*) The British government, except in India, was not keen to incur new responsibilities. Its interests were primarily economic and strategic. For details *see* XXI, **5** and **6**.

(*ii*) In contrast to the British, the French government was keen to extend French influence in the Levant, Africa and Asia. Its interests were political and religious.

(*iii*) The Russian government's attitude tended to waver between enthusiasm and lack of interest. Russian expansion across Asia was motivated primarily by political factors. Military actions were frequently undertaken without official authorisation.

(*b*) *Areas of expansion*. Significant advances after 1815 were made by the following powers:

(*i*) Russia in Central Asia and Siberia (*see* XX, **1**, **5** and **7–9**).

(*ii*) Britain in India, South-east Asia and South Africa.

(*iii*) France in Annam (South-east Asia) and North and West Africa (*see* XVIII, XIX and XX, **30** and **31**).

13. Reasons for the intensification of imperialism. An increase in the tempo of expansion took place in the 1870s. This led in the

1880s to a frantic scramble for new territories by the European powers. Reasons were as follows:

(a) *Entry of new competitors*, including:

    (i) Germany in Africa, Asia and the Pacific;

    (ii) King Leopold of Belgium in Central Africa;

    (iii) Italy in East Africa.

(b) *Stalemate in Europe* (*see* 2).

(c) *Economic reasons*. After the abandonment of free trade and the revival of high tariffs in Europe in the 1870s, European powers were anxious to obtain key trade areas in Africa and Asia. They feared that otherwise they would not benefit from the African trade since their rivals would enclose their own colonies within high tariff barriers.

(d) *Change in British policy*. During the 1870s Britain under Disraeli embarked on active imperialist policies.

(e) *Provisions of the Berlin Conference* in 1884 (*see* XVIII, 7).

(f) *Influence of public opinion*. During the late nineteenth century electorates and the popular press appeared. In the age of nationalistic ideas people became vitally interested in the fortunes and reputation of their country abroad. They were swift to condemn failures and applaud successes.

Imperialists used various arguments to gain popular support so as to influence the government. Countries which were vulnerable to public agitation for imperial ventures were Britain, France and Germany.

    (i) It made the former anti-imperialist Disraeli, in 1872, call on Britain to be "a great country, an imperial country".

    (ii) It forced Bismarck, in 1882, to embark on the acquisition of colonies, a policy he had firmly resisted before.

RESULTS OF EUROPEAN IMPERIALISM

14. Effects of imperialism. Though imperialist activities can bring some benefits to both the mother country and the colony it can also bring considerable harm. The consequences of the activities of the nineteenth-century European colonial powers have profoundly affected events in the twentieth century. The effects of imperialism are summarised below.

(a) *Benefits.*

    (i) Economic: the colonial power may actively encourage the development of natural resources, industrialisation, improved agricultural methods and irrigation, which provide work for the local population.

(*ii*) Social: the medical, educational and welfare services generally may be improved.

(*iii*) Political: the colonial power may develop the institutions of government, and provide law and order where previously existed anarchy and disorder. It may also act as a unifying influence – as the British in India – or provide training in the art of self-government.

(*b*) *Weakness.* Generally people prefer rule by their own rulers, however corrupt or inefficient, to foreign rule, however benign and efficient. One drawback of foreign rule is that it encourages the erroneous belief that subject peoples are in some way inferior to ruling peoples. If foreign rule is also corrupt the subject peoples then find the position intolerable. For instance their country might be exploited solely for the interests of the foreign country and its nationals resident there.

15. Impact of the West. Europe and Asia are opposite sides of one land-mass. They are, broadly speaking, divided by the Ural Mountains, Ural river, Caspian Sea, Caucasus, Black Sea and Dardanelles. Civilisations and nations have diverged sufficiently on either side to justify the concepts of "East" and "West".

During the nineteenth century Asia and Africa succumbed to the imperialism of European powers. Before 1914 only sporadic revolts occurred in Africa and these were soon suppressed. In many parts of this continent the natives were still not aware of the extent to which the "sovereignty" of their lands and resources had passed to the Europeans. The latter had been welcomed at first as "lost gods" or other mystic persons, equipped as they were with all the signs of advanced technology.

Asia, the centre of famous cultures, accepted western values only in part. Slowly Asians came to appreciate the importance of western technology as a means for re-establishing their independence from the Europeans. They discovered the ideas of the French Revolution – nationalism, liberalism and democracy – and of the movements which tried to realise them in Europe in the nineteenth century. To them these ideas seemed at variance with the policies of the European powers.

16. European imperialism on the wane. Between 1895 and 1905 enthusiasm for imperialistic expansion reached its climax and then started to decline. Within a few years a series of sharp crises occurred in European relations (*see* **17**) and also a number of defeats were inflicted on European powers in the colonial arena. At the same time the rising tide of protest against the West gathered momentum.

(*a*) *European defeats.*

(*i*) A revolt in Cuba (1895) against Spanish rule led in 1898 to the Spanish–American War. Spain was defeated, and Cuba became independent in 1901. Puerto Rico in the Caribbean, and also Guam and the Philippines in the Pacific, were ceded to the United States.

(*ii*) The first serious reverse for a European power in Africa was suffered by the Italians. In 1896 an Italian force intending to conquer Ethiopia was destroyed by a superior force of Ethiopians at Adowa.

(*iii*) Japan was quick to adopt the techniques of western industrial society but rejected the western "way of life". The first clear indication of the rising power of Asia was the Japanese defeat of Russia in 1905 (*see* XX, **25**).

(*b*) *Asian protest movement.* Examples of the rising revolt of the East from the mid nineteenth century onwards were as follows.

(*i*) *In China.* The Taiping rebellion was partly directed against foreign influence, especially the missionaries. Other examples were the Boxer Rebellion (1900) and the Chinese revolution (1912).

(*ii*) *In India.* Examples were the Indian Mutiny (1857) and the movement for self-government led by the Indian National Congress in the 1880s.

17. Effect of imperialism on European relations. Before 1880 France, Russia and Britain had carried on colonisation or imperialist expansion without serious clashes occurring. After 1880 the entry of new competitors for the most valuable remaining spaces of the Earth resulted in increased tension, and the negotiation of numerous secret arrangements.

Territorial disputes between European powers in Africa and Asia were less serious than they appeared. They were usually settled peacefully, for example at the Berlin Conference of 1884 (*see* XVIII, **7**). No one issue affected the vital interests of all the great powers. Also allies were not prepared to support each other and risk war for issues which did not interest or affect them.

For example, France was reluctant to aid Russia in Asia, and Russia was reluctant to aid France in Africa. However, their rivalries led to the division of Europe into two rigid alliance blocs.

The following points should be noted.

(*a*) Rivalry over Egypt and later over West Africa caused embittered relations between France and Britain in the years 1882–98.

(*b*) Partly as compensation for disappointments in Africa, Italy joined the Dual Alliance in 1883.

(*c*) The German refusal to aid Britain in the Far East against Russian expansion was a contributory factor to the Anglo-Japanese alliance of 1902.

(*d*) The Anglo-Russian Convention of 1907 was caused partly by:

(*i*) the desire of Britain and Russia to end their rivalry in Central Asia;

(*ii*) their mutual fear of Germany's policy of *Drang nach Osten*, her growing influence in Turkey and her possible designs on Persia.

(*e*) Colonial reverses were suffered by:

(*i*) France in 1898, in the Fashoda incident;

(*ii*) Russia in 1905, when she was defeated by Japan.

These led to a renewed interest by these powers in the sensitive issues of Alsace-Lorraine and the Balkans respectively.

(*f*) The decision of Germany to build a large navy after 1898 was partly motivated by:

(*i*) her inability to intervene to aid the Boers against the British after 1895 if she had wished to do so;

(*ii*) her belief that to be a "world power" necessitated a large navy.

It resulted in enmity with Britain and an arms race.

(*g*) The abrupt manner of the German intervention in Morocco, which caused the Algeciras and Agadir crises of 1906 and 1911, led to:

(*i*) a tightening of the bonds of the Franco-British *entente*;

(*ii*) an increased state of tension in Europe.

(*h*) The Italian attack on Tripoli in 1911 was a contributory cause of the Balkan Wars, as this weakened Turkey and encouraged the Balkan League to follow Italy's example.

Except for (*a*), the above provide examples of how imperialism became an indirect cause of the First World War. Colonial rivalries exacerbated relations between the powers and thus contributed to the build-up of European alliances.

PROGRESS TEST 17

1. Discuss the general motives for empire-building with special reference to the nineteenth century. **(2–7)**

2. Why did economic considerations play an important part in European imperialism? **(3)**

3. Indicate some of the features and forms of European imperialism. **(8–9)**

4. Mention the important European private groups which were interested in carrying on activities in Africa and Asia. **(10)**

5. List the major colonial powers between 1815 and 1870. Why did a "scramble for possessions" take place during the last twenty years of the nineteenth century? **(12–13)**

6. Discuss the advantages and disadvantages of colonialism and imperialism. **(14)**

7. Distinguish "East" and "West" in terms of Europe and Asia. **(15)**

8. What indication was there that European imperialism was waning by 1905? **(16)**

9. Estimate the effect of colonial rivalries on the relations between the European powers. **(17)**

CHAPTER XVIII

The European scramble for Africa

INTRODUCTION

1. Scramble for Africa. In imperial affairs the main feature of the period 1880–1900 was the "scramble for Africa". This is a more precise term than "partition of Africa" as there was no orderly division of territory and it was accomplished with great rapidity. Each power seized, by force or by fraud, areas which had not already been taken. The general causes have been discussed (*see* XVII, **2–7**).

2. The existence of native empires. Before 1879 a potential pre-European partition of Africa was in process. The important regions were as follows.

(*a*) *North-east Africa.* Egyptian rule extended south to the Upper Nile.

(*b*) *Ethiopia.* The Ethiopians made territorial claims in all directions.

(*c*) *East Africa.* The Sultan of Zanzibar claimed territory as far west as the Congo.

(*d*) *South-east Africa.* A number of African kingdoms, offshoots of the Zulus, partitioned a large part of the country.

(*e*) *West Africa.*

(*i*) Various Tukulor Sultans (Moslems) ruled from Senegal to Lake Chad, aided by Fulani chiefs.

(*ii*) South of the Niger there were a number of strong negro kingdoms, such as the Mandingo, Ashanti and Dahomey.

3. Extent of European influences in 1879. Before 1879 few Europeans had ventured into the African interior. The coastal regions were uninviting and presented a number of hazards. There were rapids or waterfalls near the mouths of many rivers, deserts or malarial forests near the coast, and few natural harbours.

European influence was primarily restricted to trading posts along the African coast, with very vague boundaries.

(a) *North Africa.* Algeria was French. Apart from this only in Egypt and Tunis was there the start of European control.

(b) *East Africa.* British political influence was strong in Zanzibar. There was no European influence on the African mainland. Portugal possessed Mozambique.

(c) *South Africa.* This was firmly under European rule, shared between the British and the Afrikaners, who were descendants of the Dutch.

(d) *West Africa.* European traders had traded with the coastal peoples for four centuries. After the abolition of the slave trade the Portuguese, Dutch and Danes gradually left. Only in French Senegal and British possessions in the Gold Coast and at Lagos were there colonial administrations. Sierra Leone had been a British possession since 1787 for freed negro slaves. British trading firms had been on the Nigerian coast since 1832.

Below the equator Portugal had Angola. German traders opened a factory in the Cameroons in 1860.

THE CONGO AND THE BERLIN CONFERENCE

4. King Leopold and the Congo. King Leopold became interested in creating a strong empire in Central Africa. Belgium had no interest in becoming a colonial power. Therefore in 1876 the King encouraged the formation of an International African Association. Its aim ostensibly was to promote scientific work and to suppress the slave trade. In reality it was intended to further his personal ambitions. Branches of the Association were founded in most European countries to raise money for African explorations.

In 1879 Leopold employed Henry Stanley, the explorer, to work for the Association. Stanley made treaties with chiefs on the Upper Congo, whereby they placed themselves under Leopold's protection.

5. European rivalry in the Congo region. The activities of Leopold and Stanley soon led to other powers taking an active interest in the region. The chief ones were as follows.

(a) *The French.* In 1880 Savorgnan de Brazza was sent out to make treaties with chiefs on the north side of the Congo. France then proclaimed a protectorate over this region. In April 1884 France secured the right of pre-emption if the development of the Congo proved too much for King Leopold.

(b) *The Germans.* In June 1884 Germany proclaimed a protectorate over the Cameroons, which were close to the upper reaches of the Congo river. German traders had had a factory there since 1860.

6. Penetration of East and West Africa. During the early 1880s Germany and France started to show an active interest in territories in East and West Africa. At this time British interest remained lukewarm. Activities involving these three powers were as follows.

(a) *Britain.* In East Africa Joseph Thomson explored Kenya for the Royal Geographical Society in 1884. Previously Britain had rejected a suggestion of Kirk, which had the approval of the Sultan of Zanzibar, that a protectorate should be proclaimed in this area.

(b) *Germany.*

(i) East Africa: in November 1884 Dr. Karl Peters arrived, representing the German Colonial Society (formed in 1882). He discovered that a few miles inland were African communities which owed no allegiance to the Sultan. Without much difficulty local chiefs were persuaded to sign treaties placing their lands under the protection of Germany.

(ii) West Africa: in July 1884 Germany proclaimed a protectorate over Togoland. This was situated between the regions of British interests in Dahomey.

(c) *France.*

(i) East Africa: in 1883 France entered the island of Madagascar, near the African coast. A protectorate was proclaimed in 1885.

(ii) West Africa: in 1883 France began to infiltrate the Upper Niger region from Senegal, planning to create a large West African empire. Her action was partly prompted by the desire to challenge British colonial interests, in revenge for her exclusion from Egyptian affairs (*see* XIX, **9–10**).

7. The Berlin Conference. It was clear that the commercial interests of King Leopold, Portugal, France and Germany conflicted in the Congo region. In November 1884 Bismarck, supported by France, called together an international conference at Berlin.

(a) *Details settled.* The Congo Free State was recognised by the powers Britain, France, Russia, the United States and Portugal.

It was to be run as an international organisation on a free-trade basis. (When King Leopold claimed the whole Congo, his claim based partly on the number of treaties Stanley had made with local chiefs, this was accepted. It became his own private property.)

The following points were also agreed.

(*i*) Natives were not to be exploited in the interests of European powers.

(*ii*) There was to be freedom of navigation on the Congo and Niger rivers.

(*iii*) European claims to African territories, to be officially recognised, had to be backed by effective occupation.

(*b*) *Colonial claims.* As a consequence of (*a*)(*iii*) above the powers refused to acknowledge the claims of the Sultan of Zanzibar to much of East Africa. Also the claim of Portugal to a vast area between Angola and Mozambique was not sustained.

Bismarck announced at the end of the conference in February 1885 that Germany had established a protectorate over Tanganyika in East Africa.

(*c*) *Results of the conference.*

(*i*) It led to an intensification of the scramble for colonies. Owing to the ruling (*a*)(*iii*) above and the action of Germany (*see* (*b*) above), other European powers took this as a signal to stake their own claims quickly.

(*ii*) The conference illustrated that European powers were able to settle their colonial disputes peaceably.

(*iii*) Many of the well-meaning resolutions were ignored. The natives were ruthlessly exploited in the Congo. Leopold used it to carve out a personal fortune through a trade monopoly in rubber and ivory.

FINAL PARTITION

8. The final partition. By 1900 European powers had partitioned among themselves most of the African continent, though Ethiopia managed to preserve her independence (*see* XIX, **27**).

The areas involved were as follows.

(*a*) *South and North Africa.* For the latter area, *see* XIX.

(*b*) *Central Africa.* A series of agreements fixed the boundaries between King Leopold's Belgian Congo and the neighbouring lands taken over by other European powers. The country was governed most inefficiently. Eventually, in 1908, King Leopold ceded the Congo to Belgium.

(c) *West and East Africa* (*see* **9** and **10**).

9. West Africa. After the Berlin Conference the rivalry between Britain and France intensified.

Partly to forestall the French, Britain proclaimed a protectorate over the Niger region in 1885. France undertook serious military campaigns, and by 1890 had crushed the power of the Mandingo ruler in the Ivory Coast and the King of Dahomey. These two regions were made into a protectorate and colony respectively. As many of her possessions were separated by those of other countries on the coast, France then worked to join them together in the interior.

A rush developed between France and Britain to sign charters with local rulers. In the process Britain crushed the Ashanti in a short war in 1896 and made their territory a protectorate. France wanted to connect territories on the Upper Niger with Dahomey. In 1897–8 this culminated in a clash in Western Nigeria and an acute crisis in Anglo-French relations, aggravated by the Fashoda incident. However, it was solved peaceably (*see* XIX, **15**).

In 1899 Nigeria was made a British protectorate. By 1903 France had gained most of North-west Africa, an area of some $3\frac{3}{4}$ million square miles.

10. East Africa. In 1885 Germany advanced claims to areas where Britain had previous treaties with local chiefs. Following the report of a Delimitation Commission (composed of Britain, France and Germany) in 1886 the two countries settled their differences. The following were the various stages by which the Zanzibarian Empire gradually disappeared and East Africa was finally partitioned.

(a) *Anglo-German agreement* (October 1886). Without consulting the Sultan of Zanzibar it was agreed that the mainland territories of the Sultan extended only ten miles (seventeen kilometres) into the interior. They agreed on their "spheres of influence" in East Africa.

Germany then secured a fifty-year lease of the coastal strip adjoining her territory of Tanganyika. The British East Africa Company leased the coastal strip adjoining Kenya for an annual payment.

(b) *Protectorate over Zanzibar* (June 1890). This was accepted by the French in return for British recognition of her rights in Madagascar.

(*c*) *Anglo-German agreement* (July 1890). This finally settled all conflicting claims. In return for the cession of Heligoland, Germany abandoned claims to Uganda and recognised existing British East African interests.

(*d*) *Anglo-Portuguese agreement* (1891). This settled long-standing disputes over claims in East Africa. British claims in Nyasaland and Manicaland (eastern Rhodesia) were recognised.

(*e*) *British protectorate over Uganda* (1894). There was controversy in Britain as to whether Uganda should be retained. Eventually it was made a protectorate, one factor being the desire to secure the approaches to the headwaters of the Nile.

(*f*) *British protectorate over Kenya* (1896).

11. Rhodesia. Cecil Rhodes, the Prime Minister of Cape Colony, was anxious to extend British power northwards. He hoped that the region north of the Boer republic of the Transvaal would be rich in mineral resources. There was the risk that the route to the north would be closed by possible annexations by Germany (trying to link her possessions in South-west and East Africa) or Portugal (trying to link her West African colony of Angola with Mozambique in the east).

Rhodes formed a company which was granted a charter by the British government. The region later known as Rhodesia was occupied by a pioneer column in 1890, the local chief Lobenguela having virtually lost his authority by agreeing to the Rudd Concession in 1888. The region was named Rhodesia in 1895.

PROGRESS TEST 18

1. Describe briefly the extent of European influence in Africa before 1879. Where were the chief native empires located? (2–3)

2. Which powers were interested in the Congo region? (4–5)

3. Describe the colonial activities of Germany in East Africa. (6–8)

4. Why was the Berlin Conference convened in 1885? What were the results? (5, 7)

5. Trace the growth of influence of European powers in West Africa after 1832. (3(*d*), 9)

6. Give an account of the agreements made by Britain with other powers in East Africa between 1885 and 1892. (10)

CHAPTER XIX

The major powers and North Africa

INTRODUCTION

1. North African states. In North Africa, bounded by the Sahara in the south and the Mediterranean in the north, four Moslem states, Tripoli, Tunis, Algiers and Egypt, were nominally dependencies of the Ottoman Empire. The fifth, Morocco, was an independent kingdom. Though these territories traded with Western Europe their religious and cultural connections and much of their trade lay with the Eastern Mediterranean and the Moslem states of the Western Sudan.

2. European involvement. At the beginning of the nineteenth century European powers showed increased interest in North Africa. The reasons were as follows.

(a) *Strategic.* During the Napoleonic Wars Britain and France established contacts with some of these states to assist their own policies.

(b) *Piracy and trade.* There was a revival of interest in the direct route to Asia through the Levant. European states became concerned to safeguard their trade from attacks by the Barbary corsairs operating from the harbours of Algeria and Tunisia. Eventually piracy was suppressed when active attempts were made at colonisation by the French and when European powers decided to suppress the slave trade.

(c) *Slavery and the slave trade.* Britain abolished slavery at home in 1772, the slave trade in 1807 and slavery in the Empire in 1832. Other European states took steps to stop their own nationals dealing in the slave trade. For example it was declared illegal by Denmark (1805), Holland (1814) and France (1818).

The Moslem pirates captured Europeans for the slave trade. In 1815 Britain undertook to take action against them on behalf of the Congress of Vienna. Tripoli and Tunis promised to abandon Christian slavery, but Algiers refused. In 1816, following an incident when 200 innocent coral fishers were massacred, a British squadron under Lord Exmouth, aided by the Dutch, bombarded Algiers and forced the ruler to abolish slavery.

EGYPT AND ANGLO-FRENCH RIVALRY

3. Growth of Egyptian power. Mehemet Ali came to Egypt in 1799 in command of an Albanian contingent. In 1811 he became absolute ruler when he destroyed the power of the Mamelukes. When in power, he was determined to build up the military power of Egypt. Colonel Joseph Sèves, a Frenchman, helped organise a powerful army. A substantial fleet was also built. To secure the necessary funds, Mehemet Ali organised state monopolies of trade, took over most of the land, introduced cotton and hemp, and developed irrigation.

Egypt became involved in numerous wars in the following areas.

(*a*) *Arabia* (1811–18). The Wahabis were a fanatical Moslem sect among Bedouin tribesmen who rebelled against the Sultan. At the request of the Sultan, Mehemet Ali intervened and finally defeated them.

(*b*) *The Sudan* (1818–22). Under Mehemet's son Hussein, Egyptian forces conquered the Sudan and founded Khartoum in 1822. The main objective was to find gold supplies and to control the White Nile slave trade. Thus a regular supply of negro slave recruits for the Egyptian army would be ensured.

(*c*) *Greece and the Morea*, 1822–5 (*see* XIV, **18**).

(*d*) *Turkey*, 1832–3 and 1839–41 (*see* XIV, **26** and **29**).

4. The rule of Pasha Said. Mehemet Ali died in 1848. The next ruler was assassinated in 1854 and was succeeded by Said, the youngest son of Mehemet Ali. He was an enlightened ruler who took steps to suppress slavery. He abandoned the state ownership of land, reorganised the administration along liberal lines, and arranged the first foreign loan, floated by British bankers, to help finance his policies. Two notable developments were the following.

(*a*) The start of the construction of the Suez Canal (*see* **5**).

(*b*) The building of the first railway from Alexandria to Cairo. This was completed by a British company in 1857. It was later extended to Suez.

5. The Suez Canal project. Though the idea of a link between the Indian Ocean and the Mediterranean dates back to Queen Hatsheput of Egypt (1480–1475 B.C.), Napoleon was the first to have precise calculations made in 1798. In 1847 Saint-Simon and Prosper Enfontin set up an international committee to study it. However, their work was opposed by the Khedive, Abbas I.

(*a*) *The construction of the canal.* In 1854 Pasha Said granted to a former French consul at Tunis, Ferdinand de Lesseps, a concession to build and operate the Suez Canal. A company was organised in 1858 and work began in 1859.

(*i*) Said assisted with gifts of land and forced labour.

(*ii*) Britain opposed the scheme. Palmerston thought that the canal would mainly benefit the French and that its completion would open India to attack by a new route.

(*b*) *The opening of the canal.* In 1869 the canal was officially opened. This resulted in the following developments.

(*i*) There was increased interest by European powers in Asia and the Middle East. The French were encouraged to build up merchant fleets to trade with Asia. The Italians formed a small colony on the Red Sea.

(ii) Britain eventually became the dominant power in Egypt and North-east Africa (*see* **11**(*c*)).

6. Ismail's policies. Since 1863 the Khedive Ismail had been modernising Egypt. Some of his projects were sound: for example, irrigation canals, a telegraph system, harbour works and primary schools were created. However, luxurious follies were also undertaken such as the new palace at Alexandria.

The Civil War in the United States created a great demand for Egyptian cotton. This caused widespread prosperity during the 1860s, and European merchants went to Egypt to benefit by this. Ismail took advantage of the favourable climate to borrow money at usurious rates of interest from European bankers to finance his public works. Unfortunately Egypt soon acquired an enormous debt and became bankrupt in 1875.

This had two consequences: *see* **7** and **8**.

7. Disraeli's purchase of shares. The British Prime Minister, Disraeli, saw the Suez Canal in relation to the dawning of the new era of *Weltpolitik*. In 1875 he learnt that the 176,602 shares in the Canal Company held by the Khedive Ismail were being offered for sale in Paris. The Rothschilds found the £4 million necessary to purchase these shares, and the British government thus became the largest single shareholder.

8. Financial control by France and Britain. A report by Stephen Cave on Egyptian finances in 1876 recommended some measure of European supervision. English and French creditors, alarmed as to the security of their loans, sent out two representatives. The Caisse de la Dette was created to manage the service of the debt. Besides France and Britain, Germany, Austria and Italy were members. Eventually by skilful manipulation Britain and France managed to establish a kind of joint control or condominium in the country. An Englishman became the Minister of Finance and a Frenchman Minister of Public Works. They recommended the adoption of a constitution and other measures to revive Egypt from bankruptcy. A vigorous effort was made to satisfy the European creditors. This caused hardship in the country and a hatred of foreigners.

9. Unrest in Egypt. In 1879 the Sultan was persuaded by Britain and France to depose Ismail for his incompetent management of Egyptian affairs. The following developments took place.

(a) *A rising of Egyptian officers.* In 1881 a rising took place, led by Colonel Ahmed Arabi, against foreign control and Turkish rule. The rebels wanted constitutional rule. The new Khedive, Tewfik, son of Ismail, appointed a nationalist ministry.

(b) *British intervention.* Tewfik feared he would be deposed by the new ministry or by a conspiracy of other groups. He appealed for aid from Britain and France. When riots broke out in Alexandria against the Europeans, a British squadron bombarded the town. The French refused to take part.

(c) *Defeat of Arabi.* British troops were landed to protect the Suez Canal. Under General Wolseley, they defeated the Egyptian forces of Arabi at Tel-el-Kebir (September 1882). The British occupied Cairo, and Arabi was forced to surrender.

10. British occupation and control. The dual control was abandoned. In January 1883 Britain informed the European powers that her troops would remain in Egypt until the Khedive's authority had been firmly established. France attempted to resume the condominium relationship but was informed that she had forfeited her rights.

Sir Evelyn Baring (later Lord Cromer) was appointed consul-general, diplomatic agent and adviser to the Khedive. He became known as "the great Pharaoh of modern Egypt" because of his skilful administration. The army and government structure was reorganised. The tax system was revised, and the economic power of the country developed. British officials were appointed to help native officials and exercised an ill-defined but effective control.

11. Results of the British occupation. The consequences of the British military occupation of Egypt in 1882 were as follows.

(*a*) *Increased Anglo-French antagonism.* This lasted until 1898. Up to 1887 France tried to accelerate the withdrawal of British troops from Egypt, insisting that Egypt constituted a European problem and not merely a British concern. Friction then occurred over the Sudan (*see* **14**).

(*b*) *Acceleration of the pace of the "scramble for Africa".*

(*i*) France during the 1880s realised that her chances of regaining influence in Egypt were remote. As compensation she became seriously interested in making Morocco a protectorate and in expanding her West African empire.

(*ii*) Germany in 1882 became seriously interested in acquiring colonies. Since Italy supported France in opposing the British in the Caisse de la Dette, Britain relied on German and Austrian support in this committee to provide moral backing for the continued British presence in Egypt. Bismarck would support Britain only on the condition that she acquiesced in future German colonial aims.

(*c*) *Permanency of the British occupation.* At first the occupation of Egypt had been regarded as temporary. In May 1887 by the Drummond–Wolff Convention, Britain agreed to evacuate Egypt within three years if conditions were favourable, but reserved the right to reoccupy the country if conditions made this necessary. Under pressure from France and Russia, Turkey refused to ratify this. British statesmen gradually became convinced that forces must remain in Egypt for some time. Their reasons were as follows.

(*i*) Failure to establish a system for effectively internationalising the canal. In 1885 a conference of the powers in Paris failed to establish a regime for the canal.

(*ii*) Need to secure the sea route to India. Britain realised that control of Egypt provided security for the route to India. As a result she became less hostile towards Russian designs at the Straits. In 1888 the Suez Canal Convention, signed by the powers, stated that the canal should be open to all ships in peace and war.

Britain, however, introduced a reservation which aimed at the possibility of her closing the canal during war.

(*iii*) Desire to secure the region of the Upper Nile and the Sudan (*see* 13).

THE MAHDI AND ANGLO-FRENCH RIVALRY IN THE SUDAN

12. Mahdist rebellion in the Sudan. In 1881 Mohammed Ahmed proclaimed himself Mahdi in Dongola. He organised a dervish movement in the Sudan to overthrow Egyptian rule, to conquer Egypt and to convert the world to Islam. In 1883 his forces defeated General Hicks, in command of an Egyptian force, near Sheken. In January 1884 the British advised the Egyptian government to evacuate the Sudan. General Gordon was sent to Khartoum to withdraw the Egyptian garrisons. He was besieged by forces of the Mahdi. Reinforcements arrived too late to save the fall of Khartoum and the death of Gordon (January 1885).

13. The Kitchener expedition. Fighting continued after 1885 between the Egyptians and the forces of the Khalifa (successor to the Mahdi) in the Wadi Halfa region. In 1896 the British government decided to send a military force under General Kitchener to recapture the Sudan. This decision was taken not so much because of the conditions of dervish rule but because of the following two important considerations.

(*a*) Awareness of the importance of the Sudan and the Upper Nile basin, notably the Bahr-el-Ghazel, to assure and increase the Egyptian water-supply.

(*b*) The knowledge that other powers were interested in the Sudan. While Britain regarded this basin as part of Egypt and subject to the conditions maintained in the north, France argued that this region was under the control of Turkey. In February 1896 a French expedition led by Major Marchand set off from Gabon, hoping to occupy the Upper Nile and thus be in a position to threaten the British in Egypt.

There was also the prospect that forces from the Belgian Congo and Ethiopia would soon intrude into the area. Emperor Menelek of Ethiopia had sent a circular to the powers in 1891 claiming all territory to the Nile.

14. Reconquest of the Sudan. In September 1896 General Kitchener took Dongola. He then advanced slowly up the Nile, building a railway as he advanced. Eventually he managed to secure Anglo-Egyptian authority over the Sudan as a result of the following developments.

(a) *His defeat of the Khalifa.* The dervishes were beaten at Atbara River (April 1898) and Omdurman (September). Kitchener then captured Khartoum, the Khalifa having fled.

(b) *His forcing the retreat of the Ethiopians and the French.* Marchand arrived at Fashoda, about 650 kilometres south of Khartoum, in July 1898. An Ethiopian force, with French support, reached the Nile just above Fashoda. The French plan was to push Ethiopian claims to the right bank while claiming the left bank of the Nile themselves.

Kitchener, hearing of this threat to the British position, moved south to eject Marchand. In September Marchand refused to evacuate without orders from France. An acute crisis occurred between Britain and France. The British claimed the territory for Egypt by right of conquest.

The French government was harassed by domestic affairs, and found no support from Russia. In November Marchand was finally ordered to evacuate Fashoda.

15. Significance of the Fashoda incident. Though at the time Anglo-French relations were poor, in the long run the incident prepared the way for improved relations culminating in the *entente* of 1904. The reasons were as follows.

(a) Colonial antagonism in Africa between the two countries diminished considerably. They agreed in March 1899 on their respective spheres of influence. France renounced all territory along the Nile, in return for some districts in the Sahara.

(b) The British position in Egypt was then secured. Britain was determined to exercise influence in Egypt for the time being to protect the Suez route to India and to counter a possible Russian occupation of Constantinople or the Straits. Any French threat was removed and British influence in the Sudan reinforced by the following.

(i) Anglo-Egyptian convention of January 1899: these powers established a condominium in the area.

(ii) Anglo-Ethiopian treaty of 1902: Ethiopia agreed to a frontier which was away from the Nile.

(c) France began to give more attention to European problems. Clémenceau said it was useless to fight over some African marshes while Germany occupied Metz and Strasbourg. In Europe British and French interests did not conflict.

EUROPEAN RIVALRY IN MOROCCO

16. The Spanish-Moroccan quarrel. Morocco had largely isolated herself from the rest of the world. The Sultan refused to help in suppressing the slave trade.

Spain in 1859 claimed that her ports of Ceuta and Melilla on the northern coast were being constantly raided by the Sultan's subjects. In 1860 a Spanish army defeated the Sultan. By the Treaty of Tetuan, Morocco promised to pay Spain a huge indemnity. This indemnity opened Morocco to further European interference to enable her to pay it. The Sultan had to raise a loan in London on the security of the Moroccan customs, and to accept control over them by foreign commissioners.

17. Partition plans considered. According to the Madrid Convention of July 1880, leading European powers and the United States agreed to recognise the independence of Morocco. The status and privileges of foreigners in Morocco were also regulated.

Despite this, plans were made for the possible division of the country between France and Spain should the Sultan cease to exercise authority. These were in secret articles contained in the following agreements:

(a) *the Anglo-French entente* (April 1904);
(b) *the Franco-Spanish treaty* (October 1904).

18. German intervention. In 1904 France assured Germany of the integrity of Morocco and the maintenance of the "open-door" policy enabling all countries to trade in that country. However, the Kaiser soon suspected that France had made secret negotiations concerning Moroccan partition. In February 1905 the French envoy made new demands on the Sultan for "reform".

The German officials Bülow and Holstein were annoyed, since the French Foreign Minister, Delcassé, had deliberately excluded Germany from any negotiations. Germany had economic interests there and felt she was entitled to be consulted in any settlement. The Kaiser was persuaded to go to Tangiers on 31st March. He landed from his yacht and declared dramatically that

Germany adhered to the principle of independence for Morocco and equal economic opportunity for all nations.

The reasons for this intervention were:

(a) to protect German interests in Morocco;

(b) to test the strength of the Anglo-French *entente* (*see* VII, 23). Germany wanted to discredit Delcassé, the architect of the *entente*, and hoped that Britain would not intervene. It was known that Russia had just suffered a heavy defeat by Japan at Mukden on 1st March, and was not in any position to intervene.

On 11th April Bülow issued a circular to all the signatories of the Treaty of Madrid. Supported by the Sultan, Bülow suggested that an international conference be held at Tangiers.

19. The French response. The French Premier, Rouvier, was prepared to offer Germany a port in Morocco. The Germans insisted on the holding of a conference. Delcassé refused to attend a conference and wanted to form a close Franco-British alliance. The French cabinet opposed this, saying it could lead to a war with Germany at a time when her eastern ally Russia was weak. Delcassé resigned in June 1905. In July the French, assured of American support, finally agreed to a conference.

20. The Algeciras Conference. At this conference (January–April 1906) Germany was supported only by Austria and Morocco. Italy joined France, Spain, Russia, Britain and the United States in opposing German demands.

(a) *Details of the conference.*

(i) The sovereignty of Morocco was asserted. Equal trading opportunities were confirmed for other nations.

(ii) The customs administration and police were to be under the joint administration of the French and Spanish.

(iii) Capital for the Moroccan state bank could be supplied by all countries. France was to be allowed to contribute the largest amount.

(b) *Results of the conference.* Though the final details embodied superficially what Germany wanted, the Kaiser knew that it had been a defeat for him, for the following reasons.

(i) The bonds of the Anglo-French *entente* were strengthened, not weakened as Germany had hoped would occur. Britain interpreted German action in Morocco as a bid for European hegemony and hence was prepared to work more closely with France. Before the conference the French and

British general staffs held discussions on military and naval co-operation in the event of war.

(*ii*) France eventually gained control of Morocco in 1912 (*see* 22(*c*)). Thus the attempt by Germany to retain any influence in Morocco failed.

(*iii*) German intervention contributed to greater European insecurity. During the crisis, war between France and Germany was contemplated for the first time since 1887. During the conference the powers, Italy excepted, took sides according to their alliance obligations. The increased rigidity of the alliance system lessened the chances of future incidents having peaceful outcomes.

21. Background to further rivalry. The various events preceding the second diplomatic crisis in Morocco were as follows.

(*a*) *The Casablanca affair.* In 1908 France occupied Casablanca and arrested several German deserters from the Foreign Legion. When Germany asked for a French apology the matter was referred to the International Court at The Hague. It announced in 1909 that France had acted legally, according to the police powers it had.

(*b*) *Spanish infiltration.* In July 1909 Riff tribes attacked the Spanish at Melilla. Despite losses the Spanish began to occupy the zone reserved to them in past agreements.

(*c*) *French occupation of Fez.* In April 1911 Berber tribes attacked the capital town, Fez. On the plea of protecting foreigners, French troops occupied the town.

(*d*) *The German gunboat "Panther" at Agadir.* Germany feared that France intended to proclaim a protectorate. To protect her interests, Germany sent a gunboat to the harbour of Agadir in July.

22. The Agadir crisis. Both France and Germany considered the possibility of war. On 21st July Lloyd George protested against the exclusion of Britain from all talks on Morocco. He used aggressive language against Germany. Britain feared that Germany had pretensions of establishing a naval base at Agadir. The determination of Britain to support France persuaded Germany to stand down.

The incident resulted in the following developments.

(*a*) *General dissatisfaction in France and Germany* over the terms of the settlement. In November Germany agreed to give

France a free hand in Morocco, with a special zone allotted to Spain. In return France surrendered the north-west part of her Congo to the German Cameroons.

(b) *Outburst of anti-British feeling in Germany.* Germany considered that "the real enemy" in the dispute had been Britain.

(c) *Eventual French protectorate over Morocco.* In the Treaty of Fez (March 1912) the Sultan was obliged to accept a French protectorate in Morocco, a zone for the Spanish, and a special status for Tangiers.

ALGERIA, TUNISIA AND TRIPOLI

23. Franco-Algerian quarrel. After 1815 the French government refused to pay Algeria for the food supplies given to Napoleon for his Egyptian campaigns. In 1827 in a fit of anger the Dey of Algiers, in the course of a discussion on this topic, struck the French consul in the face with his fly-whisk. In July 1830 France used this as an excuse to occupy northern Algeria and depose the Dey. The French also wanted to suppress pirate bands and achieve some glory for the tottering Bourbon monarchy.

24. The colonisation of Algeria. The French were uncertain how to proceed in Algeria after Louis-Philippe became king. Abdel-Kader was proclaimed Dey by the native chiefs. He attacked the French, who suffered several defeats during the period 1832–7. In 1840 the French occupied the country seriously and Abdel-Kader sought the aid of Morocco. In 1844 the Moroccans were defeated at Isly and withdrew from the conflict. In 1847 Abdel-Kader finally surrendered to the French. Arab resistance was then broken, and Algeria was made a French dependency in 1848.

During the reign of Napoleon III continued insurrections occurred in the interior. In 1863 a land law recognised private ownership and did much to break up tribal organisation. The French tried unsuccessfully to settle the country with military colonists from France. Eventually France established her authority in the country.

25. European rivalry in Tunis. Tunis was the most westernised of the North African states. In 1819 the Bey outlawed piracy. He was the first ruler in North Africa to abolish slavery and adopt a constitutional form of government in the period 1841–6.

Initially British influence was predominant. The Bey relied

on British support to maintain his independence against the French in Algiers and Turkey in Tripoli. However, during the 1860s British influence declined. French influence grew as France was determined that no other European country should occupy a position of strength on the borders of Algeria.

The various stages leading to the French protectorate over Tunis were as follows.

(a) In 1869 the Bey had to accept the financial control of Britain, France and Italy. He had borrowed heavily in Europe, and had failed to meet his obligations.

(b) In 1871 Italy sent an expedition to Tunisia, hoping eventually to annex it. This was opposed by Britain and France.

(c) In 1878, at the Congress of Berlin, Lord Salisbury offered France a free hand in Tunis as compensation for the acquisition of Cyprus by Britain.

(d) Rivalry took place between France and Italy. In the years 1879–81 both intrigued to obtain key concessions concerning railways, telegraphs, land grants, etc.

(e) In 1881, by the Treaty of Bardo, the Bey of Tunis accepted a French protectorate. There were protests from Turkey, Britain and Italy. Bismarck backed the French action.

26. Tripoli annexed by Italy. Balked of her designs in Ethiopia in 1896 (*see* **27**) and Tunisia in 1871, Italy was determined to gain Tripoli. Various understandings were reached with Russia (1909), Austria and Germany (1887), France (1900) and Britain (1890), so that her designs in this direction were not checked.

In 1911 Italy thought the moment opportune as general confusion existed over the Agadir crisis. An excuse was found in the restrictions on foreign trade imposed by the new Turkish government. Italy was anxious to take Tripoli before it was annexed by another power, perhaps Germany. Her attack was completely unjustified since The Porte, in response to an Italian ultimatum, had offered to discuss a settlement of Italian claims in Tripoli. The Turkish navy was unable to render much assistance and the Italians soon overran the province. By the Treaty of Ouchy (1912) Turkey ceded Tripoli and Cyrenaica, and allowed Italy "temporary possession" of the Dodecanese (a group of islands in the Aegean Sea).

ETHIOPIA AND THE RED SEA

27. Ethiopia and the Red Sea area. Johannes IV (1875–89), called King of Kings, ruled an ill-defined area in North-east Africa, near the Red Sea. The interests of certain European powers in this area were as follows.

(a) *Britain.* Following the Egyptian withdrawal from the Sudan and the Red Sea coast, Britain established a protectorate over part of the Somali coast in 1884.

(b) *France.* In 1884 the French expanded their station at Obock into a protectorate.

(c) *Italy.* In 1869 an Italian company bought the port of Assab on the Red Sea. In 1885 the Italians occupied Massawa, and began to expand into the highlands, but were checked by the Ethiopians.

In 1889 Johannes was killed and the succession was disputed. The Italians supported Menelek, who became emperor. By way of reward the Italians occupied some territory and claimed that Ethiopia was an Italian protectorate by the Treaty of Uccialli (May 1889). This was denounced by Menelek in 1891. The Italians consolidated their coastal colony at Eritrea and defeated the dervishes who challenged their position.

In 1895 the Italians tried to conquer Ethiopia. At the battle of Adowa (March 1896) an Italian force of 20,000, mainly African, was annihilated by some 80,000 Ethiopians under Menelek.

Italy had to recognise Ethiopian independence and to agree to restrict her activities to the coast in future.

In 1906 by a Tripartite Pact, Britain, France and Italy recognised the independence of Ethiopia. In the event of the situation becoming untenable they defined spheres of influence for themselves. Menelek protested against the implications of this treaty.

NOTE: For Ethiopia and her claims to the Nile, *see* 13(b).

PROGRESS TEST 19

1. List the five North African states. Which one was not a dependency of Turkey? **(1)**

2. Why did Egypt become involved in various wars between 1811 and 1841? **(3)**

3. Describe the Suez Canal project. **(5)**

4. How did Britain gain influence in Egypt? **(4–10)**

5. What were the important consequences of the British occupation of Egypt in 1882? **(11)**

6. Why did Britain decide to remain in Egypt? **(11(c))**

7. Why was it decided to send a British expedition to reconquer the Sudan in 1896? **(13)**

8. What was the significance of the Fashoda affair? **(15)**

9. What were the provisions of the Madrid Convention? **(17)**

10. Trace the causes of the first Moroccan crisis. **(18–19)**

11. Explain why the results of the Algeciras Conference represented a defeat for Germany. **(20)**

12. Why did Germany send a gunboat to Agadir in 1911? **(21(d))**

13. Account for the French occupation of Algeria. **(24)**

14. What steps preceded the French declaration of a protectorate over Tunisia in 1881? **(25)**

15. What arrangements did Italy make to ensure that her annexation of Tripoli would not be opposed? **(26)**

CHAPTER XX

European powers and Asia

ANGLO-RUSSIAN RIVALRY IN CENTRAL ASIA

1. Conflict in Central Asia. As the Mogul Empire disintegrated, Central Asia became an area of continuous warfare.

In the Caucasus, the region between the Black Sea and Caspian Sea, which was the gateway from Asia into Asia Minor and Arabia, there were no definite frontiers between Russia, Persia and Turkey. In the east towards China no definite frontiers existed between Persia, the Central Asian Khanates and China. A power vacuum also existed between Afghanistan in the south and Siberia in the north.

The principal powers in Central Asia were as follows.

(*a*) *Russia.* In the far north there was little resistance to Russian expansion across Asia into Siberia. Russia could not expand any further eastwards until she had established mastery of Central Asia. However, Russia had to combat the following opposition:

(*i*) stubborn resistance of native Tartar and Mohammedan tribes;

(*ii*) competition of Persia and Turkey for control of these areas.

(*b*) *Persia.* Persia engaged in continuous warfare with Turkey in the west and Afghanistan in the east. From the seventeenth century she was also involved in wars with Russia.

2. British and French involvement. Events in Central Asia became more complex when Britain and France showed interest. Britain had trade interests in Persia, and she was also interested in Persia and Afghanistan since both bordered India. Britain wanted an ally against the designs of either of these states or those of the French or Russians on India. During part of the Napoleonic Wars (1798–1807) France hoped Persia would assist her to regain influence in India and to threaten the British there.

The various see-saw arrangements were as follows.

(*a*) In 1798 Britain, fearful of Afghan influence in India, induced the Persians to attack Afghanistan. No positive results came from this.

(b) The French attempt to gain influence in India was checked when their allies the Mahratta princes were defeated at Assaye (1803). In 1806 the French offered to support Persia against Russia and in an attack on India. Nothing came of this as the French lost interest after the Treaty of Tilsit (see II, 5).

(c) In 1809 Britain feared a French or Persian attack on India. An agreement was made with Afghanistan to check either contingency. In 1816 the Afghans drove back a Persian attack on their border town of Herat.

(d) In the Treaty of Teheran (1814) Britain promised some aid for Persia against external attack. After 1812 Britain was officially at peace with Russia and so gave only lukewarm support to Persia in her wars with Russia (see 3).

3. Russian mastery of the Caucasus.
The three-cornered struggle between Russia, Persia and Turkey for possession of Transcaucasia reached a turning point in 1799. Russia occupied Tiflis in Georgia. Persia suffered defeats in two successive wars and had to accept harsh terms in the following treaties.

(a) *Treaty of Gulistan* (1813). Persia lost most of her Caucasian possessions, including Baku and Georgia.

(b) *Treaty of Turkamchai* (1828). Persia suffered further territorial losses.

4. The Afghan Wars.
Two wars occurred between British forces in India and Afghanistan. On both occasions the cause was the British fear of Afghan subservience to Russia or Persia.

(a) *First Afghan War* (1839–42). In 1837 Russia induced Persia to attack Herat. As a result of British intervention this attack was defeated.

During the war the Afghan ruler Dost Mohammed was deposed by the British and replaced by another ruler. The new ruler was unpopular and a native rising forced the British to retreat from the Afghan capital, Kabul, in 1841. The British force was massacred *en route*. As a result Dost Mohammed was restored as ruler, and Britain abandoned intervention in Afghan affairs.

(b) *Second Afghan War* (1878–9). After 1870 the Amir, Shere Ali, encouraged Russian interests as a counterweight to the British. In 1878 he concluded a treaty with Russia.

When Shere Ali refused to conclude a similar agreement with

Britain a British force marched into Afghanistan. By the Treaty of Gandamak (1879) the Amir agreed to conduct his foreign policy only on the advice of the Indian government.

5. Russian expansion. After the final capitulation of the Caucasian tribes led by Sheykh Shamil in 1859, Russian forces were released to expand Russian power eastwards. This led to the following developments:

(a) *Annexation of East Turkestan* (1868).

(b) *Annexation of West Turkestan* (1873). The Russians were then only 650 kilometres from the north-west frontier of India.

(c) *Capture of Merv* (1884). This completed the subjection of the Turkoman tribes. Russian influence in northern Persia then increased.

6. Britain's policy. After the Kabul fiasco of 1841 Britain adopted a cautious policy towards the turbulent neighbours of India. Her policy became one of "masterly inactivity". This meant embarking on no risky enterprises but being ready for action should it become necessary. It owed much to the influence of John Lawrence, who in 1864 was to become Viceroy of India. He believed that Russia "might prove a safer neighbour than the wild tribes of Central Asia". However, Britain took care to consolidate her position in the north-western part of India.

Britain refused to aid Persia or the Turkoman tribes against Russian expansion. Each fresh Russian conquest was matched by a corresponding ineffectual British protest. The Russians would reply that the Turkomans were not subjects of Persia and were hindering trade by their unruly activities. During Anglo-Russian talks at Heidelberg in 1869, the Russian Foreign Minister, Gorchakov, said the reason for recent conquests was that the military had exceeded their instructions "in the hope of gaining distinction".

7. Anglo-Russian agreements. Russia extended her sovereignty over the nomadic tribes bordering Persia and Afghanistan. Eventually a series of territorial settlements were made between Russia and Britain. These settled differences between the two countries without war. The first one was in 1873. Subsequent ones were in the following years.

(a) *1885.* Russia occupied part of the Afghan frontier at Penjdeh. This produced an acute crisis which nearly led to war. Eventually a protocol settled the frontier to the satisfaction of

Britain and Russia. In future Russia decided to concentrate on expansion towards China and not India. This was the least line of resistance for the following two reasons.

(*i*) China presented less physical difficulties to rail penetration. There were the barriers of desert and mountain to overcome in any expansion to India.

(*ii*) China was far weaker militarily than British India.

(*b*) *1894.* Russia annexed the Pamirs. On the east lay Chinese Turkestan, on the south the north-west frontier of India. Another convention was signed.

8. Rivalry in Tibet. Britain failed in her attempts through the Chinese to establish commercial agreements with Tibet. Between 1898 and 1901 the Dalai Lama, ruler of Tibet, sent three missions to Russia. He was guided by the Russian Buddhist, Dorjieff. Lord Curzon concluded that Russia was establishing influence in Tibet, and in 1904 Britain sent a mission to Tibet under Colonel Younghusband. The result was an Anglo-Tibetan treaty, placing the country in some degree under British protection. Russia protested in vain.

9. Anglo-Russian entente. In 1907 Russia and Britain decided to reach final agreement on all outstanding differences.

(*a*) *Reasons.* Some of the factors were as follows.

(*i*) Both countries were then on friendly terms with France, who encouraged them to come together.

(*ii*) Both powers were apprehensive about the German policy of *Drang nach Osten.* Germany was building the Baghdad Railway, which had a branch planned to extend to Persia. This threatened the interests of Russia and Britain. German influence in Turkey was growing.

(*iii*) Britain, with bases in Egypt, Malta and Gibraltar, was less apprehensive about Russian designs at Constantinople and the Straits. Britain also wanted to encourage Russia to have friendly relations with Japan, who was an ally of Britain.

(*b*) *Details.* The main points concerned the following areas.

(*i*) Afghanistan was recognised as within the British sphere of influence. Both Britain and Russia were to have equal commercial opportunities in Afghanistan.

(*ii*) Russia recognised British interests in the Persian Gulf. Both countries decided, without consulting Persia, that Russia would have "a sphere of influence" in northern Persia, while

Britain would have the same in the south. In between there was to be a neutral zone. Both countries were to be free to obtain political or commercial concessions there.

(*iii*) Both countries agreed to respect the integrity of Tibet. In future it was decided to deal with Tibet only through its suzerain, the Chinese government.

CHINA AND HER EARLY
RELATIONS WITH FOREIGNERS

10. Chinese military strategy. Under powerful dynasties, Chinese power had extended south to Annam and as far west as Persia and the Caspian Sea. The Great Wall was built as a customs–immigration barrier and patrol line rather than as a major line of military resistance. It was intended to keep out wandering nomads. Beyond it, China established "zones of influence". The aim was not to convert areas into Chinese colonies, but to ensure they did not attack China.

A broad distinction was made between outer protectorates and inner protectorates.

(*a*) *Outer protectorates.* These were Annam, Burma, Nepal and Korea, which were tributary states. They sent tribute missions to the Peking Court and received presents in return.

(*b*) *Inner protectorates.* These were Tibet, Chinese Turkestan, Mongolia and Manchuria.

11. Chinese civilisation. China considered that her Oriental civilisation was superior to that of the "Occidental" or "Western" countries. She justified this on the basis of achievements in the following spheres.

(*a*) *The arts.* Chinese culture was notable for its contribution to drama, literature, historiography, philosophy, pottery and music.

(*b*) *The sciences.* The Chinese invented paper-making processes, gunpowder, the mariner's compass for navigation and movable type for printing.

NOTE: In the past, China had been the centre of the Eastern world. She had been a giver of civilisation to others. Her religion, language and architecture, for example, had influenced developments in other parts of Asia.

12. Chinese policy towards foreigners. The Chinese were suspicious of foreigners and looked upon them as "devils" or "bar-

barians". The following notes give an indication of the state of Sino-foreign relations around 1800.

(*a*) *Minimum contacts.* The Chinese preferred to have as little to do with foreigners as possible.

(*b*) *Tributary relationship.* Other countries were regarded as having subordinate status to the government of Peking even when they did not pay tribute. Russia was the only country which had official relations with China.

(*c*) *Application of Chinese law.* The Chinese insisted that no law was applicable on Chinese territory except Chinese law. In 1780 a Frenchman killed a Portuguese in a scuffle. The Chinese demanded his surrender for trial, and he was publicly strangled.

(*d*) *Restrictive trade.* Direct involvement in commercial questions seemed degrading to a Confucian mandarin. Local Chinese officials erected a barrier between themselves and Europeans. This took the form of a Chinese merchant guild. After 1757 the Emperor decided that Canton would be the sole port for such trade. Foreign traders, such as the British, French, Portuguese and Dutch, had to pay duties of up to 20 per cent on all goods imported into China.

THE OPIUM WARS AND THEIR CONSEQUENCES

13. The illicit trade in opium. In 1800 the import of opium was forbidden by the Chinese authorities. However, it soon became big business. Europeans with only a limited access to the Chinese market resorted to smuggling. As a result, the Canton trade lost the legal and carefully controlled character it had possessed in the eighteenth century.

Reasons for the persistence of the trade were as follows.

(*a*) There was an enormous domestic demand for opium among the depressed classes.

(*b*) It provided an important source of revenue to pay for the administrative expenses of the East India Company in India. In 1833 the company lost its monopoly of trade to India. It did not send opium in its ships, but allowed other ships under licence to do so. The trade was important to the British government in India, which relied on the sale of opium to China to balance its imports, especially of cotton goods from Lancashire.

(*c*) Local Chinese officials connived at the trade in return for bribes.

14. Causes of the First Opium War, 1839–42. The reasons for hostilities were as follows:

(*a*) *Continuation of the illegal opium trade after 1800* (*see* **13**).

(*b*) *Chinese determination to end the opium trade.* In 1839 the Imperial Commissioner, Lin Tse-hsu, was sent to Canton to suppress the trade. When Britain refused to hand over for execution officers of ships carrying opium, British factories were blockaded.

Chests of contraband opium were confiscated and burned. In the resulting turmoil, a Chinese died in a riot. War junks were sent to compel the surrender of those responsible, and war resulted.

15. Treaty of Nanking, 1842. Peace came eventually when a British expedition went up the Yangtze and cut off food supplies to Peking.

(*a*) *Main provisions.* China had to pay an indemnity and make the following important concessions.

(*i*) Certain places were made treaty ports and thrown open to British traders. British consuls in Canton, Shanghai, Amoy, Foochow and Ningpo were also permitted.

(*ii*) Hong Kong island was ceded to Britain.

(*iii*) The principle of extra-territoriality was established. It was established that foreigners accused of crimes by Chinese in these ports were to be tried according to their own, not Chinese, law.

(*b*) *Main consequences.* The war had revealed the weakness of the Chinese Empire and the treaty was the first step to greater European intrusion in the affairs of China.

16. The Second Opium War, 1856–8. Important points to note are as follows.

(*a*) *Causes.* The Chinese were reluctant to honour the concessions made to Europeans; they felt treaties with "foreign devils" had no binding force.

The Chinese were responsible for a number of violent acts and refused to accept Anglo-French demands for reparations. Examples of Chinese violence were the following.

(*i*) The "Arrow" incident in October 1856 when Chinese authorities in Canton stopped a ship sailing under the British flag which had been engaged in the opium traffic. The Chinese crew were taken off and the ensign hauled down.

(*ii*) Attacks on European factories.

(*iii*) Assassination of a French missionary in Kwangsi province. This shocked the French. Since the Treaty of Whampoa (1844) France had been the official protector of Roman Catholics in China.

(*b*) *The war*. An Anglo-French force captured Canton. When the Chinese continued to refuse to negotiate directly with them, the British and French captured the Taku forts near the gateway to Peking. In June 1858 the Chinese agreed to the Treaty of Tientsin. However, continued Chinese lack of co-operation led to the French and British occupying Peking in 1860 and burning the Emperor's Summer Palace. Chinese archers were no match for the Anglo-French marines and this hastened the end of the conflict.

(*c*) *Concessions*. The Chinese agreed to the following.

(*i*) Western legations were to be permitted in Peking.

(*ii*) French Catholic missions were permitted to hold land. China agreed to tolerate Christianity.

(*iii*) The legalisation of the import of opium.

17. Consequences of the war. The war again revealed the extent of the weakness of China. Eventually it encouraged European powers and Japan to take advantage of China's position to gain territorial concessions.

In the short run, it resulted in a new lease of life for the Manchu dynasty. The old claim that the Chinese emperor had a mandate from heaven to rule the world now appeared extremely weak. China's humiliating defeats by small European armies convinced Chinese officials that problems created by contact with the West could not be solved by traditional methods alone.

Some of the changes made in China were as follows.

(*a*) *Increased delegation of authority to viceroys*. These Chinese officials helped in defeating rebels by levying local armies by taxes raised for the government. They were now given increased powers by Peking.

(*b*) *Coastal reforms*. The Imperial Maritime Customs were reorganised and provided a new source of revenue. Treaty-port harbours and waterways were also developed.

(*c*) *Development of mines, railways, steamships and textile mills* under official auspices.

(*d*) *The beginnings of a study of western ideas*. Feng Kuei-Fen in the 1860s advocated China's "self-strengthening". This meant the adoption of western military ideas so that China could control civil unrest more effectively and resist foreign aggression.

Feng's ideas gained popularity. In education more attention was paid to the study of international affairs.

France and Britain now believed that the Manchu dynasty was preferable to any possible alternative ruler. They decided to help maintain the Manchu in power and agreed to co-operate with China in the execution of existing treaties.

18. Russian gains. Russia took advantage of Chinese involvement with France and Britain in the Second Opium War to secure important territorial advantages. These were as follows.

(*a*) *Treaty of Aigun* (1858). The area north of Manchuria had been generally recognised as Chinese until 1858. Now Muraviev secured the land north of the Amur river for Russia.

(*b*) *Treaty of Peking* (1860). General Ignatiev, the Russian envoy, secured the cession of the Maritime province. This was a valuable and strategically located territory east of Ussuri. Vladivostok was founded.

(*c*) *Treaty of St. Petersburg* (1881). Russia occupied the Ili district on the Russo-Sinkiang border in 1871. To avert war, China eventually accepted terms in 1881.

EUROPEAN POWERS, JAPAN AND CHINA

19. The emergence of Japan. The story of China's relations with European powers is complicated by the rapid growth in power of Japan. This factor had a considerable effect on the relations between the European powers. Since the seventeenth century the Japanese had excluded foreign missionaries and had followed a policy of exclusion. Eventually Japan had to abandon this policy owing to the influence of certain foreign powers.

(*a*) *Russia.* After 1806 Russia established a settlement on Sakhalin, under the direction of Muraviev. Japan protested that she had claimed it as Japanese since 1799.

(*b*) *The United States.* After 1820 the United States made numerous efforts to open relations with Japan. One reason was the increase in the North Pacific whaling industry. The United States wanted more humane treatment of crews of whalers wrecked in Japanese waters.

In 1852 Commodore Matthew C. Perry was sent to Japan. His purpose was to improve the treatment in Japan of American seamen and to open a few ports to trade and supplies. This he managed to do in 1854, after he had threatened to use force.

(c) *Combinations of foreign powers.* After 1854 Japan signed various treaties with Britain, Russia and the Netherlands. However, trade was limited by the hostility of the Japanese to foreign influence. A strong movement existed to expel all foreigners.

In 1865 a strong Allied expedition (British, Dutch, French and American) bombarded Japanese forts. After a demonstration at Osaka they secured Japanese imperial ratification of the existing treaties.

20. Modernisation of Japan. Impressed by the foreigners' military power, Japan started to modernise herself after 1867. A strong ruler, Mutsuhito, became Meiji emperor. He assumed direct control of the nation. The remnants of military rule and feudalism were abolished. With the support of able advisers, the anti-foreigners policy was dropped. A strong centralised bureaucratic government was developed along western lines. Great progress was made in industrialisation, public education and science. In 1872 universal military service was introduced.

Reasons why Japan was able to modernise more rapidly than China were as follows.

(a) *Adaptability.* In the past Japan had learnt many ideas from China. Unlike China, she had not been the centre of a famous ancient civilisation. It was thus easier for her to learn from the West.

(b) *Military prowess.* Before 1867 Japan had had a tradition of feudal military government. The Japanese were more group-minded than the Chinese and showed a capacity for discipline and organisation.

(c) *Size of the country.* The relative compactness and small size of Japan made centralised control more effective than in China.

(d) *Non-intervention of other powers.* After Japan had abandoned her "exclusionist policies", other powers made no attempt to violate the territorial integrity of Japan. However, rivalry did exist with Russia for control of some of the outlying islands.

(i) In the first Russo-Japanese treaty, the boundary between the two countries in the Kurile Islands was settled. The boundary in Sakhalin remained ambiguous.

(*ii*) In another Russo-Japanese treaty, in 1875, Russia received all of Sakhalin, Japan all of the Kurile Islands.

21. Sino-Japanese War. In 1876 Japan forced Korea to open three ports to trade and to provide extra-territorial rights for Japanese residents. Subsequent Sino-Japanese rivalry in Korea led to war in 1894 after Japan had sunk a British ship carrying Chinese troops to Korea.

Japan destroyed the Chinese army and navy, and China was forced to make peace. By the Treaty of Shimonoseki (1895) China had to:

    (*a*) recognise the independence of Korea;

    (*b*) cede to Japan Formosa, the Pescadores Islands and the Liaotung Peninsula;

    (*c*) pay an indemnity of 200 million taels.

22. Effects of the war. These were as follows:

    (*a*) *Joint Allied intervention.* In 1895 Russia, Germany and France forced Japan to return the Liaotung Peninsula to China for monetary compensation of a further 30 million taels.

    (*b*) *Increased Chinese demands for reform.* China's humiliating defeat by Japan, equipped with modern instruments of war, led to increased demands for reform.

    (*c*) *Foreign loans.* In 1895–6, as native capital was not available, China had to rely on a Franco-Russian and an Anglo-German loan to help military, railway and industrial development. This was secured only at the expense of a further extension of foreign control. The loans were secured by the Chinese customs revenues.

    (*d*) *European scramble for concessions* (*see* **23**).

23. The scramble for concessions. Germany, France and Russia expected to be paid for their services to China against Japan. Soon a "competitive rush" for concessions took place among the major powers.

    (*a*) *Russia.*

        (*i*) In 1896 a fifteen-year defensive alliance was signed. Russia was allowed to set up military depots in the Liaotung Peninsula. By the Li–Lobanov concession, Russia was permitted to build and operate the Chinese Eastern Railway. This provided a short link across North Manchuria to the Russian port of

Vladivostok. It saved the need to travel by the longer northern route on Russian soil.

(*ii*) In March 1898 Russia secured a twenty-five-year lease of the southern Liaotung Peninsula, which included Port Arthur and Talienwan. She secured the right to construct a railway from Harbin to these ports. This action was partly prompted by Germany's gains (*see* (*b*)).

(*b*) *Germany*. Following the murder of two German missionaries in Shantung in November 1897, Germany immediately occupied the Kiaochow Peninsula. In 1898 she secured a ninety-nine-year lease of Kiaochow with the port of Tsingtao. Her action encouraged other powers to follow suit (*see* (*a*)(*ii*) above and (*c*) below).

(*c*) *Britain* secured the following concessions in 1898.

(*i*) The recognition of the Yangtze river valley as her sphere of influence (February).

(*ii*) A lease of Weihaiwei to last as long as the Russian occupation of Port Arthur (March).

(*iii*) A ninety-nine-year lease of Kowloon, on the mainland opposite Hong Kong island (June).

(*d*) *France*. In April 1898 France received a ninety-nine-year lease of Kwangchowan Bay and its vicinity.

24. Anglo-Japanese alliance. In April 1901 Count Hyashi made the first overtures for an Anglo-Japanese alliance to the British Foreign Minister, Lord Lansdowne. It was signed in January 1902.

(*a*) *Causes*. Both Japan and Britain had failed to secure allies and felt isolated as other powers had allies. They feared Russia's designs on Manchuria.

(*i*) Britain had failed to negotiate an alliance with Germany (1898–1901). She feared Germany's growing naval power and wanted an ally in Asia. Her negotiations for a Russian agreement had failed and she wanted to prevent a Russo-Japanese alliance.

(*ii*) Japan also failed to secure an alliance with Russia (1901–2). Count de Witte was not prepared to allow Japan a free hand in Korea.

(*b*) *Details*. The alliance was concluded for five years. Both powers recognised the independence of China and Korea, the special interests of each in China, and Britain recognised the special interests of Japan in Korea. Military provisions were as follows.

(*i*) If either power was at war with a third power, the other agreed to maintain strict neutrality.

(*ii*) If either power was involved in war with two other powers, the other agreed to help.

On Britain's initiative, the alliance was renewed in August 1905 and modified. It then provided for mutual support in case either was attacked by another power, and was extended to include India.

(*c*) *Results* (*see* **27**).

25. Russo-Japanese War. This started in February 1904. The relevant details were as follows:

(*a*) *Causes.* The war was due to territorial rivalry and conflicting ambitions in the following areas.

(*i*) Manchuria: Russia, instead of evacuating this area after 1900 as Japan had hoped, started to penetrate deeper into the country. Japan disliked Russian intervention in 1895 in restoring the Liaotung Peninsula to China and then securing a lease there.

(*ii*) Korea: Japan feared that Russia was becoming a rival for political influence in this country.

(*b*) *Russian defeat.* At the start of the war, Japan besieged the Russian fleet at Port Arthur. The decision was then taken to send the Russian Baltic squadron to the Pacific. *En route*, it attacked the Hull herring fishing fleet in the North Sea, under the delusion that these vessels were Japanese torpedo boats. After a seven months' cruise, it was promptly sunk by the Japanese under Admiral Togo at the battle of Tsushima on 8th April 1905.

Russian troops were defeated at Mukden at the beginning of March 1905.

(*c*) *End to the war.* Russian resources were not exhausted, but the majority of the Russian people viewed the war with indifference. In contrast, the Japanese people were enthusiastic about the war, but it was clear that Japan would soon run out of finances.

As a result of the mediation of President Roosevelt of the United States, peace terms were signed at Portsmouth in September.

(*i*) Manchuria was to be evacuated by both powers and restored to China.

(*ii*) Russia agreed to recognise Japan's paramount interest in Korea.

(*iii*) Russia ceded to Japan the lease of the Liaotung

Peninsula, the South Manchuria Railway and the southern half of Sakhalin.

26. Results of the war. Germany now had less to fear from Russia and adopted an aggressive tone in North Africa (*see* XIX, **22**). Other results of the war were as follows.

    (*a*) *A changed "balance of power" position in the Far East.*

      (*i*) Japan was established as a major Far Eastern power while Russia ceased to play an effective role in that area.

      (*ii*) China's decline was accelerated. The Russo-Chinese alliance in 1896 had been mainly directed to limit Japanese expansionist policies. Now Russia decided, in the period 1907–12, to co-operate with Japan against China through a secret agreement.

    (*b*) *A revival of Asian nationalism.* At the time, Japan's victory was regarded in Europe as a victory for Western modernised dynamism over Asiatic feudalistic inertia. However, it encouraged an awakening of the political consciousness of Asians. The Asian problem was stated by R. Grousset to be not the partition of Asia by European powers, but the "problem of Asia's revolt against her European masters".

The first suggestion for a Monroe Doctrine for the Far East came from a Burmese newspaper in 1905. An editorial suggested that the dependent lands of Asia would welcome a Japanese initiative in curbing the western colonial powers and expelling them from the Orient.

    (*c*) *A revival of widespread domestic unrest in Russia* (*see* XII, **21**).

27. Influence of Far Eastern events on European relations. During the period 1895–1905, events in the Far East, particularly in China, had a significant effect on relations between European powers. One important point was their influence in developing links between Britain and Japan, and between Britain, France and Russia.

    (*a*) The mutual interests of Russia and France in China led to increased co-operation between these two powers in the 1890s.

    (*b*) The Anglo-Japanese alliance of 1902 ended the isolation of both Japan and Britain. Contributory factors were as follows.

      (*i*) The joint co-operation of Germany, Russia and France in pressurising Japan in 1895 (*see* **22**(*a*)).

(*ii*) Germany's refusal to aid Britain in the Far East against Russian expansion.

(*c*) The Anglo-Japanese alliance played a part in eventually improving relations between the following powers.

(*i*) France and Britain: after 1902 France had less fear of being drawn into a Far Eastern dispute to help Russia.

(*ii*) Russia and Britain: Britain had hoped her alliance with Japan in 1902 would make her a less aggressive power. However, it had the opposite effect, and was a contributory factor to the Russo-Japanese War of 1905. Russia's defeat illustrated her profound weakness. Britain's fear of Russia was partially removed as a result of this and the alliance with Japan, renewed in 1905.

28. Decline of Manchu China. During the nineteenth century serious internal unrest coincided with the decline in the fighting efficiency of the Chinese armed forces and increased bureaucratic corruption and decay. China had greater problems to face than Japan in transforming her social and political institutions. Her failure to overcome them accounted largely for her slow decline. Continual foreign intervention in her affairs also complicated the process of reform. In October 1911 a revolution broke out, and a republic was declared.

FRANCE IN VIETNAM AND BRITAIN IN BURMA

29. Introduction. In this section only those areas are discussed which are close to southern China and which were profoundly influenced by Chinese culture. These were as follows:

(*a*) *Burma.* This country bordered British India. It became one cause of Anglo-French rivalry (*see* 32(*c*)).

(*b*) *Indo-China.* Its nineteenth-century history represented an interesting example of European colonialism.

30. Franco-Spanish intervention. Vietnam was predominantly Chinese in culture. The Empire of Annam acknowledged the suzerainty of the Chinese emperor. French Catholic missions had been active in the country since 1615.

France protested after 1848 against the harsh treatment of Christians and missionaries. When this was rejected, a French warship, the *Catinat*, bombarded the forts at Tourane in 1852. In 1857 the Annamese emperor, Tu Duc, had the Spanish Bishop of Tonkin put to death. A joint Franco-Spanish fleet under Admiral Genouilly then occupied Saigon in Cochin-China. French operations were held up by hostilities in China (*see* 16). Eventually, in 1860, the Treaty of Saigon was signed.

The Emperor agreed to:

(*a*) cede the three eastern provinces of Cochin-China to France;

(*b*) allow full opportunities for Catholic missionary activity;

(*c*) open three ports, including Tourane, to French trade.

China pointed out in vain that no treaty between a foreign power and Vietnam was valid without the approval of the Peking government.

31. Extension of French influence. Control of Saigon eventually resulted in the absorption of the whole Annamese Empire. In 1862 France, using the excuse of protecting missionaries and trade rights, sent troops there. Gradually territories were taken which had long been regarded as under Chinese suzerainty. The French were temporarily checked when their forces were beaten by the Chinese at Langson in March 1885, but later expansion continued and was halted in the north only when the borders of metropolitan China were reached and in the west only when they came to the sphere of British influence in Burma and India. Many years of unrest and rebellion followed. Not until 1896 was Tonkin completely "pacified".

32. Britain and Burma. Burma had been under Siamese suzerainty in the past. Modern Burma was built upon the conquests of King Alaungpaya (1752–60). His successors repulsed Chinese invasions in 1769, but in 1771 were unable to maintain their authority in Siam.

(*a*) *First Burmese War* (1824–6). The Burmese king, Bagyidau, had been pursuing a policy of expansion. In 1822 he conquered Manipur and Assam. His forces in Arakan then threatened the East India Company. To secure the eastern frontier of India, and to avert invasion, the British attacked and defeated the Burmese. Unable to find a local ruler for the territory overrun, the British annexed Assam, Arakan and the Tenasserim coast.

(*b*) *Second Burmese War* (1852–3). Burmese rulers continued to hamper the development of British trade. The Burmese were defeated in a short war, and had to accept the British annexation of Lower Burma.

(c) *Rivalry with the French.* Britain was soon drawn into rivalry with the French in Indo-China in an attempt to forestall them in the China trade. Both countries explored possibilities of finding an overland route to China. It was realised that one point on the upper reaches of the Yangtze would be only just over 600 miles from Calcutta. This compared with the sea distance of some 4,300 miles to Shanghai.

Activities of the French prompted the British into securing extra-territorial rights in Upper Burma. Britain also obtained from Burma guaranteed navigation rights for British steamships on the Irrawaddy river.

King Thibau (1878–85) was anti-British. It seemed likely that he planned to import French arms via Tonkin. In 1885 he concluded an agreement with the French, to whom he gave economic concessions.

(d) *Third Burmese War* (1885–6). Britain demanded that in future Burmese foreign relations be conducted in accordance with the advice of the Indian government. This was rejected. The Burmese were defeated again and Thibau was sent to India. Upper Burma was then annexed by Britain. In July 1886 China was forced to acknowledge the British protectorate.

PROGRESS TEST 20

1. What were the principal powers in Central Asia? **(1)**

2. Discuss the reasons for British and French interests in Persia during the period 1798–1809. **(2)**

3. Explain how Russia eventually secured mastery of the Caucasus. **(3)**

4. Why did the First Afghan War take place and what were the results? **(4)**

5. What policy did Britain adopt towards Russian expansion in Central Asia after 1841? **(6–7)**

6. Why did Britain and Russia decide to settle all outstanding differences in 1907? **(9)**

7. List the neighbouring areas of China which were regarded as protectorates. **(10)**

8. What was the traditional Chinese policy towards foreigners? **(12)**

9. What were the causes of the First Opium War? **(14)**

10. Explain the principle of extra-territoriality. **(15(a)(iii))**

11. What were the results of the Second Opium War? (16(*c*), 17)

12. Describe early Japanese foreign relations before 1860. (19)

13. Why did Japan find it easier to modernise than China? (20)

14. What were the causes and results of the Sino-Japanese War? (21)

15. Which European powers intervened on behalf of China in 1895? How were they rewarded? (22, 23)

16. Why did Britain conclude an alliance with Japan? (24(*a*))

17. What were the results of the Russo-Japanese War? (26)

18. What were the reasons for British and French intervention in Burma. (32)

CHAPTER XXI

British foreign policy

PRINCIPLES AND MAIN FEATURES

1. Introduction. A detailed coverage of British foreign policy would be outside the scope of this book. It is important, however, to note various maxims which guided the actions of Foreign Ministers. Certain principles and aims helped determine the relationships between Britain and other European powers and provided a partial explanation for Britain's world-wide interests.

Mussolini once remarked that "there is no such thing as originality in foreign policy". Certainly the principles adhered to by Britain in the nineteenth century provided a continuity to her foreign policy. Her primary aim became the preservation of peace so that secure trading conditions existed. Policies were followed, either conservative or radical, which were conducive to peace in the long run. It has been said that the nineteenth century was the period of "*Pax Britannica*". General peace was preserved, since the British navy was sufficiently strong to prevent the expansion abroad of any European power in a form likely to injure Britain's interests.

2. European balance of power. Disraeli once said that "so long as the power and advice of Britain is felt in the councils of Europe", peace would be maintained.

Britain wanted to prevent any European power from acquiring hegemony in a form which might threaten the following.

(a) *The independence of the Low Countries* (Holland and Belgium). The following should be noted.

(i) British policy during the Napoleonic Wars (*see* II).

(ii) British policy towards Belgium. The events of 1830–9 are covered elsewhere (*see* IV, **25**). In 1870, after the start of the Franco-Prussian War, when Bismarck had published Benedetti's draft treaty of 1866 for the French annexation of Belgium, Gladstone intervened. He obtained from each belligerent a treaty undertaking to join Britain in defence of Belgian neutrality against the other. This was to remain in force for one year after the conclusion of peace.

(*b*) *British naval command of the Channel and the North Sea.* Britain wished to maintain mastery in these areas for the following two reasons.

(*i*) To preserve the strategic unity of the British Isles. This meant the prevention of any attempt by another power to invade or form close relations with any part of the British Isles (England, Scotland, Wales and Ireland) since this would be detrimental to the interests of the whole.

(*ii*) To ensure the safety of her maritime trade routes, and thus her own food supplies from overseas.

3. Naval supremacy. Britain, the island power, considered naval supremacy vital for her independent role in foreign affairs and to obviate the necessity for a large conscript army. It was believed that Britain had been saved during the Napoleonic Wars by her navy and not by her allies.

When France and Russia, both naval powers, formed a close link in 1892, the British position seemed threatened. This led to the formulation of the principle of the "two-power standard". This stated that the British navy "should be equal to the combination of the two next strongest navies in Europe".

Naval power was used successfully in the following areas.

(*a*) *The Mediterranean.*

(*i*) Greek independence in 1832 was partly due to the defeat at Navarino Bay of the Turkish fleet by the British and French.

In 1850 the British blockaded the Piraeus. This helped compel the Greek government to compensate a Gibraltar Jew, Don Pacifico, who had claimed protection as a British subject.

(*ii*) Italy, 1860 (*see* XIII, **38**(*a*)(*iii*)).

(*iii*) Egypt and Syria: the successful bombardment of Acre in 1840 helped prevent Mehemet Ali conquering Turkey.

(*iv*) The Straits, 1878 (*see* XVI, **9**).

(*b*) *The Low Countries*, 1830–9 (*see* IV, **25**).

(*c*) *The Atlantic.* The Spanish and Portuguese colonies were kept free from European intervention partly owing to the work of Admiral Cochrane, who commanded squadrons in the area from 1808 to 1825. The Monroe Doctrine was really effective only for about sixty years, when it had the support of the British navy (*see* IV, **17** and **18**).

4. Splendid isolation. In the 1820s Britain withdrew from the Conference System. After their involvement in the Napoleonic Wars the British ceased being primarily interested in European events. They wanted to concentrate on home affairs and interests outside Europe, largely of an economic nature.

"Splendid isolation" characterised much of British foreign policy in the nineteenth century. It implied the following principles.

(a) *No lengthy foreign commitments.* Palmerston summed up the British approach when he said Britain had no objection to treaties for specific objects but these were not to be in force indefinitely. Britain wanted to be free to judge each case as it arose. This was merely a development of the policy of Castlereagh and Canning.

Later in the 1880s Salisbury pleaded Britain's world interests and the government's reliance on popular changing opinions as arguments against an alliance with Germany (*see* X, **27**(*c*)).

Though this policy was moderated after 1902, it was still the attitude of many statesmen up until 1914. Britain had no firm commitments to foreign powers, except Japan.

(b) *Non-intervention abroad.* Canning summed up this attitude when he stated: "Every nation for itself and God for us all." However, it was not consistently followed. Britain was not averse to utilising her naval power to defend her interests in the Mediterranean. As long as they did not conflict with the preservation of Turkey against the encroachments of Russia, Britain generally favoured liberal and national movements abroad. For example, she suggested the formation of the Quadruple Alliance in 1833–4 (*see* V, **14**(*b*)).

Examples of non-intervention abroad concerned the following areas.

(*i*) Poland (1863): Britain might have given some encouragement to the Polish revolt against Tsarism.

(*ii*) Schleswig-Holstein (1863–5): Britain was prepared to give only moral encouragement to Denmark, not military support.

COLONIAL AFFAIRS

5. Attitude to colonies. The period 1875–1900 was the "hey-day" of British imperialism. The activities of Lord Cromer in Egypt, Lord Milner in South Africa, and Joseph Chamberlain had widespread support. Before this period, however, the British attitude to Empire was slightly contradictory. The British government was not opposed to the idea of Empire as such, but was prepared actively to encourage it in certain regions only.

Two opposing views which influenced the government at various times were as follows.

(*a*) *The keeping of responsibilities to a minimum.* The reasons for this attitude have been discussed elsewhere (*see* XVII, **11**). Examples of the reluctance of the British government to acquire new responsibilities and of its readiness to abandon old ones concerned the following areas.

(*i*) South Africa: in the 1850s Britain was prepared to give virtual independence to the Boer republics.

(*ii*) East Africa: naval power had made Britain the most influential power in this area. However, she made no attempt to colonise. When Captain Owen annexed Mombassa in 1826, his action was repudiated by the government.

(*iii*) Australia, Canada and New Zealand received self-government in 1855, 1867 and 1876 respectively. These largely white-populated areas, containing people mainly of British origin, were regarded as capable of looking after their own affairs.

(*b*) *Expansion.* It must be noted that, before being granted self-government, Australia, Canada and New Zealand had been helped in their development by Britain. They soon developed from weak regions with only small white coastal populations into influential states. Along with South Africa, they were regarded as the "backbone" of the Empire by 1914.

In certain areas Britain was keen to develop her empire, but to minimise expense resorted to the practice of "indirect rule". This was first applied in India, and meant rule through local rulers, assisted by British advisers. It was later extended to Malaya, the Fiji Islands and parts of Africa.

Much of British colonial policy was dictated by the strategic-economic requirements of protecting the sea routes ("lifelines") to India, and the land frontiers of that subcontinent. The British government took every opportunity to extend its authority in India, which was regarded as the "jewel" of the Empire. Expansion elsewhere was frequently undertaken with the security of India in mind. The following should be noted.

(*i*) Strategic bases and areas: to strengthen her control over the sea routes to India, and to prevent other powers controlling these areas, Britain retained Mauritius and Cape Colony in 1815, annexed Aden in 1839, took an interest in Zanzibar and East Africa, and eventually became involved in Egypt and the Suez Canal (*see* XIX, **15**).

(*ii*) Indian land frontiers: to protect the north-west frontier Britain embarked on two costly Afghan Wars (*see* XX, **4**). Burma was gradually conquered in the process of securing the eastern frontier.

6. Strategic bases. During the nineteenth century Britain alone possessed the far-flung bases necessary to world maritime predominance. They enabled Britain to gain an extensive overseas empire.

(*a*) *Reasons for bases.* Britain was interested in acquiring strategic bases for the following reasons.

(*i*) Political: possessions served as useful "pawns" in the power politics of European rivalries. The traditional enemies of Britain had been France and Spain, major colonial powers. Britain's usual plan was for her continental allies to engage them on land, while she attacked their possessions and undermined their naval power from such bases as Gibraltar in the Mediterranean.

(*ii*) Commercial: Britain developed extensive trade with the Mediterranean countries, India and China. Possessions served as trading or refuelling stations for ships, as naval bases and as garrison outposts for forces used to suppress slavery and piracy, or to protect British economic or political interests against hostile powers.

(*b*) *Areas involved.* Britain's interests were world-wide, but were focused particularly on securing the main routes to India, China and Australia. She also wanted to defend the Straits and Constantinople (regarded by Temperley, the historian, as "the first strategic position in the world") against the advance of either Russia or France. Specific areas where bases were gained for the reasons mentioned above were the following.

(*i*) The Mediterranean: as power shifted in Europe from France and Spain eastwards towards Germany and Russia, Britain extended her influence eastwards. Malta was retained in 1815 and Cyprus was acquired in 1878. The latter was intended to be a base for defending the Straits and Constantinople against the advance of Russia. However, its significance declined after the opening of the Suez Canal when Alexandria and Egypt became more important.

In 1863 Britain voluntarily ceded the Ionian Isles to Greece.

(*ii*) The Red Sea, Persian Gulf and Indian Ocean: important posts were Mauritius in the Indian Ocean and Aden on the Red Sea (occupied in 1838). After 1896 Britain feared German designs in the Gulf as this was the likely area for one terminal of the Baghdad Railway. In 1899 an arrangement was made with the Sheik of Kuwait, who promised to cede no territory without British consent.

(*iii*) The Far East and Pacific: Singapore was acquired by Sir Stamford Raffles in 1819. Later Hong Kong was leased (*see* XX, 15). In 1874 Britain annexed the Fiji Islands.

(*iv*) The North Sea: Heligoland was retained until 1890, when it was ceded to Germany.

(*v*) South Africa (Cape Colony).

END OF ISOLATIONIST POLICY

7. End of isolation. During the 1890s the policy of "splendid isolation" seemed no longer practical, for the following reasons.

(*a*) *All European powers were linked together in alliances except for Britain.* In addition to the Triple Alliance of Germany, Austria and Italy (1883), there was the Dual Entente of France and Russia (1894). After 1895 Britain felt particularly isolated in the Far East, where Germany, France and Russia worked closely together.

(*b*) *Britain no longer had undisputed naval mastery at sea.* It was realised that the "two-power standard" (*see* 3) could no longer be maintained. The border dispute between British Guiana and Venezuela in 1895 made the British Admiralty realise that it could not concentrate a fleet in the West Atlantic to deal with any contingency there while at the same time keeping adequate ships in other areas.

They feared the growing naval power of the following powers.

(*i*) The United States and Japan in the Far East.

(*ii*) France, Italy and Russia in the Atlantic and Mediterranean.

(*c*) *Relations between Britain and some other powers were poor.*

(*i*) As relations between Britain and the Boers deteriorated after 1895 German public opinion became steadily hostile to Britain.

(*ii*) The Fashoda incident in 1898 (*see* XIX, **14–15**) showed the dangers of being on bad terms with France and a member of the Triple Alliance at the same time.

(*iii*) Britain and Russia were still on bad terms owing to numerous colonial disputes, while Britain resented the growth of Russian power in Manchuria.

8. The search for allies. In January 1898 Britain made tentative suggestions to Russia to end colonial rivalry. This was ignored, and so the British Colonial Minister, Chamberlain, made attempts to form an alliance with Germany. After negotiations had failed in 1901 Britain eventually came to arrangements with the following.

(*a*) *Japan* in 1902 (*see* XX, **24**).
(*b*) *France* in 1904 (*see* VII, **23**).
(*c*) *Russia* in 1907 (*see* XX, **9**).

PROGRESS TEST 21

1. Why did British statesmen consider the maintenance of the "balance of power" in Europe important? **(2)**

2. Give illustrations of the successful use of naval power by Britain during the nineteenth century. **(3)**

3. What was meant by "splendid isolation"? **(4)**

4. Describe the British attitude towards colonies during the period 1815–75. **(5)**

5. Why did Britain consider it necessary to have far-flung bases? **(6)**

6. Why did Britain seek allies at the end of the nineteenth century? **(7, 8)**

CHAPTER XXII

Causes of the First World War

BACKGROUND FACTORS, 1871–1914

1. Introduction. In mid 1914 some observers considered that the danger of a major war had passed. Relations between some countries had in fact improved. For instance, France and Germany concluded an agreement in February over economic spheres of influence in Turkey. Britain and Germany had co-operated in the Balkan crisis in 1913 and in June 1914 reached agreement over the future of the Portuguese colonies and the Baghdad Railway. In 1914 first Britain and the United States, and then Britain and France, agreed they would never go to war with each other without first submitting their difficulties to a third impartial party.

There were indications that governments were increasingly co-operating in the management of common affairs. For example, the establishment of the International Red Cross at Geneva (1863) had been followed by that of the International Postal Union (1875), a common system of copyright, and an International Office of Public Health (1907). Moreover, the International Court at The Hague had been created in 1899 to deal with any international disputes which states wished to refer to it. Improved means of travel, the motor car and aeroplane, and verbal means of communication, the telephone and Morse code, etc., all seemed to point towards greater unity and understanding.

However, an incident in Bosnia soon plunged Europe into the greatest war it had ever experienced.

2. Causes of the war. It was clear that though superficially Europe appeared calm in mid 1914 in fact unrest existed in many areas. The German Kaiser remarked at the time: "The whole of Germany is charged with electricity. It only needs a spark to set the whole thing off." There were a number of interrelated factors, such as the following, which each provided part of the answer to why general war occurred in 1914.

(a) *General causes.* The following factors, for which no one country was to blame, had during the previous forty years led to an acute state of tension in Europe.

(i) The alliance systems (*see* 3).

(ii) Militarism (*see* 4).

(iii) Economic influences (*see* 5).

(iv) Colonial conflicts (*see* XVII, 17).

(v) Belief in national self-determination (*see* I, 4(b), IV, 2 and XVI, 37(e)).

(b) *National rivalries.* Each power had interests which conflicted with those of other powers. Note that tension was particularly acute between the following states.

(i) France and Germany over Alsace-Lorraine (*see* VII, 13 and 20(a); X, 12).

(ii) Austria and Russia over the Balkans (*see* XVI, 35).

(iii) Austria and Serbia. Both states in their policies after 1903 sought to provoke the other (*see* XVI, 27). The immediate cause for localised war must be shared between the Pan-Serb plotters, who were determined to assassinate the Archduke, and Austria, who was determined to avenge his death (*see* 13–15 and 23).

(c) *Breakdown of European diplomacy.* No country expected or wanted a general war. That a local conflict between Austria and Serbia escalated into a major one was partly the result of the failure of the diplomats of the great powers to devise a suitable solution (*see* 20 and 21).

(d) *The policies of Germany.* The world ambitions of the Kaiser after 1890 were the prime cause of the increased tension in European relations. Though all powers must share the blame for the outbreak of war in 1914, Germany was the main culprit (*see* 24).

3. The alliance systems. The object of an alliance was to prevent war by appearing so strong as to deter other groups from warlike action. The best hope for peace was that the non-aggressive member of an alliance would restrain others (as in the Bosnian crisis of 1908) or collaborate with states of a rival grouping to reach a solution in the interests of all (as at the Algeciras Conference of 1906 and in the Balkan Wars of 1912–13). However, each succeeding crisis tightened the bonds within each group. There was always the risk that with an increase in incidents the system might work differently. The momentum of the more reckless members might drag their allies, like tied mountain climbers, over the edge of the abyss. By 1914 the system had become rigid and inflexible. There was no longer a bridge between the opposing coalitions. This meant that after Sarajevo none of the major powers made serious efforts to restrain aggressive allies, or to co-operate with the opposing coalition for fear of appearing disloyal.

In 1914 the two evenly balanced forces were as follows.

(a) *The Triple Alliance.* The Dual Alliance of Germany and Austria, concluded in 1879, had been transformed into a Triple Alliance when Italy joined in 1883. Owing to the conflicting commitments of Italy, however, the loyalty of this state to the Triple Alliance in 1914 was questionable.

(b) *The Triple Entente.* This had evolved from the following groupings.

   (i) The Franco-Russian alliance of 1894 (*see* VII, **21**).

   (ii) The Anglo-French *entente* of 1904 (*see* VII, **23**).

   (iii) The Anglo-Russian *entente* of 1907 (*see* XX, **9**).

4. Militarism. So as to take precautions in case of war, European powers embarked on a spate of activity in the early 1900s. People became increasingly more war-minded as the prospects of a general European conflict increased after successive crises and incidents. Militarism denoted a certain enthusiasm for war-preparedness, the values of military organisation and discipline, and force as a solution to problems. The development of this spirit in Europe led many senior statesmen in 1914 to accept the inevitable rather than seriously try to combat the forces of war.

Note the following.

(a) *The arms race.* After 1900 the war budgets of the major powers were increased, so that larger armed forces could be maintained, and a vast amount of arms equipment produced. This was particularly true in Germany. France and Russia followed close behind, while Austria attempted to keep pace. Britain embarked on an enormous naval programme to rival Germany, and Lord Haldane, the Minister of War, organised a strong expeditionary force for use overseas and a territorial army for defence at home.

Attempts to restrict the arms race at the following meetings failed.

   (i) The Hague Conferences of 1899 and 1907. The first one

was convened by the Tsar, anxious about the cost of rearming Russia. The second was called on the initiative of Britain. No agreement on disarmament was reached, owing largely to the obstinacy of Germany. Agreement was reached only on a number of minor issues. For example, the rules of war were defined, and certain inhumane weapons outlawed.

(*ii*) The Anglo-German naval conversations in 1912 (*see* X, **31**(*d*)).

(*b*) *Military influence on policy determination.* After 1900 in all major countries military and naval personnel were consulted more frequently. Considerations of war gradually overrode other factors as senior staff officers were permitted a larger share in policy-making. After 1905 British generals were admitted to the secrets of the French in joint military talks. While these had no binding force on Britain, it was difficult to deny that there was at least a presumption that if France was attacked Britain would help.

In 1914 the general staffs in Germany, Austria and Russia generally favoured war. As the civilian leaders acted indecisively during the crisis period of 23rd–30th July 1914, the military leaders of these countries played a decisive role in influencing their governments to mobilise and declare war (*see* **21**). Note the influence of the following.

(*i*) The German Admiral Tirpitz rigidly opposed any proposals for naval disarmament, and Moltke, the Chief of Staff, was keen on war against France. In May 1914 he told Conrad that "any delay means a lessening of our chances". Germany appeared to have reached her maximum military strength while France and Russia were still in the process of building up their forces.

(*ii*) Conrad von Hötzendorf, the Austrian Chief of Staff, had been agitating for "preventive war" against Serbia since 1906.

(*iii*) Sir John Fisher, in charge of the British Admiralty, was convinced that war would ultimately come with Germany, and once made the suggestion to "Copenhagen the German fleet" before it was too late.

(*c*) *Atmosphere of war.* This existed particularly in Germany. However, to a lesser extent, all countries were influenced by militarism. Vested interests which perpetuated the industry of war existed among groups of people ranging from arms manufacturers and their shareholders to newspaper proprietors who benefited from the state of international tension in Europe. In the early 1900s writers who examined and glorified war became more numerous and were more widely read than those writing on cultural subjects or on the need for international harmony.

5. Economic influences. In a very indirect way economic factors contributed to the growth of tension in Europe, and thus to the war of 1914. The following examples illustrate this.

(*a*) *Economic motives behind many colonial ventures* (*see* XVII, 3). Germany was one of the major industrial powers after 1871. Her economic aims were a partial cause of her activities in the Ottoman Empire and Morocco, which resulted in tightening the bonds of the Triple Entente.

(*b*) *The role of trade competition.* Some German historians after 1919 argued that German trade rivalry with Britain had caused Britain to join France against her. Certainly British businessmen resented the loss of trade to vigorous German firms which undercut British goods in many markets, notably South America, and resorted to "dumping tactics".

However, German protectionist policies did not force Britain to abandon free trade, and in fact extensive trade took place between the two countries before 1914. Thus the evidence for this argument is slender.

(*c*) *The role of finance.* An example of the influence of money in politics was the enormous French loans to Tsarist Russia after 1906. These buttressed the Russian government and meant that it continued to pursue ambitious policies abroad, particularly in the Balkans. If Russia had become bankrupt, a liberalised government might have emerged which might have given attention to urgent domestic problems.

(*d*) *The "devil theory".* It has been argued that the war was caused largely as a result of powerful industrialists who desired to make huge profits out of the production of "weapons of war". Again there is little evidence for this. However, it cannot be denied that armament manufacturers, such as Krupp in Germany and Schneider-Creusot in France, benefited from the arms race in Europe after 1900.

(*e*) *Lebensraum.* Some German authorities argued that as a result of the tremendous industrial growth of Germany after 1871 it had to expand or burst. Over-production and over-population in particular necessitated the finding of new "living space". This argument may be part of the explanation as to why militarist theories were so readily accepted in Germany before 1914. One argument put forward by Admiral Tirpitz was the "risk theory". He argued that a mercantile marine, national commerce and colonies justified the building of a large navy capable of taking the offensive.

INSTABILITY IN THE BALKANS

6. Introduction. The continued instability of the Balkans after 1879 was to be a major cause of war in 1914. The positions worsened after the Bosnian crisis of 1908–9 and the Balkan Wars of 1912–13.

Serbia and Russia were not prepared to be humiliated again by the central powers. The aim of Serbia to unite all Slavs in one state and Austria's policy of incorporating all Slavs into her empire or of having a subservient border Slav state were not reconcilable. The Hapsburg monarchy was itself becoming steadily more insecure, owing to mounting unrest in Hungary, where many Slavs avoided the draft.

Germany was determined to back Austria against Serbia, being keen to establish economic influence in the Balkans and the Ottoman Empire. Also the projected Berlin–Baghdad Railway would need to pass through Serbia. Serbia, ambitious and more powerful after the Balkan Wars, was distinctly unfriendly to Austrian and German hopes. Since neither the central powers nor Serbia were prepared to abandon their aims, war seemed the only solution. Note, however, that in 1914 Germany did advocate a policy of reconciliation with Serbia (*see* **19**).

All the factors considered in **7–10** also contributed to a highly explosive situation.

7. Albania and the Aegean islands. In 1913 the Greeks had taken Janina in southern Albania, and they failed to give it up after the Treaty of London. Following Albanian raids into Serbian territory Serbia invaded northern Albania in September. Austria forced Serbia to evacuate Albania in October, but joint Austro-Italian pressure failed to remove the Greeks.

In December Grey suggested to the powers the division of southern Albania between Greece and Albania, with compensation for Greece in the Aegean isles. This was accepted, but the dispute then continued between Greece and Turkey over the islands. In June 1914 there was the distinct danger of war between Greece and Turkey.

8. Incident of the German general. The "Young Turks", who seized power after the *coup d'état* of January 1913, were pro-German. Eventually a German military mission went to help reorganise the army. Russia protested when they learned in November that General Liman von Sanders was to command a Turkish army corps in Constantinople and to have other powers. The French supported the Russian protest but the British were lukewarm. Grey, the British Foreign Minister, wanted to keep out of the dispute since a British admiral was in Constantinople on a similar naval mission.

The Kaiser was for holding out, and a crisis occurred. Eventually Bethmann-Hollweg, the German Chancellor, gained the Kaiser's support for a compromise. Sanders was to be made an inspector-general of the Turkish army and a Turkish field-marshal, and thus had to resign his command in January 1914. The incident passed over, but Russia remained intensely suspicious of German aims.

9. Decision of the Russian Crown Council. At an Imperial Crown Council at St. Petersburg on 21st February 1914, it was agreed that only a general European war would enable Russia to realise her "historic aims". These were the control of Constantinople and of the Straits. It was also decided that Russia would not be prepared for at least two to three years.

10. Slav agitation. In 1909 the Serbian government had promised to have good neighbourly relations with Austria-Hungary and to suppress hostile propaganda. However, there was no press censorship in Serbia. Even had the Serbian government wanted to do so, it would have been unable to curb the incessant Pan-Serb and South-Slav agitation which had grown since 1908 or to prevent the close links between its own Serbs and those in the Austrian Empire in Bosnia, Dalmatia, and Croatia.

During the years 1912–14 there were frequent student demonstrations in these provinces and attempts to assassinate government officials. They were encouraged by students in Serbia and various Serb societies. Two of note were the following.

(*a*) *Narodna Odbrana* (National Defence). This was a moderate organisation, and consisted mainly of government members. It was founded in 1909 and supported the union of South Slavs.

(*b*) *Crna Ruka* (Black Hand). This was founded in 1911 and drew a small membership from Slavs in the Austrian Empire and

Serbia. It was narrowly Pan-Serb in political orientation and largely a terroristic organisation. Thus the Serbian government did not like it, but nevertheless allowed it to set up near Nish a training school for guerrillas and saboteurs.

11. The position of Romania. Romania'a role in events was to have effects on the internal affairs of Hungary as well as the foreign affairs of the Dual Monarchy. Romania had been a member of the Triple Alliance since 1883 but the Romanian people naturally disliked the continued oppression by the Magyars of Romanians in Transylvania. The Romanian alliance with Germany and Austria was known only to a few Romanian officials and was not likely to be honoured by the people.

During 1913–14 Romania started to form closer links with Russia. This apparent defection of Romania weakened the position of Austria in the southern Balkans.

12. Austrian and German plans in June 1914. The Emperor Francis Joseph wanted to try peaceful diplomacy to isolate Serbia. At Konoposht, on 12th–13th June, he informed the Kaiser that Austria favoured an alliance with Bulgaria and Turkey. This would prevent the recreation of the Balkan League under Russian auspices. It was hoped this would win back Romania, and that the new grouping would include Greece and Turkey. Germany differed from Austria on this, and advised Austria to try direct reconciliation with Serbia and Romania.

THE SARAJEVO ASSASSINATION AND THE AUSTRIAN ULTIMATUM

13. The Sarajevo assassination. In late June 1914, Archduke Ferdinand, the Hapsburg heir, went on an official tour of Bosnia. It was perhaps unwise of the Austrian government to allow this, considering the state of unrest which existed, but it was argued that it would be good public relations for the monarchy. Ferdinand was in fact well received and no serious incidents occurred until the last day of his visit, 28th June. This was Serbia's national day, St. Vitus's Day, the anniversary of the battle of Kossovo (1389), where the Serbs had been crushed by the Turks. Security measures for the visit were poor. While the Archduke and his wife were riding in a car in the capital, Sarajevo, they were assassinated by Gavrilo Princip, an agent of the Black

Hand, and his comrades. The news shocked all of Europe, and was to be the immediate cause of war.

14. Background to the incident. Colonel Dimitrievich, head of the Intelligence Department of the Serbian general staff, was a leading member of the Black Hand. He planned the murder of Archduke Ferdinand. By 14th June the leaders of the groups which were to carry out the plan had crossed into Bosnia, with the connivance of Serbian customs officials.

The Serbian government advised the colonel to scrap the plot, and the whole plan was actually rejected by the executive committee of the Black Hand on the 14th June. Agents of Dimitrievich ordered Princip to abandon the plot, but he refused to do so. Though the Serbian government had not been involved in the plot, they took little effective action to prevent it. Pashitch, the Serbian Premier, did not want to appear a traitor to Serb national ideas.

Little was done to recall Princip from Bosnia. Austria was only warned in a vague manner that an attempt might be made on the Archduke's life, and consequently no attention was paid to it.

15. Austria's reaction. At first a peaceful outcome to the incident seemed possible. Count Berchtold, the Austrian Foreign Minister since the death of Aehrenthal in February 1912, had previously wanted to co-operate with Russia and was not anxious for war. The Hungarian Premier, Count Tisza, involved in domestic problems of the forcible Magyarisation of Serbs, Slovenes and Romanians, also wanted a peaceful solution.

However, the following steps were taken which led not only to an Austro-Serbian conflict but to a world war.

(a) *A promise of unconditional German support.* On 5th July the Austrian Count Hoyos went to the Kaiser at Potsdam to discuss Balkan problems. In the absence on holiday of important German officials the Kaiser promised German support for Austria. He hoped Austria would take such steps as she deemed necessary against Serbia while European opinion was favourably inclined towards her. The Kaiser also promised full support "if matters went to the length of war between Austria-Hungary and Russia". This was known as the "blank cheque". However, the Kaiser clearly did not expect that a European war would be the outcome and expected a localised settlement to materialise.

(b) *The report of an investigation in Serbia.* Austria suspected the complicity of the Serbian government in the plot. Baron Wiesner, a Serbian special investigator, said on 13th July that no evidence could be found to substantiate this and that in fact the opposite had been true – the Serbian government had been opposed to it.

(c) *The decision of the Austrian Supreme Council.* On 14th July the Council persuaded Tisza to agree to the adoption by Austria of an aggressive policy towards Serbia. He accepted on condition that no Serbian territory was annexed by Austria.

(d) *The ultimatum.* On 23rd July Austria presented a Note to Serbia to be answered in forty-eight hours. Neither Germany nor Italy knew its contents. Among the Austrian demands were the following.

(i) The suppression of Pan-Slav propaganda by Serbia.

(ii) The dismissal of officials accused by Austria of propaganda.

(iii) Collaboration of Austrian with Serbian officials in the suppression of Pan-Slavism and an enquiry regarding responsibility for the assassination.

16. Serbia's reply. Serbia was urged by Russia, Britain and France to make all possible concessions to Austria. Serbia mobilised her army and then replied on 25th July. The moderate tone of her reply showed an attempt to make amends. She accepted all the Austrian demands except the crucial sixth point: Serbia refused to allow Austria to collaborate in criminal proceedings held in Serbia. To maintain peace, Serbia offered to submit this point to the International Court at The Hague. Serbia's refusal to accept the Austrian demands in full may have been due to reports of Russian determination to support her.

Austria immediately mobilised her forces against Serbia.

THE COLLAPSE OF DIPLOMACY

17. British attempt to prevent war. On 26th July Sir Edward Grey, the British Foreign Minister, suggested that the Serbian issue be referred to a conference in London. France and Italy agreed. Russia accepted this in principle, though she preferred the method of direct talks with Vienna, which had been started. Austria refused to consider this proposal, and was supported by Germany.

The same day Grey sent a telegram to Germany asking her to

persuade Austria to accept the Serbian reply to the ultimatum. Bethmann-Hollweg sent the message direct to Vienna but asked that the ultimatum be rejected by Austria.

18. Outbreak of Austro-Serbian war. On 28th July, Austria declared war on Serbia. She mobilised her forces, however, not only against Serbia but also against Russia. Austro-Russian talks ceased. Belgrade was bombarded the next day, but Austria did not start serious operations until 12th August.

19. Anglo-German pressure on Austria. The Kaiser did not see the Serbian reply to the ultimatum until 28th July. He believed that the conciliatory Serbian reply had removed "every cause for war". Grey proposed to Germany that Austria should cease military operations but hold Belgrade as a pledge for the settlement of her demands. Germany advised Austria to accept this British proposal and also to resume direct talks with Russia.

20. Breakdown of European diplomacy. Lloyd George later remarked that at this time Europe "stumbled and staggered into war". The diplomats were not generally of a high calibre. Bethmann-Hollweg, for instance, lacked confidence and had no firm plan. Moreover, he never realised the significance of German military strategy, that it was directed in the first instance not against Russia but against France.

By 28th July European statesmen realised that an acute crisis had arrived. However, they could find no effective alternative, particularly in Austria, Germany and Russia, but to listen to the arguments of the militarists. They vaguely thought that a local war could occur without the involvement of all the European powers. When measures for mobilisation were taken between 29th and 31st July the statesmen hoped such actions did not mean war. Britain seemed unconcerned at the time. A poster in Britain read: "To hell with Serbia." Grey was influenced by Angell's belief that there would never be another major war as the bankers would not allow it.

21. Influence of the military. By 29th July the general staff in every country had begun to have a decisive influence on policy-making.

(a) *Russia.* On 29th July the Tsar telegraphed the Kaiser that rising pressures were about to overwhelm him. He suggested that the Austro-Serbian dispute be submitted to the Hague Conference. The following then occurred.

(*i*) The Tsar was persuaded by Sazonov and the military to order a general mobilisation.

(*ii*) This was recalled and replaced by the order for a partial mobilisation against Austria alone. This followed a telegram from the Kaiser.

(*iii*) The Russian Chief of Staff was then told by his subordinates that it was impossible to carry out only a partial mobilisation. Only one plan existed. This was for a general mobilisation against both Austria and Germany. To attempt another plan would lead to chaos. If begun, a partial mobilisation, it was explained, was hard to transform into a general mobilisation.

(*iv*) The Tsar was thus persuaded on 30th July to change his mind again and order a general mobilisation.

(*b*) *Germany.* News came to Berlin on 29th July of the impending Russian mobilisation. This affected the German war plan. Germany planned a war on two fronts against both Russia and France in which she would defeat France first. She could mobilise her forces faster than Russia but would lose the advantage if she allowed Russia too long a start.

Moltke wanted mobilisation and war against France and Belgium, with whom Germany was not even quarrelling. Bethmann-Hollweg resisted pressure from Moltke but asked Britain if she would be neutral if Germany promised in a war not to take French or Belgian territory. Britain rejected this. Contradictory steps taken then were as follows.

(*i*) Bethmann-Hollweg and the Kaiser urged Austria to urge moderation and to consider Grey's peace proposal (*see* 19).

(*ii*) Moltke telegraphed Conrad saying "Germany with you unconditionally". He advised Austria to ignore Grey's proposal and to mobilise at once against Russia.

On receipt of these messages it was not surprising that Berchtold exclaimed: "Who runs the German government?"

22. Outbreak of general war. The various stages were as follows.

(*a*) Austria announced full mobilisation measures on 31st July.

(*b*) Germany declared a "state of war emergency" on the same day. A twelve-hour ultimatum was sent to Russia demanding that she cease war preparations on the German frontier. Germany enquired of France as to her attitude in a Russo-German war and demanded a pledge of neutrality. France replied on 1st August that she would be guided by her own interests.

(c) France and Germany mobilised their forces on 1st August.

(d) Germany declared war on Russia on the same day, having received no reply to her ultimatum.

(e) On 2nd August Germany invaded Luxembourg and asked Belgium for permission for German forces to cross her territory. In return Germany would promise to respect the sanctity of Belgian territory. The request was rejected.

(f) Britain assured France, on 2nd August, that her coast would be protected against German attack.

(g) Germany invaded Belgium and declared war on France on 3rd August. The latter action was prompted by military considerations, the conviction that France would support Russia and that it was necessary to deal a quick blow in the west before dealing with Russia.

(h) Britain declared war on Germany on 4th August.

(i) Austria declared war on Russia on 6th August.

THE RESPONSIBILITY OF THE POWERS FOR THE WAR

23. Austria. In 1914 Austria was the only great power which could not conceivably gain from war. Any successes in the Balkans might well saddle the monarchy with more embittered Slavs. Yet she was the only power determined on war. This was shown by the nature of the ultimatum and her refusal to listen to those advising moderation.

(a) Austria demanded harsh conditions which she expected Serbia to refuse. Sir Edward Grey called the ultimatum "the most formidable document ever presented to an independent state". However, Austria would not have sent the ultimatum had she not believed Germany would support her.

(b) Austria had virtually decided on war unless Serbia was prepared to accept all the conditions.

(c) The short time-limit allowed for a reply showed that Austria wanted to prevent intervention by other powers. The ultimatum was timed to arrive in Serbia just after the two most important French statesmen had left on a visit to Russia.

(d) Austria refused to accept the advice of Germany and Britain to moderate her demands on Serbia. She thought mistakenly that the war could be localised again as the Balkan Wars had been in 1912–13.

24. Germany. This country was primarily responsible for war for the following reasons.

(*a*) She was the strongest military power in Europe. She occupied a commanding diplomatic position, and was the only power capable of successfully restraining Austria, which was deplorably weak militarily. At the onset of the war the Austrian forces were repulsed by the Serbs.

(*b*) She made no serious effort to restrain Austria. The Kaiser in the "blank cheque" of 5th July gave Austria virtually *carte blanche* to take any action against Serbia which she deemed necessary. At the end of July, Bethmann-Hollweg's mild efforts to restrain Austria were undermined by the independent efforts of Moltke (*see* **21**(*b*)).

(*c*) She deliberately provoked war in the west. The militarists took advantage of the Sarajevo incident to advance their own plans, thus dragging Germany and all Europe into war. Germany wanted to achieve a quick "knock-out" blow against France before fighting Russia in the east. The most effective way to achieve this was to invade France via Belgium. This meant the violation of Belgian neutrality. Germany mistakenly thought that the war could be localised and Britain kept out.

25. Russia. Though this power was militarily weak she sought to achieve success abroad to divert the attention of her people from domestic problems. Russia contributed to the start of the war in the following ways.

(*a*) She made known her determination to support Serbia against Bosnia. She was determined after the humiliation of 1909 never again to abandon support of the Serbian cause. This only encouraged Serbia to adopt an intransigent attitude towards Austria after 1909 and to refuse to accept the ultimatum totally in 1914.

(*b*) She was the first major power to order a general mobilisation of her armed forces on 29th July. This greatly reduced the chance of a peaceful settlement of the Austro-Serbian dispute and increased the chances of a general war.

26. France. This country played little part in the 1914 crisis. President Poincaré and Prime Minister Viviani were on a state visit to Russia from 15th to 29th July. However, France was involved in two ways.

(a) She was the first major power, apart from Austria, to take preparatory military measures. These were taken on 27th July.

(b) She gave continued support to Russia during the Austro-Serbian dispute. Russia knew, therefore, when she ordered general mobilisation on 29th July, that, in the event of war with Austria and Germany, France would support her. However, the French leaders while on their visit did not advise Russia to refrain from action that would provide Germany with an excuse for war.

27. Britain. In July 1914 the attention of the British was primarily focused on the domestic crisis over the Irish Home Rule Bill. This was about to become law and aimed to grant self-government to Ireland. Ulster was prepared to fight rather than be ruled by Dublin. It is against this background that one must assess Britain's role abroad in 1914. Britain played little part in causing the war. However, some blame can be attributed to her on account of the following.

(a) Her failure to give whole-hearted support to France early in the crisis misled Germany. It has been argued that war could have been prevented if Grey had done this, since Germany would have exerted more pressure on Austria to prevent hostilities with Serbia. Grey's defence was that he could not make promises which might be revoked by Parliament or opposed by public opinion. However, precautionary steps were taken on 27th July. The British fleet was ordered not to disband after manoeuvres.

(b) No effort was made to restrain Russia during the crisis.

(c) No firm warning was given to Germany over Belgium. On 30th July, Grey warned Germany that the violation of Belgian territory would arouse strong feelings in Britain. It was not made sufficiently clear that Britain would intervene if Germany invaded Belgium.

PROGRESS TEST 22

1. What grounds were there for being optimistic about international relations in 1914? (1)

2. List the main causes of the world war in 1914. (2)

3. Describe the growth of alliances in Europe. In what way did the existence of rival coalitions contribute to war? (3)

4. Define "militarism". Discuss the attempts to limit the arms race and explain why they were unsuccessful.   **(4)**

5. Did economic rivalry contribute to the war?   **(5)**

6. Describe the state of Austro-Serbian relations in June 1914. **(6–7;** *see also* **XVI, 35–37)**

7. Why did German policy in the Balkans antagonise Russia? **(6, 8)**

8. Explain why Albania became an area of importance during 1913–14.   **(7;** *see also* **XVI, 34–37)**

9. Why did Slav agitation against Austria increase after 1908? **(10;** *see also* **XVI, 27, 30, 35)**

10. Give an account of the murder of the Archduke Ferdinand. **(13–14)**

11. What indication existed that Austria deliberately provoked a war with Serbia in 1914?   **(15, 23)**

12. Did Germany make any attempts to restrain Austria from going to war with Serbia in 1914?   **(14(a), 21, 24(b))**

13. Describe the role of Britain in attempting to prevent war in 1914.   **(17, 19, 27)**

14. In what way did European diplomacy break down in 1914?   **(20)**

15. What part did Russia and France play in the start of war? **(21(a), 25–26)**

Appendixes

APPENDIX I

Bibliography

HISTORY IN GENERAL

Elton, G. R.: *Political History—Principles and Practice* (Allen Lane, Penguin, 1970).
Perkin, Harold (ed.): *History—An Introduction for the Intending Student* (Routledge & Kegan Paul, 1970).

GENERAL WORKS ON THE PERIOD

Anderson, M. S.: *The Ascendancy of Europe 1815–1914* (Longman, 1972).
Ford, Franklin L.: *Europe, 1780–1830* (Longman, 1970).
Hearder, Harry: *Europe in the Nineteenth Century, 1830–80* (Longman, 1970).
Langer, W. L.: *European Alliances and Alignments, 1871–1914* (New York, 1950).
Leslie, R. F.: *The Age of Transformation, 1789–1871* (Blandford Press, 1964).
Seaman, L. C. B.: *From Vienna to Versailles* (Methuen, 1955).
Taylor, A. J. P.: *The Struggle for Mastery in Europe, 1848–1914* (Clarendon Press, Oxford, 1954).
Wood, Anthony: *Europe, 1815–1945* (Longman, 1975).
Woodward, Sir Llewellyn: *Prelude to Modern Europe, 1815–1914* (Methuen, 1972).

SPECIALIST WORKS ON THE PERIOD

Brinton, C.: *A Decade of Revolution, 1789–1799* (Harper & Row, 1934).
Charques, Richard: *The Twilight of Imperial Russia* (Oxford University Press, 1958).
Cobban, Alfred: *A History of Modern France*, Vols. 2 and 3 (Penguin, 1970).
Collins, A.: *Age of Progress* (Arnold, 1965).

413

Droz, Jacques: *Europe between Revolutions 1815–1848* (Fontana, 1967).

Grenville, J.: *Europe Reshaped 1848–1878* (Fontana, 1977).

Jones, R. Ben: *The French Revolution* (University of London Press, 1967).

Koch, H. W., Ed.: *The Origins of the First World War: Great Power Rivalry and German War Aims* (Macmillan, 1972).

Medlicott, W. N.: *Bismarck and Modern Germany* (English Universities Press, 1970).

Milne, Andrew: *Metternich* (University of London Press, 1975).

Nicolson, Harold: *The Congress of Vienna* (Constable, 1946).

Seton-Watson, Hugh: *The Decline of Imperial Russia 1855–1914* (Methuen, 1952).

Seton-Watson, R. W.: *Disraeli, Gladstone and the Eastern Question* (Frank Cass, 1962).

Taylor, A. J. P.: *The Hapsburg Monarchy* (Hamish Hamilton, 1948).

Taylor, A. J. P.: *The Course of German History* (Methuen).

Vinacke, H. M.: *A History of the Far East in Modern Times* (Allen & Unwin, 1959).

Zeldin, Theodore: *The Political System of Napoleon III* (Oxford University Press).

APPENDIX II

Examination Technique

Essay Questions

1. *Read all the questions.* Make certain you understand the meaning of each question. Note how many questions must be answered. Select the ones you think you can do.

2. *Plan your answers.* Unless time does not permit this, it is useful to set down on some rough paper the main headings which will form the basis of the paragraphs of your answer. This will help you to marshal your thoughts, particularly as success depends often on the ability to describe clearly the correct sequence of events.

3. *Present your ideas in an interesting manner.* The examiner is not impressed merely by one's wealth of knowledge about particular events or one's ability to recite "parrot-fashion" the main dates. He wants to know whether one understands the relative importance and significance of certain facts connected to an event and can skilfully present them in the most effective manner.

4. *Be specific rather than vague.* Avoid too many general statements, and use factual material wherever possible (*e.g.* statistics, quotations, dates, names of persons and places, etc.).

5. *Be concise rather than long-winded.* You are being tested not on your ability to express yourself in grand literary style but on your ability to cover as many aspects of the question in as brief a manner as possible. Do not use many long words when a few short ones will suffice to illustrate your answer. However, avoid using abbreviations, lists or short notes as alternatives to short, lucid sentences.

6. *Avoid bad grammar.* You are not being tested on your literary or grammatical ability. However, the art of clearly expressing your ideas in short, lucid sentences will be of great benefit. Avoid slang, hackneyed or loose expressions, familiar or informal language and journalese. Make certain of the correct spellings of important words relating to the period. It creates an

415

impression of "slipshod" work when well-known names are spelt incorrectly.

7. *Define terms clearly*. Sometimes an answer requires an understanding of certain historical-political terms. Examples are balance of power, Congress System, Eastern Question, *Weltpolitik* and liberalism. In such cases a short sentence explaining the meaning of the term provides a useful introduction to an answer.

8. *Allocate equal time to all questions*. One gains more credit for completely answering a question than for giving lengthy answers to some questions and scanty attention to others.

9. *Make certain your answer is relevant*. Credit is not given for any information, however accurate, which has no bearing on the actual question and what the examiner wants to know.

Objective tests. There are a variety of types. The multiple-choice item is the most widely used and can be very easily adapted, using additional materials such as graphs, pictures, cartoons, maps and written material. It consists of a stem in the form of an introductory question or an incomplete statement together with a number of possible answers, of which only one is correct.

An objective test usually has a wide content coverage. The candidate who knows his subject-matter well, is familiar with the format of objective tests, and has some knowledge of the thinking behind them and the work that goes into their preparation should have little difficulty in coping with this type of examination.

Candidates should note carefully the instructions, and particularly the following:

(*a*) the time allocated for the test, or for each part of it;

(*b*) the total number of questions;

(*c*) instructions for marking the answer sheet and procedure to adopt if erasure of incorrect answers is necessary.

Examination Questions

THE FRENCH REVOLUTION AND ITS AFTERMATH, 1789–1848

1. "The fate of the French monarchy was sealed by the flight to Varennes." Do you agree? (*"A" Level*)

2. Account for the successful resistance of the French to the intervention of foreign powers. (*"A" Level*)

3. "It exists in every country in Europe; and among all orders of men in every country, who look up to France as to a common head." (Burke, 1796). On what grounds is it possible at that time to describe the French Revolution as a European movement? (*Historical Tripos, Part I, Cambridge, Degree*)

4. Why was the French Revolution followed by the dictatorship of Napoleon? (*B.A. General, London*)

5. Discuss the character of Napoleon I. What benefits did his career bring to France? (*"O" Level*)

6. What were the principal points of conflict which led to the Franco-Russian War of 1812? (*"A" Level*)

7. How important a part did Britain play in the downfall of Napoleon I? (*"A" Level*)

8. Why did Spain lose her American empire? (*"A" Level*)

9. What was restored in Europe in 1815? (*"A" Level*)

10. Discuss the origins of Congress diplomacy and examine its place in the conduct of international relations during the decade 1815 to 1825. (*B.A. General, London*)

11. "A Holy Alliance was impossible before the French Revolution." What light does this throw upon the aims and the significance of the Congress System? (*Historical Tripos, Part II, Cambridge, Degree*)

12. Explain the causes of the Belgian revolt and trace the stages by which independence was achieved. (*"O" Level*)

13. Why did Russia play so important a part in European affairs during the first half of the nineteenth century? (*Historical Tripos, Part I, Cambridge, Degree*)

14. Political idealism or economic discontent: which was the

more important cause of the Revolution of 1848 in *either* (a) France *or* (b) Germany and Austria?   ("*A*" *Level*)

EUROPEAN HISTORY, 1815–1870

1. How and why did Charles X lose his throne?   ("*O*" *Level*)

2. Describe the policy of Louis-Philippe at home and abroad and explain why he lost his throne in 1848.   ("*O*" *Level*)

3. Attempt a justification of Metternich's policy in foreign affairs.   ("*A*" *Level*)

4. What effects did the spread of revolutionary ideas between 1815 and 1848 have on political development in *either* Germany or Italy?   ("*A*" *Level*)

5. Why did the Frankfurt Parliament meet in 1848? Explain its lack of success.   ("*O*" *Level*)

6. Account for Radetzky's victory over Charles Albert in the campaigns of 1848–9.   ("*A*" *Level*)

7. Why did so many Italians, friends of the Risorgimento, dislike and disagree with Mazzini?   ("*A*" *Level*)

8. Why did France suffer so many changes of regime in the first half of the nineteenth century?   (*Joint Scholarship and Entrance Examination, Women's Colleges, Cambridge*)

9. What was the Schleswig-Holstein problem and how was it dealt with?   (*B.A. General, London*)

10. Was Napoleon III a statesman or a political adventurer?   ("*A*" *Level*)

11. Why did war break out between Austria and Prussia in 1866? Describe the war and its results.   ("*O*" *Level*)

12. "The conquest of Italy by Piedmont." Is this an accurate description of the events of 1859–71?   (*B.A. General, London*)

13. Account for the swift and overwhelming defeat of France in 1870.   ("*A*" *Level*)

14. Consider the importance of the reign of Alexander II in Russian history.   ("*A*" *Level*)

15. Examine the part played by the Polish Question in European affairs between the Third Partition and the rising of 1863.   (*Historical Tripos, Part II, Cambridge, Degree*)

EUROPEAN HISTORY, 1870–1914

1. Did the emancipation of the serfs in Russia modify or strengthen the autocracy of the Tsars?   (*Foreign History, Cambridge Entrance*)

2. Give some account of the nature and working of the Austro-Hungarian Compromise between 1867 and 1914. (*"A" Level*)

3. How successful was Bismarck in building internal unity in Germany after 1871? (*"A" Level*)

4. "As ruthless in maintaining peace as in preparing for war." Do you agree with this verdict on Bismarck? (*B.Sc. (Econ.), Part I, London*)

5. What domestic problems faced France after the Franco-Prussian War and to what extent had they been solved by 1904? (*"O" Level*)

6. Discuss the view that the Reinsurance Treaty was dishonest. (*"A" Level*)

7. Show how Europe had become divided into two hostile armed camps by 1904. (*"O" Level*)

8. Explain how Great Britain's emergence from "splendid isolation" between 1890 and 1907 was affected by her relations with (*a*) Germany, (*b*) France and (*c*) Russia. (*"O" Level*)

9. What aims did Italy have in Africa between 1880 and 1914 and what effects did they have on her relations with the powers? (*"O" Level*)

10. Trace the causes of friction in Anglo-German relations between 1900 and 1914. (*"O" Level*)

11. Why was there increasing discontent with Tsarist rule in Russia between 1894 and 1914? (*"O" Level*)

12. Why was it impossible to localise the Austro-Serbian quarrel in 1914? (*"A" Level*)

13. What were the chief differences in the relations between the Great Powers in 1914 as compared with 1871, and what had brought them about? (*Historical Tripos, Part II, Cambridge, Degree*)

14. What effect did the internal difficulties of the Hapsburg Empire have upon the international situation and upon the foreign policy of the Court of Vienna, 1900–14? (*Historical Tripos, Part II, Cambridge, Degree*)

THE EASTERN AND BALKAN QUESTIONS

1. Outline the story of the struggle for Greek independence in this period. (*"O" Level*)

2. Give an account of the Syrian Question between 1831 and 1840. (*"O" Level*)

3. Analyse Russian policy towards the Ottoman Empire during the period 1814–41. (*B.A. General, London*)

4. Analyse the problems involved in the "Near Eastern Question" and discuss the extent of their solution at the Peace Congress of Paris in 1856. ("*A*" *Level*)

5. Explain how events in the Balkans affected the relations of the great powers between 1875 and 1878. ("*O*" *Level*)

6. Do you agree that the Congress of Berlin merely ratified agreements already concluded between the Powers? (*B.A. Combined Honours, Southampton*)

7. What evidence was there by 1900 that Britain had "backed the wrong horse" at Berlin in 1878? ("*A*" *Level*)

8. Using the following material, write an account explaining the foreign policy of Austria-Hungary between 1900 and 1914:

The change in her relations with Serbia at the beginning of the twentieth century.

The Bosnian Crisis, 1908–9.

The Balkan Wars, 1912–13.

The Sarajevo Crisis, 1914.

("*O*" *Level*)

IMPERIALISM, AFRICA AND ASIA

1. In what respects did the Opium Wars mark a turning-point in the history of China's relations with the modern world? (*Historical Tripos, Part I, Cambridge, Degree*)

2. To what extent did Far Eastern questions seriously affect relations between the great powers in this period? ("*A*" *Level*)

3. What effect did African problems have on relations between France and Britain in the period 1871–1904? ("*A*" *Level*)

4. Discuss the significance of the "triple intervention" which followed the Sino-Japanese War of 1894–5. (*B.A. Honours, Southampton*)

5. Why did Britain and Japan make an alliance in 1902? ("*A*" *Level*)

6. What were the causes, events and results of the Russo-Japanese War, 1904–5? ("*O*" *Level*)

7. What part did problems presented by (*a*) Persia, (*b*) Afghanistan play in Anglo-Russian relations in the late nineteenth and the first decade of the twentieth century? ("*A*" *Level*)

8. What were the motives for European expansion overseas, 1880–1914? (*B.A. General, London*)

9. Trace the effect on international relations between 1880 and 1914 of international rivalries in one of the following:

(*a*) Egypt and the Nile.

(*b*) The Congo.

(*c*) Morocco.

(*d*) China.

(*e*) Albania and Macedonia.

(*B.A. General, London*)

Objective-test questions. The following are examples of simple objective-test questions suitable for revision work when one has been studying a topic only for a short time.

1. "In accordance with the words of the Scriptures which command all men to regard one another as brothers, the three contracting monarchs will remain united by the bonds of a true and indissoluble brotherhood."

(*a*) The brotherhood to which this quotation refers was known as: (1) the Triple Alliance, (2) the Holy Alliance, (3) the *Drei Kaiser Bund*, (4) the Triple Entente.

(*b*) The three contracting monarchs referred to were the rulers of: (1) Britain, Austria and Prussia, (2) Britain, France and Russia, (3) Austria, Russia and Prussia, (4) Austria, France and Russia.

2. Which of the following most accurately describes the effect of the Peninsular War? (1) Spanish involvement presented Britain with another weak ally. (2) Spanish resistance drained Napoleon's resources for seven years. (3) Spanish participation gave Britain control of Gibraltar. (4) Spanish victories encouraged Spain to grant independence to her colonies in South America. (5) Spanish defeat by France encouraged the revolt of her colonies.

3. All of the following countries fought at the Battle of Waterloo *except*: (1) Britain, (2) Prussia, (3) Russia, (4) France, (5) Holland.

4. During the nineteenth century, Russian control of the Straits uniting the Black Sea and the Mediterranean was most strongly opposed by: (1) Austria-Hungary, (2) France, (3) Great Britain, (4) Italy, (5) Germany.

5. Which one of the following was *least* effective in achieving the unification of Germany? (1) Reduction in the number of

German states. (2) Nationalistic fervour. (3) Gradual abolition of tariff barriers. (4) Leadership of the Diet of the German Confederation.

6. The government of the German Empire was practically absolute because of the: (1) power of the Kaiser as Emperor of Germany, (2) absence of universal suffrage, (3) absence of a representative assembly, (4) power of the Kaiser as King of Prussia, (5) power of the Chancellor.

7. Which one of the following was not a factor tending to hold together the Dual Monarchy of Austria-Hungary? (1) Common loyalty to the Emperor. (2) Economic advantage. (3) A common language and literature. (4) The advantage, in power and prestige, of being a part of a large empire. (5) The Roman Catholic Church.

8. Austria-Hungary made an alliance with Germany chiefly in order to gain support in the event of a clash with: (1) France, (2) Italy, (3) Russia, (4) Turkey, (5) Britain.

9. Cavour sought to unify Italy by: (1) allying with Prussia against Austria, (2) appealing to the masses to rise in revolt, (3) commissioning Garibaldi to conquer Rome, (4) making an alliance with France.

10. Why, principally, was Louis Napoleon elected President of the Second French Republic? (1) His writing showed that he had unusual abilities as a statesman. (2) His name recalled the glorious career of his uncle. (3) He had demonstrated his military leadership in the Revolution of 1848. (4) He promised to regain Alsace-Lorraine from Germany.

11. Which one of the following was the most important cause of China's remaining isolated for centuries? (1) The mountainous and desert regions along the frontier. (2) The Great Wall. (3) The hostility of the Japanese. (4) The military might of the Chinese. (5) China's attitude to foreigners.

12. The "Eastern Question" was concerned with: (1) how India should be ruled, (2) what should be done about the Turkish Empire, (3) how the Russians could change their government, (4) whether British merchants should be allowed to trade in opium, (5) the decline of Manchu China.

Index

Index

425